On the Definition
of Learning

# On the Definition of Learning

Edited by
Ane Qvortrup, Merete Wiberg,
Gerd Christensen & Mikala Hansbøl

University Press of Southern Denmark 2016

On the Definition of Learning

Copyright © 2016 The authors and
University Press of Southern Denmark
ISBN: 978-87-7674-876-0

Typesetting and cover design by
Donald Jensen, UniSats
Printed by Tarm Bogtryk a-s
Printed in Denmark 2016

Printed with support from
the Danish Council for Independent Research (Culture and Communication)

University Press of Southern Denmark
Campusvej 55
DK-5230 Odense M

www.universitypress.dk


Distribution in the United States and Canada:
International Specialized Book Services
www.isbs.com

Distribution in the United Kingdom and Ireland:
Gazelle Book Services
www.gazellebookservices.co.uk


All rights reserved. No part of this publication may be reproduced,
distributed, or transmitted in any form or by any means, including
photocopying, recording, or other electronic or mechanical methods,
without the prior written permission of the publisher, except in the
case of brief quotations embodied in critical reviews and certain other
non-commercial uses permitted by copyright law.

# Contents

Introduction    7
*Ane Qvortrup, Merete Wiberg, Gerd Christensen & Mikala Hensbøl*

What should we demand of a definition of 'learning'?    21
*Esben Nedenskov Petersen, Caroline Schaffalitzky de Muckadell
& Rolf Hvidtfeldt*

Articulating a base for the development of a concept of learning    39
*Nina Bonderup Dohn*

The normative aspect of learning    59
*Merete Wiberg*

Realism and learning    75
*Oliver Kauffmann*

How we learn    101
*Steen Beck*

'Situated learning'
– beyond apprenticeship and social constructionism    125
*Gerd Christensen*

On defining learning from a social-ontological perspective    141
*Klaus Nielsen*

The mistake to mistake learning theory for didactics    163
*Ane Qvortrup & Tina Bering Keiding*

Student notes as a mediating tool for learning in school subjects    189
*Torben Spanget Christensen*

What's space to learning?    213
*Rie Troelsen*

Learning from a social practice theoretical perspective    229
*Maj Sofie Rasmussen*

An interview with Paul Cobb    245

An interview with Christopher Winch    273

An interview with Knud Illeris    299

An interview with Anna Sfard    323

Contributors    337

# Introduction

*Ane Qvortrup, Merete Wiberg, Gerd Christensen & Mikala Hansbøl*

Since the end of the last century the phenomenon of learning has received increasingly more attention. Both nationally and internationally there is a political focus on learning and a "call for harnessing knowledge about learning and applying it more systematically to education" (Dumont, Istance & Benavides, 2013). This development changes both the main purpose of education and its modes of delivery. The education system has witnessed a shift from content-based to outcome-based curricula, and schools have become heavily influenced by pedagogical concepts such as 'visible learning' (Hattie 2009).

According to A. Hargreaves (2003), the change can be linked to globalization, the emergence of 'the knowledge society' and an enhanced focus on innovation and creativity. Knowledge and learning are considered as fundamental resources for future development. Sustainability, learning in terms of learning outcomes, and lifelong learning have become increasingly recognized as important factors in the 'global competition' (Jarvis 2007). The focus on education, however, took off in the Western world already in the early part of the 20th Century. The so-called 'second industrial revolution' demanded an educated work force and this led to a view of workers as 'human capital' (Becker 1964; Mincer 1958). In the Western countries in the post war period, the interest in education was closely connected with the development of the welfare state. As illustrated our interest in education and learning can be considered as closely connected to the diffusion of a variety of ideas about the kind of society and world humans live in: Today, concepts are the global world (Giddens 1991, 1994), the competition state (Pedersen 2011), the network society (Castells 2010), the knowledge society (Jarvis 2007), the learning society (Hargreaves 2005) – just to mention a few widely used. In relation to developments in society, new concepts of education and learning have also appeared, such as 'lifelong learning', 'informal and non-formal learning', 'digital learning', 'work place learning', 'blended learning', 'cooperative learning, 'responsibility for his own learning', 'facilitation of learning', 'evidence-based education', etc.

Parallel to these changes in education and learning, and in the net of social relations, a variety of theories of learning have evolved. The field of research on learning has become very complex, with different foci, founders and proponents, schools, and disciplinary approaches (Qvortrup & Wiberg 2013). Thus, the phenomenon of learning as it appears today is manifold. It has emerged as an evolving object, with multiple connections to various disciplines of research and fields of interest.

Within the multi-faceted landscape of theories and definitions of learning, there exists no general agreement on what learning really is, or on what is demanded of a definition of learning. Some proponents of theories of learning tend to advocate their own viewpoint and to consider learning theories as mutually exclusive and therefore incompatible. Some try to unify the field of learning into *one* comprehensive theory of learning (Illeris, 2006; Jarvis, 2006), while others claim to focus on particular aspects of learning (e.g. creative learning), on places for learning (e.g. workplace learning), or on perspectives on learning (e.g. individual, social, child, adult, organizational learning).

This indicates that learning cannot be defined once and for all. Instead, the field must be considered as a collection of perspectives on and conceptualizations of learning. Conceptualizations of learning often base themselves on particular metaphors, such as learning as 'acquisition', 'participation' and/or 'knowledge creation' (Sfard 1998, Qvortrup & Wiberg, 2013). Furthermore, different conceptualizations of learning often imply different and definite assumptions about the relationships of subject and object, individuality and context, inside and outside, thinking and action, cognition and body, and knowledge and practice. Thus, it is important to be sensitive to the variety of concepts and theories of learning in the field, and to continue to cultivate that variety. However, currently there doesn't seem to be a way to locate theories of learning within a unified field of research, where concepts of learning are thoroughly and systematically discussed across the field. There seems to be a lack of mutual discussion and inspiration among the different fields, interests and positions. As a consequence, the development of strong theory building is inhibited.

An important aspect involved in building a strong field of learning theory is to clarify how learning concepts and theories can prove useful in relation to different contexts, interests, problems and situations. This aspect can be judged in terms of whether it is 'viable' (von Glasersfeld, 1996), 'operationally useful' (von Foerster, 1984) or if it takes the form of 'ideas as plans of operations to be performed' (Dewey, [1929]1990) or of 'instruments of finding one's way around' (Terhart, 2003). Any concept of learning must be considered in the light of the empirical studies it is based on, and the various definitions and conceptualizations of learning it adheres to.

One difficulty, therefore, involves coming to terms with constantly changing definitions of learning; another relates to the question of how to move from learning, learning objectives and learning theory to educational settings, teaching strategies and teaching theories. Learning theories help us to understand learning as a phenomenon, but they do not reflect upon what, how and why something should be taught and learned in education (Qvortrup & Keiding 2016). However, some researchers claim that a theory of teaching includes both a theory of student learning and a theory of teacher behavior (Hattie, 2009; Terhart, 2011). Biggs and Tang (2007) call for a focus on 'constructive alignment' between teaching activities, learning objectives, and different students' learning through participation. But this is no simple matter, and often the attempts to establish connections between theoretical concepts of learning and teaching are based on educational designs attached to particular views of knowledge and learning. Examples of this can be found in some (social) constructivist theories of teaching activities, which take their point of departure in the view of knowledge and learning as always socially situated, and as arising from collective and personal constructions (Lave & Wenger 1991; Wenger 1998). Manifold teaching or pedagogical patterns (Laurillard, 2012), such as student-orientated inquiry teaching, problem-based teaching, cooperative learning, and computer-supported collaborative teaching, have been conceived and referred to as if they inherently belong to particular social constructivist notions of knowledge and learning. Several of these attempts tend to focus on the teachers' proactive efforts to design teaching activities that facilitate students' learning through encouraging individual and collaborative/cooperative efforts to construct knowledge (Qvortrup & Keiding, 2015a; Hattie, 2009, p. 26, Cobb, 2007, p. 5). The problem with many of these approaches seems to be that the alleged interdependence referred to above is often only postulated as a claim. As argued in the chapter by Qvortrup & Keiding in this book, the theory is applied in very general form, where the analytical contribution from the theory is neither explicit nor evident (Tight, 2007), but mainly functions as a kind of ideological statement, "empty category" (Koselleck 2004: 187) or "empty signifier" (Laclau 1996: 36-47). Very often there is a lack of thorough investigation of the actual relationships involved in practice between the different ways of enacting education and the intended trajectories of learning.

With the increased emphasis on the capability of educational programs to generate learning results in a globalized world, (ref. OECD, PISA etc.) there is a need to discuss how conceptualizations of learning are put to work in educational contexts. (Richardson, 2003; Sfard, 1998; Cobb, 2007). Furthermore, there is a need to conceptualize the normative aspects of learning in relation to discussions of what is considered worth learning, and to how different forms of learning influence the formative processes of human development. Formational concepts such as 'Bildung' and worth-whileness (Peters 1972) can help us discuss the limitations of the concept of learning, by including reflections on the overall aims of education in present day societies.

This book is a first product of the 'On the definition of learning' network. It is a result of the network's first collective efforts to discuss the topics outlined above at a conference held by the network at the University of Southern Denmark on August 28th – 29th, 2014. The network arose out of the aspiration to study the phenomenon of learning in depth and to understand its complex relationship to empirical investigation and teaching. Its aim is to discuss different conceptualizations and theories of learning in a qualified fashion, so that it becomes possible to better understand how concepts of learning influence our understanding of the empirical phenomenon of learning, as well as our sense of the relationship between learning and teaching. At the same time, the network hopes to highlight the need to develop new ways to analyze these matters as both things apart and partially co-existing.

As such, the book grapples with difficult issues related to learning and education in a postmodern, always emerging and highly digitalized world. The book takes the first steps towards actively and critically engaging the various approaches in the field, at the same time that it emphasizes the complex relationships that exist between conceptualizations of learning and the empirical phenomenon of learning and teaching. All the chapters contribute in various ways to break new ground towards understanding how learning has been investigated in the past through the use of various tools, such as models, concepts and metaphors. Furthermore, they contribute to the discussion of how different conceptions of learning help educators and empirical researchers in their endeavor to optimize and identify learning respectively. The book aims to encourage further development in these areas. As such, it is a call to a heightened awareness of the importance of considering learning and educational constructions as complexly intertwined; that is to say, that different definitions of learning originate in different modes of analyses, they are situated within different fields of research, and have connections to different social interests.

In the **first part** of the book the field of investigation is concerned with how various theories define and delimit the phenomenon of learning. This inquiry will facilitate a synthesis that moves from individual theories of learning towards theoretical reflections on learning as a central discipline in education research and practice. The first part of the book identifies, clarifies and discusses fundamental aspects of learning in a trans-theoretical perspective. These aspects are considered fundamental to the aim of acquiring a varied and comprehensive understanding of the phenomenon of learning. These aspects include intention, normativity, subjectification, knowledge forms, prerequisites and obstacles to learning.

In the **second part** of the book the field of investigation and discussion is how to use research and knowledge in the field of learning theory to develop theories of teaching on the basis of practice. The chapters in this part of the book discuss the relationships between teaching and learning theory, at first on a meta-level and secondly, with the aim of exemplifying how the insights and concepts of learning theory may contribute to the development of teaching activities.

These discussions in the second part are further qualified and developed in the **third part** of the book. The chapters in this part investigate the interplay between theories of learning, empirical research, and emerging practices of learning. This part focuses on questions like how various theories of learning can provide us with specific ways of identifying learning empirically in educational settings, as well as in other contexts.

The **fourth part** of the book in a way cuts across the other parts. It discusses theoretical concepts, as well as aspects related to empirical investigation and to teaching. It consists of interviews with the four professors: Paul Cobb, Christopher Winch, Anna Sfard and Knud Illeris, all of whom kindly accepted the invitation to participate in the network. The interviews with Paul Cobb and Christopher Winch took place during network visits to Nashville and London respectively, while the interview with Anna Sfard is based on email-correspondance. The interview with Knud Illeris was conducted in Denmark.

## The contents of the book

Part 1: *Theory building within the theoretical field of learning*

As mentioned, Part 1 of the book investigates how various theories define and delimit the phenomenon of learning. It is divided into two sections. The first section, which consists of 3 chapters, identifies, clarifies and discusses fundamental aspects of learning across theories. The first chapter in this section by Esben Nedenskov Petersen, Caroline Schaffalitzky de Muckadell and Rolf Hvidtfeldt discusses the problems involved in defining learning. Clear and precise definitions of theoretical terms are commonly held to be crucial to fruitful theoretical exchanges and development in the humanities, as well as in the natural and social sciences. But while the value of definitions is widely acknowledged, it is often overlooked that there exist different kinds of definitions with different purposes and distinct criteria of adequacy. The chapter examines different types of definition, and argues that the purposes we intend a definition of learning to serve are essential to determining what kind of definition we look for. The argument is illustrated by the authors applying their considerations to the assessment of the particular definition of learning proposed by the influential Danish educational researcher, Knud Illeris.

The second chapter, Nina Bonderup Dohn's "Articulating a base for the development of a concept of learning", also pursues the question of how to define learning. It asks the questions of what a theory of learning must be able to account for; what it must take into account in doing so; and how much both these criteria must be taken into account in the very concept of learning utilized in developing the theory. The chapter concentrates on the subjects of learning, their relationship to the world (including other subjects), and the ontology of the result of learning. It argues that 4 basic claims about learning must be taken into account, not only in developing the theory, but in developing a particular conception of learning. It further suggests that some theoretical assumptions will be inherent in the concepts used in a theory, and that these theoretical assumptions will develop as the theory is developed. Moreover, it argues that a theory, generally speaking, will typically have a wider theoretical and empirical scope – it will say more about the world – than what is implied in its concepts alone.

The third chapter in the first section, by Merete Wiberg, is called "The normative aspect of learning". It addresses how normativity, in terms of individual understanding, motivation and valuation, is part of the learning process. In order to understand motivation as more than just a psychological process, we need to conceptualize how motives of learning are constituted from the perspective of the individual struggling to come to terms with what it considers valuable to learn. In this chapter, learning is conceptualized as the interplay between the individual and the world, while the individual – according to Hegel – is considered as standing in between particularity and universality. Inspired by the philosophy of John Dewey and G.W. Hegel, Wiberg considers learning as a process of inquiry, consisting of the continuous evaluation of the individual's own understanding. The focus on normativity, individuality and learning is not meant to prescribe how learning must be facilitated, but to emphasize the normative aspect that must be taken into account when learning is intended and required.

The second section of part 1 investigates how various theories define and delimit learning. The first chapter in this section, chapter 4, is called "Realism and Learning" and is written by Oliver Kauffmann. Oliver Kauffmann argues for a realistic approach to learning. In this case, the realistic approach mean a defense of two assumptions: (i) that learning from an epistemological point of view to a large extent involves asymmetrical processes of knowledge- and skill-acquisition and; (ii) that acquired knowledge and skills cannot be understood without reference to a mind-independent world to which the subject has cognitive access. The argument in the chapter initially points out a number of possible problems with the epistemological underpinnings of so-called "radical constructivism", proposed by Ernest von Glasersfeld. Secondly, the chapter argues for the claims of realism as an approach to learning, by taking advantage of insights taken from the field of implicit learning and cognition, as well as from the supervenience approach to the relation between body and mind.

The second chapter in this section, chapter 5, is called "How we learn" and is written by Steen Beck. The chapter looks at some depth into the theories of Piaget and Vygotsky, who are often seen as the founders of two very different approaches to learning and teaching. Piaget considered rational knowledge to be the result of the individual's spontaneous cognitive activity and a process of equilibrium. Vygotsky's method of analysis focused particularly on instruction, as it combined with the ways in which scientific concepts emerge in the asymmetric relationship between teacher and student in the Zone of Proximal Development. In this chapter, differences and similarities between the two positions are discussed by analyzing the two theoretical pioneers' fundamental postulations about learning and teaching, as well as their reactions to each other. The main thesis presented in the chapter is that the two theories of learning and teaching are less antagonistic than is often thought. The equilibrium process with its stabilizations and changes of scheme from "within" can be seen as the mechanism that facilitates social learning in the Zone of Proximal Development. In recognizing this, we are made to realize that human learning is not by nature either biological or cultural, but that an understanding of both psycho-genesis and socio-genesis is vital if we want to understand how we learn.

The third chapter in this section, chapter 6 of the book, "'Situated learning' – beyond apprenticeship and social constructionism", is written by Gerd Christensen. The chapter discusses the theoretical and philosophical fundament of Jean Lave & Etienne Wenger's theory of 'situated learning'. In Denmark, the theory has been categorized as a theory of 'apprenticeship' and as 'social constructionism'. The chapter outlines these perceptions, and argues that the comprehension of the theory has significant implications for how it is viewed as contributing to the understanding of learning and to analyses of learning in actual contexts. The chapter can thus be considered as not only a contribution to a more specific discussion of 'situated learning', but also to the wider discussion of how to conceptualize 'learning' as such. In addition, the chapter discusses some of the analytical perspectives, which are presented in some of the other chapters in this anthology. To give one an idea of the range of perspectives, we can note that while Klaus Nielsen uses Lave & Wenger's theory for his analysis, Ane Qvortrup and Tina Bering Keiding try to analyze its impact; Helle Plauborg uses Karen Barads approach in her analyses, while Steen Beck looks at the theory of Vygotsky.

Based on work in the field of situated learning and on Honneth's work, Klaus Nielsen's chapter (chapter 7) "On defining learning from a social-ontological perspective" aims to develop a social-ontological approach to learning in which Honneth's focus on the struggle for recognition is central. The chapter reads Honneth, as well as Lave and Wenger's work in keeping with a tradition from humanistic psychology, in which ontology is considered important when addressing issues of learning. In this context, the notion of a social-ontological approach to issues of learning is used to formulate a critique of the tendencies found both in the current regime of homo economicus, and in theories of learning with strong focus on technology and instrumentality. Following this critique and inspired by the analyses of Honneth and Lave and Wenger, the chapter tries to develop an understanding of what a social-ontological perspective on learning would look like. It concludes by returning to the notion of homo economicus, to analyze what kinds of critical questions it will be possible to pose through a social-ontological perspective on learning.

Part 2: *Building relationships between the field of learning theory and teaching theory.*
Part 2 investigates the relationships between the field of learning theory and teaching theory, and it consists of two chapters. Chapter 8, "The mistake to mistake learning theory with didactics", is written by Ane Qvortrup and Tina Bering Keiding. It discusses and explains how the concept of learning in a teaching context can be understood, and how learning theories may contribute to teaching. It shows, especially in the Denmark, how broad concepts of constructivism and socio-cultural learning theories seem to have replaced educational theory and didactics as conceptual frameworks for reasoning on teaching and choices of design in the Scholarship of Teaching and Learning in Higher

Education. The chapter also illustrates how and why didactical theory and practice cannot be deduced from learning theory, and discusses the possible consequences of an over-reliance upon learning theory. Finally, the chapter argues that both learning theories and didactics are fundamental for a systematic reflection on teaching and learning, and that the two cannot be replaced by each other.

Chapter 9 is entitled "Student notes as a mediating tool for learning in school subjects" and is written by Torben Spanget Christensen. This chapter presents data from an empirical ethnographic field study, which examined the role of student note-writing in the transition from Danish lower to upper secondary school with regard to its potential as a tool for learning. The impetus for the study was an observed disparity between the significance that students in this transition phase attach to note writing, and the actual quality of their notes. The chapter presents two male students and their note writing, and addresses two central research questions: Can note writing serve as a mediating tool between everyday language and subject discourse language? And furthermore, can it function as a tool for a change in identity from pupil to student? These two proposed learning strategies are considered as closely related, but each with a key contribution to make to the overall learning process. Note writing as a mediating tool is considered as a way to capture and acquire the subject discourse, while note writing as a tool of identity change is considered a way to participate in the academic and disciplinary social community of the class and school.

The third and final part of the book investigates the relation between learning theory and empirical research on learning practices. The first chapter, chapter 10, is entitled "What's space to learning?" and is written by Rie Troelsen. In this chapter, preliminary findings from a small-scale research project are presented with the aim of exploring ways of investigating learning from a spatial perspective. The research project focuses on teachers' perceptions of the impact of space on their personal experiences of learning. By using a threefold method, consisting of investigations of how teachers act in, conceive and perceive the impact of space on learning, the results from the project indicate that teachers include space as a didactical category in their planning and conducting of learning activities. It is, however, important for the teachers to feel a sense of ownership of learning space in order for space to become a didactical category. In a time where many learning spaces at university are rebuilt, renovated and redesigned, this is an important point. Moving from traditional spaces, like the lecture auditorium, to more flexible learning spaces, like those employed for project-based activities, point at new and different ways of learning. One possible consequence is that many teachers could become uncertain and lose their sense of ownership over learning space. Another possible consequence is that teachers might plan and conduct their teaching on the grounds of theories of learning more relevant and suited to the new learning spaces, than the ones they used while teaching in traditional spaces.

The second chapter in the final section of the book, is called "Learning from a social practice theoretical perspective" (chapter 11) and it is written by Maj Sofie Rasmussen. It addresses the use of learning theories in the educational field, and discusses a theory of learning that distances itself from institutionalized definitions. Based on a case study in lower-secondary school at *Fryshuset* in Stockholm, Sweden, it argues that an understanding of learning may be developed into a theoretical framework of social practice, which would allow us to empirically discover and explore learning as expansive, meaningful mo(ve)ments (Mørck, 2014) that take place in and across particular situations and social settings. This approach suggests and introduces theoretical distinctions into the landscape of learning. In a social practice theoretical understanding, learning is connected to the learner's understanding of himself or herself as part of a community (or as an 'outsider'), as well as to his or her participation in changing social practices (Lave, in press). In addition, learning is seen in relation to significant, expansive and/or constraining mo(ve)ments involved, e.g., in becoming a more (or less) recognized member of different communities of practice. This is an essential point when studying transcending and potentially marginalizing processes in schools.

It is a pleasure for us to be able to present the work of these researchers in this first book from the network 'On the definition of learning'. We wish to thank all the authors for their very interesting, strong and groundbreaking work presented in the book, and for their contribution to the network in general. Furthermore, on behalf of several of our contributors, we would like to thank the anonymous reviewers for their effort. Finally, we are grateful to Anna Sfard, Paul Cobb, Christopher Winch and Knud Illeris for providing us with very interesting and stimulating interviews. Discussions like these are what propel us to continue our work in the field.

## References

Becker, G. (1964). *Human capital.* New York: Columbia University Press.
Castells, M. (2010). *The Rise of The Network Society - The Information Age: Economy, Society and Culture.* John Wiley & Sons.
Cobb, Paul (2007) Putting Philosophy to Work. In: Lester, Frank K. (ed.) *Second Handbook of Research on Mathematics teaching and Learning.* Charlotte, NC: Information Age Publishing Inc. p. 3-38.
Dewey, J. ([1929]1990). *The Quest for Certainty. John Dewey, The Later Works, Vol. 4.* J. A. Boydston (ed.) Carbondale and Edwardsville: Southern Illinois University Press.
Dumont, H.; Istance, D. & Benavides, F. (2013). The Nature of Learning. Using Research to Inspire Practice. OECD: http://www.educ.ethz.ch/pro/litll/oecdbuch.pdf.
Hargreaves, A. (2003). *Teaching in the Knowledge Society.* New York & London: Teachers College Press.
Hattie, John (2009). *Visible Learning.* Abingdon: Routledge.
Illeris, K.(2006). *Læring.* Frederiksberg: Roskilde Universitetsforlag.
Jarvis, P. (2006). *Towards a Comprehensive Theory of Human Learning,* London and New York: Routledge Taylor and Francis Group.
Jarvis, P. (2007). *Globalisation, Lifelong Learning and the Learning Society. Sociological Perspectives.* New York & London: Routledge Taylor and Francis Group.
Koselleck, R. (2004). *Futures Past.* New York, NY: Columbia University Press.
Laclau, E. (1996). Deconstruction, Pragmatism, Hegemony. In Mouffe, C. (ed.) *Deconstruction and Pragmatism,* p. 49-70. London: Routledge.
Laurillard, D. (2012): *Teaching as a Design Science - Building Pedagogical Patterns for Learning and Technology.* Routledge.
Lave, Jean; Wenger, Etienne (1991). *Situated Learning: Legitimate Peripheral Participation.* Cambridge: Cambridge University Press.
Mincer, J. (1958). Investment in Human Capital and Personal Income Distribution. *The Journal of Political Economy* 66(4), p. 281-302.
Pedersen, O.K. (2011). *Konkurrencestaten.* København: Hans Reitzels Forlag.
Peters. R.S (1972). *Ethics and Education.* London: Unwin University Books.
Qvortrup, A. & Keiding, T. (2015) DUT som didaktisk felt - en empirisk analyse af didaktiske temaer i perioden 2006-2013. In: *Dansk Universitetspædagogisk Tidsskrift* 10(19), p. 8-21.
Qvortrup, Ane & Wiberg, Merete (2013) *Læringsteori og Didaktik.* København: Hans Reitzel Forlag.
Richardson, V. (2003). Constructivist pedagogy. *Teachers College Record,* 105(9), p. 1626-1640.

Sfard Anna (1998). On two Metaphors for Learning and the Dangers of choosing Just one. In: *Educational Researcher.* Vol. 27 No. 2, p. 4-13.

Terhart, E. (2003). Constructivism and teaching: A new paradigm in general didactics? *Journal of Curriculum Studies*, 35(1), p. 25-44.

Tight, M. (2007). Bridging the Divide: A comparative analysis of articles in higher education journals published inside and outside North America. Higher Education, 53(2), p. 235-253.

von Foerster, H. (1984) *Sicht und Einsicht.* Germany: Viehweg.

von Glasersfeld, E. (1996) *Radikaler Konstruktivismus. Ideen, Ergebnisse, Probleme.* Frankfurt: Suhrkamp.

Wenger, Etienne (1998). *Communities of Practice: Learning, Meaning, and Identity.* Cambridge: Cambridge University Press.

# What should we demand of a definition of 'learning'?[1]

*Esben Nedenskov Petersen, Caroline Schaffalitzky de Muckadell and Rolf Hvidtfeldt*

## Introduction

Clear and precise definitions of theoretical concepts are commonly held to be crucial to fruitful theoretical exchanges and development in both the humanities, and the natural and social sciences. Bluntly put, the function of definitions is to unambiguously point out the phenomena theories are about, and they do so by spelling out the meanings of central terms in the theoretical framework. But while the value of definitions is widely acknowledged it is often overlooked that there are various kinds of definitions with different purposes and distinct criteria of adequacy.[2] So before searching for a definition of 'learning' one should consider the definition types available, the purposes they may serve, and the purpose the sought definition is intended to serve.[3]

This contribution distinguishes definitions from theories, examines different types of definition, and shows that the purposes we intend a definition of 'learning' to serve determines what kind of definition we should look for. The relevance of these issues to the project of defining 'learning' is demonstrated by applying our considerations to the assessment of the particular definition of 'learning' proposed by the influential Danish educational researcher Knud Illeris.

## Definitions and theories

Before we turn to the discussion of what we should demand of a definition of 'learning' and the various kinds of definitions available, we first want to clarify the relation between definition and theory. As we shall see, the two are interrelated, but ought nevertheless to be distinguished analytically.

The classical Aristotelian approach to definition is to see it as the attempt to answer the question "what is so-and-so?".[4] Stated in this succinct manner, however, definitions are easily conflated with theories. Let us look at the question: "What is learning?". One way of answering this question is to say that learning is something we cannot help do because it is deeply rooted in our human genes. Or it may be said that learning is something which helps us adapt to the world. Or that learning is an important part of socialization. These responses, however, are clearly not offering definitions of the word 'learning'. Instead, they are *theories* about why people learn things, what the effects of learning may be, and the role learning plays in society. In contrast, the *definition* of 'learning' could be something along the lines of "the meaning of the word 'learning' is acquiring insight or skills" or perhaps "By 'learning' I mean taking lessons and practicing skills". Let us try to spell out further the difference between definitions and theories. Definitions are usually understood either as identifying the essential properties characteristic of things belonging to a specific category or as formulations which state the meanings of words or concepts. Some hold that definitions do both (e.g. Fine, 1994, p. 14) and there are numerous variants of these two views on how to define 'definition' (cf. Robinson, 1950, p. 2-3 for famous examples from the history of philosophy). According to all of them, definitions can be seen as tools for classification: having a definition of 'learning' will allow one to decide whether something (such as a public whipping) belongs in that category or not. In contrast, theories are (relatively) coherent sets of propositions. They can provide, for instance, causal, functional and structural explanations of a matter (depending on the kind of theory), and sometimes also be used to predict or evaluate something.

So, what is the relation between definitions and theories? Let us consider this question by focusing on concepts other than 'learning'. Some definitions, such as that of 'sunburn', will explicitly rely on theories because it incorporates the causal explanation about the origin of the skin burn. Others, such as the definition of 'fossil', presuppose considerable theoretical knowledge of, for instance, paleontological facts. Such examples might appear to suggest that definitions are simply theories on a par with other theories about a subject matter. But a little reflection will show that this is not the case. For instance, there are endless numbers of theoretical claims which are clearly not part of the definitions of what their terms refer to. The claim that Aristotle was responsible for Alexander's learning about the Greek philosophers, for example, is clearly not something that a definition of 'learning' needs to include.

But even though definitions are distinct in aims and structure from theories, and cannot generally be characterized as short versions of theories, they are still crucially related to theories. This is because definitions are necessary for theories and theorizing. A theory of learning must contain a clear understanding of the meaning of 'learning' so as to make it clear what the theory is about and what it applies to. Often the meanings of theoretical terms are merely implicitly present in a theory, and in some cases this is as it should be because their meaning is sufficiently clear and obvious. For instance, a book on theories on how to break in dogs need not include a definition of 'dog'. But in other cases where key theoretical terms are used with several different meanings across the literature, one may have to compare theories and analyze core examples to provide a definition of, for instance, 'punishment', 'domestic animal', or 'learning' in order to settle which phenomena the theories are about.

Definitions are necessary in advancement of academic efforts because they are the markers needed in evaluating a theory. Without a precise definition of the subject in question, it will remain unclear whether a theory covers all relevant possible instances under discussion. For example, if a theorist claims that learning can only occur when discipline is strict, one must be able to identify what counts as instances of learning to determine whether the theorist is right. Furthermore, attention to definitions is important to make sure that they are not unnecessarily packed with theoretical content. One should be aware of the relation between definition and theory.

On the whole, research is advanced by definitions because they can reduce vagueness and ambiguity, clear up homonymies, and force researchers to make precise categorizations. Definitions are hence crucial in improving theories (see Schaffalitzky, 2014, p. 510-511 for similar points). However, as will be apparent in the following, there are different kinds of definition with different aims and different standards of adequacy.

## Lexical definitions and its challenges

Now that we have distinguished theories and definitions, let us take a closer look at what work we can reasonably expect definitions to perform. It should, however, be noted that the range of phenomena referred to as 'definitions' is so broad and heterogeneous that some of its members must be left out of the discussion here. In what follows, what we refer to as 'definitions' will be limited to the most common and prominent types of definitions: namely those intended as specifications of the meanings of words On this understanding, what a definition characterizes is the meaning of a term, not the phenomena that the term refers to.

Among such definitions of word meaning there are two main varieties that we want to consider: first, lexical definitions which aim to capture the meanings particular words have in their common usage, and, secondly, definitions which assign to a term a particular meaning that does not necessarily correspond with the meaning commonly attached to the term. In addition, to illustrate the relevance of the distinctions between these varieties of definitions we will hold them up against Knud Illeris' definition of 'learning', according to which 'learning' is defined as 'any process that in living organisms leads to permanent capacity change and which is not solely due to biological maturation or aging' (Illeris, 2009, p. 7).[5]

## What is a lexical definition?

We begin by considering lexical definitions. A lexical definition of a term is meant to provide a characterization of the meaning attached to a term in ordinary, common usage. To say that the lexical definition of a term is such and such hence implies the claim that such and such corresponds to what ordinary speakers mean by the term. A lexical definition of 'learning', for instance, should be such that how the meaning of 'learning' is characterized correlates with how the term is used. If it does not, the definition is incorrect because it then mischaracterizes the term's meaning.

Let us then consider, how Illeris' definition fares when evaluated as a lexical definition (noting all the while that Illeris does not explicitly say whether his definition is intended as a lexical definition rather than another type of definition). To decide this question we should ask whether the proposed definition corresponds with the ordinary use of 'learning'. This does not seem to be the case. Permanent changes in the capacities of a subject which are neither solely nor partly due to biological maturation or aging encompass a range of phenomena which are not readily thought of as examples of learning. Castration and laser eye surgery, for example, are instances of such permanent changes in a subjects capacities. Yet, we hardly want to say that the castration of someone is an instance of learning, so that, for instance, the voice of a castrato singer is the effect of pre-pubertal learning. Illeris' definition of 'learning' then seems inadequate as a lexical definition because it is too broad. It misrepresents the ordinary meaning of the word 'learning' by including phenomena that we would not ordinarily categorize as examples of learning. If we want an adequate lexical definition of 'learning' we need a less inclusive definition.

The task of providing adequate lexical definition of terms in ordinary language, however, is not an easy one. One major difficulty concerning attempts to specify lexical meaning is due to the largely tacit nature of the knowledge that ordinary speakers have of word meaning. While knowledge of what their words mean enables us to apply and understand the terms in our vocabulary, such knowledge does not come in the form of consciously held beliefs about explicitly stated definitions. Instead, its contents are typically implicit in how we think and tend not to be directly accessible to conscious awareness, which means that the meanings speakers attach to words can only be made explicit with great difficulty, if at all.

Therefore, providing an adequate lexical definition of a term from ordinary discourse is not simply a matter of looking up the right entry in the mental lexicon. Rather, producing an adequate explicit formulation of a term's meaning will require an extensive, systematic effort to think through the conditions under which the term can be applied and the conditions under which it cannot.

Moreover, as we will discuss in the following, there may be further considerable, perhaps even insurmountable, obstacles to achieving a lexical definition of 'learning' which retains the clarity and precision that we seek to achieve when pursuing definitions. In particular, contrary to widespread orthodoxy, our word meanings might not be structured in a way that can be adequately represented by means of definitions taking so-called "classical form", that is definitions that draw the boundaries of categories by stating the necessary and jointly sufficient conditions on category membership.

The idea that categorization is structured as definitions of the classical form has been the dominating view – not least in philosophy, psychology, and linguistics – from antiquity at least up till the last quarter of the twentieth century (Taylor, 2003, p. 20). The origin of the classical view on categorization is customarily thought to be Aristotle's Metaphysics (1984, sect. 996b & 1011b). An important advantage of the classical view is that once the proper definition has been sorted out, one will know the definite boundaries of the category in question and so be able to deduce exactly if something meets the definition or not. For instance, if one defines 'bachelor' as an unmarried man, it means that 'bachelor' applies to everything that is both a man and is unmarried. Each of these conditions is necessary, but neither is individually sufficient.

Historically, the classical view of definitions has dominated attempts to provide lexical definitions in philosophy. Recent research within experimental psychology, however, has revolutionized the understanding of categorization (Rosch, 1973; Rosch, 1975; Rosch et al., 1976; Lakoff, 1987, p. 6-7) and this has had a profound influence on discussions about definitions. Today it is uncontroversial, at least within the cognitive sciences, that there are a number of important aspects of human categorization that the classical definition-based model is unable to account for. So let us take a look at some of the central problems.

## Fuzziness as a challenge

The first major problem is this: if categories were structured by necessary and sufficient conditions, it would entail definite categorial boundaries. Either something is a member of some category, or it is not. Either you fulfill the conditions or you don't. One can find many examples of categories that work in this way. Take for instance the category prime number, which can be defined, as *all natural numbers that have exactly two distinct divisors: 1 and itself.* Even though it may take a while to figure out that $(2^{43.112.609} - 1)$ is a prime, once you do there is no discussion. Any natural number is either totally in or totally out.

However, inspired by Wittgenstein's concept of family resemblance (Wittgenstein, 1990), Eleanor Rosch and her colleagues designed experimental research which demonstrated convincingly that there are many categories where this is not the case (Rosch, 1975). While tables and chairs are obviously part of the class of phenomena which 'furniture' refers to, it is less obvious whether carpets or TV sets enjoy the same status. Linguistic vagueness is by no means a new discovery, but even though the vagueness of predicates such as 'obese' is uncontroversial, the fuzziness of the reference of natural kind terms such as 'vegetable' and 'fruit' may still come as a surprise. No one doubts that apples and oranges are convincing candidates for membership of the category we call 'fruit', but think of coconuts or cucumbers. Many might be tempted to use 'vegetable' when referring to the latter. The fuzziness of categories, thus, in many cases speaks strongly against the possibility of capturing the meaning of terms by use of classical definitions.

## Prototypicality structure as a challenge

Another major problem is the following. If categories can be adequately represented in the form of classical definitions, then fulfilling the necessary and sufficient conditions should make any object a full member of the specific category on a par with all other members; all members should be equally typical and no member should be better than any other. But some members are generally found to be more central than others. The classical example in the literature is that the robin is thought of as a better example of the category 'bird' than the penguin or the ostrich. The issue of prototypicality is very much related to the problem of conceptual fuzziness above. But while fuzziness concerns what is going on at the boundaries of categories, prototypicality focuses on the structure at the centre of the category in question. Categories that exhibit typicality-effects are called graded categories, and it is not the case, as one might suspect, that gradedness is only a feature of fuzzy categories. Even categories with distinct boundaries turn out to be graded on close examination. Experiments have shown that for instance the category 'even numbers', which have quite clear boundaries, display typicality-effects: experimental participants consistently rate numbers like '2', '4', '6', and '8' as better examples of even numbers than, say, '34' (Armstrong et al., 1983, p. 276).

## Trouble for the lexical definition of 'learning'?

How are these objections against the classical conception of lexical meaning relevant for the issue of a definition of 'learning'? They are relevant, we claim, because if the meaning of 'learning' is structured as word meanings are most, attempts to provide a definition of 'learning' which has the sharp distinctions of the classical form and still captures the meaning of 'learning' in common use may be in vain. There is hence little reason to think that a classical definition of 'learning' can be easily achieved. Both prototypicality and gradedness appear to stand in the way of this pursuit.

Are some instances of learning more prototypical than others? We believe so. To see this, compare (1) "acquiring mathematical skills through the solving of equations in a textbook" with (2) "acquiring the ability to run a marathon in under 3 hours". Here (1) is definitely more prototypical than (2). Indeed, some might even be hesitant to think that building up the physique to run a marathon in an impressive time amounts to learning. It is simply not entirely clear whether such a change in physical capacity would qualify as learning. And there are likely many other (and perhaps better) examples involving fuzziness and gradedness due to the psychological, physiological, and sociological complexity of learning as a real-world phenomenon.

The central point is that the meaning of 'learning' appears to be fuzzy as well as graded. Consequently, a classical definition, however ingeniously constructed, simply seems unsuitable to capture the meaning of this term. So it seems that we have to choose between, on the one hand, a vague definition[6] referring to prototypical instances which might to some extent capture the common use of 'learning' and, on the other hand, something clear and precise which is not apt to represent the term's ordinary meaning.

A further worry one might have is that in everyday speech we use 'learning' to refer to quite disparate phenomena which may be very different in nature. For instance, the phenomenon of *learning to walk* might be a case of actualizing an innate biological potential, whereas *learning to read* is a case of acquiring a set of culturally based skills. *Learning to sit still* or *control ones temper* on the other hand might be cases of acquiring the ability to suppress specific natural reactions in order to live up to certain social norms (which, of course, presupposes yet another form of learning).

It is obviously an empirical question to what extent these different phenomena of learning differ in nature. But if they do, this might be a significant part of the answer to the question why it is especially hard to come up with a single concise comprehensive definition of 'learning'.

If, indeed, this is the situation, the recommendation could be to opt for the development of several (as many as required) definitions each targeting a distinct kind of the various phenomena we currently cram together and label as 'learning'.

In the remaining part of the chapter we want to consider two types of definition which escape these difficulties since they are not supposed to correspond with the lexical meaning of a term.

## Stipulative definitions and explicative definitions

As we have seen, clear-cut lexical definitions of the words theorists get from ordinary discourse may be more difficult to achieve than is usually assumed.

### Simple stipulative definitions

While a lexical definition of 'learning' in the form of necessary and sufficient conditions on learning might seem desirable for the sake of clarity, there may be good reasons not to strive for this type of definition after all. But rather than giving up on clarity and precision, we may look for alternative ways of defining the term, which do not fall prey to the difficulties related to lexical definitions.

One option, often seen in academic work, is to go for a *stipulative definition*. A definition is stipulative when we simply stipulate that for the purposes of certain contexts the meaning of a word is such and such, that is, when we simply decide to attach a specific explicitly stated meaning to a term or symbol in specific contexts. Thus, rather than trying to capture or represent a meaning that a symbol already has, a stipulative definition assigns a meaning to a symbol without any commitment to capturing, or even taking into consideration, the meaning others have attached to the symbol.

Accordingly, since we may decide to assign a symbol whatever meaning we like, stipulative definitions can neither be said to be correct nor incorrect. Indeed, this is one reason why they are useful for academic purposes. When a word has a long history of use, and has been understood differently by different theorists belonging to different research traditions it may eventually become impossible to employ the word in a way which does not conflict with one or the other of the interpretations previously thought to be the correct lexical definition of the word. In that case, by stipulating that one will use the word with a particular meaning, one can employ the word with a clear and precise meaning without a commitment to the further claim that one has represented its meaning in ordinary discourse correctly. So while Illeris' definition of learning is problematic as lexical definition it could still be an acceptable stipulative definition.

With respect to stipulative definitions what matters is not correctness but whether the stipulated meaning is precise and picks out a category of phenomena with properties such that regarding them as belonging to the same type is useful for our theoretical and communicative purposes. In biology, for example, a concept representing human hearts, as well as toe nails and tree sap would be much less useful than one which refers to the fetuses of mammals at a particular developmental stage.

However, since a stipulative definition is free to fix the meaning of a term in any way one finds useful there is no guarantee that it will retain the meaning that a term has in ordinary language. Thus, as Frank Jackson notes, stipulating the meaning of a term involves the risk that one might end up discussing something completely different from what ordinary folk are interested in and 'think is up for discussion' (Jackson 1998, p. 42) when the term is used. So when theorists define the meaning of a common or familiar term they are typically not content merely to assign it a stipulative meaning without any relation to how ordinary speakers and other theorists usually use the term. Instead, they attempt to carve out a meaning for the term which is both suitable for theoretical purposes and close to the term's ordinary meaning. This leads us to the so-called explicative definitions.

*Explicative definitions*
While the ideal of both capturing ordinary meaning and providing terms with a meaning fruitful for theorizing is usually implicit when terms are defined, it is closely related to the aims of what philosophers, following Carnap (1947; 1950), refer to as explicative definitions, or explications. Roughly speaking, an explication makes "a vague or not quite exact concept used in everyday life or in an earlier stage of scientific or logical development..." exact by replacing the concept "... with a newly constructed, more exact concept" (Carnap, 1947, p. 7-8). And this seems to be exactly what we look for in stipulative definitions of pre-existing terms.

However, we should not simply adopt Carnaps requirements on adequate explications as the aims of our definitions. In particular, we should be critical of the idea that a sufficiently exact explication of a term requires its meaning to be specified in scientific terms. Thus, to avoid impossible, or inappropriately demanding, requirements on explicative definitions we should relinquish the requirement that they have to consist only of scientific vocabulary. Indeed, for the most part, something relatively exact seems to be all that we can ask for when we look for a definition of a term. This is commonly the case in explorative settings or when the development of novel theoretical frameworks requires that one initially operates with less than the highest standards of scientific accuracy.

In addition, we should be careful not to automatically assume that the speakers of a language, e.g., English, all attach the same meaning to every term they use. For instance, the meanings attached to 'culture' by anthropologists may well be different from the meaning that ordinary speakers attach to the expression. Orthographically identical expressions may hence have different meanings in different sociolects and idiolects, so that it is misleading to refer to something in the singular as *the* meaning attached to the expression in common usage. Thus, rather than simply saying that an explication should make the meaning of a term more precise, how we think of explication should reflect that what we want to make more precise may be the meaning attached to a term by a particular group of speakers in their common usage of the term.[7]

By modifying Carnaps original conception of explications to reflect these considerations, we get an account measuring the adequacy of explications in terms of criteria closely linked to the theoretical and communicative roles we generally want our explicatively defined terms to play.[8] According to this modified conception of explicative definitions, an adequate explication should satisfy the following four criteria to a sufficient degree.

### a. Similarity
Relative to a particular group of speakers, the explicative definition of a term, e.g., the term 'learning', should be such that for the most part where the explicated term has been used by speakers in the relevant group the explicative definition would have applied equally well. But it is not required that the similarity is very extensive.

**b. Exactness**
The explicative definition of a term should have an exact form, possibly the familiar form of a classical definition, which places the term's meaning within a framework of relatively exact, interrelated concepts.

**c. Fruitfulness**
The explicative definition of a term should be such that it can be used in many generalizations, or universal claims.

**d. Simplicity**
And, finally, the explicative definition of a term should be as simple as the requirements of the other three criteria (similarity, exactness, and fruitfulness) allow.

Let us now examine, what happens if we evaluate Illeris' definition of learning against these criteria. First, with respect to Similarity, the proposed definition seems to do fairly well. It seems that in most cases the definition can replace 'learning', despite of some situations where it is wrong to say that so and so is a case of learning but right to say that it is a lasting change in the capacities of a subject which is not due to biological maturation or aging. So when we take into account that there does not have to be a very extensive similarity Illeris' definition may be adequate as an explication in this regard.

Further, the notion of a change in a subject's capacities, as well as the notions of biological maturation and aging, appears to be reasonably precise notions, which either have or can be given an exact scientific interpretation. So, arguably, the definition is also sufficiently precise to be acceptable as an explication. It should be mentioned, however, that the verdict concerning this question is not entirely clear, since particularly the notion of aging is a matter of dispute.

With respect to fruitfulness, however, Illeris' definition looks problematic due to its inclusive nature. Its inclusiveness may ensure that every instance of learning falls within its purview but this broadness comes at a considerable cost, since the broadness of the category tends to preclude interesting generalizations about its extension. In other words, the proposed conception of learning becomes so broad that very little of interest can be said about learning in general. To see this, consider Illeris' own general claim that all learning incorporates three dimensions, or aspects, namely the content dimension, the motivational dimension and the relational dimension, which concerns the social and societal aspects of learning (Illeris, 2006, p. 35-43; Illeris, 2007, p. 16-18). Despite of being phrased in very abstract and somewhat vague terms this general claim still appears to conflict with the definition we are discussing. Getting your legs amputated while you are in a coma hence qualifies as learning if 'learning' is defined as any lasting change in the capacities of a subject which is not due to biological maturation or aging. But the claim that such a change in a subject's capacities has a motivational dimension or a content dimension appears questionable, unless we interpret the thesis regarding the three dimensions of learning so loosely that it becomes void of any interesting consequences.

Moreover, while we have introduced the notion of sufficient fruitfulness as a requirement on explications, the criterion is not merely an arbitrary condition on satisfying a technical predicate. The demand for fruitfulness is motivated by thoughts about how the categories we employ in scientific research best serve the growth of our knowledge. Accordingly, if we group together phenomena with very little in common only very few insights about a particular phenomenon in a category will carry over to other phenomena in the category. So there would be little theoretical interest in concepts denoting widely disparate phenomena, since knowledge of one phenomenon would not permit us to infer anything about the other things that the category subsumes. On the other hand, if our categories instead comprise phenomena with extensive similarities what we learn about a particular phenomenon in a category will extend more readily to the others.

Therefore, while nothing prevents Illeris from relying on his definition of 'learning' as a stipulative definition, his proposal seems problematic both as a lexical definition of 'learning' and an explication of the term. Its broadness implies that it includes phenomena which we would ordinarily reject as examples of learning. But even if we disregard its ability to capture the ordinary meaning of 'learning' the definition seems to have a problem, since its broadness tends to undermine its theoretical significance by making it a common label for a very heterogeneous set of phenomena. Whether it is a lexical definition or an explication we want, we should be looking for something narrower.

## How should we proceed to define 'learning'?

Now that we have distinguished lexical definitions from mere stipulations and explications, how should we proceed with the project of defining 'learning'? As we have argued, there may be insurmountable obstacles to obtaining an adequate lexical definition, and a more or less random stipulation is clearly an unattractive alternative. So rather than pursuing these types of definitions, we want to suggest how Illeris' definition might be amended to provide a more suitable explication of the term.

To that end, we want to suggest a definition of 'learning' adopted from psychological research. According to this definition, something is learning if and only if it is a 'process by which relatively permanent changes occur in behavioral potential as a result of experience' (Anderson 1995, p. 4-5). With minor variations this definition is the one we find in typical psychology textbooks, e.g., (Gray 2011; Gross 2010; Klein 2012; Poling et al. 1990).

This definition has two important advantages over Illeris' proposal. First, Anderson's definition is not vulnerable to those counterexamples to Illeris' definition that we put forward. Amputation of a person's leg influences the person's behavioral potential in various ways, but does not qualify as learning on Anderson's psychological definition because the change does not result from experience (although it may be accompanied by experiences that the person might learn from). Second, while it may not yet be the optimal explication, the fact that Anderson's definition is narrower than Illeris' definition means that it is likely to allow more interesting generalizations about the phenomena it refers to. For example, the general claim that motivation is important to learning seems highly plausible on this proposal, since motivation is likely to influence how experience affects neural states in order to change behavioral potential. Anderson's definition hence seems to fare better than Illeris' proposal with respect to both Similarity and Fruitfulness.

We do not, however, mean to suggest that this proposal should end the discussion of how 'learning' should be explicated. It may only be an initial step towards a more optimal definition, or a wide range of individually distinct narrower explications. Thus, whereas Anderson's definition reflects the very broad theoretical assumption that experience affects behavioral potential, future research may allow us to say more precisely which of our experiential psychological processes our research on learning should investigate. But while the proposal here is modest in this sense, it is not without ramifications. If we think of learning as something primarily related with psychological conditions and phenomena, then it stands to reason that learning should be investigated with methods suitable for settling psychological questions. In addition, theories of learning built on concepts without psychological respectability would have to be left by the wayside. So although we do not purport to have the optimal explication of 'learning', the potential consequences of our proposal are considerable.

## Concluding remarks on the work ahead in providing a definition of learning

A main conclusion of our discussion is that clear and precise definitions are of extreme importance in academic theorizing in general. This requirement also applies to learning theory. One attempt to provide the definition of 'learning' required in this area can be found in the work of Knud Illeris. But as we have shown, his proposal is problematic.

The question, then, is how to proceed from here. We consider two options: A lexical definition or a (partly or fully) stipulative definition. Problems loom for lexical definitions because of the fuzziness and prototype structure of word meanings, which together pose a non-trivial challenge to the idea of pinpointing the meaning of a word in ordinary usage. It may be that these challenges can be overcome, but even if one is optimistic that they will be so eventually, there is currently no common agreement on a definition of 'learning'. For this reason one might prefer to bracket the search for a lexical definition and move on by opting for a stipulative definition instead.

This is perfectly legitimate, and may even be recommendable in the light of the above. But it should be noted that stipulative definitions in the simplest form will be of little use or merit unless they are guided by criteria akin to the criteria of adequacy Carnap suggested for explicative definitions, namely similarity, exactness, fruitfulness and simplicity. A definition which meets these criteria will be of great value to theories of learning and the discussion of it deserves a central place in the scholarship of teaching and learning. As a step towards achieving this goal, we recommend replacing Illeris' definition of 'learning' with Anderson's psychological definition.

Focusing on the task of providing a definition of the meaning of 'learning' in the way we have proposed here, will also minimize the risk of conflating definitions with theories. Such conflation will deflect attention from the need for a definition. Theories are of course essential to scholarship of learning, but before the question of definition is settled there is no way to be sure what the theories actually describe and explain.

## Notes

1. This paper was presented at the conference On the definition of learning, University of Southern Denmark, 2014. We are grateful to the audience for their comments.
2. For a brief overview, see Gupta (2014).
3. To avoid confusion we will use single quotation marks to indicate whenever we are *mentioning* a word, e.g., when discussing a given definition of the word 'learning', rather than *using* a word to refer to certain phenomena, as in "An adequate theory of learning presupposes an accurate definition of 'learning'."
4. See, for instance, Robinson (1950) for a historical overview and p. 8-11 for an account of Aristotle's view on definition.
5. For the wording of the definition in Danish, see Illeris (2006, p. 15).
6. I.e., a definition so vaguely formulated that using it for its intended purpose will require that theorists implicitly supplement it with an additional level of interpretation. The need for such further interpretation, however, severely limits the utility with respect to ensuring theoretical clarity.
7. Thanks to Christopher Winch for discussion here.
8. For further discussion of Carnaps notion of explication, see e.g. Boniolo (2003) and Hanna (1968).

## References

Anderson, J.R. (1995) *Learning and Memory: An Integrated Approach*. Chichester: Wiley.

Aristotle (1984). *The Complete Works of Aristotle*. Barnes J. (ed.). New Jersey: Princeton University Press.

Armstrong S. L., Gleitman L., & Gleitman H. (1983). What some concepts might not be. *Cognition, 13*, p. 263-308

Boniolo, G. (2003). Kant's explication and Carnap's explication: The Redde rationem, *International Philosophical Quarterly, 43*(3), p. 289-298.

Carnap, R. (1947). *Meaning and Necessity*. Chicago: The University of Chicago Press.

Carnap, R. (1950). *Logical foundations of probability*. Chicago: Chicago University Press.

Fine, K. (1994). Essence and Modality: The Second *Philosophical Perspective* Lecture. *Philosophical Perspectives, 8*, p. 1-16.

Gray, P. (2011). *Psychology*. New York, Worth Publishers.
Gross, R. (2010). *Psychology. The Science of Mind and Behaviour*. London: Hodder Education
Gupta, A. (2014). Definitions. In: Edward N. Zalta (ed.). *The Stanford Encyclopedia of Philosophy* (Spring 2014 Edition). Retrieved from http://plato.stanford.edu/archives/spr2014/entries/definitions/.
Hanna, J. F. (1968). An explication of explication. *Philosophy of Science, 35*, p. 28-44.
Illeris, K. (2006). *Læring*. Roskilde: Roskilde Universitetsforlag.
Illeris, K. (2007). Læringsteoriens elementer - hvordan hænger det hele sammen, in Illeris, K. (ed.) *Læringsteorier*, (p.11-38). Roskilde: Roskilde Universitetsforlag.
Illeris, K. (2009). A comprehensive understanding of human learning. In Illeris K. (ed.): *Contemporary theories of learning*, (p. 7-20). London: Routledge.
Jackson, F. (1998). *From Metaphysics to Ethics: A Defence of Conceptual Analysis*. Oxford: Oxford University Press.
Klein, S. (2012). *Learning: Principles and Applications*. London: Sage.
Lakoff, G. (1987). *Women, Fire, and Dangerous Things*. Chicago: The University of Chicago Press.
Poling, A. et al. (1990). *Psychology*. New York: Plenum Press.
Robinson, R. (1950). *Definiton*. Oxford: Clarendon Press
Rosch E. (1973). On the Internal Structure of Perceptual and Semantic Categories. In: Moore, T. E. (ed.): *Cognitive Development and the Acquisition of Language*. New York: Academic Press.
Rosch, E. (1975). Cognitive Representations of Semantic Categories. *Journal of Experimental Psychology: General, 104*(3), p. 192-233.
Rosch, E., Mervis, C. B., Gray, W. D., Johnson, D. M., & Boyes-Braem, P. (1976). Basic Objects in Natural Categories. *Cognitive Psychology. 8*, p. 382-439.
Schaffalitzky de Muckadell, C. (2014). On Essentialism and Real Definitions of Religion. *Journal of the American Academy of Religion, 82*(2), p. 495-520.
Taylor, J. R. (2003). *Linguistic categorization*. Oxford: Oxford University Press.
Wittgenstein, L. (1990). *Philosophische Untersuchungen*. Werkausgabe Band 1. Frankfurt am Main: Suhrkamp [1953], p. 225-580.

# Articulating a base for the development of a concept of learning

*Nina Bonderup Dohn*

## Introduction

As pointed out by Qvortrup, Wiberg, Christensen and Hansbøl in the introduction to this anthology, in contemporary educational and societal debates the term 'learning' is used in a variety of ways, not all of them compatible, to denote a range of phenomena, the relationship between which is unclear to say the least. 'Lifelong', 'cooperative', 'organizational', 'informal', 'inquiry-based', are just a few of the terms put in front of 'learning' in the literature; each of them implicating (rather divergent) units of analysis, entities of learning, and, more generally, epistemological and ontological assumptions about person, world, knowledge, and coming-to-know. Clarifications and development of the conceptions of learning involved in these uses are needed, as is the articulation of a (theoretically and empirically informed) concept of learning which may be used in the evaluation of the varying conceptions.

The aim of this article is to take a first step towards such an articulation. A seemingly reasonable way to start is to ask oneself what a theory of learning must be able to account *for*; what it must take *into* account in doing so; and how much of this must be taken into account in the very concept of learning utilized in developing the theory. Now, the question of how theories and concepts relate to one another is itself a complex one since concepts will be theory-informed, or even theory-loaded (Kuhn 1970; Lakatos 1980; Popper 1972). Suffice it here to say that some theoretical assumptions will be inherent in the concepts used in a theory, and that these theoretical assumptions will develop as the theory is developed, but that the theory in general will have a wider theoretical and empirical scope – it will say more about the world – than what is implied in its concepts alone.

Engeström has pointed out four questions that any theory of learning must be able to account *for*: 1) *Who* are the subjects of learning,

2) *Why* do they learn, 3) *What* do they learn, and 4) *How* do they learn (Engeström, 2001). Similarly, Lave and Packer claim that A) the relationship between subject and world, B) the telos of change, and C) the mechanisms whereby this change is accomplished are "the minimum components of any theory of learning worthy of the name" (Lave & Packer 2008). Here, some assumptions about *at least* Engeström's points 1 and 3 and Lave & Packer's point A will be inherent in the concept of learning employed in the theory: one will need an initial idea of who the subjects of learning are (and this idea will involve an idea of how the subjects and the world relate ontologically), and what the learning process may result in (a basic notion of the ontology of the result – is it skills, knowledge, identity, life, etc.; and what is the nature of these?) to even be able to identify instances of learning. Arguably, why subjects learn and how they do it (and similarly the telos and mechanisms of the process) will be more empirical questions to be answered through developing the theory in dialogue with empirical research. In the following I therefore concentrate on *the subjects of learning, their relationship to the world (including other subjects)*, and *the ontology of the result of learning*. I shall argue for 4 basic claims about these matters that must be taken into account, not only in developing the theory, but in developing its concept of learning itself. The claims are all philosophically and empirically corroborated. They are:

1. We need a concept of learning focused on the individual.
2. A focus on the individual does not imply neglecting sociality. The individual is a "person-in-the-world", and the world has social aspects.
3. These 'social aspects' play different roles in learning (ranging from constitutive ones to contingent mediatory ones) at different analytical levels, in different content domains, and in different situations.
4. Knowledge fundamentally has tacit, actionable embodied aspects and acquires essential context-dependent content and form from its situated realization.

I should stress that my contention is not that these 4 claims exhaust all possible claims which must be taken into account in articulating a concept of learning. They are necessary aspects, but are probably not jointly sufficient. Other claims might be necessary to take into account, too. There is for instance ample evidence that representations, both in the form of mental models and in the form of linguistic propositions, also play a role in learning (e.g. Gentner & Stevens 1983; Held, Knauff, & Vosgerau 2006; Johnson 1987; Lakoff & Johnson 1999; Magnani & Nersessian 2002). Even the starkest proponents of tacit knowledge accept this (Molander 1992, 1996; Wackerhausen 1991), at least for some stages of learning (Dreyfus 1979; Dreyfus & Dreyfus 1986) and perhaps building on tacit aspects (Polanyi 1962, 1966). I choose to focus on the proposed 4 claims because they form a middle ground between individualist cognitivist theories (which tend to neglect the significance of tacit knowledge as well as the constitutive role which social context plays for some domains in some situations) on the one hand and situated learning theories (which tend to neglect that sociality is not constitutive of learning in all domains, at all times, at all analytical levels) on the other. My aim is precisely to point out that this middle ground holds promise of being a viable position from which to articulate a concept of learning.

## Line of argumentation – 'philosophizing with'

Before turning to the argument for the claims, however, a metaphilosophical comment about the line of argumentation – and especially about the way it integrates different philosophical and empirical perspectives – is in order. I shall undertake a kind of 'philosophizing with' (Hansson 2008) the academic field of learning; more specifically the kind of 'philosophizing with' where one is a 'dialogue partner with a voice of one's own' (Dohn 2009a, 2011b).

This role implies applying 'traditional' philosophical methods such as conceptual analysis, 'armchair intuitions', hermeneutical and phenomenological analysis, commonsense observations etc. to issues within the empirical sciences. Not in the manner of an a priori (and thereby final) arbiter of the meaningfulness of concepts and views as envisaged by e.g. the logical positivists (Ayer 1936; Carnap 1928) and practiced today by Bennett and Hacker (Bennett & Hacker 2003). Nor solely as 'conceptual clarifier' or 'interpreter of empirical results' on the platform of and within the limits set by present day empirical science such as e.g. Dennett, Jackson, and Searle do (in very different ways and with very different results) (Dennett 1991; Jackson 1998; Searle

1983). Instead, 'philosophizing with' as a dialogue partner amounts to utilizing input from 'traditional' philosophical methods together with all available empirical evidence to construct reasonable theories. The expectation is not that all pieces may be brought to fit nicely together – most often the philosophical input will be diverse as will empirical results, with contradictions within each type of input as well as between types. Nor do I accord more initial credibility to one form of input over the other: Armchair intuitions may be proven wrong empirically (the shortest distance between two points is not a straight line if space is curved, as it has turned out – against intuition – to be in our universe). Empirical observations may be shown to be based on untenable conceptual presuppositions and therefore to be misconstrued (as the presupposition of a clear-cut observer-phenomenon distinction led to problematic observations concerning the nature of light a hundred years ago). As others have argued, too, the goal is to reach 'reflective equilibrium' (Goodman 1955; Rawls 1971) where diverse forms of input are weighed against each other, some pieces are discarded (with explanation of why and of why they were formerly thought to be acceptable), others reinterpreted and the most reasonable account construed. Philosophy has a distinct voice of its own in this dialogue for 'reflective equilibrium' because it pursues normative and foundational issues beyond empirical investigations.

Utilizing this type of integrative and dialogically minded 'philosophizing with', I shall in the following formulate and provide evidence (philosophical and empirical) for the abovementioned 4 claims.

## Claim 1:
## A concept of learning must be focused on the individual

This claim is corroborated by a *philosophical argument*, more specifically by an example of 'armchair' *conceptual analysis* in the vein of Anglo-American analytical philosophy. The outset for the argument is Jackson's point that when a theory makes use of a term which is also used in everyday 'folk' parlance, then it is essential to accommodate the 'folk' understanding of the concept to which the term refers (Jackson 1998). This does not mean that a theory cannot define and articulate new concepts – on the contrary, this is a fully legitimate and often necessary move. It only means that when one does, one should not choose words in use in folk parlance to denote these new concepts if they do not incorporate the concepts implied by the everyday usage of the words. Otherwise equivocations and misunderstandings will ensue, because one is not "addressing the subject we folk suppose is up for discussion", but will in point of fact have "changed the subject by stipulating new uses of the words" (Jackson 1998, p. 38, 42).

Now, learning is certainly a term in (wide) use in everyday folk parlance so Jackson's point is highly relevant here. Further, it is key to the pre-understanding of learning inherent in this folk usage that it takes its outset in the individual human being: Learning is seen as a phenomenon (process, state, disposition, etc.) which takes place in, happens to or is undertaken by the individual person. Therefore, in articulating a concept of learning, focus must be on the individual.

However, establishing this necessary focus does not imply that we cannot find – empirically, philosophically or both – that an individual's learning can only be fully understood with reference to the evolvement of a system (e.g. a system of interactions between people). Nor does it rule a priori against speaking of a system's learning as in 'learning organizations', 'group learning' or 'computer learning'. But it does mean that the relationship to individual human learning must be explicated. In the latter case (system's learning) by arguing for why the given system's learning is similar to individual human learning in ways significant enough to make it reasonable to use the same term. In the former case (dependency on a system) by explicating in detail (probably both empirically and philosophically) how the individual's learning comes about as part of the evolvement of the system.

Therefore, more specifically, claim 1 does imply that some theoretical uses of the term 'learning' are problematic as they stand. Talk of "learning as social practice" (translated subtitle of Nielsen & Kvale 1999) or "learning as an aspect of the activities in which persons are constituted by, and constitute themselves in participation in communities of practice" (Lave & Packer 2008, p. 33) is incomplete at best if no discussion is provided of how these ways of using the term relate to everyday conceptions of learning as an individual phenomenon. Similarly, talk of "learning as neuronal connecting" (as opposed to e.g. 'learning facilitated by neuronal connecting') compels an explication of exactly how the neuronal connecting 'is' the same process (or state, disposition, etc.) as the phenomenologically well-known situation of for instance coming to know a new fact or becoming able to exercise a new skill.[1]

## Claim 2:
## The individual is a 'person-in-the-world' which implies sociality

Claim 1 postulates a need for a focus on the individual. This might be understood as directing the concept of learning 'inwards', away from social interaction, into the mind (or brain) of the individual. The gist of claim 2 is to counter this interpretation by pointing out that the individual is a "person-in-the-world", not an entity in radical independent existence from the world. Focus on the individual therefore directs the concept of learning to the world and entails analysis of the significance of world for individual being. Further, the world has social aspects and for this reason a focus on the individual does not entail neglecting sociality. Claim 2 is substantiated by two types of *philosophical* argument – a Heidegger-Merleau-Pontian *phenomenological* analysis and a Hegelian *hermeneutic* one – and by a host of *empirical* corroborating examples from *sociocultural theory*, especially situated learning.

Firstly, as Heidegger and Merleau-Ponty argue, we are as humans always already in the world as acting beings, meeting and making use of the world in its *Zuhandenheit* for us (Heidegger 1986; Merleau-Ponty 1962), i.e. meeting the world as always-already a meaningfully structured place which we 'know our way around' in as we 'go about our business'. This 'being in the world' is prior to any distinction between subject and object – a distinction which does not in fact arise before a 'breakdown' of the *Zuhandenheit* (to use Dreyfus' expression, cf. Dreyfus 1991) into a *Vorhandenheit* of the things present. Breakdowns, on their part, happen when things perform in ways not anticipated in our 'going about our business', such as when a hammer breaks in use or the computer program crashes in the midst of writing.

Now, in and through our acting in the world, we have a pre-reflective understanding of it. It is precisely this pre-reflective understanding which is challenged in breakdowns – but which on the other hand is necessary for breakdowns to occur: It is our pre-reflective understanding which lets us have (unarticulated and non-reflected) anticipations that can be disappointed, thereby effecting the awareness of self-and-anticipations as different from object-and-what-happened. Our pre-reflective understanding of the world is holistic and gestaltlike – aspects and traits are constituted *as* aspects/traits by the overall meaningfulness of the situation. They get their more specific meaning through their significance for the overall meaningfulness. A hammer is a hammer (as opposed to e.g. a metal block on a stick) in virtue of being used in human practices of building and joining things together; practices that take place in certain types of settings such as workshops, building sites etc. Actually, 'metal blocks on sticks' are metal blocks on sticks in virtue of human practices, too, e.g. the human scientifically inspired practice of attempting to define artefacts in 'neutral' terms.

Thus far, the argument establishes that the individual is a 'person-in-the-world'; which means that to understand the individual's learning, one has to understand its outset in human agency in the world and the pre-reflective understanding established in and through it. The further argument is that the human practices and settings in which meaningfulness is rooted are developed culturally and that people are 'initiated' into them through interaction with others. Therefore the world (as the meaningful whole that meets us and of which we always already have a pre-reflective understanding) has social aspects. For this reason, even though a concept of learning must focus on the individual's learning (to accommodate to claim 1), this does not imply neglecting sociality. The focus on the individual of itself leads to the requirement of taking sociality into account.

This phenomenological argument for the non-negligibility of sociality, even given the individual as outset and focus, may be supplemented with the hermeneutic analysis of Hegel and Marx concerning how man's 'nature' is constituted (an analysis which, it should be noted, at least in its Hegelian version to some extent was a source of inspiration for Heidegger): We become who we are through the interaction with others, and the interpretation and self-interpretation which this interaction allows us to make. With Hegel's example: The Master and Slave co-constitute each other's identities – the Master is as dependent on the Slave's recognition of him as Master to be, and understand himself to be, Master, as the Slave is of the Master's recognition of him as Slave to be (and understand himself to be) Slave. Both need the other and the other's recognition to be who and what they are (Hegel 1807/1952). Or with more modern examples: Teacher and students are mutually dependent on each other's recognition of these identities to actually be teacher and students (and not just persons coincidentally happening to be simultaneously in the same room); employer and employees similarly depend on each other for their interpretation and self-interpretation of these identities. In this sense, too, the world has social aspects, and the person-in-the-world is a social being.

Empirically, the claim is corroborated by research within sociocultural theory, especially situated learning. Examples of more concrete ways in which 'the world has social aspects' abound, from Vygotsky, back to the theory's roots in Hegel and Marx (Packer & Goicoechea 2000), and onwards to phenomenologically inspired sociology and anthropology, with Bourdieu's investigations of 'habitus' and 'field' as an obvious focal point. To mention just a few of these:

- Vygotsky initially demonstrated the significance of internalization of cultural practices for the development of the "higher psychological processes" (Vygotsky 1978). He did this both with semi-empirical examples, supported by non-rigorous observation, of language acquisition, and with empirical investigations of how children develop cognitive functions and learn through guidance from others, within their 'zone of proximal development'.
- Vygotsky's Western heirs have supplied several detailed examples. These include Wertsch's analyses of individual action as tool-mediated (Wertsch 1998), Cole and Scribner's research on reasoning in different cultures (Cole & Scribner 1974; Scribner & Cole 1973) and Hedegaard's studies of classroom learning (Hedegaard 1995). Säljö (2000) provides a nice overview of empirical evidence within this field, as well as a developed theoretical argument for the socio-cultural approach.
- Holland, Lachicotte Jr, Skinner, and Cain report from a range of empirical cases, including studies of the lives of Nepalese and Japanese women, of 'initiation' into Anonymous Alcoholics, of views on women within a college world, and of the self-understanding of a man diagnosed with a mental disorder (Holland, Lachicotte Jr, Skinner, & Cain 1998). These cases all document that individuals acquire and improvise their identities as persons living in worlds which are already socially figured.
- Greeno and others have provided detailed studies of the significance of classroom interactions for creating (or withholding) opportunities

to learn for given students and for the resulting cognitive understandings which the students develop (Greeno & Gresalfi 2008; Greeno & van de Sande 2007; Gresalfi 2009; Hand 2010). These studies thus show how the individual's learning is dependent upon and inherently bound up with the individual's being in the world of social interaction.
- Lave and Wenger, building on Lave's empirical research, describe tailor apprentices' learning as a learning of "who is involved; what they do; what everyday life is like; how masters talk, walk, work, and generally conduct their lives..." (Lave & Wenger 1991, p. 95). This 'social' learning is an integral part, they argue, of developing the craftsmanship of tailoring. Individual 'skill acquisition' must be understood through the person's being in the world of social negotiation of tailor identity.
- Bourdieu's analyses of the habitus and field of both indigenous cultures and cultures within the Western world, notably the academic one(s), provide documentation for the immersion of the individual in a social world (Bourdieu 1977, 1990, 2000). These analyses provide the empirical analogue to Heidegger's philosophical claims about *das Man* that we always already are part of and think with, as well as to Merleau-Ponty's argument that we meet the world first and foremost as acting, bodily beings whose understandings of the world are incorporated in their doings.

## Claim 3:
## The role of 'social aspects' in learning depend on content domain and situation

Claim 2 posits that 'the world has social aspects'. However, claiming this does not necessarily imply that the world is socially mediated, constituted, or determined in the same way and to the same degree across different content domains and across diverse kinds of situation. It certainly doesn't imply a full-blown social constructivist ontology, i.e. that the world is fully constituted through social interaction, as (one might interpret) e.g. Barnes and Bloor (to) hold (Barnes & Bloor 1982). Jumping from the demonstration of 'social aspects' to the claim that the world is socially constituted and constructed, thus neglecting possible differences between domains and situations, amounts to making an 'overgeneralization mistake'. Sociocultural theorists are prone to make this mistake because they take their outset in the 'system of social interaction', be this in terms of the 'social practice' (e.g. Lave & Wenger 1991; Nielsen & Kvale 1999), 'activity system' (Engeström 1987), 'communities of practice' (Wenger 1998) or the like. Such an outset makes it easy to overlook differences in social mediation between domains and situations because the investigating hereof involves questioning the dominance of sociality which to some extent is presupposed in their formulation of their outset.

Opposing this tendency, claim 3 states that the role of 'social aspects' in learning does in fact depend on content domain and situation. Corroboration of this claim is given through a philosophical analysis, in the vein of *analytical philosophy*. The analysis supplies a framework of analytical levels at which a given situation poses demands, possibilities, and restrictions on a person – what I term the 'requirement characteristics' of the situation. The plausibility of the framework is illustrated by indicating its applicability to *empirical examples*. In addition, reference is made to *empirical research* which independently of the framework documents that at least one of the levels (the domain-internal context level, cf. below) is not fully constituted by socially mediated or constituted requirements at the other levels.

The framework is inspired by Wedege's distinction between 'situation context' and 'problem context' (Wedege 1999), put forward to qualify the discussion of what is involved in knowing mathematics in different situations. The idea is to enable an analytical teasing out of different social, material, psychological, domain-specific etc. aspects that contribute in intertwinement to forming the situation's 'requirement characteristics'. At least five analytical levels at which a situation shows 'requirement characteristics' may be distinguished, and the degree of social mediation will vary between these levels. The levels are:

- The *domain-internal context level* (concerned with the domain, e.g. literary novels or set theory)
- The *activity-internal context level* (concerned with the activity itself, e.g. writing a wiki entry, reading a book, solving a math problem, buying groceries)
- The *activity-framing context level* (the setting in which the activity takes place, e.g. a classroom or a supermarket)

- The *activity-enabling structure level* (the general societal structuring of practices of a certain kind, e.g. the structuring of learning practices within schools)
- The *cultural practices level* (the very general level of cultural tools and ways of behaving which are prevalent in a culture across its practices; e.g. the manufacturing of stone into tools in the Stone Age; the practice of today of communicating extensively through information technology such as emails or websites).

The more general levels are culturally dependent and therefore socially mediated to a high degree. For the lower levels, the degree of social dependency varies across domains and settings. Thus, for example, the activity of mountaineering is much less socially constituted at the domain-internal and activity-internal context levels than is interior decorating. This is perhaps most easily seen by considering that what constitutes 'absolute failure' of meeting the requirement characteristics in the first case (falling to one's death) is not socially negotiable, but depends entirely on the lack of meeting certain physical requirement characteristics at the domain-internal level (e.g. demands concerning friction and balance) and at the activity-internal context level (the movement of one's body along the cliff side). In contrast, what constitutes 'absolute failure' in the case of interior decoration is socially negotiable, also at the domain-internal and activity-internal context levels, though not fully socially constituted, since there will also be requirement characteristics concerning material aspects and physical movement.

Despite this general difference between the domains of mountaineering and interior decoration, the former might in specific situations, such as a mountaineering contest, have quite a high degree of socially constituted requirement characteristics. The activity-framing context level may lead to socially constituted requirement characteristics at the lower levels as well, e.g. by setting rules for which equipment may be used and precisely how the feet may be placed. This situation might be contrasted with one where the activity-framing context is not one of mountaineering at all, but instead that of a person traversing a mountain because it is the quickest way to fetch a doctor on the other side. In this situation, 'anything goes' as concerns outfit, equipment, and 'styles of walking and climbing' – the only thing that matters is coming safely and quickly to the other side.

Extending this perspective to the field of learning, 'social aspects' play different roles in learning, depending on which analytical level, domain, and situation one is focusing on. Intuitively, physical reality constrains the building of a bridge more than it constrains reading, though of course the latter is (amongst others) dependent on light conditions and physical functioning of the perceptual system and of the brain (but so is building a bridge). Learning to undertake these two forms of activity in a competent way thus seemingly involves social mediation to different degrees.

Only few empirical examples have been analyzed with this framework. I have utilized the first three levels in an assessment of the validity of the claims put forward by the *Programme for International Student Assessment* (PISA) that they test students' 'knowledge and skills for life' (Dohn, 2007). I analyze test items to illustrate how requirement characteristics at the activity-framing context level (participating in an international test of individuals' skills and knowledge) influence requirement characteristics at the activity-internal context level (e.g. length restrictions and argumentation strategies acceptable in an essay-like answer) and at the domain-internal context level (e.g. characterizations of form and genre in the provided text). To give one example, a test item concerning two letters about graffiti includes the question "Regardless of which letter you agree with, in your opinion, which do you think is the better letter? Explain your answer by referring to *the way* one or both letters are written" (OECD, 2002, p. 45) According to PISA's scoring rules, the following two answers are adequate: A) "I like Helga's letter. She was quite dominant getting her opinion out." B) I think Helga's letter was the better one of the two. I thought Sophia's was a bit biased." But C) "Helga had a better argument" is deemed not to supply sufficient explanation and thus to be inadequate. Now, in most other situations than a PISA test (i.e. in most other activity-framing contexts), A), B) and C) would count as on a par at the domain-internal level. If for instance a quick impression of viewpoints in a class was needed to form discussion groups, all three responses would be adequate. If, on the other hand, the activity-setting context was one of writing an essay, A) and B) would be just as much in need of explanation as is C, i.e. they would all be inadequate. But the requirement characteristics of the special setting of a two-hour survey to assess skills put narrow limits on the length of writing appropriate per test item, whilst still demanding *some* argumentation, and therefore in *this* specific situation the three answers are evaluated differently. The upshot of my analysis with the framework thus is that social mediation at higher levels frames and delimits requirement characteristics at lower levels without on the other hand fully determining or constituting them.

I have also used the framework to analyze the competence demands actually, implicitly, placed on students when web 2.0-mediated learning activities building on bottom-up, many-to-many interaction and user-generation of content are utilized within educational practices (Dohn 2009b, 2009c). Similarly, the framework would serve to explain results of research within situated learning and activity theory. For example, a study by Säljö and Wyndhamn shows students to have difficulties in solving an everyday problem of finding the right postage for a letter when this activity takes place in the formal school setting (Säljö & Wyndhamn 1993). My framework would help explain how requirement characteristics of the activity-setting context of school for the students (wrongly) frame applications of math (domain-internal context level) and postage considerations (activity-internal context level). Similar analyses could be made of Schoultz, Säljö, and Wyndhamn's study of students' understanding of TIMMS test items (Schoultz, Säljö, & Wyndhamn 2001), of Lave's example of math in the supermarket (Lave 1988) and of de la Rocha's example of math in the kitchen (de la Rocha 1985).

Finally, the empirical research of e.g. Yackel & Cobb and Greeno & collaborators shows the significance of the content domain in itself in establishing what counts as adequate reasoning within the domain (Greeno & Gresalfi 2008; Greeno & van de Sande 2007; Gresalfi 2009; Yackel & Cobb 1996). That is, their research shows the necessity of distinguishing requirement characteristics at the domain-internal context level and of attributing them weight in analysis of classroom interactions in addition to socially constituted requirement characteristics at higher levels. Arguably – though they do not have this focus themselves – their concrete examples also show that what constitutes the requirement characteristics at the domain-internal level is an interplay of socially mediated and non-socially mediated domain features which vary in degree of social mediation between domains.

## Claim 4:
## Knowledge has tacit, actionable, context-dependent, embodied aspects

The corroboration of Claim 4 combines *analytical philosophical arguments, phenomenological analysis,* and *empirical results* from *distributed cognition* and *situated learning theory.*

The analytical philosophical argument takes its outset in the rule-following considerations of Wittgenstein and Ryle (Ryle 1949; Wittgenstein 1984), especially in their Scandinavian reception (Johannessen & Rolf 1989; Josefson 1998; Molander 1992, 1996; Rolf 1991) which interprets them as focusing on the tacit understanding of practice which makes rule-following possible. Thus, according to this reception, to follow a rule is not a question of interpretation, at least not if 'interpretation' is understood as involving any kind of articulation, reflection or consideration. Instead, it involves a tacit, practical, embodied understanding present in the action itself – a 'feel for' the unique situation and for what amounts to 'following the rule' here. This explains the need for examples in learning how to follow a rule. It also explains why it is necessary for learners to work through examples themselves rather than just have them explained by a teacher: Only through doing applications of the rule – examples – can one acquire the practical 'feel for' the situation. This practical 'feel for' is the 'gut feeling' whereby we (in practice, not intellectually) evaluate the rule and sometimes find that an exception to it has to be made. I should stress that this practical feel for the situation is part of what I above with Heidegger described as our pre-reflective, non-articulated understanding of the world. My viewpoint here is in line with the Heidegger-inspired phenomenological descriptions of Merleau-Ponty and Dreyfus (Dreyfus 1979, 1991, 2002; Merleau-Ponty 1962), but part company with those followers of Heidegger who would claim that being in the world involves *interpretation* of it, rather than 'non-reflective understanding-in-acting'. Interpretation, on the other hand, to my mind, *is* involved, in our coming into being as *persons*, as I suggested above with Hegel.

Phenomenological analysis, drawing in particular on Merleau-Ponty (Merleau-Ponty 1962) and his reception by Dreyfus and Dreyfus (Dreyfus 1979, 2002; Dreyfus & Dreyfus 1986), enables a more positive characterization to be given of the tacit, practical, embodied understanding postulated by the analytical philosophical argumentation.

This characterization determines practical understanding as grounded in immediate (intuitive) recognition of the overall gestalt of the situation and "holistic pairing of new situations with associated responses produced by successful experiences in similar situations" (Dreyfus & Dreyfus 1986, p. 35). Gestalt recognition and response pairing are flexible forms of identification, i.e. they accommodate situational variations instead of grouping situations into rigid categories.

Empirical results from especially the fields of distributed cognition (Hutchins 1993, 1995; Hutchins & Klausen 1996) and situated learning (Lave 1988; Lave & Wenger 1991; Nielsen 1999; Nielsen & Kvale 1999; Wenger 1998) serve to flesh out knowledge and competence as relationships-in-action between the agent and the environment, including tools and people present. Thus, the detailed studies provided by these researchers of (among others) sailors maneuvering a ship to port, pilots navigating a plane in a plane simulator, people grocery shopping in the supermarket, claims processors processing insurance claims, all clearly illustrate how knowledge is always locally realized and negotiated with aspects of situational specificity which are essential to its realization and cannot be abstracted away.

As I stated in the beginning of the article, there is amble evidence that mental and linguistic representations play a role in learning. However, the combination of Wittgensteinian and phenomenological arguments throws serious doubt on the claim that knowledge is *constituted* by mental or linguistic representation. Instead, these approaches strongly suggest that the primary ontology of knowledge is situated realization in the action it enables. This suggestion is corroborated by the cited empirical research. But if this is so, representation will necessarily involve fundamental ontological reconstruction, i.e. change in ontology. Conversely, making use of mental models or propositions in action requires ontological transformation, too. Thinking and language quite obviously play large roles in human practices, but in general these are roles they have as part of *exercising* competence; they do not *constitute* competence. Thoughts and linguistic statements are important for expressing, articulating or redirecting understanding, but they are grounded in the tacit situational 'feel for' the situation; not the other way around.

In sum,[2] and taken together, these different arguments integrate to demonstrate the reasonableness of Claim 4: Knowledge fundamentally has tacit, actionable embodied aspects and acquires essential context-dependent content and form from its situated realization. It is grounded in immediate recognition of and response pairing to the situation's gestalt. Thinking and communicating are phenomena of knowledge-in-doing and as such take their meaning in part from the situation in which they arise.

## Concluding remarks

In this article I have utilized a form of integrative and dialogically minded 'philosophizing with' to argue for 4 basic claims concerning *the subjects of learning, their relationship to the world (including other subjects)*, and *the ontology of the result of learning*. These claims are:

1. We need a concept of learning focused on the individual
2. A focus on the individual does not imply neglecting sociality. The individual is a "person-in-the world", and the world has social aspects
3. These 'social aspects' play different roles in learning (ranging from constitutive ones to contingent mediatory ones) at different analytical levels, in different content domains, and in different situations
4. Knowledge fundamentally has tacit, actionable embodied aspects and acquires essential context-dependent content and form from its situated realization.

These claims must be taken into account in developing a theory's concept of learning. This means, at the very least, that a concept of learning should be consistent with them. Furthermore, it will count as a point in favor of a proposed concept of learning if it not only complies with the four claims in the negative sense of not contradicting them, but actually builds positively on them. A strong case will be made for a concept of learning if it not only builds positively on the four claims, but even supplies a platform on which they can be further nuanced and developed. This is so, because such a platform will itself supply new possibilities of the kind of 'philosophizing with' which I have been contending-through-use in this article: It will allow the development of a set of arguments integrating philosophy with other theoretical and empirical disciplines to the end of helping us better understand what learning is.

## Notes

1   This last comment corresponds to the well-known criticism of mind-brain-identity theories that it is not clear precisely what it means to postulate e.g. that a thought is identical to neuronal firing.
2   More elaborate versions of the argument may be found in (Dohn 2005, 2011a, 2013, 2014).

## References

Ayer, A. J. (1936). *Language, Truth and Logic*. London: Victor Gollancz.
Barnes, B., & Bloor. D. (1982). Relativism, Rationality and the Sociology of Knowledge. In: M. Hollis & S. Lukes (Eds.), *Rationality and Relativism* (p. 21-47). Oxford: Blackwell.
Bennett, M., & Hacker, P. M. S. (2003). *Philosophical Foundations of Neuroscience*. Oxford: Blackwell.
Bourdieu, P. (1977). *Outline of a Theory of Practice" translated by R. Nice*: Cambridge.
Bourdieu, P. (1990). *The logic of practice*: Stanford University Press.
Bourdieu, P. (2000). *Fascalian Meditations*. Stanford: Stanford University Press.
Carnap, R. (1928). *Logische Aufbau der Welt*. Berlin: Weltkreis Verlag.
Cole, M., & Scribner, S. (1974). *Culture and Thought: A Psychological Introduction*. Oxford: John Wiley & Sons.
de la Rocha, O. (1985). The Reorganization of Arithmetic Practice in the Kitchen. *Anthropology & Education Quarterly, 16*(3), p. 193-198.
Dennett, D. C. (1991). *Consciousness explained*. New York: Little, Brown and Co.
Dohn, N. B. (2005). *Læring i praksis - fremstruktureringen af et handlingsorienteret perspektiv*. Aalborg: Aalborg University.
Dohn, N. B. (2007). Knowledge and Skills for PISA—Assessing the Assessment. *Journal of Philosophy of Education, 41*(1), p. 1-16.
Dohn, N. B. (2009a). Erkendelsesteori og læringsteori - to sider af viden eller samme side med forskellige ord? In: M. Etemadi, M. Wiberg, M. Paulsen, & S. H. Klausen (Eds.), *Læring og Erkendelse*. Aalborg: Aalborg Universitetsforlag.
Dohn, N. B. (2009b). Web 2.0-Mediated Competence - Implicit Educational Demands on Learners. *Electronic Journal of E-learning, 7*(1), p. 111-118.
Dohn, N. B. (2009c). Web 2.0: Inherent tensions and evident challenges for education. *International Journal of Computer-Supported Collaborative Learning, 4*(3), p. 343-363.
Dohn, N. B. (2011a). On the Epistemological Presuppositions of Reflective Activities. *Educational Theory, 61*(6), p. 671-708.
Dohn, N. B. (2011b). Roles of Epistemology in Investigating Knowledge: "Philosophizing With". *Metaphilosophy, 42*(4), p. 431-450.
Dohn, N. B. (2013). 'Viden i praksis" - implikationer for it-baseret læring. *Res Cogitans, 1*, p. 94-128.
Dohn, N. B. (2014). On the necessity of intertwining 'knowledge in practice' in action research. *International Journal of Action Research, 10*(1), p. 54-97.
Dreyfus, H. (1979). *What Computers Still Can't Do*. New York: Harper & Row.

Dreyfus, H. (1991). *Being-in-the-world: A commentary on Heidegger's Being and Time, Division I.* Cambridge, Massachussetts: Mit Press.
Dreyfus, H. (2002). Intelligence Without Representation–Merleau-Ponty's critique of mental representation the relevance of phenomenology to scientific explanation. *Phenomenology and the Cognitive Sciences, 1*(4), p. 367-383.
Dreyfus, H., & Dreyfus, S. (1986). *Mind over machine. The power of human intuition and expertise in the era of the computer.* New York: Free Press.
Engeström, Y. (1987). *Learning by Expanding: An Activity-Theoretical Approach to Developmental Research.* Helsinki: Orienta-Konsultit.
Engeström, Y. (2001). Expansive learning at work: Toward an activity theoretical reconceptualization. *Journal of education and work, 14*(1), p. 133-156.
Gentner, D., & Stevens, A. L. (Eds.). (1983). *Mental models.* Hillsdale, N.J.: L. Erlbaum Associates.
Goodman, N. (1955). *Fact, fiction, and forecast.* Cambridge, Mass.: Harvard University Press.
Greeno, J. G., & Gresalfi, M. S. (2008). Opportunities to learn in practice and identity. In: P. A. Moss, D. C. Pullin, J. P. Gee, E. H. Haertel, & L. J. Young (Eds.), *Assessment, equity, and opportunity to learn* (p. 170-199). New York: Cambridge University Press.
Greeno, J. G., & van de Sande, C. (2007). Perspectival understanding of conceptions and conceptual growth in interaction. *Educational Psychologist, 42*(1), p. 9-23.
Gresalfi, M. S. (2009). Taking up opportunities to learn: Constructing dispositions in mathematics classrooms. *The Journal of the learning sciences, 18*(3), p. 327-369.
Hand, V. M. (2010). The co-construction of opposition in a low-track mathematics classroom. *American Educational Research Journal, 47*(1), p. 97-132.
Hansson, S. O. (2008). Philosophy and other disciplines. *Metaphilosophy, 39*(4-5), p. 472-483.
Hedegaard, M. (1995). *Tænkning, viden, udvikling.* Aarhus: Aarhus Universitetsforlag.
Hegel, G. W. F. (1807/1952). *Phänomenologie des Geistes.* Hamburg: Felix Meiner Verlag.
Heidegger, M. (1986). *Sein und Zeit; 16. Auflage.* Tübingen: Max Niemeyer Verlag.
Held, C., Knauff, M., & Vosgerau, G. (Eds.). (2006). *Mental models and the mind: Current developments in cognitive psychology, neuroscience, and philosophy of mind.* Amsterdam: Elsevier.
Holland, D., Lachicotte Jr, W., Skinner, D., & Cain, C. (1998). *Identity and agency in cultural worlds.* Cambridge Massachusetts: Harvard University Press.
Hutchins, E. (1993). Learning to navigate. In: S. Chaiklin & J. Lave (Eds.), *Understanding practice: Perspectives on activity and context* (p. 35-63). New York: Cambridge University Press.
Hutchins, E. (1995). *Cognition in the Wild.* Cambridge, Massachusetts: MIT Press.
Hutchins, E., & Klausen, T. (1996). Distributed cognition in an airline cockpit. In: Y. Engeström & D. Middleton (Eds.), *Cognition and communication at work* (p. 15-34). New York: Cambridge University Press.
Jackson, F. (1998). *From metaphysics to ethics: A defence of conceptual analysis.* Oxford: Clarendon Press.
Johannessen, K. S., & Rolf, B. (1989). *Om tyst kunskap: två artiklar.* Uppsala:

Uppsala Universitet.
Johnson, M. (1987). *The body in the mind: The bodily basis of meaning, imagination, and reason.* Chicago: University of Chicago Press.
Josefson, I. (1998). *Läkarens yrkeskunnande.* Stockholm: Studentlitteratur.
Kuhn, T. S. (1970). *The structure of scientific revolutions* (2 ed.). Chicago: The University of Chicago Press.
Lakatos, I. (1980). *The Methodology of Scientific Research Programmes: Volume 1: Philosophical Papers*: Cambridge University Press.
Lakoff, G., & Johnson, M. (1999). *Philosophy in the Flesh: The Embodied Mind and Its Challenge to Western Thought.* New York: Basic Books.
Lave, J. (1988). *Cognition in Practice - Mind, Mathematics and Culture in Everyday Life.* Cambridge: Cambridge University Press.
Lave, J., & Packer, M. (2008). Towards a social ontology of learning. In: K. Nielsen, S. Brinkmann, C. Elmholdt, L. Tanggaard, P. Musaeus & G. Kraft (Eds.), *A Qualitative Stance* (pp. 17-46). Aarhus: Aarhus University Press.
Lave, J., & Wenger, E. (1991). *Situated Learning - Legitimate Peripheral Participation.* New York: Cambridge University Press.
Magnani, L., & Nersessian, N. J. (Eds.). (2002). *Model-based reasoning: science, technology, values.* New York: Kluwer Academic.
Merleau-Ponty, M. (1962). *Phenomenology of Perception.* London: Routledge and Kegan, Paul.
Molander, B. (1992). Tacit knowledge and silenced knowledge: fundamental problems and controversies In: B. Göranzon & M. Florin (Eds.), *Skill and education: Reflection and experience* (p. 9-31). London: Springer Verlag.
Molander, B. (1996). *Kunskap i handling.* Göteborg: Diadalos.
Nielsen, K. (1999). *Musical Apprenticeship: Learning at the Academy of Music as Socially Situated.* PhD dissertation. Aarhus: Psykologisk Institut, Aarhus Univeristet.
Nielsen, K., & Kvale, S. (Eds.). (1999). *Mesterlære - Læring som social praksis.* København: Hans Reitzels Forlag.
OECD. (2002). *Programme for International Student Assessment. Sample tasks from the PISA 2000 assessment of reading, mathematical and scientific literacy.* Paris: OECD Publications.
Packer, M. J., & Goicoechea, J. (2000). Sociocultural and constructivist theories of learning: Ontology, not just epistemology. *Educational Psychologist, 35*(4), 227-241.
Polanyi, M. (1962). *Personal knowledge: Towards a post-critical philosophy* (Vol. 1158). Chicago: University of Chicago Press.
Polanyi, M. (1966). *The tacit dimension.* New York: Doubleday & Co.
Popper, K. R. (1972). *Objective knowledge: An evolutionary approach.* Oxford: Clarendon Press.
Rawls, J. (1971). *A theory of justice.* Cambridge: Belknap Press.
Rolf, B. (1991). *Profession, tradition och tyst kunskap: en studie i Michael Polanyis teori om den professionella kunskapens tysta dimension.* Övre Dalkarlshyttan: Nya Doxa.
Ryle, G. (1949). *The concept of mind.* London: Hutchinson's University Library.

Schoultz, J., Säljö, R., & Wyndhamn, J. (2001). Conceptual knowledge in talk and text: What does it take to understand a science question? *Instructional Science, 29*(3), p. 213-236.

Scribner, S., & Cole, M. (1973). Cognitive consequences of formal and informal education. *Science, 182*(4112), p. 553-559.

Searle, J. R. (1983). *Intentionality: An Essay in the Philosophy of Mind*. New York, NY: Cambridge University Press.

Säljö, R. (2000). *Læring i praksis - et sociokulturelt perspektiv*. København: Hans Reitzels Forlag.

Säljö, R., & Wyndhamn, J. (1993). Solving everyday problems in the formal setting: An empirical study of the school as context for thought. In: S. Chaiklin & J. Lave (Eds.), *Understanding practice: Perspectives on activity and context* (p. 327-342). New York: Cambridge University Press.

Vygotsky, L. S. (1978). *Mind in Society: The Development of Higher Psychological Processes*. Harvard: Harvard University Press.

Wackerhausen, S. (1991). Teknologi, kompetence og vidensformer. *Philosophia, 20*(3/4), p. 81-117.

Wedege, T. (1999). To know or not to know – mathematics, that is a question of context. *Educational Studies in Mathematics, 39*(1-3), p. 205-227.

Wenger, E. (1998). *Communities of Practice*. New York: Cambridge University Press.

Wertsch, J. V. (1998). *Mind as action*. New York: Oxford University Press.

Wittgenstein, L. (1984). *Philosophische Untersuchungen* (Vol. 1). Frankfurt a.M.: Suhrkamp.

Yackel, E., & Cobb, P. (1996). Sociomathematical norms, argumentation, and autonomy in mathematics. *Journal for research in mathematics education*, p. 458-477.

# The normative aspect of learning

*Merete Wiberg*

## Introduction

Human intention in terms of aiming and searching for standards of living, it will be argued, is an important element of learning processes and gives direction to personal learning. Learning is a complex phenomenon involving processes of change and adaptation. This chapter will address and discuss the normative aspect of learning as an inherent part of the processes of inquiry and problem solving which, according to John Dewey, characterize learning. Defining and trying to solve a problem by conducting processes of inquiry entails ongoing judgment of what might be valuable aims of and means for defining and solving the problem. The ongoing inquiry and dealing with ideas of how and why certain elements, such as means and aims in the process, are valuable constitute the dynamics of normativity. The *Bildung* tradition should be recognized for the insight that development of personal as well as societal values is an important aspect of learning and teaching (Humboldt [1797]1960). Learning is, seen from the perspective of the *Bildung* tradition, a personal formational process during which an individual realizes its own role as a particular person as well as a person connected with a universal level. When looking at human learning as change and development of a person's knowledge, understanding and competences, it should follow that learning must constitute what a person considers valuable. What, why and how we learn are important aspects of personal formation and influences and develops the spectrum and content of values in the personal horizon of meaning.

Gaining insights, knowledge and competences is important because what we learn eventually serves as a pathway and instrument to realizing what we believe is good and valuable. Therefore, education is important. From the personal perspective, what we assume to be 'good' and worthwhile directs our desire and will to learn, but because the person who is about to learn is not sure what is good or worthwhile, the individual needs to examine this as part of the learning process.

When teachers emphasize judgment and critical thinking, it is typically because they view investigation and inquiry of what is worthwhile learning important in the process of learning itself. Learning consist to a large extent of exercising, practicing and adapting to situations and conditions, but what drives these efforts must be ideas that both transcend and are part of these processes, such as the idea of perfection, enjoyment, happiness, desire to participate or the idea of creating a better life for oneself and others.

Moral learning is part of this approach to learning because dealing with what, from a personal perspective, is worthwhile learning influences moral thinking and conduct. Many circumstances, such as family background, educational policy and what Hans-Georg Gadamer (Gadamer 1986) described as 'horizons' influence what we consider worthwhile. The important point is that values not only influence learning processes but that dealing with values is part of processes of learning themselves.

The chapter contributes to a discussion of whether learning is or should be an instrument for promoting certain societal values or should rather be seen as an act where developing and dealing with standards and values is important in terms of formation of the student. Actual focus on learning outcomes in educational institutions across the world seems to further the view that learning is an instrument for achieving certain outcomes determined before the actual process of learning, and therefore the emerging and not foreseen aspects of learning, such as the development of personal values in the process, seem to be valued less than effective learning. It seems to sometimes be forgotten that effectiveness in itself is a value that will be at work in processes of learning.

The chapter will proceed with a discussion of how the dynamic aspect of normativity in learning is to be understood, by focusing on Dewey's concept of inquiry which, from a pragmatic point of view, is seen as the key concept in relation to understanding the phenomenon of learning, and subsequently understanding how values as operational ideas are at work in acts of inquiry. It will be concluded that the dynamic aspect of normativity in learning is to be found in the act of inquiry, where the individual learns to come to terms with the world and become an individual between particularity and universality.

The first section addresses the concept of normativity.

## Normativity and standards of learning

Normativity in the context of learning will in this chapter be defined as the way a person evaluates their own understanding and sets implicit or explicit standards for their aims of learning with respect to the role of learning as improving, changing or sustaining their way of living. Standards might explicitly be set by an individual, a group of individuals or society or they might be set as a matter of course. Values alone do not guide our desire to learn something, but they are inherent in the process of learning because, it will be argued, dealing with various standards and values is part of how learning takes place when seen as a process of inquiry. This might happen in the form of a challenge of standards of how to perform within a certain discipline or in the form of adopting the standards already given. If learning takes place in an educational institution, values and criteria within a disciplinary area would implicitly or explicitly be part of teaching and learning. Therefore, it should be emphasized that processes of learning not only result in outcomes of something decided beforehand but are also permeated with values which the students either conform to or are critical towards. The students are to deal with ideas of criteria and standards within a disciplinary field, and learning might be characterized by being a struggle where the individual strives to cope with what is considered valuable. Looking at learning from the perspective of the individual learner, the normative aspect of learning is to be found in the interplay between individual and world, when the individual in an inquiring process tries to come to terms with the world. The Hegelian concepts of particularity and universality, which will be addressed later, will help us to understand the interplay between individual and world.

The aim, when focusing on normativity and learning, is not to prescribe how learning should be facilitated. The idea is rather to address individuals' desire and motivation to learn and their understanding and evaluation of what is worthwhile learning. The view on values in this chapter is inspired by Dewey's concept of ideas as operational tools (Dewey [1929]1990]. Values are seen as a certain kind of ideas which, along with other ideas, are operational in acts of inquiry. Values address what is considered valuable and worthwhile, such as questions of what a certain competence or ability contributes to personal and societal development. For example, a young person who has decided to study journalism will during the studies train certain skills, techniques and competences, while at the same time, as part of the learning process, dealing with standards and norms of the discipline and therefore going through a process of personal development because their repertoire and understanding of values are developed. According to Christopher Winch, who deals with professional knowledge from a philosophical perspective, the way a skill is exercised tells something about the person and not the technique itself (Winch 2012, p. 64). Winch's perspective will be addressed later in the chapter, but it might be added that dealing with disciplinary standards and values will inevitably constitute the way the skill in question is exercised.

The spectrum of human learning covers basic aspects of life, such as learning to walk, as well as more existential aspects of life, such as personal development. Human learning includes more than adjustment to an environment. 'More' might be understood in terms of human searching and striving for meaningfulness, which includes valuation of what is good or bad to strive for. Seen in a learning perspective, it includes valuation of what is worthwhile learning. "For education is not just, as is often said, for life. It is the search for a quality of living" (Peters 1974, p. 416). We might say that an important aim of education is to develop 'seer of values' to use an expression from the German philosopher Nicolai Hartmann: *"Ethical man is in everything the opposite of the precipitate and apathetic man. He is the seer of values, he is sapiens in the original sense of the word: the "taster". He it is who has a faculty for the fulness of life's values, that "moral faculty."* (Hartmann[1932] 2007, p. 45)

Being 'normative' means to set and describe standards for what is considered valuable. Underlying these standards are an ongoing search for and valuation of what is good and bad standards for how to lead a life. Learning is a means of change, development and improvement of human life, and therefore the concept of learning must address how standards for change and improvement are inherent and developed in processes of learning when an individual tries to cope with the world. Normativity concerns the concept of learning when it comes to motivation, because motivation to learn can be seen as closely related to an individual's interests and valuation of what is worthwhile learning, for example when they wish and intend to learn a skill or a discipline, either because they find it important and meaningful for their own life or maybe because they find it important for society. When asking a person why they want to learn something, for example to play an instrument, the answer might be that learning to play this instrument is valuable because it will contribute to joy and beauty in life. Other answers might be that somebody told the person to learn something the person does not see the point in learning. This is often the case in schools and something that troubles teachers and politicians. What is considered valuable and meaningful stems from the perspective of both individual and community, because the community sets standards for what is valuable to learn and constantly requires individuals to meet the standards.

In the education system, it is seen as a problem if students do not show interest in learning and therefore do not engage themselves in the processes of learning they are intended to. In order to solve this societal problem, various methods, some of them characterized as evidence based, are developed by researchers and other professionals to motivate and bring about learning; however, the problem is that these methods usually focus on change of behaviour, rather than seeing learning as a process where a person tries to come to terms with the world. Whether students pay or do not pay interest in the intended learning, we need to understand what influences intentions of learning and how intentions of learning are related to a search for individual meaningfulness and social standards of living. In order to discuss the concept of learning with respect to individuality and normativity, Dewey's concept of inquiry and Hegel's dialectical philosophy will be applied to address the individual's inquiring process of coming to terms with the world. In the next section the concept of inquiry will be addressed.

## The concept of inquiry

The concept of inquiry in relation to learning applied in this chapter is developed by John Dewey, who understood the act of inquiry as an important aspect of the transformative process that occurs in learning. Dewey defined the concept of inquiry in the following way: "Inquiry is the controlled or directed transformation of an indeterminate situation into one that is so determinate in its constituent distinctions and relations as to convert the elements of the original situation into a unified whole" (Dewey 1991, p. 108). Jim Garrison argues in the chapter

"The "Permanent Deposit" and Hegelian Thoughts in Dewey's Theory of Inquiry" (Garrison 2006) that learning and the concept of inquiry are closely connected in Dewey's philosophy, and furthermore that Dewey was strongly inspired by Hegel in how he understood the inquiring process. In order to discuss the interplay between individual and world, and the role of inquiry in the process of learning, approaches to Dewey's use of G.W. Hegel's dialectical philosophy will be included (Good 2006, Shook & Good 2010; Garrison 2006). Dewey was simultaneously inspired by and critical towards some aspects of Hegel's dialectical method, especially the idea of absolutism (Garrison 2006). Many Dewey researchers agree that Hegel's way of switching between identifying conflicts in what appears to be coherent wholes and overcoming the conflicts by developing new concepts (Hegel [1807]1977) is to be found in a reconstructed version in Dewey's philosophy. An ongoing shift between indeterminate and determinate situations can be seen in the processes of development that Hegel described in the *Phenomenology of Spirit*. James A. Good, who has done research on the influence of Hegel's philosophy on Dewey's, describes Hegel's theory of knowledge as a theory of learning or discovery, and he emphasizes how Hegel – like Dewey – struggled to overcome the gap between the subject as the knower and the object as what is known.

> Because he [Hegel M.W.] rejected Cartesian dualism and developed a functionalist psychology, Hegel's theory of knowledge is more accurately described as a theory of learning or discovery (...) Hegel emphasized that there is no unbridgeable opposition between the knower and the known, and truth is the way the world is for subjects (...). This characterization of learning was based upon a novel conception of the self and its relationship to the world (Good 2006, p. 24).

The Hegelian conceptualization of the relationship between the self and the world is also clear in Dewey's work *Knowing and the Known*, where Dewey and Bentley developed a transactional theory in order to conceptualize the relation between the knower and the known as an entangled relation (Dewey and Bentley [1949] 1989). The development of 'consciousness' in *Phenomenology of Spirit* is characterized by shifts between indeterminate and determinate situations. The mechanism or logic of change[1] is that consciousness builds up what appears to be a meaningful explanation of how reality is to be understood, but again and again it collapses due to flaws in understanding (see also Dewey [1897]2010).

Human learning might, inspired by Hegel, be understood as a 'struggle' that helps individuals come to terms with being social beings: the struggle which, in the *Phenomenology of Spirit*, is the story of how 'consciousness' develops through stages of different shapes of consciousness, and during the process learns to understand the relationship between self and the world in terms of a mediation process between an individual and a social (Allgemeine) level. An example of the Hegelian dynamics of normativity in a process of learning is given in the section "The law of the heart and the frenzy of self-conceit" (Hegel 1977: p. 221-228) ("Das Gesetz des Herzens und der Wahnsinn des Eigendünkels") (Hegel 1973, p. 275-283). The consciousness believes that its own understanding of what it is to be good, in terms of following the law of the heart, conforms to the understanding of all other individuals.[2] The problem, Hegel points out, is that the consciousness's understanding of goodness is only for itself and not for the other: "The consciousness which sets up the law of its heart therefore meets with resistance from others, because it contradicts the equally *individual* laws of their hearts" (Hegel 1977, p. 227). The struggle here, which might be seen as a process of learning, is for the consciousness to come to terms with the conflict between its understanding of its own goodness and other individuals' different understandings. In order to move on in life, the individual at this stage must challenge its own understanding and definition of goodness and explore the meaning of the phenomenon of goodness. In order to move on from this situation, which is confusing because of the resistance the individual meets from other individuals, it must transform its understanding of the concept and develop its concept of goodness into something else. This may lead to conforming or non-conforming to the understanding of other individuals.

During the process that Hegel unfolded in *Phenomenology of Spirit*, processes of development, which we here understand as processes of learning, might be seen as a description of how the personal striving of learning – or perhaps resistance to learning – is challenged when it meets other individuals and other understandings and how mediation between a particular individual and a universal level, represented by other individuals, takes place. The normative aspect in this process must, from the perspective of the individual, be seen as the ongoing change of understanding, evaluation and valuation of what it is facing.

Dewey's conceptualizing of development as the move from an uncertain situation to certain situations, and the idea of understanding problem solving as moving from an uncertain situation to a kind of wholeness, very clearly illustrates the inspiration from Hegel (Dewey [1938] 1991). According to Jim Garrison, Dewey reconstructed the Hegelian dialectics and transformed it into a naturalized theory of inquiry. Garrison stresses that Dewey, like Hegel, thought that knowledge proceeds from the vague individual to the more determinate individual, not from either the concrete to the abstract or from the particular to the generalized (Garrison 2006 p. 6). The role of concepts and ideas is to be tools in creating connections between particulars and to move towards a more determined situation characterized by wholeness (Dewey [1938] 1991, p. 108). Dewey's understanding of ideas is interesting and relevant when trying to conceptualize how and why dealing with values is essential in processes of learning. The next section addresses Dewey's concept of ideas as working and operational.

## Ideas and values

Ideas are, according to Dewey, operational and are working in knowing (and thinking) acts of inquiry and therefore in processes of learning (Dewey [1938] 1991; Dewey [1929] 1990). The understanding of ideas as working and operational is as follows: "First, the active and productive character of ideas, of thought, is manifest (...) Ideas are anticipatory plans and designs which take effect in concrete reconstructions of antecedent conditions of existence" (Dewey [1929] 1990, p. 133). This is very useful when dealing with how values and valuation plays a role in the process of learning, because values are without doubt a certain kind of ideas. Following Dewey's view on ideas, values must be a kind of ideas that address what we as human beings consider valuable and worthwhile to strive for, and in this sense they work operationally when learning takes place; also, ideas are essential for reconstruction of valuation. The role and status of ideas has been discussed throughout the history of philosophy, for example in the Medieval Problem of Universals, but whether values are real in terms of having a certain ontological status or are a result of human negotiations, their role in an act of inquiry is always operational. An important insight from Dewey is that conceptual dualisms between the material and the ideal are very problematic. Dewey's anti-dualistic claim has the consequence that ideas are not ideals in the sense that they can be isolated from material and human action. Ideas are – and here Dewey probably follows Aristotle and Hegel – always embodied and situational and therefore active and working. Furthermore, they are active in forming human action with respect to the process as well as the result of the act. Ideas are mediating tools between particularity and universality because they simultaneously transcend and work in a particular situation, for example a situation where learning is taking place. Ideas work as standards and ideals for what a student is to achieve, and therefore ideas are operational in mediating between the individual student and the community of a disciplinary area in which the student to some extent aspires to participate.

## Mediation between subject and object – particularity and universality

One of the problems that occurs when trying to get a conceptual grip of the normative aspect of learning is how to understand the interplay between what in philosophy is conceptualized as subject and object. If learning is understood as an act that in some way establishes a relation between a subject and an object, the analytical point of view must be the interplay between an acting subject and 'an object' that is characterized by being shared by other individuals and therefore belongs to the social sphere or common world. The object might be material (physical) or symbolic (spiritual) or both, which is the case if the object is another human being. The 'subject' is, in modern philosophy, usually understood as consciousness, I, individual or self, while the object is understood as 'something' the subject relates to, for example through perception, intention (intentionality), use, etc. If a sharp distinction between subject and object is drawn – as for example in some cognitive theories of learning that focus on learning as something that takes place *in* the subject, where the metaphor for 'in' is the 'mind' as a kind of place for either storing knowledge or performing network activities (Bereiter 2002) – it will lead to a dualistic position. Trying to avoid a sharp distinction between subject and object, on the other hand, will lead to a non-dualistic position. There are problematic aspects to both positions: a dualistic position has a tendency to isolate parts of an individual, for example the mind or intellect, while a non-dualistic position falls short of answering how to differentiate between a subjective and an objective, intersubjective level.

Dewey's philosophy, including his philosophy of learning, has an inherent focus on how to avoid dualisms; Hegelian philosophy was an inspiration, although he transformed the Hegelian dialectics. To understand what it means to be a person in relation to anything other than oneself is an issue that has been dealt with in the *Bildung* tradition, which deals with the interplay between individual and sociality while trying to conceptualize how an individual process of becoming is at the same time a process of coming to terms with oneself as a social being. Gadamer referred to Hegel's understanding of *Bildung* as the ability of an individual to move beyond particularity and understand themselves as part of the universal: "Whoever abandons himself to his particularity is ungebildet (...) – e.g., if someone gives way to blind anger without measure or sense of proportion" (Gadamer 2013, p. 11).[3] The individual stands midway between particularity and universality due to being both particular and universal (Good 2008, p. 29).

Gadamer's concept of 'horizon' (Gadamer 1986 p. 307) and the concept of 'historical horizon' (Gadamer 1986, p. 308) indicate the interplay between subject and world and between particularity and universality, while including a historical perspective:

> All self-knowledge arises from what is historically pregiven, what with Hegel we call "substance" because it underlies all subjective intentions and actions, and hence both prescribes and limits every possibility for understanding any tradition whatsoever in its historical alterity (Gadamer 2013, p. 313).

From a learning perspective it is important to add that Gadamer did not understand horizons as closed, or the idea of an individual to move beyond a horizon as impossible. Horizons are, according to Gadamer, "something into which we move and that moves with us. Horizons change for a person who is moving" (Gadamer 2013, p. 315). The concept of 'horizon' is useful for understanding the dynamics of the normative dimension of learning. If we understand ourselves metaphorically as situated in a landscape, the horizon(s) we are embedded in must inevitably influence our movements, while at the same time being changed by our movements. From a learning perspective there are several affinities with Dewey's view of learning as undergoing and trying at the same time (Dewey [1916] 1985, chapter 11). The learning individual is 'caught' in a certain context, because it is a living organism in historical time, while at the same time having the ability to think and reflect and therefore to take action and change and transcend the environment. A criterion for learning is, according to Dewey, when the combination of undergoing consequences and change caused by action is loaded with significance: "When an activity is continued into the undergoing of consequences, when the change made by action is reflected back into a change made in us, the mere flux is loaded with significance. We learn something" (Dewey [1916] 1985, p. 146). The central insight here is the understanding of learning as loaded with significance. To be aware of significance, which is Dewey's criterion for learning, is to be aware of the values inherent in the situation – for example whether the consequence of an action is valuable or not, or whether the elements of the action were suited for attaining the result wanted. It is important to remember that the unit of analysis i.e. situation consists of both the person (subject) who intends and acts and the social and material world (object).

## Mastery of skills and standards of learning

If learning is loaded with meaning, and processes of learning include a dynamic aspect of normativity, learning must have consequences for the development of character. Christopher Winch focuses on this aspect and discusses, from a Wittgenstein inspired perspective, how human activity, such as mastery of a skill, should be seen as normatively constituted, due to being part of a culture with evaluative practices and norms of conduct (Winch 2012, chapter 5). Winch's concept of culture might, from a Gadamer perspective, be seen as horizon of meaning. Winch stresses the normative dimension from the perspective of the subject when he discusses the connection between the ability to exercise a skill in a certain way and the character of the person who exercises that skill (Winch 2012, p. 62-64). Exercising a skill does not, according to Winch, in itself constitute personal character. It is the way the skill is exercised that tells something about the person, rather than the technique itself (Winch 2012 p. 64). An important point, according to Winch, is "that a skill is a personal attribute and a technique a way of doing things that can be described or enacted within the exercise of skill" (Winch 2012, p. 59-60).

According to this understanding, differentiation of the subject or the particular individual is to be found in the way a skill is exercised and in the way the individual understands its own role while exercising the skill. In a learning perspective, the ability to exercise a certain skill might be seen as a result of a process of learning. Skill as a personal attribute can be understood with respect to individual standards of how to exercise the skill, while at the same time it should not be forgotten that individual standards are influenced by social and disciplinary standards. An important dimension of standards is that they transcend the here and now: "Standards, as it were, take a 'stand' in relation to the flux of experience, operating by bringing an element of definition and permanence which enables a transcendence of the here and now. They bring meaning through constancy" (Bonnett 1986, p. 115). Setting standards is what takes place in the interplay between individual and world, and it is an important element of the normative aspect of learning, bringing about a temporary permanence in terms of underlying values in processes of learning.

Part of a process of becoming a person is to learn to perform a set of skills in a certain way (compare Winch 2012). If normativity is understood as human striving towards what is considered worthwhile and meaningful in a certain context or culture, the aspect of normativity in learning might be seen as the personal striving and search towards what is worthwhile to learn, from the perspective of the individual or a group of individuals. The concept of standard is useful in the argumentation because setting a standard includes a process of inquiry in order to 'fix' a standard, at least for the time being. Standards must be seen from the perspective of the individual as well as the social context. Therefore, setting standards and searching for standards in an inquiring process might contribute to identifying what takes place in the mediating process between individual and world.

## Conclusion: The dynamics of normativity in learning and coming to terms with the world

What is so special about the concept of learning is that it addresses concrete processes in situations. This is what makes the field of learning different from the *Bildung* tradition, where focus is on stating overall aims for education beyond concrete situations of learning. If striving for worthwhileness is to be understood in a learning perspective, there must be a focus on how normative processes take place in concrete situations, such as the classroom or the kindergarten.

Theories of learning are primarily analytical and descriptive with regard to how and why the phenomenon of learning is to be understood; however, following the line of this chapter, theories of learning must include and be aware of the normative aspect of learning, if the interplay between human intentions to learn and a world with standards of evaluation and norms is to be understood. The 'struggle' of the individual trying to learn and understand its own role and position in the world might be seen as processes of coming to terms with understanding other individuals, including understanding what other individuals understand as worthwhile (which includes the search for truth or development of the best possible ways to do or deal with things). This means that human learning might be seen as interplay between conflict and conciliation, or between a particular and a universal stance: me and what appears as the other.

It has been argued that normativity is important for understanding the phenomenon of learning and the normative aspect of learning found in the interplay between individual and world. In order to deepen the understanding of the interplay between individual and world, it was discussed as a subject/object relation and, inspired by Hegel, it was argued that the individual stands midway between particularity and universality, being both particular and universal. If the reasoning concerning the concept of learning is based on this premise, the process of learning must be understood as both particular and universal. An important argument for this statement is a dialectic position that stresses differentiation between subject and object and therefore offers an alternative to dualistic and non-dualistic positions of learning. The contribution to teaching and learning practices is helping to clarify how normative processes of learning, in terms of individual understanding and evaluation, are part of the learning process itself. In order to understand motivation as more than just inner psychological processes, learning is conceptualized in terms of how valuable learning, from the perspective of the individual, is constituted when struggling to come to terms with the world.

## Notes

1. Logic in the philosophy of Hegel (and Dewey) is to be understood as a practical logic, or a logic of life (Good 2006, p. 27)
2. According to Charles Taylor, this section in the *Phenomenology of Spirit* refers to the understanding of natural goodness in the Enlightenment, such as it might be understood by Rousseau (Taylor 1977, p. 165).
3. Like Dewey, Gadamer disputed Hegel's idea of absolute Spirit. This will not be discussed in this chapter, where Hegel's philosophy of development will be seen in a pragmatic perspective as an ongoing, never-ending process – a process of learning.

## References

Bereiter, Carl (2002). *Education and Mind in the Knowledge Age*. Mahwah: Lawrence Erlbaum Associates, Inc. Publishers.

Bonnett, Michael. (1986). Personal authenticity and public standards. In: Cooper, D.E.(ed.) *Education, values and mind. Essays for R.S.Peters*. London, Boston and Henley: Routledge & Kegan Paul.

Dewey, John ([1916]1985). *Democracy and Education*. John Dewey The Middle Works, Vol. 9. Edited by J. A. Boydston Carbondale and Edwardsville: Southern Illinois University Press.

Dewey, J. ([1929]1990). *The Quest for Certainty. John Dewey, The Later Works, Vol. 4*. Edited by J. A. Boydston. Carbondale and Edwardsville: Southern Illinois University Press.

Dewey, John ([1938]1991) *Logic: The Theory of Inquiry. John Dewey The Later Works*. Edited by J.A.Boydston Volume 12, Carbondale and Edwardsville: Southern Illionois University Press.

Dewey, John & Bentley, Arthur ([1949]1989). *Knowing and the Known*, In: *John Dewey The Later Works*, Volume 16. Edited by J.A.Boydston Carbondale and Edwardsville: Southern Illionois University Press.

Dewey, John ([1897]2010). Hegel's Philosophy of Spirit: 1897, University of Chicago. In: Shook,. J.R. & J.A.Good. *John Dewey's Philosophy of Spirit*. New York: Fordham University Press.

Gadamer, Hans-Georg (2013). *Truth and Method*. London/New York: Bloomsbury Academic, revised second edition 2004.

Hans-Georg Gadamer. (1986) *Wahrheit und Methode*. Tübingen: J.C.B.Mohr (Paul Siebeck).

Garrison, Jim (2006). The "Permanent Deposit" and Hegelian Thoughts in Dewey's Theory of Inquiry, *Educational Theory* 56(1) p. 1-37.
Good, John.R..(2006). *A Search for Unity in Diversity*. Oxford: Lexington Books.
Hartmann, Nicolai. ([1932]2007). *Moral Phenomena. Volume 1 of Ethics*. New Brunswick, New Jersey: Transaction Publishers.
Hegel, G. W. F. (1977).*Phenomenology of Spirit*. USA: Oxford University Press.
Hegel, G. W. F. ([1807]1973). *Phaenomenologie des Geistes*, Frankfurt am Main: Suhrkamp.
Humboldt, W. von. (1797]1960). Theorie der Bildung des Menschen. In: *Wilhelm von Humboldt. Werke 1*. herausgegeben von Andreas Flitner und Klaus Giel: Darmstadt: Wissenschaftliche Buchgesellschaft.
Peters, R.S. (1974). *Psychology and Ethical development*. London: George Allen&Unwin Ltd.
Shook, John.R.& Good, James A.(2010). *John Dewey's Philosophy of Spirit*. New York: Fordham University Press.
Taylor, Charles (1984). *Hegel*. Cambridge: Cambridge University Press.
Winch, Christopher (2012). *Dimensions of Expertise*. London: Continuum.

# Realism and learning

*Oliver Kauffmann*

## Introduction
In this chapter, I argue for a realistic conception of learning. Basically, this means a defense of two assumptions: (i) that, to a large extent, learning from an epistemological point of view involves asymmetrical processes of knowledge- and skill-acquisition; (ii) that acquired knowledge and skills cannot be understood without reference to a mind-independent world to which the subject has cognitive access. In addition, I also defend an ontological claim (iii) about an irreducible bifurcation between mind and world.

Would anyone object to the foregoing claims? Although (i) and (ii) in particular are probably very much in line with common sense, the three assumptions are certainly not commonly accepted in academia, at least not among learning and didactics researchers in the humanities and social sciences in the English-speaking world. Also, the falsehood of (ii) may appear to follow from the truth of (iii), illuminating a blatant inconsistency on my part. Anyway, a realistic conception of learning along the lines sketched is certainly up against the strong dominance of various constructivist positions in the domains mentioned, and in particular, in the field of teacher education.

Let me begin with a few introductory remarks to help the reader understand the background and motivation for writing this chapter. The driving force behind my work with the constructivism-realism issue in the field of learning is an amalgam of two factors: First and foremost, it grows out of the recognition of what I see as inherent epistemological problems with specific versions of constructivism – which is the raison d'etre for writing this piece. Secondly, I must admit to a certain feeling of discomfort with the widespread "I am a constructivist," academic lip service witnessed in educational circles (cf. e.g. Phillips 1995), and also recognized by constructivists themselves (e.g. Bauersfeld 1995, p. 137). Denis C. Phillips has described this "descent into sectarianism" as the ugly side of constructivism (Phillips 1995, p. 5). Some constructivists very likely believe that critical discussions of the epistemological foundations of constructivism "are over and done with many years ago," and/or that the rise of constructivism in the 1980s really meant the appearance of a new paradigm (cf. e.g. (Fosnot & Perry 2005, p. 34; Glasersfeld & Varela 1987, p. 29) – a new paradigm that should simply be recognized as the leading game in town.[1]

What *is* constructivism, then? And, how are my arguments "constructed," and how is the chapter organized?

## Constructivisms

"Constructivism" refers to a plethora of different positions and ideas in the human and social sciences, and constructivist approaches to the specific *analysandum*, "learning," is likewise a rag rug of different theories. Still, certain basic, common threads may be identified. Thus, according to constructivist learning theory, learning, very briefly put, is conceived as changes in cognizing systems by the building up of viable, adaptive, meaningful structures in those systems and/or their social relations, in contrast to a gradual discovery and apprehension of mind-independent facts. To put it differently, there is a conceptual distinction between "learning as active construction," and "discovery learning," as it has been termed by constructivists themselves (cf. e.g. Wood, Cobb & Yackel 1995). Also, it should be noted that although constructivist theories of learning in general are distinguished from constructivist descriptions of teaching (e.g. Fosnot & Perry 2005, p. 33; Larochelle & Bednarz 1998), many researchers see an intimate relation between these areas:

> Constructivism is a theory of learning that rejects the idea that it is possible to transfer the content of teaching to pupils. (Rasmussen 1998, p. 554)

Although Rasmussen pushes the envelope by characterizing the constructivist position of learning in terms of a problem with teaching, the important point is that constructivist theories of learning and teaching converge on the denial of knowledge transfer. Learning is not a question of the transference of knowledge, and teaching is not a question of mediating processes of such transferences.

Considered strictly as a theory about learning and knowledge, which is my focus, the following quote from Catherine Fosnot's preface to her reader (Fosnot 2005) is revealing:

Constructivism is a theory about knowledge and learning; it describes both what "knowing" is and how one "comes to know." Based on work in psychology, philosophy, science, and biology, the theory describes knowledge not as truths to be transmitted or discovered, but as emergent, developmental, nonobjective, viable constructed explanations by humans engaged in meaning-making in cultural and social communities of discourse. (Fosnot 2005, p. ix)

Positions such as Ernst von Glasersfeld's "radical constructivism" and Niklas Luhmann's "operative constructivism" fit in here. But research approaches to education that emphasize the situatedness of activity along cultural and social dimensions are also within Fosnot's scope. Contributions such as Brown et al. (1989) and Greeno's (1991) are classic examples (see also Cobb, 2005 for an overview). And, to the extent that these kinds of research emphasize a non-individualistic approach to learning, and typically exhibit no particular interest in (positioning themselves against) the epistemological mind-world-divide debate, they differ from the von Glasersfeld- and Luhmann-inspired research. Still, this (socially oriented) "second kind of constructivism" needs to be carefully dealt with, as it sometimes runs the risk of neglecting – or even eliminating – the mind,[2] whereas the (individualistically oriented) "first kind of constructivism" runs "the opposite risk": a neglect of the mind-independent world. Only instances of such a potentially "world-neglecting" kind of constructivism are in the focus of this chapter. The issue of "constructivism of the second kind" will not be dealt with here.

With respect to "the first kind of constructivism," von Glasersfeld has played a particularly prominent role, and perhaps he was the one who really defined the theoretical groundwork for other constructivists (cf. Meyer 2009, p. 332). With respect to Luhmann, his constructivist thoughts have indeed had some impact outside of Germany, in particular, in Denmark and Norway. However compared to von Glasersfeld's so-called "radical constructivism," Luhmann's influence on learning, and, more broadly, the educational field, including teaching and teacher education, is minor. Therefore, I primarily take advantage of Von Glasersfeld's approach in what follows, and leave my specific criticism of the epistemological underpinnings of the Luhmannian system's approach and its application to the learning field to more local arenas.

In the next section, I target von Glasersfeld's constructivism (von Glasersfeld 1995b; von Glaserfeld 2007). Firstly, I advance a concern with respect to the epistemological underpinnings of the theory, in particular, what I interpret as a premise about the existence of a basic, sensory *stratum* from which each of us constructs our conception of reality. This assumption plays a crucial, epistemic role in von Glasersfeld's theory of learning. At least one understanding of this assumption gives rise to well-known problems with how a cognizing subject constructs knowledge of a world from simple, conscious sensations. Secondly, I problematize the suggestion often advanced by von Glasersfeld, that realism is basically a matter of a specific *prejudice* – the prejudice according to which an organism perceives an experience-independent reality. Finally, in this section, I point out that the mind and its properties appear very different compared to the physical properties of the world. Despite immense efforts, so far we haven't solved this so called "explanatory gap." Apparently we are confronted with an ontological divide here, which learning theorists of a constructivist persuasion sometimes overlook.

In the next section, I turn to the positive task of delivering an elaboration of the two basic elements of a realistic conception of learning (i-ii), mentioned above. In the fifth and final part of my presentation, I give an argument for realism from the perspective of "implicit learning." In the context of the agenda of this chapter, what implicit learning demonstrates is that learning takes place passively, "under the radar of constructivism." Thus, at the level of brute neurophysiological processes, constraints with respect to mental processes at a higher ontological level are to be found. And some of these constraints are discovered by the demonstration of various forms of implicit learning. The final section sums up.

## Constructivism with respect to the world

I think that there are strong reasons that von Glasersfeld's radical constructivism must go. I would also like to add, *en passage*, that my criticism of von Glasersfeld's position does no harm to the epistemology of Piaget, von Glasersfeld's important source of inspiration. In contrast to von Glaserfeld's outlook, my belief is that their epistemological underpinnings are very different from each other. Or, to put it differently:

(also) considered as an interpretation of Piaget's epistemological work, von Glasersfeld's position is false.[3]

What is von Glaserfeld's position, then – and why, precisely, is it probably flawed?

Here are the central tenets of von Glasersfeld's radical constructivism (cf. von Glasersfeld 1976; von Glasersfeld 1982; von Glasersfeld 1995b; von Glasersfeld 2007): (i) cognitive states do not represent an experience-independent reality; (ii) knowledge of reality is a construction, in the sense that the human individual constructs its own conception of reality, and (iii) therefore, there is no basis for talking about an experience-independent reality. Von Glasersfeld believes that this is relatively close to what Piaget (really) meant. I do not. But forget about the complicated, interpretative questions about "the real Piaget." With respect to radical constructivism *an sich*, the problem is that its epistemological foundations are not obviously true. On the contrary, the very idea that subjects fundamentally construct their own worlds has been heavily criticized in epistemology and psychology for almost a century now, including by Piaget himself, and I shall come to this issue shortly.

Let me charitably put forth a fuller picture of von Glasersfeld's epistemology, which hinges on a number of Piagetian – or "Piagetian" – assumptions.

According to von Glasersfeld, Piaget's thinking radically rejects the classical epistemological tradition's understanding of central concepts such as "reality," "truth," and "knowledge," and the conception of how we acquire knowledge (von Glasersfeld 1995b, p. 54; von Glasersfeld 2007, p. 91). The essence is that each of us constructs a conception of reality, but has no reason whatsoever for believing that we are in the possession of knowledge of an experience-independent reality. But how does this come about? The fundamental premises for the above-mentioned tenets of radical constructivism are explicitly formulated in the following way by von Glasersfeld:

> 1. Knowledge is not passively received either through the senses or by way of communication; knowledge is actively built up by the cognizing subject. 2. The function of cognition is adaptive, in the biological sense of the term, tending towards fit or viability; cognition serves the subject's organization of the experiential world, not the discovery of an objective ontological reality. (von Glasersfeld 1995b, p. 51)

In fairness to von Glasersfeld, it should be noted that he also delivers an argument for his position independent of his Piaget exegesis, by building on a semantic premise about the fundamental impossibility of intersubjective understanding through language. I take the liberty of ignoring this parallel line of argument, since the inspiration from (his reading of) Piaget is the essential one.

From the quote above, it is clear that biological inspiration is crucial to the radical constructivism von Glasersfeld endorses: The basic idea is about organisms adapting to their surroundings, but transformed into a question about human beings' *mental* adaptation. In itself, this thought is not controversial; it is a central tenet of Piaget's thinking. Assimilation and accommodation are adaptive functions of learning. However, the controversial issue appears, when von Glasersfeld argues that assimilation has two very different meanings, one of which is not noted in the standard reception of Piaget. Thus, as pointed out by von Glasersfeld, "assimilation" may also mean adaptation in the sense that human beings do not have knowledge of an experience-independent reality, but *construct* knowledge, in the sense that experiences are attuned, in relation to existing expectations. Also, the concept of "knowledge" is replaced with the concept of "viability," a concept to which I return in the next section.

From von Glasersfeld's perspective, the focus is not the external mind-world relation, but on the internal mind-mind relation, one might say. An organism, for example, a child, is, in a cognitive sense, confirmed in what it already understands *via* its contact with its surroundings. According to von Glasersfeld, this is something very different from the tradition's understanding of assimilation, which, in accordance with a dominant biological use, means transfer of, and absorption of (physical), material from the external world. In an analogous way, it is used in learning theory to describe cognitive transfer of information about the external world, justifying the assumption that the child will gradually acquire a more adequate understanding of reality.

Von Glasersfeld admits that this orthodox reading of "assimilation" may be found in Piaget's writings. Here is an example:

> One can say [...] that all needs tend first of all to incorporate things and people into the subject's own activity, that is, to "assimilate" the external world into the structures that have already been constructed, and secondly to readjust these structures as a function of subtle transformations, that is,

to "accommodate" them to external objects. From this point of view, all mental life, as indeed all organic life, tends progressively to assimilate the surrounding environment. (Piaget 1967, p. 7-8)

However, he points out that Piaget also writes about assimilation in a more radical, bio-cybernetic sense, which has nothing to do with the organism's (*in casu*, the child's) access to reality through the construction of a gradually more adequate model of reality, but instead is to be understood as a construction of a model of reality, in the sense of *an internal organization of its experience*:

In my interpretation, assimilation must instead be understood as treating new material *as an instance of something known*. (von Glasersfeld 1995b, p. 62)

It is this difference between two understandings of assimilation that gives rise to the difference between "radical constructivism" and "trivial constructivism." The latter may be briefly described as the position that the child gradually constructs cognitive resources (schemata, concepts, models) that enable it to cope with a mind-independent reality through adequate representations.

How should we evaluate von Glasersefeld's position? According to himself, the sole reason people might find his position strange, when compared to "trivial constructivism," is that we rely on *a realist prejudice*, according to which an organism perceives an experience-independent reality. Instead, we should see perception as a continuing "equilibration," relative to the given experiences.

Von Glasersfeld is not right, however, about one's feeling of discomfort with his position, that it comes from a mere realist *prejudice*. One problematic issue stems from what follows from his own position: how - from his premises - is an organism really able to learn anything beyond its own constructed "world"? If not, one may, *via modus tollens*, argue that his position is logically falsified, from the obvious fact that we do learn about the world. The argument would run like this: if the consequent, Q (Q = nothing about a mind-independent world can be learned) of von Glasersfeld's position (G) may be falsified (¬ Q, that is, it is *not* true, that nothing can be learned about a mind-independent world), it follows logically that G is false - Glasersfeld's position is untenable. But this would be a mistaken reasoning. Von Glasersfeld would not admit that Q could be falsified, because he would (rightly) point out that Q (and not ¬ Q) follows directly from G. So the strategy against von Glasersfeld – if one feels uncomfortable with Q – is to look into the premises of G itself. To put it slightly differently, and stronger: whether or not one would endorse the claim that we actually learn something about a mind-independent world (¬ Q ∨ Q), one should deal with his premises for G. This neatly shows the interrelation between epistemology and learning theory: in order to address and evaluate basic questions about learning, one will sometimes have to deal with the epistemological underpinnings of the concept in question. If (and only if) these underpinnings may be demonstrated to be problematic, one would be able to deal with the question of whether learning is really about a mind-independent world, *without begging the question* against G(lasersfeld).

We might then, for the sake of argument, admit, that "a feeling of uncomfortableness with his position stems from a mere realist prejudice," and see whether the premises of G themselves are problematic. And I believe that they are – or at least, might be.

Take a look at this neat summary of the epistemological underpinnings of von Glasersfeld's position, by Denis C. Phillips and Jonas F. Soltis:

> In brief, von Glasersfeld argues that the individual learner is *not* the recipient of knowledge that is pressed onto his or her consciousness by some "external reality." In this regard he differs markedly from Locke and also from Plato. But, similarly to Locke, he seems to hold the view that each individual is only in "contact" with the impressions (or stimuli or experiences) that are received via the sense organs. Thus the task for the learner is to construct a body of knowledge on the basis of these sense impressions [...]. (Phillips & Soltis 2009, p. 50)

The problem with the two central epistemological premises – that each individual is only in "contact" with the impressions (or stimuli or experiences) received via the sense organs, from which the learner's task is to construct a body of knowledge on the basis of these sense impressions – is that they may give a distorted picture of what it is to experience the world. The idea of a clear divide between conceptualization and the "sensory given" has, for more than a century, been under attack from very different quarters, for example, gestalt psychology, analytical epistemology, phenomenology, and pragmatism, not to mention from the (late) Wittgensteinian approach (e.g. Wittgenstein 1953). In addition, to the extent that von Glasersfeld believes himself to build on Piaget's thinking, it is striking that he never considers that Piaget, too, criticizes the empiricist idea of "something given to the senses." More specifically, Piaget identifies the demonstration of the gestalt character of perceptual experiences delivered by the so-called "gestalt psychologists" as a premise in the argument against Ernst Mach's phenomenalism (cf. e.g. Piaget 1972b, p. 45-48). Furthermore, via his conception of equilibrium, Piaget explicitly develops Wolfgang Koehler's and Max Wertheimer's gestalt psychological considerations of the structuring of sensory experiences (see Piaget 1973, p. 125-141).

I will be a bit more specific about what is – or may – be wrong with the idea that each individual is only "in contact" with the stimuli (or experiences) received via the sense organs, apparently endorsed by von Glasersfeld.

Considered from an experiential point of view, it may be simply pointed out that "the sensory given" does not exist. What do I mean by this? I mean that this idea does not fit "the phenomenal structure" of our sensory experiences. By "phenomenal structure," I refer to what may be objectively known about the formal conditions for having sensory experiences of the world, as uncovered by adopting a descriptive, first person stance. This peculiar perspective has been particularly highlighted and applied by the phenomenological tradition along multifarious dimensions, a tradition initiated by Edmund Husserl's explorations.[4] For example, Husserl (1913) presents an early, classic catalogue of examples and results. A central phenomenological distinction that may figure as a general example is *the division between "immanence" and "transcendence"*: To have sensory experiences of physical objects means, among other things, to experience a world of intentional objects, the properties of which are never fully uncovered for the observer, that is, by "presenting" all sides at once. Nevertheless, concrete objects are present to us as fully individuated objects; we anticipate the not yet presented sides of objects, an anticipation exhibited most clearly in the mature organism's mastery of sensory-motor interactions with familiar, concrete objects. This peculiar epistemological feature – that concrete objects *present* themselves as concrete, in conjunction with the fact that, at the same time, they *escape full, simultaneous appearance*, is what phenomenologists call "transcendence." "Immanence," on the other hand, denotes the idea of the subject's fully epistemic mastery of its objects, owing to the transparency of its intentional objects, a feature typically ascribed to (some or all the properties of) the mind (cf. e.g. Husserl 1913, § 38).

In order to evaluate whether the phenomenologically-based criticism of the idea that each individual is only in contact with the impressions (or stimuli or experiences) received via the sense organs, is correct, it would have been useful if von Glasersfeld engaged in the discussion of the phenomenological approach to the questions of transcendence and immanence, which he does not. He probably considers the phenomenological tradition an inherent part of the Western history of philosophy, a long tradition he is clearly against through and through (cf. e.g. von Glasersfeld 1995b, p. 24-52; von Glasersfeld & Varela 1987). Whereas phenomenologists believe that we are directly presented with, and live in a common world, according to von Glasersfeld, we are, on the contrary, in a fundamental, epistemic sense, closed off from an external world:

> Our "knowledge," whatever rational meaning give to that term, must begin with experience – such as, for instance, the cut we make between the part of our experience that we come to call "ourself" and all the rest of our experience, which we then call our "world." Hence, this world of ours, no matter how we structure it, no matter how well we manage to keep it stable with permanent objects and recurrent interactions, is by definition the "subjective" world of our experience and not the ontological reality of which philosophers have dreamed. (von Glasersfeld & Varela 1987, p. 6-7)

The problem here becomes how to manage to build up our "knowledge" of our individual, subjective "worlds," if the material merely consists of simple sense impressions, which do not have any inherent phenomenal structure whatsoever. One might retort that this is not what von Glasersfeld means. But this is what he writes. Consider this:

> Any specification or description of the constraints, therefore, must be formulated in terms of the availability of single, as yet uncoordinated signals (i.e., particles of experience) and of the regularities or interdependence of these signals which the knowing organism, as a result of his own cognizing

activity, singles out from his initially undifferentiated continuous stream of experience. (von Glasersfeld 2007, p. 80)

In other words, according to von Glasersfeld, an organism must rely on "signals" it receives from an undifferentiated stream of consciousness. This is really a sort of empiricism, where the data, as well as the "world" the individual constructs of them, are internal, in relation to the organism's cognitive system: "all invariances and regularities are our construction" (von Glaserfeld & Varela 1987, p. 7). However, this leads to solipsism, which von Glasersfeld denies, saying that it is precisely the philosophical tradition that wants us to accept that we really already *do* have this knowledge of an external world (ibid.; cmp. also with von Glasersfeld 1995a, p. 7). However, this is not an argument, but it certainly is an interesting response, because it flies in the face of common sense, and although much of science has common-sense phenomena as its *explananda*, the *explanans need not be*, and very often are not. Still, even if we admit that a counterintuitive position such as solipsism may be correct, this claim amounts to nothing more than the proposition being metaphysically and logically possible. And it does not remedy the fact that the epistemological premises of von Glasersfeld's position appear problematic to the extent that the phenomenal structure of sense impressions as possible paths to knowledge of an external world is ignored (or ruled out by *fiat*).

Let me point out another problem with von Glasersfeld's position. One might say that the burden of proof lies with the one who obviously goes against a generally accepted, justified claim. And *realism* – not constructivism – is that generally accepted, and by default, justified, claim. From a didactic perspective, constructivist-oriented science teachers often find it very difficult indeed to get their students to "play around" with their realist scientific prejudices, and adopt a reflective stance from which this view has merely relative value, that is, to give up the claim's default epistemic status (cf. Duit 1995, p. 279-280; Mitchell & Baird 1986).

From conversational conventions, one would have to take the burden of proof seriously, and answer the question of why solipsism or weaker versions of constructivism are true, instead of realists being obliged to lift the burden of proof with respect to the correctness of realism. I hasten to add that this is not to say that the default claim is true, of course. But a consideration of conversational implicature makes it a reasonable claim that the burden of proof lies with those who believe this claim to be false. This is important, to the extent that some proponents of realism are themselves on the edge of begging the question against constructivists by relying on the truthfulness of this realist background assumption (e.g. Fox 2001, p. 26-27; Searle 1995).

Consider this analogy: A person who asks, "How do you know that there are not 489 invisible angels in this room?" might be answered in the following way: "Well, first give me a reason for believing that there are 489 (and not 0, 5679, or 21...) angels in the room." This response expresses a reasonable expection with respect to getting the other part qualify what justifies *his* belief. In an analogous way, Glasersfeld's argument simply doesn't get started by disputing realism *as a mere prejudice*. It is much more than that: *It is our default epistemological perspective on a world as being there, waiting to be explored*. Husserl's conception of "the natural attitude" captures this idea.

Finally, it should be mentioned that von Glasersfeld apparently limits the set of data from which an organism "constructs its own worlds" to *consciously presented data* – to conscious experiences. Thus, he seems to overlook the information an organism receives below the conscious threshold, or at least such information does not seem to play any role in his theory.[5] This is strange, to the extent that the child's dynamic sensory-motor interaction with its environment, which plays a central role in "its construction of reality," is orthogonal to the conscious/unconscious divide, from Piaget's perspective.[6] As other critics have pointed out (e.g. Martínez-Delgado 2002, p. 843), von Glasersfeld, to the extent that he sometimes *does* mention "an environment," takes advantage of this notion as placeholder for mind-*independent* objects. In other words, there appears to be an implicit realist element in the theory, which is not consistent with the intended constructivism. The following quote illustrates this implicit realist element:

> [...] in Piaget's constructivist theory [...] the actions take place in an environment and are grounded in and directed at objects that constitute the organism's experiential world, not things in themselves that have an independent existence [...]. (von Glasersfeld 2005, p. 4)

Hence, on top of the theory-inherent problem with the epistemological premises raised above, other lacunas might be found in radical constructivism. Surely, it is radical – but it apparently harbors inconsistencies and problems that make it difficult to get away from a realist grounding and turned into constructivism *proper*.

## Realism with respect to the world (and the mind)

What is meant by "realism," in the context of learning? "Realism" means (i) that, to a large extent, learning involves asymmetrical processes of knowledge- and skill-acquisition, and (ii) that acquired knowledge and skills cannot be understood without reference to a mind-independent world to which the subject has cognitive access. In addition, I also advance an ontological claim (iii) about an irreducible bifurcation of mind and world. I will now add some details to these points.

Learning (at any level, and in any form and aspect) is a relational phenomenon, like thinking, desiring, and perceiving. This means that there are (at least) two *relata*: a subject, and specific content, skills, expertise, and so forth, to be learned. A learning subject is a subject who acquires beliefs or knowledge that x, skills with respect to y, competence to z, and so on. Whatever it takes to learn, if learning does not result in a change with respect to the subject, as a result of the learning process, we would not say, at the end of the day, that learning took place. Although I believe there are good (and well known) reasons for not saying that learning takes place on the part of subjects, still, subjects learn, just as subjects perceive, think, desire, and act. Subjects as *loci* for learning that does not imply that learning *itself* is a feature (property) of subjects, just as little as "dancing" would be. Remember: Learning is a relational phenomenon. But, to the extent that over time (perhaps a whole life) a subject has learned, it follows that certain characteristics of that subject have changed; maybe the specific content, "the world," the organizations, facilitators, and so on, that are involved, have changed, too. But necessarily, the subject has undergone some change as a result of the learning process, such as "transformation of life," acquiring the mastery of a technique, skill, rule, and so forth. Among other things, learning results in the transformation of a subject. Again: this is not to exclude the occurrence of other transformations, as well. Learning as a transformational process is different from the conditions making this transformation possible. Thus, in principle, the transformation may be studied apart from these conditions.

A human subject can be understood as an embodied entity with certain mental features, (normally) part of, and engaged in a societal context. And, to the extent that mental and bodily features are influenced by the subject's learning process, the mind and the body are fields of potential interest for those studying learning. Remember: If you accept that there is a change in the subject over time due to learning, this change necessarily involves physical features (physical dispositions, neural firing-patterns, etc.) and/or mental features (life attitude, acquiring knowledge in various forms, schematas, etc.) Also, to the extent that mental features supervene upon physical features (a widely accepted, although fundamentally ontological assumption, which itself is not fully understood), the body must be of a peculiar interest to those studying learning. Again, this does not deny that there is a social level of learning (which has received much attention in learning theory), where societal features are in particular focus, in contrast to "subjective features." Still, learning necessarily involves embodied subjects. A learning society, S, which learns something, but where its members s1, s2, s3....sn do not learn anything, does not make sense. Whether or not societies and organizations may *also* be properly said to learn, *per se*, is another question, irrelevant here. In addition, this is not to deny that societal features are emergent, and as such have a specific ontological feature (cf. Durkheim, etc.). These features are studied in the social sciences, and a subset of these plays roles in the subject's learning, as studied in sociology and anthropology of education.

Theorists of learning must, for the above-mentioned reasons, acknowledge the creature (the embodied subject with certain mental features entangled in a society) as having a special status, *qua* the one who learns (whatever is learned, and whichever way learning takes place). Therefore, what is going on *in*, *at*, and *with* the subject's mind and body is of peculiar interest for understanding learning. Furthermore – by accepting the metaphysical supervenience claim above – what is going on *in*, *at*, and *with* the subject's *body* is essential to understand learning. Hence, even if learning itself is not a property of a subject, what is going on in, at, and with the subject is of special interest for a learning theory.

Learning has mind-to-world "direction of fit" (Anscombe 1957; Searle 1979), in the sense that the subject's take on the world is changed as a result of the learning process, in ways that give the subject an enhanced understanding of, mastery of, and ability to cope with her life, body, and/or features of the world. This is an asymmetrical relation, to the extent that changes in or with *the subject* (or set of subjects) primarily are what makes the proposition "learning is taking place" become true – and not changes in *the world*. Here, learning is like perceiving, but unlike desiring (and its derivatives). When I want you to pass the salt, I have an interest in the world's change to the effect that I get x. The world (*in casu* you) is to change, not I, in order to satisfy my desire for salt. But in learning, as in perceiving, I am (ultimately) the one who is to change, for learning and perceiving taking place and not (only) the world.

Learning has mind-to-world direction of fit, since there are worldly features that cannot be *contingently* dealt with through learning. These features are uncovered in various ways by the environment's giving us feedback. This is the fact regarding feedback that is often forgotten by constructivists, or that figures as a more or less implicit (but underdetermined) realist component of their theory. This was already mentioned at the end of section 3 (also see Fox 2001, p. 27-29; Martínez-Delgado 2002, p. 843-846). It is certainly true that learning sometimes (perhaps often) involves the active engagement of, movement of, and acting out by the subject, as pointed out by so many researchers of learning, since the days of Dewey. But the world "strikes back": there are constraints in the world that shape my learning (about the world) by setting limits to my physical "engagement" with and within this world. These features are features of a mind-independent world, and include the mental worlds of other minds, reacted upon by proxy through their bodies and language.

The existence of objective features is not only implicit in von Glasersfeld's account; but the choice of the concept of "viability" as a replacement for the concept of knowledge (with its implications of truth) has the effect of blurring this fact (see e.g. von Glasersfeld 1980, p. 970-974; von Glasersfeld 1982, p. 614 *et passim*; von Glasersfeld 1995b: 14; 68-69; see also Martínez-Delgado 2002, p. 843f on this point). The role of mind-independent features as truth makers is downplayed, or simply neglected.

Our world, with its individual worlds of other minds included – through our engagement with it and in it – has an impact to our minds and bodies. And learning is the specific set of processes through which subjects become more able to cope with their worlds, which, to a large extent is *the* world, *our* world. Not a world that is mind-independent in the Kantian, *an sich* sense, but in the sense that the experienced features *of this world* are different from – implying that they may be distinguished from – the mind itself and its features. The Husserlian distinction between transcendence and immanence in experience, mentioned above, is just one exemplification of this realist, epistemic outlook. These distinctions are not arbitrary, varying from subject to subject; they direct our attention to invariant features of perception, thinking, and learning, which help us to acknowledge the central bifurcation of mind and world, a bifurcation that does not exclude that it is possible to epistemically transcend the ontological divide between mind and world, *by learning about this world.*

The foregoing does not deny that there exist significant, culturally-based differences with respect to what is learned, dependent as it is on societal, cultural, and other features. Also, there is perhaps no limit to fantasy, story-telling, and similar kinds of discursive acts in which we talk about our worlds and ourselves. But there are still limits to forms and the content of learning, because learning is not like freely confabulating, dreaming, or otherwise making up stories. Learning is part of our culture, sure. But it also part of our nature, as much as perceiving and thinking are.

There are normative constraints on thinking (Aristotle gave us insight to this with his elementary logic). There are structural and content constraints on perception. And similarly, there are natural constraints on the processes of learning. These limits are invariants of the world in which we live and of the mind that makes us experience this world. That there is no natural *vehicle* for learning (in contrast with the case of perception) makes it seem much easier and justifiable to either study learning completely apart from the mind, that is, from a social perspective, or by moving in the opposite direction, into the subject, conceiving learning as a mere construction of the individual mind. And both these moves, downplaying the mind and the world respectively as they do, are not ontologically coherent to the extent they ultimately do not acknowledge a difference between mind and world:

an epistemological difference, and an ontological one. Compressed into one sentence, the ontological difference is that the mind and its properties, for all we know, appear different from the (physical) world. But whereas the ontological difference exemplifies an "explanatory gap" (cf. e.g. Chalmers 1995), the epistemological difference describes a condition and a possibility: that the mind (somehow supervening upon the body) *is able to learn about our world.*

## Implicit learning – below the radar of constructivism

There is a domain of research in learning, where constructivism has no foothold at all. This is the field of implicit learning. In this last part of my chapter I briefly launch a criticism against constructivism along a different path, which in a peculiar way is complimentary to the criticism raised above.

I believe that the existence of implicit learning demonstrates that there are facets of learning that go against the assumptions about how learning subjects construct their realities, or how cognitive systems observe by making differences, to paraphrase what learning is about from constructivist points of view. I also believe that this criticism has the potential to target constructivism more broadly; that is, widening the scope, compared to the narrow focus of a von Glasersfeld type of position. The premises of my critique also add some flesh and bone to the somewhat formal outline of the realist picture of learning I sketched above.

Why is implicit learning a problem for constructivism? Let me briefly outline the implicit-explicit learning distinction, before I address this question.

"Implicit learning" is defined as an organism's capacity for unintended learning, without being conscious of what is learned or how it is learned. Explicit learning takes place when an organism consciously learns. A related assumption is that a precondition for an organism's capacity to articulate what has been learned is that it is (or was) conscious of it. It was Polanyi's conception of "tacit knowing" that influenced the early studies of 'implicit learning" (Reber 1967; Reber 1993b; Reber, Allen & Reber 1999), and through the development of this research field, grounded by Reber's early studies, the distinction between implicit and explicit learning has gained strong empirical support (Reber 1993a; Berry & Dienes 1993; Goschke 1997; Stadler & Frensch 1998; Cleeremans et al. 1998; Frensch & Cleeremans 2002; Seger et al. 2000), although a number of methodological problems have also been identified (see e.g. Shanks & St. John, 1994; Gaillard et al. 2006), which still perplex the research field (Nakamura 2013).

Within cognitive neuropsychology, for almost half a century, a similar distinction between "implicit" and "explicit" abilities has played a pivotal role in the understanding of cognitive and emotive capacities, and their neural underpinnings (see e.g. Weiskrantz 1997; de Gelder et al. 2001). For example, people with prosopagnosia, that is, the inability to consciously recognize persons by their faces, despite otherwise normal perceptual capacities, may be demonstrated to have retained implicit knowledge with respect to faces. Thus, a significant positive galvanic skin response was measured when pictures of known faces were presented together with the matching name, in contrast with a non-matching name (Bauer 1984). Another much studied neurocognitive syndrome is blindsight, a visual syndrome where, owing to damage to their primary visual cortex, the patients have acquired blindness in the corresponding part of the visual field. Despite this damage, it may be experimentally shown that they retain certain perceptual and visuomotor abilities. Thus, by applying forced choice methods, these patients demonstrate the abilities to detect and discriminate among perceptual properties of a stimulus in their visual field, such as location, spatial orientation, form, direction of movement, and even color, despite the fact that they report no conscious experience of the presented stimuli (cf. e.g. Cowey 2010).

With respect to constructivism, implicit learning is problematic for a number of reasons. Firstly, in contrast to the idea of learning conceived as *active* construction, processes of implicit learning are *passive*. By "passive," I mean without reach of knowledge and the control of the conscious subject. We react to our environment, to meeting other people, to minute changes in the surfaces with which we are in contact, by standing, running, sitting on chairs; we react to subtle and not-so-subtle changes in pitch, light intensity, saturation of colors, minute changes of facial expression, humidity, temperature, and a world of other properties with which we are confronted. We react to things done *to* us and *with* us; we are immersed in an environment with all sorts of simple, complicated and complex, concrete, abstract, physical, mental, and social things, processes, and events. We exhibit instinctive, adaptive, conditioned, and habituated responses, which in the heyday of behaviorism were considered core examples of learning behavior. Behaviorism had its problems, but no one would deny that the underlying mechanisms may be implemented, and that the behavioral response patterns may be elicited, whereas the idea that behaviorism lends us the full picture of learning is certainly wrong. The point is that we exhibit a vast number of reactions to our environment, without intention to (re)act, or without having knowledge-in-action of these reaction patterns. Thus, implicit learning goes against a conception of learning as an active, deliberate "process of construction," with the conscious subject in command.

Secondly, a central part of the foregoing picture is that we are not *conscious* of these reactions to our environment. Constructivism clearly builds on an active, personal component in the subject's construction of "its world," but we are not always conscious of our constructions, and sometimes rely on processes that are completely non-mental, to the extent that they are not cognitively penetrable by consciousness at all, and their content – although paraphrasable in language in an elliptical way – is not itself semantically structured, for example, David Milner and Melvyn Goodale's highly influential work on the ventral-dorsal bifurcation of information processing in primates' visual systems (Milner & Goodale 1995; Milner & Goodale 2008).

Thirdly, implicit processes exemplify cognitive features that are *primary*, from an evolutionary point of view, compared to explicit, conscious, and semantically structured mental states (see in particular Reber 1992 and Reber & Allen 2000). Hence, to the extent that the processes exemplify that organisms rely on *reliable*, implicit, cognitive reactions to the environment, these features cannot be ignored, when compared to conscious, language-driven "constructions." Humans and other mammals share the cognitive abilities to react and respond to the physical world And, from an evolutionary point of view, it would be strange, if our consciously accessible cognition of "a world" were connected to our implicit cognition in no important way. Quite the contrary, we do have reason to think that the conscious mind and the unconscious mind are not epistemically quite separate, and that, from an ontological point of view, the mind supervenes upon the body and its neurobiological properties, although – I admit – this relation is not understood.

Finally, let me add *en passant*,[7] that although constructivists such as von Glasersfeld, Luhmann, and their followers, often point out that constructivism is consistent with biological research, neurophysiology, and the cognitive sciences, this is a truth with important caveats. It is true that the neurobiological research on cognitive, living systems done by Francisco Varela and Humberto Maturana is often referred to by constructivists, particularly those of a Luhmannian sort, but this represents a very small fraction of research in (neuro)biology, the impact of which has been minor. And, more importantly, the cognitive perspectives of the biological system and "the system of the mind" of the systems approach are mutually incompatible, thus, there *really* is no common ground between such systems, from an epistemic point of view. Therefore, the huge amount of neurobiological and -physiological research dealing with the interfaces between mind and body is not really interesting, not revealing, not relevant to the systems approach at all. At bottom, it is instead the idea of *autopoiesis* (and related properties) as a central feature of living systems and of the cognizing mind, which matters to this approach. Certainly, the transformational aspects of sensory processing, as revealed by neurophysiological and -biological research are also highly important to constructivists adopting a systems approach (cf. e.g. von Glasersfeld & Varela 1987). But the interpretation of these facts is always seen in light of the systems approach itself, epitomized by the axiomatic idea of *autopoiesis*, revealing the risk of running into a vicious circle.

Needless to say, constructivist restrictions with respect to the *compatibility of the cognitive perspectives of different systems*, with respect to considering the complicated transformations of sensory signals as *enabling cognition of our world*, and with respect to *the prospects of inter-systems (neuro)biological research*, are very alien to – and incompatible with – the realist perspective on learning that I have sketched out.

## Conclusion

I have argued for a realist approach to learning. On the one hand, I have argued by *indirect means*, through a critique of one specific, influential constructivist position, that is, von Glaserfeld's radical constructivism. The epistemological foundations of this theory were in focus. On the other hand, I have also argued *directly* for realism, by delivering a number of arguments for this position, by taking advantage of insights from phenomenology, implicit learning and cognition, as well as the supervenience approach to the relation between body and mind.

## Notes

1  One should bear in mind that "paradigm" is used in at least three different ways in educational research. The chapters referred to in Fosnot & Perry (2005) and Glasersfeld & Varela (1987)) apparently intend the meaning of "paradigm" that implies semantic incommensurability with respect to the meaning of key terms across different paradigms. i.e. a standard (strong), Kuhnian sense of paradigm. If constructivists use "paradigm" this way, they should at least be aware of the extensive criticism of Kuhn's conception of semantic incommensurability that follows from it: basically, that it refers to something non-existent.

But also, very often researchers in the humanities and the social sciences use "paradigm" in a much looser sense, and the field of learning and education is certainly no exception to this. Thus, Ernest (1995) enlists no fewer than seven different educational paradigms, three of which happen to be constructivist. And, according to Ernest, the most important issues that are central to distinguishing among paradigms are the underlying metaphors for "mind" and "world" (Ernest 1995, p. 466). But firstly, since there are several instances of overlap among metaphors across paradigms – for example, the metaphor for "world" is identical in the paradigms of empiricism and in information-processing theory (ibid. p. 458) – and secondly, since Ernest also describes how paradigms develop into each other, semantic incommensurability is clearly not implied by him – and rightly so, I should like to add. But if so, a constructivist cannot use "the paradigm umbrella argument" to avoid criticism – just as little, of course, a realist can avoid this.

Finally, a normative use of "paradigm" in educational contexts can be identified. Thus, Clifford Konold refers to "paradigms" as something like normative efforts to transfer epistemological insights from learning theory to didactics (*in casu* teaching of mathematics, cf. Konold 1995, p. 180). An instance of this is the consideration showed to "the replacement paradigm" in teaching science. In accordance with this paradigm, students' everyday conceptions ought to be replaced by scientific ones (cf. e.g. Duit 1995). This paradigm is criticized by constructivists; epistemological concerns along constructivist lines result in their opting for everyday conceptions replacement by multiple coexisting scientific views, rather than a single one (Duit 1995, p. 278).

2  "The" situated learning approach may, in some of its instantiations, exemplify this. In a forthcoming paper I argue that this position is unsound precisely

to the extent that it ignores three real, cognitive features of subjects, in order to understand a specific learning task; introspection, attention, and consciousness. Put differently, in at least one version, this approach relies implicitly on a cognitive perspective, in order to be able to specify the precise conditions for a subject's access to a community of practice. The case I have in mind, and exploit, is the case of wine tasting, often described and used by Etienne Wenger – the so-called "purple-in-the-nose" case (Wenger 2006). This case is particularly interesting, because – in contrast with most of situated learning scenarios – it specifically addresses consciousness. Or, it apparently does.

3   I believe that, at the same time, Piaget's genetic epistemology harbors an acknowledged realist position with respect to the existence of the external world, and a "genetic-transcendental constructivism," when it comes to the question of the development of knowledge in the child. If true, this sits fairly uneasily with the reading of Piaget that forms the core of von Glasersfeld's constructivism. In other words, I think von Glasersfeld is on his own here – Piaget would not agree with von Glasersfeld, if he had had the chance to discuss it. In particular, several explicit, realist comments in Piaget's *opus* make von Glasersfeld's interpretation contentious, although these comments also make the estimation of where precisely to place Piaget on the constructivism-realism map rather difficult. Even the book to which von Glasersfeld refers as essential to his interpretation of Piaget as a radical constructivist (Piaget 1954) harbors this double epistemological perspective. Whether Piaget's position is really an unstable one, comprising both realist and transcendentally constructivist elements, I cannot address here. For an explicit acknowledgment and discussion of Piaget's realism, see Kitchener (1986). For a discussion of an inherent constructivism-realism paradox in Piaget's genetic epistemology, see Kauffmann (2013).

4   It should be noted that one does not have to subscribe to phenomenology to investigate the phenomenal structure of sensory experiences. Piaget, for example, although acknowledging the gestalt ordering of our sensory world, at the same time also embodied a rather critical stance toward a number of transcendental elements of phenomenological thinking (cf. Piaget 1972a, chapters 3 and 4).

5   I am indebted to an anonymous referee, for raising a number of critical points with respect to this issue. Perhaps von Glasersfeld does not restrict the scope of "sensory signals from which a subject constructs its 'world'" to simple, conscious sensations. But I find no clear evidence in his writings of this possibility. On the other hand, it is probably not correct to attribute to von Glasersfeld an (implicit) acceptance of the empiricist "Myth of the Given," as I claimed in an earlier draft of this chapter.

6   This is implicitly recognized by von Glasersfeld, when he (correctly) points out that Piaget "does not supply a model of what consciousness might be and how it works" (Glasersfeld 1995c, p. 377).

7   These final remarks are very sketchy. The ideas and arguments will be spelled out in full, in further publications.

# References

Anscombe, G. E. M. (1957). *Intention*. Oxford: Blackwell.
Bauer, R. M. (1984). Autonomic recognition of names and faces in prosopagnosia: A neuropsychological application of the Guilty Knowledge Test. *Neuropsychologia*, 22, p. 457-469.
Bauersfeld, H. (1995). The structuring of the structures: Development and function of mathematizing as a social practice. In: Steffe, L. P. & J. Gale (Eds.): *Constructivism in Education*. Hillsdale, New Jersey: Lawrence Erlbaum Associates, Publishers, 137-158.
Berry, D. C. & Dienes, Z. (1993). *Implicit learning. Theoretical and Empirical Issues*. Howe, UK: Lawrence Erlbaum Associates Ltd.
Brown, J.S., Collins, A., & Duguid, P. (1989). Situated cognition and the culture of learning. *Educational Researcher*, 18 (1), p. 32-42.
Chalmers, D. (1995). *The Conscious Mind. In Search of a Fundamental Theory*. Oxford: Oxford University Press.
Claxton, G. (2012). Turning thinking on its head: How bodies make up their minds. *Thinking skills and creativity*, 7, p. 78-84.
Cleeremans, A. (1993). *Mechanisms of Implicit Learning. Connectionist Models of Sequence Processing*. Cambridge, Massachusetts: MIT Press.
Cleeremans. A. (2008), 'Consciousness: The radical plasticity thesis'. In: R. Banerjee & B.K. Chakrabarti (Eds.) *Progress in Brain Research*, 168, p. 19-33.
Cleeremans, A., Destrebecqz, A. & Boyer, M. (1998). Implicit learning: news from the front. *Trends in Cognitive Sciences*, 2 (10), p. 406-416.
Cobb, P. (2005). Where is the mind? A combination of sociocultural and cognitive constructivist perspectives. In: Fosnot, C.T. (ed.): *Constructivism. Theory, Perspectives, and Practice*. New York: Teachers College, p. 39-57.
Cowey, A. (2010). The blindsight saga. *Experimental Brain Research*, 200, p. 3-24.
de Gelder, B., de Haan, E. & Heywood, C. (Eds.) (2001). *Out of Mind. Varieties of Unconscious Processes*. Oxford: Oxford University Press.
Dienes, Z. & Berry, D. C. (1997). Implicit learning: below the subjective threshold. *Psychonomic Bull. Rev.*, 4, p. 3-23.
Duguid, P. (2006). What talking tells us. *Organization Studies*, 27 (12), p. 1794-1804.
Duit, R. (1995). The constructivist view: A fashionable and fruitful paradigm for science education research and practice. In: Steffe, L. P. & J. Gale (Eds.): *Constructivism in Education*. Hillsdale, New Jersey: Lawrence Erlbaum Associates, Publishers, p. 271-285.
Ernest, P. (1995). The one and the many. In: Steffe, L. P. & J. Gale (Eds.): *Constructivism in Education*. , Hillsdale, New Jersey: Lawrence Erlbaum Associates, Publishers, p. 459-486.
Eysenck, M. W. & Keane, M. T. (2010). *Cognitive Psychology: A Student's Handbook*. Hove: Lawrence Erlbaum Associates.
Fosnot, C. T. (2005). Preface. In: Fosnot, C.T. (ed.): *Constructivism. Theory, Perspectives, and Practice*. 2$^{nd}$ edition. New York: Teachers College, ix-xii.
Fosnot, C.T. & R. S. Perry (2005). Constructivism: A psychological theory of learning. In Fosnot, C.T. (ed.): *Constructivism. Theory, Perspectives, and Practice*. 2$^{nd}$ edition. New York: Teachers College, p. 8-38.

Fox, R. (2001). Constructivism examined. *Oxford Review of Education, 27* (1), p. 23-35.
French, R. M. & A. Cleeremans (2002). *Implicit learning: An empirical, philosophical and computational consensus in the making.* Hove, UK: Psychology Press.
Gaillard, V., Vandenberghe, M., Destrebecqz, A., & A. Cleeremans (2006). First- and third-person approaches in implicit learning research. *Consciousness and Cognition, 15*, p. 709-722.
Goschke, T. (1997). Implicit learning and unconscious knowledge: mental representation, computational mechanisms, and brain structures. In: K. Lamberts & D. Shanks (Eds.) *Knowledge, Concepts, and Categories.* Hove, UK: Psychology Press, p. 247-333.
Greeno, J. G. (1991). Number sense as situated knowing in a conceptual domain. *Journal for Research in Mathematics Education 22*, p. 170-218.
Husserl. E. (1913). *Ideen zu einer reinen Phänomenologie und phänomenologischen Philosophie I.* Dordrecht.
Kauffmann, O. (2013). Om realisme og konstruktivisme i Piagets læringsteori og genetiske epistemologi. *Studier i Pædagogisk Filosofi 2* (2), p. 53-77.
Kitchener, Richard F. (1986). *Piaget's Theory of Knowledge. Genetic Epistemology and Scientific Reason.* New Haven: Yale University Press.
Konold, C. (1995). Social and cultural dimensions of knowledge and classroom teaching. In: Steffe, L. P. & J. Gale (Eds.): *Constructivism in Education.* Hillsdale, New Jersey: Lawrence Erlbaum Associates, Publishers, p. 175-183.
Larochelle, M. & N. Bednarz (1998). Constructivism and education: Beyond epistemological correctness. In: Larochelle, M., Bednarz, N. & J. Garrison (Eds.) *Constructivism and Education.* Cambridge: Cambridge University Press, p. 3-20.
Lowe, E. J. (1995). *Locke on Human Understanding.* London: Routledge.
Martínez-Delgado, A. (2002). Radical Constructivism: Between realism and solipsism. *Issues and Trends*, p. 840-855.
Meyer, D.L. (2009). The poverty of constructivism. *Educational Philosophy and Theory, 41* (3), p. 332-341.
Milner, A. D. & M. A. Goodale (1995). *The Visual Brain in Action.* Oxford: Oxford University Press.
Milner, A. D. & M. A. Goodale, (2008). Two visual systems re-viewed. *Neuropsychologia, 46*, p. 774–785.
Mitchell, J. & J. Baird (1986). Teaching, learning and the curriculum: I. The influence of content in science. *Research in Science Education, 16*, p. 141-149.
Nakamura, D. (2013). Methodological considerations in studying awareness during learning. Part 1: Implicit learning. *Polish Psychological Bulletin, 44*, p. 102-117.
Phillips, D. C. (1995). The good, the bad, and the ugly: The many faces of constructivism. *Educational Researcher, 24* (7), p. 5-12.
Phillips, D. C. & J. F. Soltis (2009). *Perspectives on Learning.* 5th edition. New York & London: Teachers College, Columbia University.
Piaget, J. (1954). *The Construction of Reality in the Child.* New York: Basic Books.
Piaget. J. (1967). *Six Psychological Studies.* New York: Random House, Inc.
Piaget, J. (1972a). *Insights and Illusions of Philosophy.* London: Routledge & Kegan Paul.

Piaget, J. (1972b). *Psychology and Epistemology. Towards a Theory of Knowledge.* Harmondsworth: Penguin Books.

Piaget, J. (1973). *The Child and Reality. Problems of Genetic Psychology.* London: Frederick Muller Ltd.

Prigatano, G. P. & Schachter, D. L. (1991). *Awareness of Deficit after Brain Injury: Clinical and Theoretical Issues.* Oxford: Oxford University Press.

Rasmussen, J. (1998). Constructivism and phenomenology what do they have in common, and how can they be told apart? *Cybernetics and Systems: An International Journal,* 29 (6), p. 553-576.

Reber, A. S. (1967). Implicit learning of artificial grammars. *Journal of Verbal Learning and Verbal Behavior,* 6, p. 855-863.

Reber, A. S. (1992). The cognitive unconscious: An evolutionary perspective. *Consciousness and Cognition,* 1, p. 93-133.

Reber, A. S. (1993a). *Implicit Learning and Tacit Knowledge. An Essay on the Cognitive Unconscious.* Oxford: Oxford University Press.

Reber, A. S. (1993b). Personal knowledge and the cognitive unconscious. *Polanyiana,* 3, p. 97-115.

Reber, A. S. & R. Allen (2000). Individual differences in implicit learning. In R. G. Kunzendorf & B. Wallace (Eds.) *Individual Differences in Conscious Experience.* Philadelphia: John Benjamins, p. 227-247.

Reber, A. S., Allen, R., & P. J. Reber. (1999). Implicit and explicit learning. In: R. Steinberg (Ed.) *The Nature of Cognition.* Cambridge, MA: MIT Press.

Reich, K. (2000). *Systemisch-Konstruktivistische Pädagogik. Einführung in Grundlagen einer interaktionistisch-konstruktivistischen Pädagogik.* Weinheim: Beltz Verlag.

Searle, J. R. (1979). A taxonomy of ilocutionary acts. In: J. R. Searle *Expression and Meaning.* Cambridge: Cambridge University Press, p. 1-29.

Searle, J. R. (1995). *The Construction of Social Reality.* London: Allen Lane, Penguin Group.

Seger, C. A., Prabhakaran, V., Poldrack, R. A. & Gabrieli, J. D. E. (2000). Neural activity differs between explicit and implicit learning of artificial grammar strings: An fMRI study. *Psychobiology,* 28 (3), p. 283-292.

Shanks, D. R. & St. John, M. F. (1994). Characteristics of dissociable human learning systems. *Behavioral and Brain Sciences,* 17, p. 367-447.

Stadler, M. A. & P. A. Frensch (Eds.) (1998). *Handbook of Implicit Learning.* Thousand Oaks, CA: Sage Publications.

von Glasersfeld, E. (1976). Radical constructivism and Piaget's concept of knowledge. In: Frank B. Murray (ed.) *Cognitive Psychology: The Impact of Piaget.* New York: Plenum Press, p. 109-122.

von Glasersfeld, E. (1980). Adaptation and viability. In The Sociobiological Challenge to Psychology, *American Psychologist* 35 (11), p. 970-974.

von Glasersfeld, E. (1982). An interpretation of Piaget's constructivism. *Revue Internationale de Philosophie* 36 (4), p. 612-635.

von Glasersfeld, E. (1995a). A constructivist approach to teaching. In: Steffe, L. P. & J. Gale (Eds.): *Constructivism in Education.* Hillsdale, New Jersey: Lawrence Erlbaum Associates, Publishers, p. 3-15.

von Glasersfeld, E. (1995b). *Radical Constructivism: A Way of Knowing and Learning.* London: Routledge Falmer.
von Glasersfeld, E. (1995c). sensory experience, abstraction, and teaching. In: Steffe, L. P. & J. Gale (Eds.): *Constructivism in Education.* Hillsdale, New Jersey: Lawrence Erlbaum Associates, Publishers, p. 369-383.
Von Glasersfeld, E. (2005). Introduction. Aspects of constructivism. In: Fosnot, C.T. (ed.): *Constructivism. Theory, Perspectives, and Practice.* 2$^{nd}$ edition. New York: Teachers College, p. 3-7.
von Glasersfeld, E. (2007). *Key Works in Radical Constructivism.* Rotterdam: Sense Publishers.
Von Glasersfeld, E. & F. J. Varela (1987). Problems of knowledge and cognizing organisms. *Methodologia 1*, p. 29-46.
Weiskrantz, L. (1997). *Consciousness Lost and Found.* Oxford: Oxford University Press.
Wenger, E. (2006). Social learning theory – current issues and challenges. Manuscript.
Winch, C. (1998). *The Philosophy of Human Learning.* London: Routledge.
Wittgenstein, L. (1953). *Philosophische Untersuchungen/Philosophical Investigations.* London: Blackwell.
Wood, T., Cobb, P. & E. Yackel (1995). Reflections on learning and teaching mathematics in elementary school. In: Steffe, L. P. & J. Gale (Eds.): *Constructivism in Education.* Hillsdale, New Jersey: Lawrence Erlbaum Associates, Publishers, p. 401-422.

# How we learn

A critical-constructive discussion of Piaget's and Vygotsky's theories of teaching and learning and their reactions to each other

*Steen Beck*

## Introduction

The concept of learning plays an important role in contemporary considerations about education. Almost all leading learning theories today are based on the view that learning in school demands students with the ability to relate actively to the academic subject and through dialogue, experiment, reflection etc. thereby creating a personal academic identity. This point of view is called *constructivist* and the Swiss biologist and epistemologist Jean Piaget (1886-1980) is an important figure in the classical constructive idea of learning as a subjective and cognitive construction. According to Piaget learning is closely connected to possibilities and limits of the individual cognitive capacity and development. While Piaget emphasized the mechanism of individual auto-regulation without leaving social factors out of account in the formation of rationality, other psychologists have paid much more close attention to social situated learning and the mechanisms involved in learner's appropriation of cultural knowledge which in fact is what academic subjects can be said to be. This point of view can be called socio-cultural and Lev Vygotsky (1896-1934) is a central figure in this approach. While Piaget studied the individual construction of knowledge 'from within' through assimilation and accommodation, Vygotsky showed how instruction 'from without' creates a *zone of proximate development* whereby an important link between individual learning and cultural appropriation is created.

From my point of view the difference between Piaget's and Vygotsky's approach should not be exaggerated (for a more detailed unfolding of my analysis in this chapter, see Beck 2015). They both stressed interaction as fundamental to development and learning, and there are many similarities in their approach to changes in cognitive structures and their ideas of how concepts are created in the individual's developmental proces. But also the two theorists conceptualized the relation between the individual and its social environment with different foci and ideas of the importance of 'the social'. The difference does not only concern the difference between Piaget's biological and Vygotsky's socio-cultural approach (although this difference – as we shall see – should not be exaggerated), but also the relation between (teacher) control and (student) freedom: Piaget stressed with his foundation in protestant individualism the autonomy of the individual towards the societal authorities, while Vygotsky with his foundation in Marxism and revolutionary ideas of 'the new socialist man' stressed the importance of social technologies in the transformation of human cognition.

In this chapter my thesis is that Piaget's and Vygotsky's cultural contexts and philosophical and scientific orientations for sure created some important differences in their approach. At the same time I argue that they both contributed with important perspectives on the relation between teaching and learning. Therefore the differences between their approaches should not be discussed in a manner where *the winner takes it all*, but with respect to the complexity of development as a proces where biological, psychological and cultural levels are all involved.

It is in the light of such efforts to reopen the debate on the relation between teaching and learning that I want to revisit the two great theorists of learning with a deconstructive as well as a constructive purpose in mind. My *deconstructive purpose* is to show that neither Piaget's idea of psycho-genesis nor Vygotsky's idea of socio-genesis is sufficient to explain what learning is while my *constructive purpose* is to show that both of their contributions to learning theory are necessary even though what they add up together does not suffice. The chapter is structured as follows: In the first two sections, Vygotsky's and Piaget's respective theories of concept formation and the relation between learning and teaching are introduced in a historical context which seems important if the meaning of their theories are to be fully understood. Also their critique of one another is introduced: My intention is here to locate what Vygotsky and Piaget pay attention to regarding each other's position and what they ignore. In section three, I discuss some strengths and weaknesses of their positions and of their reactions to each other. In section four, some fundamental differences between the two theoretical giants' approaches to teaching and learning are discussed, and, in section five, I attempt to integrate the viable parts of Piaget and Vygotsky's theories, thereby revitalizing and actualizing central insights from both.

## Vygotsky's theory of instruction – and his critique of Piaget
*Vygotsky's theory of learning*
Vygotsky created his world famous theory about children's cognitive development and the importance of instruction-based learning only a few years after the Russian Revolution in 1917. He wanted to contribute to Lenin's and the Bolsheviks' ideas about the new socialist man and from the beginning of the 1920s he considered education a vital part of this project (Au 2007). An educated population was necessary in order to modernize Russia – but how should teaching and learning be understood and practiced from a Marxist point of view? With Marx, Hegel, Spinoza, the Russian behaviorists and linguistics such as Potebnya and Shpet as his starting point, Vygotsky developed a view of man as an individual who learns to master his own nature. This theory was founded on extreme rationalism and adopted the utopian point of view that the individual within the realized communist society becomes transparent to himself (Vygotsky 1997/1927; 1994/1930).

Vygotsky was a child of the *historicism* of Dialectical and Historical Materialism in which "laws" of history are revealed and higher as well as lower forms of civilization and consciousness are analyzed (Popper 1962; Gielen and Jeshmaridian 1999). Man had developed his thinking historically and in the future it would be possible to develop it even further, thereby creating a humanity of social individuals whose levels of cognitive and emotional self-mastery were so high that they would in reality constitute a new kind of human beings. To Vygotsky, education was crucial for this development to take place (Vygotsky 1926/1997; 1934/1987). With his sense of dialectic thinking and his interest in the interplay between different factors that come together as a totality or, as Vygotsky termed it, a "unit of analysis" or a "cell", he definitively transgressed a more primitive form of materialism by showing that phenomena cannot be understood simply by reducing them to "the material", e.g. the brain, but that it is the interplay and the productive contrasts between phenomena, e.g. between thought and language, between lower and higher mental processes etc., that generates development and thereby renders possible the emergence of qualitatively new aspects.

From Vygotsky's point of view, higher mental functions include language, which at first exists *outside* the individual as an inter-mental phenomenon, but it soon becomes an intra-mental tool for reflection and self-reflection, thereby becoming the base for the production of meaning. This is in brief terms the developing line of the individual, moving from the imitation of words heard from others, to the expression of scientific concepts used in problem solving. In this way, the individual is closely linked to the development of society and of the species, but in a dialectical manner wherein the relation produces affirmation and negation, a process which explains the emergence of new cognitive abilities.

According to Vygotsky, the function of language changes during a child's development. In early childhood, language is used for emotional expression and social interaction. Later, it is used for communication and intellectual purposes. Although biological considerations are not at the forefront of Vygotsky's thinking, he is aware that biological maturation is involved in concept-development. He talks about neo-formations and 'crises' in the development of the child (Vygotsky 1932), and he defines the child's first efforts to create concepts or concept-like words as *syncretism*. During this phase, the child tries to create abstractions in a chaotic and unsystematic way. In the next phase, the child creates *complexes*; now concepts are established, but they are closely related to everyday experiences and without any system. After a period wherein the child creates what Vygotsky calls *pseudo-concepts* and *potential concepts*, which hold traceable elements of systematic thinking, but still no ability to reflect on his own use of concepts, the child is ready to form real or *scientific concepts*. Unlike everyday concepts, scientific concepts are formed as part of the instructional process and do not belong to the child's own "empirical" register, but to the collective thinking of mankind.

From here, the route to Vygotsky's famous concept of *the Zone of Proximal Development* ran very straight: To learn is to acquire skills that were at first outside of the learner, held by more able learners and were then internalized. In this way, rudimentary functions are used to develop proper skills. What the child is able to do in collaboration today he will be able to do independently tomorrow (Vygotsky 1984/1934, p. 211). Children with the same biological age have different mental ages and accordingly different potentials. According to Vygotsky, it is not possible to say anything of significance about an individual's intelligence from a given test, because you have to consider that individual's potential for learning as part of the IQ. The child who profits the most from the help of another has the greater intellectual potential.

## Vygotsky's critique of Piaget

In Vygotsky's *Thinking and Speech*, Piaget takes a prominent place as both a celebrated and a criticized figure. Vygotsky agrees with Piaget that a child's ability to use scientific concepts is dependent on development and must be interpreted as an emergent phenomenon. Concepts cannot, in Vygotsky's own words, be compared to hot cakes being served to the child (ibid. p. 179), but become possible in a developmental perspective where the active child "does" something and thereby changes himself. At the same time, however, Vygotsky is not satisfied with Piaget's understanding of the dialectical relation between the child's contribution to concept development and the importance of the cultural context. Piaget promotes the idea that the only authentic thinking performed by the child is spontaneous and self-constructed, while instruction-based thinking is more superficial and, in fact, alien to the child because it is not in accordance with the child's own logic. In Vygotsky's interpretation, Piaget's point of view is that scientific concepts are forced upon the child from the outside; they are alien to the child itself (ibid. p. 175). Vygotsky's conclusion is that, to Piaget, the child's characteristic way of thinking has no constructive, positive and formative function in the child's mental development and growth (ibid. p. 175). Vygotsky holds the opposite to be true: There is no antagonism between spontaneous and non-spontaneous concepts. As the child develops, its use of language is re-structured, hence making it possible to develop a capacity for higher mental functions through the appropriation of the cultural tools, which in turn become the foundations of conscious attention, verbal memory, systematic thinking etc.:

> "Finally (in opposition to Piaget's mistaken and contradictory third position), we would argue that – in the process of concept formation – the

relationship between the processes of instruction and development must be immeasurably more complex and positive in nature than the simple antagonism proposed by Piaget" (ibid. p. 177).

It is Piaget's psychoanalytically influenced interpretation of egocentric mentality that prevents him from obtaining a genuine understanding of the child's concept-formation. Vygotsky notices that, from Piaget's point of view, the egocentric thought must be destroyed before anything new can enter and Piaget's point of view seems to be that the destruction of egocentrism is realized through an intervention from without. Scientific concepts, however, are not created from without, but rather by an extraordinary effort of the child and his readiness for comprehending them as a result of his development of conceptual capacity. This is the reason why non-spontaneous concepts are in no way contrary to spontaneous concepts or, as Vygotsky terms them, everyday concepts. He speaks of a fluid limit or a complex process wherein the two concepts influence one another. The development of non-spontaneous concepts influences everyday concepts – and the two kinds interact in a continuous process (ibid. p. 178).

Vygotsky's analysis of the child's emerging realism and its development towards conscious self-mastering as well as his critique of Piaget's theory of the egocentric nature of the child's mentality are important premises for his approach to the learning of school subjects. Children learn to use scientific concepts when they are introduced to these in a systematic and well-defined form, and by using and discussing them in ways that accord with their actual cognitive abilities and in respect of concepts containing challenges realized in the zone of proximal development where the less able learn from the more able.

Vygotsky's critique of Piaget is absolute and leaves no room for compromise. However, the question is whether he actually interpreted Piaget's position correctly. I will return to this question after introducing Piaget and his response to Vygotsky.

## Piaget's theory of learning – and his response to Vygotsky
*Piaget's theory of learning*
A good starting point for an understanding of Piaget's approach to development and learning is the spiritual crisis he experienced in his

early years (Ducret 1984; Vidal 1994). This crisis was taking place in the Protestant environment of his childhood, in the wake of the successes obtained by the natural sciences, but also on a personal level in the form of a young man's effort to reconcile science with faith, knowledge and ethics. By taking up ideas from Henri Bergson and Auguste Sabatier, he developed a set of ideas about the relationship between consciousness and evolution. These considerations can be found in his early works *Le mission de l'idée* (Piaget 1916) and *Recherche* (Piaget 1918) wherein he took the first steps towards a biological theory of life as a process of becoming and of equilibrium processes. Although Bergson was replaced by other sources of inspiration and discourses, the ideas about *duration (la durée)* and *the vital impulse* became lasting platform to Piaget (Bennour & Vonèche 2009).

Piaget viewed the particular mode of thought held by the child as qualitatively distinct from that of the adult. His point which was – as Vygotsky rightly emphasizes – clearly inspired by psychoanalysis (Piaget 1920 a+b) was that the child develops from having a non-socialized, autistic and ego-centric mentality towards a more socialized and decentralized mode of thought, which is logical and rational. Here we find important brick stones for his famous theory about the four developmental stages caused by assimilatory and accommodative processes involving both internal regulation and experiences of the exterior world, such as objects and people (Piaget 1936/1948; 1937; 1945/1994; 1970/1979).

Piaget's view of Protestantism and his defense of immanence, which values the human desire for balance as well as the unification of the particular and the general, were decisive to his understanding of human development and moral judgment. This allowed him to defend the individual right to develop an autonomous morality founded on reason rather than a heteronomous morality founded on tradition and superstition (Piaget 1928; 1930/1998; 1932; Piaget & Inhelder 1955/1970). In extension of this idea about the formation of an autonomous morality and mode of thought, he argued for a new kind of school based on a new pedagogy: *l'école active*. Here, the learning processes made it possible for a child to develop an autonomous morality by means of interacting and collaborating with other children.

Piaget's theory of learning was founded on the close connection between biological and cognitive processes (Piaget 1970). Starting out from the theory of the human being as a living organism, he formed a theory about its basic mental processes. He emphasized the self-regulative character of the psychological system (Piaget 1968) while regarding cognitive development as the result of interaction between the individual and its surroundings. Although Piaget stressed the individual character of learning, he did not – as is often postulated by social-constructivists – ignore the importance of interaction with the exterior environment. We develop and learn by acting upon objects and we learn to correct our "egocentric" thoughts through cooperation with others: Operations and co-operations refer to the same fundamental cognitive processes (Piaget 1965/1977). Also he was aware that different cultural environments create different possibilities for cognitive development and learning (he even mentioned "lazy" cultures as a thread to individual development) although he at the same time stated that we have to consider universal aspects of development and learning; he talked about possible delays in cognitive development due to under-stimulation from the environment and also he discussed if abstract thinking is developed in 'primitive' societies in the same degree as in modern societies (Piaget 1966).

According to Piaget, humans have the ability to maintain knowledge and experiences in relatively stable ways, which he calls "schemes". Learners improve their schemes because they need to adapt to the environment with its tasks to be solved and skills to be learned. In functional terms, the adaptation process is identical with a continuous effort to attain equilibrium by assimilation (whereby we translate new experiences to already existing meanings) and accommodation (whereby we adjust our schemes according to new experiences). Piaget's basic idea is that human beings are problem-solving creatures trying to re-establish an interrupted balance between part and totality and between the interior self-regulations and the exterior environment. This is Piaget's theory of learning in a nutshell: Learning takes place when the individual knows that there is something he wants to know or do, which he or she is currently not capable of knowing or doing. The recognition that one is not able to solve the problem, but has to learn something new sets in motion a learning process whereby the individual changes his capacity for learning while also learning something specific. In other words, Piaget's epistemic subject is driven towards "the new" by its need for a new balance, which in turn catalyzes the emergence of new cognitive capacities.

The neo-Piagetian scientist Juan Pascual-Leone (2012) refers to Piaget as a "dialectic constructivist" and emphasises the fact that, in terms of an actual understanding of Piaget's theories of the processual nature of thinking, the issue is not one of structures, but rather of *structurations* and *de-structurations*: Piaget operates with affirming and negating cognitive processes; the affirming processes, relating to assimilative thinking, are linked to the schemes and enable the individual to act in accordance with intentions and understandings. Accommodative processes, however, create negations in relation to the existing schemes of understanding; they are incongruent, dialectically anti-polar and create the basis for new forms of *practice* (for a comparison of the dialectical thinking of Piaget and Hegel, see Kesselring 1981).

Piaget was first and foremost interested in the cognitive development of human beings and in kinds of thinking made possible through spontaneous practice and not through cultural forming, such as via school education. On the other hand, this does not mean that his research was without pedagogical implications. According to Piaget, traditional teaching created overly passive learners left without the possibility of making the necessary operations, such as analysis, experiment, suggestions, communication etc. The exterior world certainly is influential, but not in any direct way. Its importance consists mainly in stimulating operations and actions.

*Piaget's answer to Vygotsky*
In 1962, Vygotsky's main text, which included his critique of Piaget, was translated into English with the title *Thought and Language*. Piaget was asked to respond to Vygotsky in an afterword and, although he had heard of Vygotsky from Russian colleagues such as Luria and Leontjev, this English translation was his first opportunity to become acquainted with Vygotsky's critique, by then almost thirty years old. Piaget's task was not easy; in 1962, he was to give a response to a long-dead colleague, who in 1934 had reacted to Piaget's first texts from 1923-24.

In his commentary, Piaget does not find the difference between his own and Vygotsky's approaches to children's concept development as fundamental as Vygotsky does. Moreover, he finds Vygotsky's criticism of the fact that he ignores the importance of scientific concepts in cognitive development misunderstood. Piaget's point of view is that this is exactly what his genetic theory is about:

"Vygotsky concluded from his reflections on my earliest books no doubt without suspecting that this was exactly my research-program [...], namely that the essential task of child psychology was to study the psychological formation of scientific concepts by following in sequence the process 'before our eyes'" (Piaget 1962, p. 250).

In the same paragraph, he says that he later – which Vygotsky could not know – published studies of children's understanding of basic scientific concepts, namely the development of children's understanding of numbers, quantity, movement, time, space, etc. Vygotsky accuses him of ignoring scientific thinking, which is nothing less than the hard core of his research program on how scientific thinking is possible for human beings. From his point of view, the development of spontaneous concepts leads to fundamental logical-mathematical structures, which are the preconditions for scientific thinking and the "taking in" of school subjects.

Piaget also finds Vygotsky's critique of his approach to teaching and learning unsatisfactory. Once again, it is the question of how to understand the development of concepts that puts Vygotsky on the wrong track. Piaget emphasizes that he actually links spontaneous concepts to learning in school and he also emphasizes that there ought to be some connection between teaching and learning. Teachers should stimulate children's thinking by giving them exercises and discussing the subjects with the children. School education is, he thought, very important to children's cognitive development and can to a certain degree even accelerate cognitive processes (although Piaget was in other comments rather critical towards what he called "the American question" as he thought that cognitive development takes time and should not be pushed which is the problem with traditional 'adult-centered' school teaching). According to Piaget, it is important to stress the phrase 'to a certain degree' and by investigating other causal mechanisms than Vygotsky did, he wanted to understand the coupling mechanisms that influence the relationship between teaching and learning.

Piaget's position towards the existing teaching in contemporary schools can best be summed up as a critique of an ideology founded on authoritarian beliefs and "heterogeneous' morals, forced upon the individual from without. In the existing school, teachers generally lack an understanding of the psychological preconditions of learning. This is the reason why teachers are not able to use children's spontaneous thinking and can at best enhance reproductive and figurative thinking. Piaget's main point of view is that children from about the age of seven are cognitively able to learn in an experimental and analytical way; therefore the teacher's understanding of age-relevant adaptation strategies is highly important if he is to relate didactical aims to real learning. In some respects, this sounds very much like Vygotsky's theory of learning in the Zone of Proximal Development; the teacher has to know the actual level of a student in order to come up with exercises that match the student and thereby enhance learning. This proximity of Piaget's and Vygotsky's positions towards pedagogy is probably the reason why Piaget finds it a little odd that Vygotsky is so eager to emphasize the differences between their approaches to the relation between learning and teaching. It also explains why Piaget finds that Vygotsky misunderstands him in a very fundamental way, namely in taking his opinion to be that teachers should teach the students spontaneous concepts in order to be able to fight against them. In fact, Piaget's point is the exact opposite, namely that teachers should use children's spontaneous intellectual development much better than they often do and in order to create much better connections between scientific concepts (school subjects) and the child's actual abilities to perform rational mental operations (the student's cognitive development).

Piaget's point is not that students are not able to learn non-spontaneous concepts, but rather that the relation between spontaneous and non-spontaneous concepts is far more complex than Vygotsky with his somewhat rough understanding of the student's actual level of learning (one of the two poles in his concept of the zone of proximal development) postulates (Piaget 1962, p. 252).

Piaget agrees with Vygotsky that two lines of thinking meet in effective learning at school, namely non-spontaneous concepts being introduced by the teacher and spontaneous concepts founded in the operational capacity of the child. Spontaneous concepts are quite different from what Vygotsky calls every day concepts. It is not possible to learn anything that is not grounded in assimilation processes and, likewise, accommodation without an assimilative platform is not possible. This is what teachers in the existing school often forget. In other words, the school should recognize the assimilation structures of students and not push forward knowledge that is not the result of experimental learning. From Piaget's point of view, the discrepancy between himself and Vygotsky does not concern "development before learning" or "learning before development" in any simple way because he also thinks that learning enhances development by simulating new cognitive structures. More accurately, he is not satisfied with teaching that does not stimulate curiosity and problem-based learning. His conclusion, however, is not that the teacher is without importance:

> "Indeed, even from the perspective of the general coordination of actions (either as overt behavior or interiorized as operations), the adult, being more advanced than the child, can help him speed up his development during educational processes in the family or school." (ibid. p. 257).

As we can see, Piaget explicitly agrees with Vygotsky's statement that learning is important to development, a statement which corresponds to Piaget's cultural thesis about the environment's importance to especially the abstract-formal phase and his general remarks on "lazy" and "engaged" milieus (Piaget 1966). One explanation of why Piaget stresses the importance of the psycho-genetic factors, somewhat at the expense of socio-genetic factors, is that he is dissatisfied with sociological and socio-cultural explanations (Piaget's critique of Foucault is significant for his position, see *Structuralism* from1968) that ignore the active and biological nature of learning and also confuse real learning with the fact that teaching and learning often take place in a school context. This confusion results in a rather naïve optimism, which to his mind exists in Vygotsky's idea of learning as appropriation of the existing culture (Glassman 1994, p. 205).

## Discussion

There seems to be a great deal of misunderstanding in Vygotsky's critique of Piaget and even though some unclear points can be detected in Piaget's early theories. Vygotsky misunderstood him at very fundamental levels, making too much of an Hegelian antithesis out of his Swiss colleague, an attitude which unfortunately was passed on to many of his followers later in the twentieth century. Piaget never thought that society and the adult in a mono-causal way change the mentality of the child, although both play important roles. Ironically, Vygotsky seems to criticize Piaget from a child-centered position, which is very similar to the position that gave Piaget his international fame (Miller 2011, p. 81). The main point in Piaget's genetic epistemology is that, thanks to the child's mental self-regulation in the equilibrium process, the child contributes very actively to the formation of rationality as a precondition for scientific thinking. Neither does Piaget posit that new stages destroy earlier ones. Rather, his point of view is that new stages emerge from potentialities and conflicts within earlier stages and sub-stages. This is exactly what his theory of assimilation and accommodation is about. What Piaget points to when he talks about scientific concepts being forced upon the child is not a universal antagonism between the child's way of thinking and the adult's way of thinking, but rather a certain kind of socialization and teaching whereby a particularly adult logic of scientific concepts is taught and "forced upon" the child without sensitivity towards the psychological and developmental aspects of the relation. In Piaget's (later) terminology, Vygotsky only sees his critique of a specific method of teaching, but not his promotion of the necessity for operational learning matching the child's cognitive capacity.

Another problem in Vygotsky's critique is his identification of Piaget's spontaneous thinking with non-scientific concepts, which he further identifies with everyday concepts (Vygotsky 1994/1934, p. 177). But the validity of this parallel is highly problematic. When Piaget defines spontaneous thinking, he is not referring to concepts, but to types of thinking or mental operations developed through the transformation of cognitive structures that leads to more mature conceptions of time and space such as reversibility, conservation etc. Spontaneous concepts are not, as Vygotsky seems to think, empirical concepts related to everyday life, but rather to the kind of thinking closely connected to the child's cognitive capacity. His spontaneous concepts are logical-mathematical concepts constructed by the child itself, such as conservation, classification, time, space, causality etc. These are very similar to Kantian categories of understanding (Miller 2011, p. 138) constructed through processes of self-regulation specific to the dynamic intelligence of the individual child. And, contrary to what Vygotsky thinks, Piaget talks about types of thinking wherein separate elements are integrated into a system, which becomes clear when we study Piaget's structural understanding of the mechanisms realized in human self-regulation. From Piaget's point of view, scientific concepts understood as academically transmitted knowledge can only be approached as far as the child is able to assimilate and accommodate properly the concepts and systematic ways of understanding with which it is presented. His point is not, as Vygotsky believes, that there is a clear difference between spontaneous and scientific thinking, but rather that there is a possible and historically constituted contradiction between the ways in which science is taught by teachers and the ways in which cognition operates.

However, Piaget misunderstands Vygotsky as much as Vygotsky misunderstands him. Piaget's definition of scientific concepts is not identical to Vygotsky's definition, even though he seems to believe so (Feldman & Fowler 1997). When Vygotsky speaks of scientific concepts, he is not referring to concepts that become possible as a consequence of the child's cognitive and spontaneous development, but to concepts belonging to school subjects such as social science, physics and history.

Piaget misses Vygotsky's point about cultural knowledge as something the adults introduce to the child because he does not find "adult thinking" interesting, as it is contingent and irrelevant to the development of the child's capacity to think. As Ronald Miller has stated:

> "... Piaget's spontaneous operations are not part of the cultural repertoire that is handed down across the generations but constitute part of the universal human condition that renders culture possible. In drawing the distinction between spontaneous and non-spontaneous concepts, in an important sense Piaget was limiting the scope of this theory in much the same way that he preferred to describe his work as 'genetic epistemology' rather than 'cognitive psychology'" (Miller 2011, p. 40).

It is clear that Vygotsky could not see the point in limiting the scope like this. From his point of view, cultural knowledge, including science, is not a contingent phenomenon, but rather a mediating resource, which makes it possible to understand and enhance cognitive development by teaching us to generalize, make abstractions etc. Piaget refers to a fundamental level of universal, spontaneous adaption and understanding or knowledge; his interest is rather formalistic, while Vygotsky refers to non-universal, non-spontaneous appropriation of knowledge and understanding, which is appreciated within a specific cultural context and within specific domains.

## An important difference

A major difference between Piaget and Vygotsky, which is not brought to the surface in their debate, but which can be regarded as a decisive subtext if the aim is to understand the differences between their arguments, concerns their views on the student's process of formation, i.e. the question of what sort of person and citizen is to be encouraged by the school's academic and social processes. It is evident that Piaget and Vygotsky represent two separate approaches to the school's educational and cultural aims and this difference plays a latent role in their debate, albeit without either of them apparently aware of the significance of this. As was mentioned above, Piaget combines a radical Protestant individualism with the vision of a democratic school, which turns societal differentiation into a strength and which praises the individual's autonomy as the very kernel of modern society. As I have also shown, Vygotsky combines the theory of an intellectual elite's education of the people into socialism with the vision of a polytechnic school wherein the foundations are laid for scientifically enlightened and self-transparent persons who are able to independently contribute to the development of a rational society. The contrast between Piaget's Protestant individualism and Vygotsky's Marxist historicism surfaces in their dissimilar views on which mechanism of development and learning is the most important. Piaget argues in favour of the student's immanent cognitive resources, thus locating the potential for rationality within the individual human being, while Vygotsky argues in favour of the teacher's systematic instruction, thus emphasizing the structural conditions for the emancipation of people's 'freedom'. In that sense, the distinction between Piaget's "inside-out" approach and Vygotsky's "outside-in" approach, which is commonly employed as a key to explaining the differences between them, has a certain amount of explanatory power. Piaget highlights the potential for conflict and transgression in the relation between student and teacher, while Vygotsky highlights the potential for harmonious cooperation and for shaping the student's consciousness. According to Lourenço, one can go as far as to say that the major difference between Piaget and Vygotsky is that the former takes as his staring point the individual's autonomy, while the latter understands the individual as a heteronomous being and as such dependent on its social surroundings (Lourenço 2012).

Piaget's views on the school's task are, as mentioned, linked to a critique of the authoritarian school and the unilateral respect associated with the moral and religious notions of traditional society. His argument in relation to the child's possibilities for establishing a rationality that emerges from within is ultimately linked to his notion of a rational individual who, given the right conditions, is able to think authoritatively and voluntarily contribute to society. A good society is, in other words, a society wherein differentiation creates the conditions for development and wherein the individual stands out as a resource for the development of knowledge. There is a clear coherence between Piaget's emphasis on the learning outcome as an individual phenomenon (although learning takes place in cooperation with others) and his notion of democratic education; people learn from one another, but it is up to the autonomous subject to decide the extent to which he or she wants to subscribe to the values that others, including the teacher, promote via their communication. In the relation between student and teacher, values are exchanged and the teacher is forced to employ his own values in guiding the student. But in a modern, democratic society the teacher also has to accept that it is up to the student to evaluate the teacher's values in order to come to his own understanding and that this is an individual issue. In the words of Leslie Smith: "... it is for me to make my mind up, whether rightly or wrongly, even when you are assisting me. This is Piaget's individualism, and it is the best tradition of 'education for intellectual freedom'" (Smith 2009, p. 330). In this sense, Piaget's contribution to the discussion of the relationship between learning and teaching is not about learning of one's own accord, but about learning as part of one's interaction with others and through the intellectual and moral culture that emerges, developing one's skills and moral constitution, thereby becoming not only a culture-appropriating, but also a culture-creating individual. One might thus say that the Protestant educational ethics, elevating the individual to a moral and responsible subject with all that this entails in terms of an authority-critical potential that ultimately denies any transcendence, including its views of the 'teacher-deity', is never so far away in Piaget's argumentation that it cannot be detected – just as it remains discernible in his debate with Vygotsky whom he criticizes for emphasizing too heavily the teacher's control techniques and too lightly the student's internal development and autonomy.

Vygotsky's position does, indeed, contain certain characteristics that point in the direction of determinism because, although he has a dynamic understanding of the developmental stages of cognition through childhood and youth, these dynamics concerns predominantly increasing degrees of appropriation and internalisation – i.e. an increasing ability to receive cultural "learning". When Vygotsky ascribes to the teacher the function of the person who by diagnosing the students' zone of proximal development can predetermine the direction of their learning process, and when he ascribes to the scientific concepts to which the teacher introduces the students a significance that is decisive to their higher mental processes, he is really saying that the teacher is speaking from a position, which the students must attain during the course of their development. In that sense, Vygotsky's theory concerns the ways in which a society and its educators can develop control techniques, not least in continuation of the double-stimulation techniques that shape the individual.

It seems to me that exactly the issue of Piaget and Vygotsky's backgrounds within, respectively, Protestant individualism and Marxist historicism constitutes the reason why Vygotsky lets teaching and learning 'merge' within the instruction category in order to show how culture is internalised, while Piaget maintains the importance of distinguishing between teaching and learning so as to maintain the autonomous individual's ability to act.

## Towards a synthesis

The great debates on what learning is have often focused on whether a biological or a cultural view of the phenomenon is the correct one. Cognitivists usually subscribe to the former stance while social-constructivists subscribe to the latter (Wiben Jensen 2011). Most, however, will probably agree that it is hard to imagine learning that does not link to some evolutionarily developed abilities particular to the given species just like most will probably also agree that in reality it is hard to isolate theories of learning from the cultural contexts within which they exist. The processes of adaptation are mainly of a biological nature (in the sense that what is to be understood is humankind's species-particular ability to perform specific actions), while the use of tools, including language, is primarily culturally shaped. Instead of partaking in endless and dichotomous discussions of an either-or between humans as biological or cultural beings, one could make the salomonic suggestion that learning encompasses both bio-genetic and socio-genetic aspects, which during the course of an individual's development merge in the processes of consciousness and changes of capacity that we connect to learning, and which may, as far as the individual's learning course goes, be both reproductive and transformative in relation to the cultural and social input that necessarily surround learning.

Feldman and Fowler have made a very fruitful contribution to an understanding and critique of both Piaget and Vygotsky and their misunderstandings of each other (Feldman & Fowler 1997). The two researchers present the thesis that Piaget and Vygotsky refer, in fact, to separate areas of development when they speak of cognitive development and learning (Feldman & Fowler 1997, p. 199), but neither Piaget nor Vygotsky is sufficiently aware of this, which is why to some extent they talk at cross-purposes. Piaget is interested in mechanisms of development within the field of universal development. Piaget's ambition was to get behind the relation as it unfolds between student and teacher during education in order to find the hidden mechanism within the individual, which sparks its interest in learning through cooperation with others. He found his explanation in a biological regularity, namely the process of adaptation with its assimilation and accommodation that in a sort of twin-like interplay creates equilibrium processes. According to Piaget, then, the central learning mechanism is the *mentally regulated equilibrium process*. Feldman and Fowler's point here is that Piaget pinpoints cognitive abilities that are quite essential within the universal area of development, but that Piaget also misses something. He is interested in certain universal cognitive development characteristics, but not in why people develop different skills – a factor that relates to the learning of specific skills and which must be regarded as a major issue in understanding of the learning process. Because how can it be that children in different cultures acquire such different skills if they are fundamentally guided by the same need to establish equilibrium? It must, of course, have something to do with the culturally determined contents that they learn. In other words, it is no use to separate the person who learns from the subject that the person learns if one is to understand how human beings learn.

As we have seen, Vygotsky, too, harboured the ambition to understand a number of relations on a universal level, e.g. certain universal aspects of mental development, which he termed 'crises' and 'neo-formations' and went on to analyse in relation to the first stages of concept development as well as the development from outer to inner speech. Nonetheless, his primary research field was *the cultural development* area and the individual's ability to absorb culture-historically knowledge accumulated. Vygotsky's fundamental thesis is that the development towards higher mental functions is embedded within processes of cultural history – processes that follow the laws of historical materialism and reduce the sort of biological and universal mechanisms that Piaget focuses on to secondary phenomena. Vygotsky, then, was more interested in *differences* than in similarities between human beings cross-culturally. According to Vygotsky, the central learning mechanism within the cultural development area is the relation between the person who is learning and a more experienced person. For example, the teacher or a more skilled student who has understood and is able to employ an aspect of a subject discourse can help the student who is still wavering between everyday concepts and scientific concepts to comprehend new connections. One could call this the *theory of cultural learning through a mechanism of subject-related transfer.*

Vygotsky, however, experiences problems when it comes to explaining what it is inside of the individual that motivates him to acquire different forms of knowledge. He makes a suggestion for what happens when you learn, but *not* for what happens inside the individual who focuses her attention on another individual in order to enable herself to do something she has not hitherto been able to do. Vygotsky's approach is simply *not* precise enough to explain learning as an activity that emanates from a subject in possession of motives and interests and that cannot be reduced to internalisation or acquisition.

Two important points can be deduced from this attempt to deconstruct Piaget and Vygotsky's debate with a view to putting it together in new ways. *Firstly*, there is no reason to choose between Piaget's and Vygotsky's respective positions on development and learning; universal as well as cultural mechanisms are in play when we learn and reducing the phenomenon to one extreme or the other is an expression of reductionism that evades the fact that both biological and cultural processes are at work when we learn (Glassman 2001; Lourenço 2012). Psychogenetic (and biogenetic) as well as socio-genetic knowledge is required in order to pinpoint what learning and development are. *Secondly*, Piaget's equilibrium mechanism may be interpreted as less universal than he thought. The equilibrium mechanism that is related to the specifically human form of adaptation to the surroundings always occurs within a specific cultural environment and is thus closely linked to the forms of leaning particular to it. This is why a 10-year old boy living in a tribal society where learning to use bow and arrow is essential learns something different from a 10-year old boy in Denmark who must learn how to read and write. This also makes it clear that the equilibrium process is in fact more area-specific and culturally shaped to a greater degree than Piaget seemed to think. On the other hand, the equilibrium process, when it is related to the development mechanism within cultural and subject-specific learning, explains something that Vygotsky finds hard to account for by means of his theory of learning within the field between current and future skills in the zone of proximal development – because Piaget's theory explains what happens to us on our inner mental stage when we learn from and with one another.

## Conclusion

As shown in the above analyses, the historically a-synchronic discussion between Vygotsky and Piaget was in many respects highly problematic and filled with misunderstandings and efforts to assimilate the other's terminology to their own position instead of searching for their common dialectical point of departure. However, although neither Piaget nor Vygotsky can be seen as the winner of the debate, both contribute interesting points to the understanding of teaching and learning, and some interesting conclusions may be drawn from their difficulties in defining the relation between learning and development in the formal learning situation. Piaget and Vygotsky's respective approaches to the formation of concepts should be seen more as a question of nuances, research interests and different degrees of "optimism" on the part of teaching rather than a question of entirely different theories.

As I have shown, both Piaget and Vygotsky can be interpreted as dialectical theorists, contributing different but equally important fundamental insights into the highly complex relation between intra- and inter-mental as well as between psychogenetic and socio-genetic aspects of the learning process. Piaget's dialectic is concerned with the twin processes of assimilation and accommodation as a combined process of oppositions, dynamics and emergency resulting in constantly new transformative totalities. Also his dialectical approach to the relation between individual cognition and the reality outside of the individual (being of a social, physical and human nature) is important, although his approach to instruction and socialization is somewhat under-theorized. Vygotsky's dialectics can be found in his approach to semantic word meanings which he called "units of meaning"; he showed how the relation between word and meaning changes during the ontogenetic development of the child because of the transformation from egocentric language as a tool of communication with others to inner language as a tool of communication with oneself. Also Vygotsky's idea of learning and instruction as a unit of analysis or a totality, where everything should be understood as relational, is dialectical. Moving from model-learning to self-mastering during the course of the learning process is something that takes place within the individual (here Vygotsky seems to agree with Piaget, but he does not elaborate as much as Piaget on the self-regulative nature of the process), but it also happens when other people, for instance the teacher or more cognitively able students in the classroom, facilitate the learning of the individual by making it perform with others what it cannot yet perform alone.

I will not hesitate to express my agreement with Piaget when he suggests a radical distinction between learning and teaching, although Vygotsky's point regarding the importance of the teacher as the person, who brings the discourses of school subjects into the classroom, thereby creating possibilities for learning within the zone of proximal learning, is also valid. Still, what happens within that zone is always a question of the learner's operations, which means that the results of teaching are in fact unpredictable and the communication between teachers and students vulnerable at a very fundamental level.

The dialectics between spontaneous thinking and the appropriation of scientific thinking is not a matter of shifting from one way of thinking to another, thereby repeating the quite un-dialectical discussion about what "came first": development or learning. It is, rather, a matter of understanding the complex relation between the individual's emerging inner capacities and his or her assimilation and accommodation of cultural resources in co-operation with others. When it comes to learning, this points to the conclusion that the equilibrium process (as explained by Piaget, only more closely related to a given practice and learning of a specific skill than Piaget seemed to believe) is best understood as taking place within a zone of proximal development (as explained by Vygotsky, only less influenced by the teacher than Vygotsky thought). We learn with and from others – yet we learn in individual ways; this is the precondition not only for our search for models to learn from, but also for our – hopefully well-deserved – position as models to others.

## References

Au, W. (2007). Vygotsky and Lenin on learning: The parallel structures of individual and social development. *Science & Society 71/3*, p. 273-298.

Beck, S. (2015). *Veje til viden – Piagets og Vygotskys læringsteorier i historisk og teoretisk belysning*. Frederiksberg: Frydenlund Academic.

Bennour, M. & Vonèche, J.J. (2009). The Historical Context of Piaget's Ideas. In: U. Müller, J. L. M. Carpendale & L. Smith (red.): *The Cambridge Companion to Piaget*. Cambridge: Cambridge University Press.

Ducret, J.-J. (1984). *Jean Piaget - savant et philosophe b. 1 og 2*. Genève: Librairie Droz.

Feldman, D.H. (1980). *Beyond Universals in Cognitive development*. Norwood, New Jersey: Ablex Publishing Corporation.

Feldman, D. H. og Fowler R. C. (1997). The nature(s) of developmental change: Piaget,Vygotsky, and the transition process. *New Ideas in Psychology 15/3*, p. 195-210.

Gielen, U. & Jeshmaridian, S.S. (1999). Lev S. Vygotsky: The man and the era. *International Journal of Group Tensions 28/3-4*, p. 273-30.

Glassman, M. (1994). All Things Being Equal: The Two Roads of Piaget and Vygotsky. *Developmental Review 14*, p. 186-214.

Glassman, M. (2001). Dewey and Vygotsky: Society, Experience, and Inquiry in Educational Practice. *Educational Researcher 30/4*, p. 3-14.

Kesselring. T. (1981). *Entwicklung und Wiederspruch – Ein Vergleich zwischen Piagets genetischer Erkenntnistheorie und Hegels Dialektik*. Frankfurt am Main: Suhrkamp Verlag.

Lourenço, O. (1212). Piaget and Vygotsky: Many resemblances, and a crucial difference. *New Ideas in Psychology* 30: p. 281-294.

Miller, R. (2011). *Vygotsky in Perspective*. Cambridge: Cambridge University Press.
Pascual-Leone (2012). Piaget as a Pioneer of Dialectical Constructivism: Seeking Dynamic Processes for Human Science. In: E. Martí & C. Rodríguez (red.): *After Piaget*. New Brunswick (U.S.A.) og London: Transaction Publishers.
Piaget, J. (1916). *La mission de l'idée*. Lausanne: Édition la Concorde.
Piaget, J. (1918). La biologie et la guerre. *Feuille centrale de la Societé suisse de Zofingue 58/5*, p. 374-380.
Piaget, J. (1918) *Recherche*. Lausanne: Édition la Concorde.
Piaget, J. (1920a). La psychanalyse dans ses rapports avec la psychologie de l'enfant. *Bulletin mensuel/Societé Alfred Binet 1*.
Piaget, J. (1920b). La psychanalyse dans ses rapports avec la psychologie de l'enfant. *Bulletin mensuel/Societé Alfred Binet 2-3*.
Piaget, J. (1923/1966). *Le langage et la pensée chez l'enfant*. Neuchatel: Delachaux et Niestlé.
Piaget, J. (1928). Deux types d'attitudes religieuses: Immanence et transcendence. *Br Chure publiée en 1928 par l'Association Chrétienne d'étudiants de Suisse romande*. Version electronique réalisée par les soins de lad Fondation Jean Piaget.
Piaget, J. (1930/1998). Les procédés de l'éducation morale. In: S. Parrat-Dayan & A. Tryphon (red.): *De la pédagogie*. Paris: Editions Odile Jacob.
Piaget, J. (1932). *Le jugement moral chez l'enfant*. Paris: Librairie Félix Alcan.
Piaget, J. (1936/1948). *La naissance de l'intelligence chez l'enfant*. Neuchatel and Paris: Delachaux & Niestlé S.A.
Piaget, J. (1937). *La construction du réel chez l'enfant*. Neuchâtel/Paris: Delachaux & Niestlé S.A.
Piaget, J. (1945/1994). *La formation du symbole chez l'enfant*. Lausanne and Paris: De-Lachaux & Niestlé.
Piaget, J. (1948 & 1972/1988). *Ou va l'education?* Paris: UNESCO. Delachaux et Niestlé, 1976.
Piaget, J. (1962/2000). Commentary on Vygotsky's criticisms of Language and thought of the child and Judgment and Reasoning in the child. *New Ideas in Psychology 18*, p. 241-259.
Piaget, J. (1965). *Sagesse et illusions de la philosophie*. Paris: Presses Universitaire de France.
Piaget, J. (1965/1977). Études sociologiques. Genève: Librairie Droz.
Piaget, J. (1966). Nécessité et signification des recherches comparatives en psychologie Génétique. International Journal of Psychology 1/1, p. 3-13.
Piaget, J. (1968/1974). *Le Structuralisme*. Paris: Presses Universitaires de France
Piaget, J. (1970/1979) *L'épistémologie génétique*. Paris: Presses Universitaires de France.
Piaget, J. (1970/1983) Piaget's Theory. I Kessen, W. (red.): *Handbook of Child Psychology b. 1*. New York: John Willey & Son.
Piaget, J. (1980). *Les formes élementaires de la dialectique*. Paris: Gallimard.
Piaget, J. & Inhelder, B. (1955/1970). *De la logique de l'enfant a la logique d l'adolescent Essai sur la construction des structures opératoires formelles*. Paris: Presses Universitaires de France.
Popper, K. (1962). *The Open Society and its Enemies, Vol. II*. New Jersey: Princeton University Press.

Smith, L. (2009). Piaget's Pedagogy. In: U. Müller, J. L. M. Carpendale & L. Smith (red.): *The Cambridge Companion to Piaget.* Cambridge: Cambridge University Press

Vygotsky, L. S. (1925/1971). *The Psychology of Art.* Cambridge, Massachusetts, and London: The M.I.T. Press.

Vygotsky, L. S. (1925/1997). *Consciousness as a problem for the psychology of behavior.* In: *The Collected Works of L. S. Vygotsky b. 3.* New York & London: Plenum Press.

Vygotsky, L. & Luria, A. (1925/1994). *Introduction to the Russian translation of Freud's Beyond the pleasure principle.* In: R. van der Veer and J. Valsiner (red.): *The Vygotsky Reader.* Oxford UK & Cambridge USA: Blackwell.

Vygotsky, L.S. (1926/1994). *The methods of reflexological and psychological investigation.* In: R. Van der Veer & J. Valsiner (red.): *The Vygotsky Reader.* Oxford UK & Cambridge USA.

Vygotsky, L. S. (1926/1997). *Educational psychology.* CRC Press: Boca Raton, Florida.

Vygotsky, L. S. (1927/1997). *The historical meaning of the crisis in psychology: A methodological investigation.* In: *The Collected Works of L. S. Vygotsky b. 3.* New York & London: Plenum Press.

Vygotsky, L. S. (1930/1994). *The socialist alteration of man.* In: R. van der Veer og J. Valsiner (red.): *The Vygotsky Reader.* Oxford UK & Cambridge USA: Blackwell.

Vygotsky, L.S. (1931/1997). The problem of the development of higher mental functions. In: *The collected works of L. S. Vygotsky b. 4.* New York: Plenum.

Vygotsky, L.S. (1932-34/1998). *Part 2: Problems of Child (Developmental) Psychology.* In: *The Collected Works,* b. 5, New York: Plenum Press.

Vygotsky, L. S. (1934/1987). *Thining and Speech.* In: *The collected works of L. S. Vygotsky b.1.* New York: Plenum.

# 'Situated learning' – beyond apprenticeship and social constructionism

*Gerd Christensen*

## Introduction

Since its release in 1991, Jean Lave and Etienne Wenger's book 'Situated Learning' (Lave & Wenger 1991) have had a significant impact on the ways in which 'learning' is conceptualized. This is not least the case in Denmark, where the book was immediately enrolled in some current debates that had stirred through the 1980s: the interest in 'the intuitive expert' (Dreyfus & Dreyfus 1986), and the focus on the philosophical concept of 'tacit knowledge' (Polanyi 1966). Both concepts were applied to research of professional knowledge i.e. the use of knowledge in professions like nursing, where the competent practitioner's skills and knowledge cannot always be made explicit (Benner 1995; Heggen 1997; Rognhaug 1993).

Through the concept of 'tacit knowledge' as a special form of knowledge, the professions could boost their legitimacy: the knowledge that the professional possesses is perhaps different from academic (theoretical, explicable) knowledge, but is not therefore (as practice-based, non-explicable) inferior. Referring to Donald Schön's distinction between reflection-in-action and reflection-on-action the practice-based knowledge was understood as the former, which also contributed to the legitimacy of practiced-based knowledge (Schön 1983).

Chronologically, this focus on tacit and practice-based knowledge was largely coinciding with educational policy discussions of a 'rehabilitation of apprenticeship' as an educational strategy in Denmark (Kvale 1993; Kvale & Nielsen 1999; Laursen 1993). In addition, the discussion was associated with the practical-creative professions' demands for legitimacy at all levels of the educational system (Wackerhausen & Wackerhausen 1993; Molander 1996; Nielsen 1995).

Hence, the impact of the concept of 'situated learning' can hardly be understood in isolation from these discussions. This is also manifested by the way the theory in Denmark was understood as a theory of apprenticeship (Kvale 1993; Kvale & Nielsen (ed.) 1999). However, as it will be shown in this chapter, Lave & Wenger's approach contains some qualities that make it very different from a traditional theory of apprenticeship. As an analytical concept, the theory can contribute to analyses of learning in all settings. As such, it urges the researcher to change perspective from the intentions for learning to what is actually going on in the practice.

But first, I will give a brief introduction to Lave & Wenger's approach.

## Learning as legitimate peripheral participation in a community of practice

In their presentation, Lave & Wenger underscores that 'situated learning' is written as a dissociation with: 1) that learning is something, which is only related to schooling and education; and 2) that learning is an individual cognitive exercise (Lave & Wenger, 1991, p. 49). Based on empirical examples, among other Jean Lave's anthropological studies of apprenticeship (training of tailors and midwives in traditional societies), the authors analyze, how the novice becomes a competent practitioner through non-teaching based learning. According to Lave & Wenger, the process of learning cannot fully be understood as something that only takes place inside the individual participants. Instead, it must be considered as a contextual occurrence, which means as something going on in between the participants. And when it comes to the question of cognition, this must be understood as 'distributed cognition' (see e.g. Ibid. p. 73 ff.).

The theory of learning, that Lave & Wenger develops, is based on three interrelated concepts: *community of practice*, *situated-ness* and *legitimate peripheral participation*. According to the authors, any context is potentially a community of practice. Thus, a community of practice is not an empirical, but an analytical concept. Basically, a community of practice is constituted through of a set of relations between the participants:

> A community of practice is a set of relations among persons, activity, and world over time and in relation with other tangential and overlapping communities of practice. A community of practice is an intrinsic

condition for the existence of knowledge, not least because it provides the interpretive support necessary for making sense of its heritage. [...] The social structure of this practice, its power relations, and its conditions for legitimacy define possibilities for learning (i.e., for legitimate peripheral participation). (Ibid. p. 98)

Communities of practice are characterized by the fact that all the actors involved are carrying out activities related to the community and to a mutual product. Thus, a community of practice is characterized by having a common task, which is structuring its activities. The task or product can be explicitly defined; such as it appears in several of the examples in the book *Situated learning* (Ibid.). Or it may be non-explicit, but (tacitly) implied by the participants who nevertheless are acting on the basis of a (tacit) mutual understanding that they are part of a common and meaningful activity – regardless of how its meaningfulness is evaluated from outside.

The concept of the 'community of practice' as a foundation for learning emphasizes that learning is not restricted to the school, but is something that can – and will – occur everywhere. The only prerequisite is the participants' explicit or implicit agreement on what the community is about, i.e. the mutual product that regulate the practice and the process of learning.

Hence, a community of practice is a community that only exists when the participants have access to complete certain functions, which the community consider as a relevant part of the mutual practice. Learning is thus attached to the community of practice, which means that it is situated. While the community of practice set the context for what can be learned, Lave & Wenger differentiates between two different forms of participation: *legitimate peripheral participation*, which is characterized by learning, and *full participation*, which is characterized by competence and 'mastering'. The position as *novice* is characterized by legitimate peripheral participation and the position as *experienced* is characterized by full participation.

While the term 'peripheral' and 'periphery' in other cases bear quite negative connotations, Lave & Wenger stresses, that the way in which they use the term, is positive: as antonym they mention *un-relatedness* (Ibid. p. 37). Thus, being 'peripheral participant' does not mean being marginalized, but rather being relevant to the community of practice.

'Legitimate' and 'peripheral' are therefore concepts to be understood as a coherent complex: legitimate-peripheral. This is underlined by the fact that the legitimate peripheral position is described as powerful ('*empowered*') unlike the position where someone is denied participation; a position that is power-less or '*dis-empowering*' (Ibid. p. 76).

The key to legitimate peripheral participation and thereby to learning, seem to be that the newcomers gets access to the community of practice and to everything that the membership entails (Ibid. p. 100). Thus, 'belonging' has a vital bearing on what you learn and whether what you learn is related to the practice of the community (Hasse 2002). However, being denied participation does not mean that you do not learn: you will learn how to acquire and maintain the position as marginalized.

## Learning as socialization?

As it may be realized, Lave & Wenger conceptualizes learning as the property of the community of practice. This is an alternative to the traditional understanding of learning as cognitive activity in the human individual (e.g. Piaget and Vygotsky). In those cases, learning must be understood as the person's property. Lave & Wenger's comprehension of cognition as something, which is distributed in the community of practice, means that learning is inscribed in the social practices of the context (Hasse 2002).

This means that learning is understood as a rather open concept compared to what we traditionally consider as learning. Traditionally, learning is understood as a change in the individual, which is partly individual (cognitive, emotional), partly social (see e.g. Illeris 2015). Lave & Wenger's 'situated learning' is less defined as a specific activity that differs from all other activities. Learning seems to be considered as a byproduct of human activity-in-context.

Hence, Lave & Wenger's concept of learning can be criticized for being too extensive and all-encompassing: that their theory makes it impossible to differ between practice and learning (Hansen 1998). This critique is also aimed at critical psychology: that everything is hence comprehended as learning, which makes it impossible to comprehend 'learning' as a specific activity (Ibid.). Learning dissolves or becomes equal to socialization. This is of cause quite problematic and as far as I see it, one of the weakest points of the theory.

Furthermore, it is important to notice that Lave & Wenger perceive learning not as transference of a curriculum, but as appropriation of the standards for how things should be done: 'A learning curriculum unfolds in opportunities for engagement in practice. It is not specified as a set of dictates for proper practice.' (Lave & Wenger 1991: 93). Hence, 'situated learning' can by no means be handled as a didactic theory that sets out requirements for 'good teaching'. In this case the boundary between a theory of learning and a theory of teaching must be maintained.

Thus, the concept of 'situated learning' is analytical rather than prescriptive (Lave 2011). This has a significant consequence for the application of the theory as an analytical tool, which I will demonstrate later in the chapter.

## Learning and apprenticeship

Although, Lave & Wenger presents 'situated learning' as a general perspective on learning, the examples in the book are all derived from traditional and practical settings such as a seamstress' workshop, midwifes practices or a butcher's shop (Lave & Wenger 1991). Due to the fact that the opportunities for learning in those examples are defined by the community of practice, there will be a significant rigidity in what can be learned: 'In this view, learning only partly – and often incidentally – implies becoming able to be involved in new activities, to perform new tasks and functions, to mater new understandings.' (Ibid. p. 53).

The quotation show that the authors consider learning as both intentional – which means occurring through activities aimed explicitly at learning – and as non-intentional, i.e. randomly occurring in communities of practice. As Kvale & Nielsen points out, this is also the case in apprenticeship (Kvale & Nielsen (ed.) 1999). The processes of learning in apprenticeship are defined by the norms of the context and must – at least to some extend – involve imitation, which is both intentional and non-intentional.

Kvale & Nielsen's conceptualization of 'situated learning' as apprenticeship may be considered as an attempt to ground the rather open and unclear learning concept. But there are some fundamental differences between 'situated learning' and 'apprenticeship' that Kvale

& Nielsen neglect when they appoint Lave & Wenger's approach as 'decentered apprenticeship' and thereby positions the approach as a theory of apprenticeship (Ibid.). Apprenticeship has as its core premise that 'mastering' is located in a person, a 'master', who is a particularly competent practitioner, and who therefor must be imitated by the lesser-experienced practitioners. This is not the case in Lave & Wenger's approach. When learning is considered as a product of the community of practice, something that exists in the space between the individuals, the 'master' cannot continuously be 'master', but will be 'master' concerning some activities and 'newcomer' or 'apprentice' concerning others.

In apprenticeship learning is considered as imitation of the competent practitioner's behavior. Hereby the learner will become a competent practitioner. But while apprenticeship is focused on the master *as a person*, Lave & Wenger's approach is focused on the community of practice. Thus, in the process of learning, the learner undergoes from legitimate peripheral to full participation in interaction with the community of practice. While traditional theories of apprenticeship have the master as the center, there is no center in Lave & Wenger's community of practice. Or rather: given that cognition is considered as distributed and the community of practice as dynamic, the center of learning will continuously be flowing and retained only momentarily by the norms of the community of practice.

The consistent rejection of an individual focus on learning in Lave & Wenger's approach thus means that 'situated learning' is not a theory of apprenticeship - not even in the form of 'decentered apprenticeship', as Kvale & Nielsen suggests. Although the concept is interesting, there is a danger that even this approach concentrates skills in a 'master', who will distribute mastery in the context.

## The inherence from dialectical materialism

The conceptualization of cognition - and thus of learning - as distributed in the community of practice, raises another question in relation to Lave & Wenger's approach: which role does the individual play for what is learned? And what are the mechanisms of learning? Does 'learning' lead to individual progression or is it so closely linked to the community of practice, that transfer is considered impossible? In other words: how does Lave & Wenger understand the relation between the human subject (person, individual) and the context?

According to Kirsten Grønbæk Hansen (1998), Lave & Wenger's emphasis on the community of practice has as its consequence that the authors in fact operate with a 'blank' or 'empty' human subject who carries nothing either into or out of the community of practice. The subject, in other words, only exists in and through the community of practice. Therefor, Grønbæk Hansen accuse Lave & Wenger to operate with a concept of the human subject that is identical with the subject in social constructionism. 'Though Jean Lave's theory is based on activity theory and critical psychology, the approach distance itself from these inspirations; a distance that allows her to approach the social constructionist project, or more broadly, the poststructuralist' (Grønbæk Hansen 1998: 6: my translation).

Grønbæk Hansen find that Lave & Wenger actually dissociate their approach to the human subject from the one you find in the theory of Vygotsky, that is in fact their source of inspiration (Ibid.). Whether you consider this accusation as valid is, however, a question of weighting respectively cognitivism and contextualism in Vygotsky's theory. According to Vygotsky learning and personal (cognitive) development will occur through the individual's encounter with the outside world, particularly through the encounter with a more competent other' (Vygotsky 2004). Although this is actually cognitivism, the contextualism in Vygotsky's approach implies that the-subject-in-the-world is the smallest unit of analysis. The dialectical approach in the learning theory of Vygotsky is defining this concept of the human being.

Thus, in this approach one cannot understand the human subject without understanding it embedded in an external world. The American interpretation of Vygotsky's approach, which among others is continued by Michael Cole and Ray McDermott, is highlighting contextualism above cognitivism. It seems obvious that it is this approach to activity theory, which has inspired Lave & Wenger (Lave & Wenger 1991). This is marked by the theory's emphasis on the situated-ness of the community of practice. According to this conceptualization, learning is closely linked to the context in which the learning has occurred.

## Dialectical materialism or social constructionism?

According to Grønbæk Hansen, the contextualism of Vygotsky's theory must be reflected in the light of dialectical materialism (Ibid.). This means, that the relationship between the individual and the society is basically considered as contradictory. The conflict between the individual and the society in dialectical materialism can be found in the tradition's distinction between the social (objective) significance on the one hand and the personal (subjective) experience on the other (Ibid.). This distinction is not present in Lave & Wenger's approach, where the human subject is considered as formed in and through the community of practice.

Consequently, the social criticism of dialectical materialism dissolves in Lave & Wenger's approach, and the process of learning (and thus becoming an individual) seems to be conceptualized as a seamless and unproblematic process. In *Situated Learning* there is almost no focus on the individual's struggle, controversies or relations of power in the context of learning (except for the butchers' example; Lave & Wenger 1991). This is of cause a weak point in Lave & Wenger's approach, and a problem, which Jean Lave retrospectively has addressed (Lave 2011). Never the less, the missing point in the theory will evidently lead to analyses that has difficulties in capturing the struggles of learning and the implications of the relations of power in the context (Christensen 2013).

Apart from this, Lave & Wenger's concept of the human subject differs in other important aspects from Vygotsky's concept of the human subject, which among others is reflected in his theory of development. Although Vygotsky considered development as a relationship between the individual and the context (mediated by 'a more competent other'), his concept of 'the zone of proximal development' (Vygotsky 2004) indicate that the individual must be in possession of a form of personal 'core' or 'essence', even though this is only in the form of individual cognition.

In contrast, Lave & Wenger subscribe for a fundamentally anti-essentialist concept of the human subject. This can be found in the way they rejects cognitivism and shifts the focus on learning from being a matter of acquiring a specific content or subject matter to becoming a person: 'Learning thus implies becoming a different person with respect to the possibilities enabled by these systems of relations. To ignore this aspect of learning is to overlook the fact that learning involves the construction of identities.' (Lave & Wenger 1991, p. 53). Thus, the world, the human subject and practice are considered as at one time existing and socially constructed:

> Briefly, a theory of social practice emphasizes the relational interdependency of agent and world, activity, meaning, cognition, learning, and knowing. It emphasizes the inherently socially negotiated character of meaning and the interested, concerned character of the thought and action of persons-in-activity. This view also claims that learning, thinking and knowing are relations among people in activity in, with, and arising from the socially and culturally structured world. This world is socially constructed; objective forms and systems of activity, on the one hand, and agents' subjective and inter subjective understanding of them on the other, mutually constitute both the world and its experienced forms. Knowledge of the social constructed world is socially mediated and open ended. (Ibid. p. 50-51)

Although Lave & Wenger uses the term 'identity', which is alien to social constructionism, their approach must be considered as such a strong contextualistic variant of activity theory that it approaches social constructionism. Whether Lave & Wenger's perspective is actually social constructionism, can only be identified by examining the ontological assumptions on which the respective approaches are based.

## A question of ontological foundation

As mentioned, there are considerable similarities between social constructionism and Lave & Wenger's approach to the human subject. However, Lave & Wenger denotes their theory as a *practice theory*. Practice theories are characterized by the basic assumption that the individual must be comprehended in the context and in the activity-in-the-world (practice) in which it participates. Analytically, it may not be possible to separate the individual, the activity and the context and thus not to analyze these phenomena separately. The group of practice theories also contains the historical-dialectical materialism of Vygotsky and Leontjev, Bourdieu's 'praxeology' and critical psychology. Lave & Wenger's affiliation to critical psychology is emphasized by the fact that Jean Lave has had a significant collaboration with the Danish critical psychologist Ole Dreier (Lave & Wenger 1991).

Analogous to Lave & Wenger's approach, all practice theories are characterized by their foundation in dialectical materialism, which is the philosophical basis of Marxism. Dialectical materialism is grounded in a materialistic, i.e. a realistic, ontology. A realistic ontology implies the basic assumption that the world exists and that it is possible for human beings, through their cognition (perception and experience), to comprehend the phenomena in the world. The human subject is considered as situated in the (material) world, and is, as such at one time separate from its surroundings and interacting with these surroundings.

The distinction between the individual and the outside world leads dialectical materialism to the aforementioned distinction between the objective (societal) structures and the subjective (individual) experiences. This distinction constitutes the foundation of the dialectic. The individual and the society are considered as connected in a dialectical relationship. This means that the individual on the one hand is considered as subject to the conditions of the society, and on the other hand is regarded as an active co-creator of the very same conditions (the process thesis-antithesis-synthesis). Although the society forms the basic conditions for the individual, the individual is, thus, not determined by the societal structures. Though the societal structures may be considered as a 'frame' for the individual, the individual is considered as an autonomous and rational agent whose subjectivity is the outset for thinking and action.

In contrast, the basic assumptions in social constructionism and post-structuralism are grounded on an anti-realistic ontology. This implies that the world is considered as produced in and through our social interaction and communication (Gergen 1991; 1994; 2001). According to this approach there are no objective (material) societal structures, which sets the frame and thus the limits for the individual. The human subject is considered as formed through discourse, i.e. the individual's historical, cultural, social and societal framework. The individual is thus not considered as in possession of a specific individuality (personality, psyche or essence), which is determining the person's schemata for actions. Alternatively, human subjects are regarded as constructed through discourse, i.e. through their relations to others and to the opportunities in the context.

The difference between a realistic and an anti-realistic ontology can best be illustrated by an example of how an analysis will be radically different depending on which paradigm, the researcher choses. A realistic based analysis will build on the assumption that certain categories such as gender, class and ethnicity exists and sets specific conditions for individuals by virtue of the societal structures (e.g. politics, institutions and economy). Assuming that these categories objectively exist, it will give rise to studies of e.g. the correlations between gender and education, and ethnicity and class as genuine groupings. A realistic ontology is thus a prerequisite for the meaningfulness in analyses of social heritage (or habitus like Bourdieu). Such an investigation is based on the assumption that the societal structures set the framework for individual life and possibilities.

In contrast, an anti-realistic grounded researcher will consider 'gender', 'class' and 'ethnicity' as social constructions. Hence, the researcher will examine how these categories are articulated and how the articulations create and exclude certain possibilities for specific groups e.g. 'men' and 'women'. What does it for instance mean that certain characteristics, capabilities and competencies on the one hand are attached to being 'a man'? And what does it on the other hand mean that this is contrasted with being 'a woman'? And how does these mechanisms function in a specific context?

Additionally, there will be a difference in what the researcher will consider as a relevant research subject. A realistic based research will deal with 'reality' in the form of materiality, as the concept of *the community of practice* in Lave & Wenger's approach. The community of practice is, thus, considered as an existing occurrence in the world. In contrast, an anti-realistic grounded researcher will take as his outset that 'reality' is created or constructed. Therefore it makes more sense to investigate the medium through which this takes place: language. There is substantially more rigidity in practice than there is in language. And there is significantly more developmental potential in language, considered as the medium through which human subjects are constructed, than there is in practice. In Lave & Wenger's conceptualization, the human subject (individual, identity) is generated in and through the community of practice. This means that the subject is considered as formed in and through the structures of the practice and is, thus, not just a social (linguistic) construction.

## Bridging the gap between anti-realism and realism

In order to assess whether Lave & Wenger's approach places itself in a realistic or an anti-realistic ontology one also has to analyze what their concept of 'practice' embraces. In this case, it appears that Lave & Wenger refer to a *situated* practice, which means a practice-the-world. Although Lave & Wenger's concept of practice is sufficiently spacious to include linguistic practice, the authors maintain a fundamental division between not only language and practice, but also between different forms of linguistic practice (Lave & Wenger 1991, p. 108; Lave 2011, p. 49). An anti-realistic based approach would not establish this kind of distinction, but would (in theory) analyze both practice and language through the analysis of the discourse. Lave & Wenger's conceptualization of the community of practice is in other words founded on a realistic ontology.

However, Lave & Wenger's approach can be considered as a perspective that, so to say, 'bridges' between realism and anti-realism. This is also the case with the philosopher Karen Barad, whose theory of *agential realism* (Barad 2007) specifically is intended to convey this distinction, but in a clearer theoretical form than Lave & Wenger.

In the concept of *agential realism,* Barad points out, that one has to understand the world as existing in an ontological (material) sense and that the prerequisite for existence is activity-in-the-world. However, materiality and discourse are considered as separate but co-existing domains, which are created through the same single event. Materiality clearly cannot be comprehended separate from or prior to linguistic practice, as well as linguistic practice cannot be comprehended separate from materiality. Practice (also linguistic practice) is always practice-in-a-material-world:

> Discourse does not refer to linguistic or signifying systems, grammars, speech acts, or conversations. To think of discourse as mere spoken or written words forming descriptive statements is to enact the mistake of representationalist thinking. Discourse is not what is said; it is that which constraints and enables what can be said. Discursive practices define what counts as meaningful statements. Statements are not the mere utterances of the originating consciousness of a unified subject; rather, statements and subjects emerge from a field of possibilities. This field of possibilities is not static or singular but rather it is a dynamic and contingent multiplicity. (Ibid. p. 146-147)

As it appears, Barad consider the human subject and materiality as at the same time created through discursive and material practices. As Lave & Wenger, Barad stresses that language, practice and materiality stands in an internal rather than an external relation to each other: 'Rather, the point is that these *entangled practices* are productive, and who and what are excluded through these entangled practices matter: different intra-actions produce different phenomena.' (Ibid: 58).

As such, Barad's perspective can be considered as supporting Lave & Wenger's emphasis on the importance of grasping the individual-in-the-context as an active agent in both a discursive and a material sense. Through this practice, the individual becomes a subject. This demands a simultaneous connectedness and separateness between the subject and the context, which stresses that it makes no sense to discuss what comes first: whether the individual initiates discourse, or is determined by discourse.

In other words, Barad seems to deliver a substantial analytical perspective, which can support conceptions of how individuals are adapted to and included in a learning community in which they are assigned different positions with different implications for their learning (Hasse 2002). As such, both Lave & Wenger and Barad can be considered as offering interesting perspectives to the endeavor to conceptualize and define learning.

## Concluding remarks: the analytical possibilities of Lave & Wenger's perspective

Until this, the chapter has been focusing on a science-philosophical analysis of Lave & Wenger's concept of 'situated learning'. This discussion has been quite theoretical and with less focus on the practical application of the theory. Thus, the aim of the concluding remarks is to sketch the possibilities and limitations of 'situated learning' as an analytical tool.

As mentioned, 'situated learning' is an analytical perspective and not a prescription for practice. This means that the perspective by no means can be considered and applied as a didactical theory i.e. as recommendations for teaching. Thus, it is by no means the intentions of the perspective to animate the teacher to organize 'communities of practice' in class (Lave 2011). Alternatively, Lave & Wenger's approach is an analytical perspective. This means that the theory can be applied for analyses of learning in different contexts. Though Lave & Wenger are focusing on learning in apprenticeship-like settings, the perspective is not limited to analyses of such settings. In principle, it can be used for analyses of any setting – at school and outside school. Hence, the subject of research does not limit the applicability of the perspective.

Foremost, Lave & Wenger's theory changes the perspective of the researcher. This means that the researcher will have to focus otherwise than if the theoretical perspective was more like a traditional theory of learning and teaching (e.g. a didactical theory). Of cause, the consequence of this change in perspective also has significant effects for what the researcher will be able to capture through her research.

Applying 'situated learning' means that the researcher will have to focus on what is *actually* going on in the context in order to identify the activities and interests of 'the community of practice'. An example could be research of what is going on in a class at school i.e. a traditional teaching- and learning setting. In this case, Lave & Wenger's approach would urge the researcher to focus on the central activities in class instead of the intentions of the teacher. Thus, the activities in class may very well be quite different from the intentions of the teacher, and the learning outcome may very well be another than what the teacher anticipated and planned.

In this case, 'situated learning' can serve as a device to change the researcher's perspective. Hence, 'situated learning' would urge the researcher to identify the center of activity in the group (the (imagined) 'product' of the community of practice), the different positions that the members of the group were allowed to enter and to possess (as marginalized, as legitimate peripheral (learning) or as full participant) and how language and practice were intertwined in these activities (Christensen 2013).

As such, Lave & Wenger's perspective is not limited to certain research subjects but can be considered as an analytical tool that provides the researcher with a different and fruitful perspective. Although the science-philosophical ambiguities in the theory, the perspective can serve as a means for very interesting analyses of learning-in-practice.

# References

Barad, Karen (2007). *Meeting the Universe Halfway. Quantum Physics and the Entanglement of Matter and Meaning*. Duke University Press.
Bourdieu, Pierre & Fierre Passeron (1990) [1977]. *Reproduction in education, society and culture*. London: Sage.
Benner, Patricia (1995). *Fra novice til ekspert. Mesterlighed og styrke i klinisk sygeplejepraksis*. [*From novice to expert. Mastery and strength in the clinical practice of nursing*]. København: Munksgaard.
Christensen, Gerd (2013). *Projekt Grupper – en undersøgelse af subjektiveringsmekanismer i gruppe- og projektarbejde på universitetsniveau*. Ph.d.-afhandling. Institut for Uddannelse og Pædagogik, Aarhus Universitet.
Dreyfus, Hubert & Stuart Dreyfus (1986). *Mind over Machine. The Power of Human Intuition and Expertise in the Erea of the Computer*. New York: The Free Press.
Gergen, Kenneth J. (1991) *The Saturated Self*. Basic Books.
Gergen, Kenneth J. (1994) *Realities and Relationships*. Harvard University Press.
Gergen, Kenneth J. (2001) [1999]. *An Invitation to Social Construction*. London: Sage.
Hansen, Kirsten Grønbæk (1998). 'Er læring mere end situeret praksis?' ['Is learning more than situated practice?'] In: *Dansk Pædagogisk Tidsskrift*. 2/1998.
Hasse, Cathrine (2002). *Kultur i bevægelse. Fra deltagerobservation til kulturanalyse – i det fysiske rum*. [*Culture in motion. From participant observation to cultural analysis - in physical space*]. Frederiksberg: Samfundslitteratur.
Heggen, Kristin (1997). 'Taus kunnskap'. [*Tacit Knowledge*] In: *Nordisk Pedagogik*, Vol. 17, nr. 1, 1997.
Illeris, Knud (2015). *Læring*. Forlaget Samfundslitteratur.
Kvale, Steinar (1993). 'En pædagogisk rehabilitering af mesterlæren?' ['An educational rehabilitation of apprenticeship?'] In: *Dansk Pædagogisk Tidsskrift*. 1/1993.
Kvale, Steinar & Klaus Nielsen (red.) (1999). *Mesterlære. Læring som social praksis*. [*Apprenticeship. Learning as social practice*]. København: Hans Reitzel.
Laursen, Per Fibæk (1993). 'En ny ydmyghed overfor praksis?' ['A new humility to practice'] In: *Dansk Pædagogisk Tidsskrift*. 1/1993.
Lave, Jean & Etienne Wenger (1991). *Situated Learning*. Cambridge University Press.
Lave, Jean (i samarbejde med Eva Bertelsen) (2011). 'Situated Learning og skiftende praksis.' ['Situated learning and changing practice'] In: Christensen, Gerd & Eva Bertelsen (red.) (2011). *Pædagogiske perspektiver på arbejdsliv*. København: Frydenlund.
McDermott, Ray (1993). 'The Acquisition of a Child by a Learning Disability'. In: Seth Chaiklin & Jean Lave (eds.). *Understanding Practice. Perspectives on Activity and Context*. Cambridge University Press.
Molander, Bengt (1996). *Kunskap i handling*. [*Knowledge in action*] Stockholm: Daidalos.
Nielsen, Mogens. (1995). *Den tyste kundskab i idehistorien*. Konferencebidrag ved 'Nordforum, Forum for Sløjd & Håndarbejde'. [*The silent knowledge of the history of ideas*. Conference contributions to 'Northern Forum, Forum for Woodwork & Crafts]. København: Undervisningsministeriet.

Polanyi, Michael (1966). *The Tacit Dimension.* London: Routledge & Kegan Paul.

Rognhaug, Berit (1993) 'Taus Kunnskap og specialpedagogisk virksomhet.' ['Tacit knowledge and special educational activity'] In: *Nordisk Tidsskrift for Specialpedagogikk.* 1/1993

Schön, Donald A. (1983). *The Reflective Practitioner: How Professionals Think in Action.* New York: Basic Books.

Vygotsky, Lev (2004). 'Problemstillinger i undervisningen og den intellektuelle udvikling i skolealderen.' In: Lindquist, Gunilla (red.). *Vygotsky om læring som udviklingsvilkår.* ['Issues in education and the intellectual development of school age.' In: Lindquist, Gunilla (ed.). *Vygotsky on learning as development conditions*]. Århus: Klim.

Wackerhausen, Birgitte & Steen Wackerhausen (1993). 'Tavs viden og pædagogik.' [Tacit knowledge and education'] In: *Dansk Pædagogisk Tidsskrift.* 4/1993

# On defining learning from a social-ontological perspective

*Klaus Nielsen*

The aim of this chapter is, based on Honneth's notion of recognition and Lave and Wenger's ideas about situated learning, to formulate a perspective on processes of learning that includes social interaction as a dynamic and genetic dimension in theories of learning. In this respect, Honneth's notion of struggle for recognition will be central. This ambition will, throughout the chapter, be termed as an aim to define a social-ontological perspective on processes of learning. In relation to the issues raised in this anthology, this chapter will be focusing on *Theory building within the field of learning*.

One of the reasons for trying to develop a social-ontological perspective on learning is to formulate a critical alternative to what can be termed "homo economicus" being the evident and unquestionable gestalt for organizing educational activities today. It goes without saying that the image of homo economicus plays a significant role as the dominant perspective on human change within the educational system today, with a strong focus on the "input/outcome" and evaluations (examinations, tests, and grades) to paraphrase the dominating discourse of the PISA examinations. Homo economicus allows for a view of the person as rational, individualistic, utilitarian, calculative, and instrumental (Houston 2010; Ferguson 2007). Within this context, action is directed toward the achievement of predetermined ends to enhance personal well-being, whether defined in monetary or social terms. As will be outlined below, this means that human actions are understood within a frame of means–end thinking, hence defining issues of learning within a technological frame of reference. Crucially, homo economicus drives forward the neoliberal theme of "individualization" with its stress on the agent's choice and freedom. As I will discuss further, the main problem as I see it with the image of homo economicus is that this perspective naturalizes the idea that social struggle as competition between individuals is the structuring force in the development of society.

This being said, the main aim of this chapter is not directly to formulate a critique of the dominance of homo economicus in relation to how the educational system is being organized today.[1] The aim is more to develop a social-ontological frame that will make it possible to formulate an alternative to the image of homo economicus in educational thinking and with a special focus on processes of learning. In this pursuit, I will outline Honneth's notion of recognition as a central part of a social-ontological approach to human existence (Honneth 2008). Honneth's analyses of recognition point to the primacy of intersubjectivity in human life, and he grounds an ontology of the human subject in the light of the human subject's radical social, or intersubjective, dependency. The fundamental idea is that the intersubjective element is the condition of possibility, both genetically and conceptually, for all forms of interaction, not just between social agents, but even for social actions by social agents taken individually. In his work, Honneth stresses recognition as a dynamic and genetic dimension in social life and hence a central dimension in a social-ontological approach to issues of learning.

The concept of ontology will be defined as "the consideration of being: what is, what exists, what it means for something—or somebody—to be" (Packer & Goicoechea 2000, p. 227). As will be outlined below, this understanding of ontology is inspired by Heidegger (1988) who argues for the notion of meaning and understanding as being crucial for comprehending the essence of human existence.

A short outline of the chapter is as follows: I will briefly outline how mainstream theories of learning in general contain very little potential for developing a critical stance toward current developments. On the contrary, mainstream learning theories seem to fit nicely into the regime of homo economicus. Thereafter, the chapter will outline how the discussion of ontology and the critique of homo economicus within learning theory are not new. Within the frames of humanistic psychology, Colaizzi and Rogers took up this discussion in the 1960s and 1970s. However, they formulated an alternative to the notion of homo economicus with a strong focus on the individual and the potential the individual has to develop an authentic self through unconditional reinforcement (Rogers & Freiberg 1994). Following this critique and inspired by the analyses of Honneth and Lave and Wenger, I will try to develop an understanding of what a social-ontological perspective on learning could look like. I will conclude by returning to the notion of homo economicus, to see what kinds of critical questions it will possible to pose through a social-ontological perspective on learning.

## Learning Theory, Homo Economicus, and Technology

Before turning to the social-ontological dimension, it is important to expand the themes of this chapter to theories of learning. As it will be outlined below, in this context, mainstream learning theory will be defined as cognitive learning theory (information processing psychology) and behavioristic learning theory (for an elaboration, see Nielsen 2008). In this paragraph, it will be argued that mainstream conventional learning theories do not reflect ontological questions explicitly. Rather, they are embedded in means-end thinking and have a strong focus on technology (Nielsen 2008; Kvale 1977). Even though these conventional theories of learning are not constituted directly by the dynamics of homo economicus, it is easy to see how they fit into the present economic regime in educational thinking. I will briefly outline the main ideas of conventional learning theories.

Two different schools of thought are central in conventional learning theories: the empiristic and the rationalistic (Packer 1985). Most mainstream definitions of learning have their roots in these two positions (Omrod 2012). The empiristic position is the principal epistemological school of thought that claims that all knowledge of reality is based on sensory experiences. Rationalism applies the epistemological approach by arguing that individuals obtain knowledge of reality solely through the use of reason (see also Packer 1985, and Merleau-Ponty 1981). The empiristic position in psychology discloses itself in behavioral psychology, while the rationalistic position is primarily formulated as an information processing theory of human cognition.[2] The information processing theory can be considered a frame concept that covers many different research programs, rather than a comprehensive theory. Characteristically, these theories focus on describing how the individual gathers, processes, and produces information about the surrounding world (Miller 1983). Learning from an empiristic point of view is defined as "a relative permanent change in [behavior] due to experience," while learning from a cognitive point of view is defined as "a relatively permanent change in mental associations" (Packer 1985,

p. 3). The first definition focuses on people's change in observable behavior, while the other focuses on changes in mental associations.

As mentioned above, the image of homo economicus is that the person is rational, individualistic, utilitarian, calculative, and instrumental. It will be claimed that these features are easily identified in mainstream learning theory. This is not coincidental. According to Kvale (1976, 1977), conventional learning theories have had huge impacts on how we conceptualize human change. The instrumental approach to learning has manifested itself as a basic assumption in mainstream learning theories claiming that the only way to understand human change is to think in instrumental terms. This means–end instrumentality is, as Kvale formulates it, a technological approach, and it comprises a significant part of modern learning theories:

> the theories of learning have had the ideological function of making a technological approach to learning self-evident and dominating.... However, the latent ideological function of this research has not been trivial – namely of letting a technological approach to fellow human subjects appear as the only possible and valid scientific psychology. (Kvale 1977, p. 106–107)

In this seminal work, Kvale claims that the only thing mainstream theories of learning add to educational practice is a specific technological approach to our understanding of how human subjects change. If we take a close look at the educational debate today, I believe it is easy to recognize the technological approach Kvale is identifying. Furthermore, if we turn to mainstream learning theories looking for a social dimension, we will often look in vain. The social dimension (the importance of the other) is highly neglected or kept to a minimum. It is the individual who is the unquestioned analytical unit (Lave & Wenger 1991). For example, if you take four standard textbooks about learning theory (see Anderson 1999; Deese & Hulse 1975; Driscoll 2005; Omrod 2012), you will find that the social dimension is scarcely mentioned.[3] Following this line of critique, it can be argued that conventional modern learning theories lack a reflection on the ontological questions of human existence. The relationship between human ontology and learning will be discussed further in the next paragraph.

## Returning to the Critical Ontological Discussion About Learning

The concept of ontology is closely related to the German philosopher Heidegger, who in Being and Time develops a profound analysis of what it means to be a human being (Heidegger 1988). In his analysis of the characteristics of human's existence, or being-in-the-world, as Heidegger terms it, he outlines the ontological dimension in his analysis of human existence. Put a bit simplistically, focusing on the ontological question allows for an analysis of the distinctive and necessary characteristics of human existence. According to Heidegger, "understanding of Being is itself a definite characteristic of Dasein's Being. Dasein is ontically distinctive in that it is ontological" (Heidegger 1988, p. 32).[4] The ontological understanding of the human being has to do with the fact that we, as human beings, are always in the process of understanding ourselves. The problem that Heidegger raises is related to Western philosophy and thinking in general. According to Heidegger, Western thinkers tend to forget that we as human beings are being-in-the-world first and foremost, before we start asking questions about how we know the world. Heidegger is launching a critique of the epistemological tradition in Western thinking (founded by Descartes) as only being concerned with epistemological questions, questions about knowledge of the world. Heidegger's claim is that Western thinking should concern itself with ontological questions instead (Dreyfus 1997, p. 3). Based on his analysis of human's being-in-the-world and its ontological dimensions, Heidegger develops a critical stance, especially in relation to the cognitive sciences, toward reifying and alienating human existence (for an elaboration, see Dreyfus 1995).

If we return to learning theory, Heidegger in particular, but also Kierkegaard, Sartre, and Merleau-Ponty's analyses of the ontological dimension of human existence, made a great impact on the formulation of humanistic psychology in the 1960s. In the tradition of the growing field of humanistic psychology, Rogers, May, and Colaizzi criticized mainstream learning theory for leading to superficial learning, dehumanization, and alienation. Following Heidegger's general critique of Western thinking, they argued that behaviorism and cognitive trends in modern learning theory neglected human existence and questions of ontology. Fundamentally, the critique raised by humanistic psychology concerning learning theory has two dimensions. Firstly, Rogers and

Colaizzi particularly criticize cognitive psychology (information processing psychology) for not providing a proper learning theory when it comes to identifying what constitutes change in human existence. Colaizzi is especially precise in his critique, arguing that cognitive psychology does not provide us with a genuine understanding of human learning. Rather, he argues, cognitive psychology provides us with an understanding of how human beings remember delimited symbolic material for a short time in order to reproduce it at a specific time and at a specific place, within a specific institutional order. In this sense, cognitive psychology does not provide us with a genuine learning theory that makes it possible to understand how we as human beings learn in relation to our existence:

> For all of us there are certain life lessons which we read or hear spoken hundreds of times before they finally click in. Until they do click in, we haven't really learned them, regardless of how glibly we can verbalize them. Prior to the point where they become significantly interwoven in our existence, they are merely bits of information that we have acquired (1978, p. 127).

Secondly, according to Colaizzi, there is a hidden agenda in making cognitive psychology the dominant learning theory in education-institutional life. This hidden agenda is that cognitive psychology helps socialize students into social conformism, teaching them to forget about their own existence. As Colaizzi claims,

> In fact, most of the time I do not act, feel, perceive, think, or experience as essentially my own person, my authentic selfness, is typically lost to me insofar as I lose myself in self-alienated anonymity and inasmuch as I become dissolved in what phenomenologists call 'the they' (Colaizzi 1978, p. 131; see also Kvale 1977).

The "they" is a clear reference to Heidegger's "Das Man" which, according to Colaizzi, pinpoints the essence of social conformism, teaching students to focus on how one (das Man) is acting in a given situation rather focusing on how they as existing beings feel in the concrete situation and acting according to their own existential needs.

Based on these considerations, both Colaizzi and Rogers develop conceptual differentiations in which they try to identify, on one hand, processes of learning that have a significant impact on how persons genuinely change in a personal and existential sense and, on the other hand, processes of learning that are merely a matter of learning in a cognitive sense. Colaizzi and Rogers denote learning processes with an impact on students' existence as genuine learning and experiential learning (Colaizzi 1978; Rogers & Freiberg 1994). The more cognitive learning processes described by mainstream learning theory, on the other hand, they term information acquisition (Colaizzi 1978) and cognitive learning processes.

There are, however, a number of problems in the way that both Colaizzi and Rogers approach the ontological perspective when it comes to issues of learning. It goes without saying that humanistic psychology has made a significant contribution to learning theories, as it highlights the importance of the personal existential dimension as a key component in learning. Questions about meaning, in this view, are crucial to processes of learning. However, one of the problems, one could interject, is whether humanistic psychology poses an alternative to the individualization introduced with the image of homo economicus mentioned above. Both Rogers and Colaizzi uncritically see a decontextualized individual as the locus of analysis when they wish to disclose how meaningful learning unfolds. Only when the individual is part of a nonjudgmental environment does genuine and meaningful learning become possible. Social arrangements of any other kind seem only to repress the person's genuine learning process and, in that sense, the gaze of the other is seen as objectifying.[5] In later years, the strong focus that humanistic psychology has on individual self-realization has been critiqued for, in reality, developing a kind of egocentrism (Brinkmann 2005) or developing a concealed way of manipulating subjects in institutional contexts (Nielsen 2005).[6] If we want to take the notion of ontology in relation to learning seriously, we need to approach the social dimension in another way than that suggested by the human psychologists.

## Introduction to a Social-Ontological Perspective

In the following section, I will outline Honneth's notion of a social-ontological perspective. The aim of this paragraph is to outline the dynamic and genetic dimension that Honneth suggests is a crucial part of social life and hence a central dimension in a social-ontological approach to learning. As will be elaborated below, the central concept in this context is Honneth's understanding of recognition. The overall idea is to consider how processes of recognition are related to human change and processes of learning.[7] This will be done in the next paragraph.

The question about social ontology as formulated by Honneth is inspired by a Hegelian and Marxist tradition in which the subject's existence is not given by the subject itself, as assumed by humanistic psychologists. For Hegel, the individual self is in no sense an immediately given element of consciousness; rather, the individual becomes a subject through being in relationships with others (Hegel 1998). It is solely through our activities in a social frame that we learn to think of ourselves as individuals in the first place (Solomon 1983; Packer & Goicoechea 2000). It is in this context that the idea of recognition becomes important. The idea of recognition as central in human relations is part of a long philosophical tradition. In the works of Hobbes, Rousseau, Kant, and Fichte, there is an acknowledgment of the need for respect and honor in life. Hegel, however, was the first theorist to give recognition in social life its proper place. For him, the act of recognizing and being recognized led to self-awareness. By understanding the other, one's own self-understanding was enlarged. This process reflected an anthropological association between self-consciousness and intersubjectivity, the isolated individual and reciprocity within community, an individual's perspective and a "fusion of 'horizons" with the other (Gadamer 1975; Houston 2010).

In "The Struggle for Recognition" (1996), Honneth took these ideas as his starting point in order to construct a critical theory of recognition. According to Honneth, the notion of recognition points to the primacy of intersubjectivity in human life, and he grounds an ontology of the human subject in the light of the human subject's radical social, or intersubjective, dependency.[8] The strong focus on the intersubjective element is fundamental to Honneth and also the condition of possibility for all forms of interactions not just between persons, but even for social actions by persons taken individually (Deranty 2009). In this context, recognition can be defined as the process of affirmation as someone by someone, in the form of being loved or cared about, being granted equal rights and being treated as an equal, or being approved of and appreciated for who one is or what one does (Carleheden, Heidegren, & Willig 2012). In this sense, recognition, for Honneth (2008; Honneth & Margalit 2001), suggests a precognitive affirmation of the social-affective bond between members of social life. In other words, before "cognizing" the identities, traits, and preferences of a person, we have to "recognize" their status as autonomous and agentic (Houston 2010). The intersubjectivistic model developed by Honneth contrasts and critiques what Honneth terms an atomistic and solipsistic perspective on the subject formulated by a Western tradition of thinking (e.g., Machiavelli and Hobbes) to which "the being of the individual is the first and the highest" (Honneth 1996, p. 12). This tradition seems to forget or neglect the communal ground underpinning individuation. Individuation is never simply a pure separation. To some extent, Honneth is formulating a critique of an early version of what we have described as homo economicus above.

It is important not to identify recognition in Honneth's description with psychological processes alone. There is both a functional and a normative dimension in Honneth's understanding of recognition as pivotal for social life (Deranty 2009).

The idea of recognition has, first of all, a functional perspective: it explains the central problem that social theory is concerned with, the problem of the coordination of individual actions (Deranty 2009). Inspired by Mead (1997), Honneth argues that the perceiver must be able to change his or her perspective in relation to the same object so that one perspective can be connected with another, and the different perspectives united into one object (Honneth 1996). This ability is well accounted for by the capacity to "take the role of the other." If I am able to take the perspective of the other in social actions, I can project myself into his or her "decentered" perspective on an object, and I can understand why the other is acting as he or she is and act accordingly myself (Honneth 1996). Just as different perspectives are unified in successful communication, the perspectives on the object are unified in successful perception. In other words, human perception is dependent on skills that are learned as a result of social interaction. Communication becomes synonymous with intersubjectivity pitched at a more fundamental level than language (Deranty 2009). According to Honneth, it is important not to identify the fundamental structure of intersubjectivity and communication with speech alone: "it is, ontogenetically speaking, beyond all doubt that the acquisition of the ability to identify one's objectual-instrumental body as properly one's own clearly precedes the 'practical acquisition of an understanding of the system of personal pronouns'"(Honneth & Joas 1988, p. 84). It is precisely the processes by which human agents are able to see themselves from the perspective of the other, which also explains how the reproduction of social life is possible (Deranty 2009; Honneth 1996). This is a fundamental intuition that the basic processes of social life are in fact made up of recognitive interactions. According to Honneth, all social phenomena need to be approached from a social-ontological perspective because it is that perspective, as Mead demonstrated (1997), which provides the proper explanation of social interactions as coordination of individual actions.

The functional aspect of recognition is closely related to the normative dimension, which constitutes the second dimension of recognition according to Honneth. The processes explaining the possibility of social coordination are the same processes that account for the conditions for personal autonomy (Honneth 1996; Deranty 2009). The normative conclusion that Honneth draws from Mead's theory of social integration is that, since the subject can achieve an identity through relations of reciprocal recognition, those relations in turn have not only a functional dimension but also a normative one. In other words, the recognitive interactional processes provide the subject the capacity to achieve an identity. In this perspective the notion of "self-realization" becomes important. It is important to understand self-realization as something other than the superficial understanding in which self-realization is the full flourishing of an otherwise already established self, as suggested by the humanistic psychology described above. Self-realization in this context refers to the social-ontological possibilities of subjective identity formation. In this sense, "processes of recognition" refers precisely to the conditions that enable a subject to develop a minimal sense of his or her own value; a "self-value" that is the most basic requirement for any action with an amount of autonomy.[9] According to Honneth, "the only way in which individuals are constituted as persons is by learning to refer to themselves from the perspective of an approving or encouraging other, as beings with certain positive traits and abilities" (1996, p. 173). At a very basic level, the normative demands for recognition are therefore not secondary demands stemming from preconstituted selves, but demands for the realization of conditions without which there can be absolutely no autonomy because there would be no self to exercise autonomy (Deranty 2009; Honneth 1996). Honneth is arguing that there is a fundamental moral and normative dimension in social life based on mutual recognition. As mentioned above, processes of recognition are closely related to a sense of self-value. This means that issues of value and normativity are also part of the essence of processes of recognition in general. In this respect, Honneth's perception of normativity is that it is a constructive dimension in both social and individual life. Social life is based on a kind of precognitive notion of recognition that fundamentally understands others as having the same needs and the same fragility that we have. Accordingly, we can never approach ourselves or the world in any neutral, objective way. Rather, the normative moral approach is always a part of our approach (Fraser & Honneth 2003). If I am recognized for who I am and what I am doing, it is tacitly assumed that I do the same with other participants in social practice (Houston 2010).

When Honneth is approaching issues of recognition, he goes beyond close relations of love and friendship to include legally institutionalized relations of universal respect for the autonomy and dignity of persons, their networks of solidarity, and their shared values, within which the particular worth of members of a community can be acknowledged (Honneth, 1996). In this sense, Honneth is not only concerned with analyzing issues of recognition in close, intimate relations but also as central component in social life in general. In Honneth's work, he claims that three distinct interactional spheres of mutual recognition (and consequently interaction of disrespect) can be mapped out: love, rights, and solidarity. It is beyond the scope of this chapter to account for all of these dimensions of the concept of recognition. However, it is important to add that the notion of solidarity seems to be central in this chapter when addressing issues of learning. "Solidarity" is the term Honneth uses for the cultural climate in which the acquisition of self-esteem has become broadly possible (becoming a part of social practice). In Honneth's view, one can properly speak of "solidarity" only in cases where shared concerns or values are at play.

Honneth emphasizes that when he is addressing recognition as a central concept he is also concerned with notions of struggle in relationship to recognition. It can be argued that social conflicts are central to Honneth's conceptualization of recognition. However, according to Honneth, social domination and social conflicts should not be understood in terms of conflicts of interest, but more as struggles over moral matters in relation to processes of recognition. As mentioned above, Honneth is critical of the conception of man as utilitarian (man as solipsistic); hence, social conflicts cannot be understood in terms of competition over material opportunities but more in terms of processes of recognition, social contempt, and disrespect (Honneth 1996). In this respect, Honneth is developing a set of categories that can be used to analyze processes, social conflicts, and individual pathologies in terms of processes of recognition, social contempt, and disrespect.

Above, there has been a short account of the general premises of a social-ontological approach to human existence. In the following sections, I will take a closer look at issues of learning from a social-ontological perspective.

## A Social-Ontological Approach to Learning

In what follows, I will pursue in detail more how we could understand learning from a social-ontological perspective. In this pursuit, Honneth's social-ontological outline will be supplemented by the insights developed from a situated perspective on learning (Lave 1992; Lave & Wenger 1991; Lave & Packer 2008). In Lave and Wenger's work on situated learning, and later in Lave and Packer's "Towards A Social Ontology of Learning" (2008), there is great sensitivity to the issue of understanding learning from a social-ontological perspective. This is underlined in the following quote by Lave: "Learning, viewed as a socially situated activity, must be grounded in a social ontology that conceives of the person as an acting being, engaged in activity in the world" (Lave 1992).

One of the central points is that processes of recognition are in themselves, as defined above, an essential part of the learning processes. When Honneth writes of processes of recognition that "the only way in which individuals are constituted as persons is by learning to refer to themselves from the perspective of an approving or encouraging other, as beings with certain positive traits and abilities" (p. 173), it is hard not to see these processes as a matter involving learning. However, it is important to underline, as also indicated in the central idea of situated learning (Lave & Wenger 1991), that learning is always a part of the subject's participation in social life and not something in itself.

The point is that while Honneth is talking about recognition, Lave and Wenger are adding the learning dimension more systematically. When Honneth writes about recognition in a transformative sense, he mainly addresses it from a developmental-psychological perspective; however, Lave and Wenger add that recognition understood as processes of learning must be understood as a recurrent and open-ended process happening in a variety of communities.

Before outlining the learning perspectives, I will briefly outline a couple of central similarities between Honneth and Lave and Wenger in order to legitimize using insights about learning from situated learning.

As in Honneth's understanding of recognition, the notion of coordination and understanding is central in Lave and Wenger's definition of communities of practice as a matter of "participation in a system of actions where the participants share a common understanding of what they are doing, of what it means to their lives and to the community" (p. 98). We are thus all participants in different communities of practice, which frame our lives and make them meaningful. To be a participant in a community of practice is thus the starting point in an understanding of ourselves and the world. Furthermore, and in accordance with Honneth, to become a part of communities of practices is also a matter of developing an identity and autonomy. The original idea Honneth has developed from Hegel, that social integration and the development of personal autonomy are not two antagonistic processes, but two dimensions of the same process, is also pivotal in situated learning. Lave outlines that everyday practice is where "central identity-generating activities take place," (Lave 1992).

Even though there are differences between Honneth and Lave and Wenger, I believe that Lave and Wenger are addressing the importance of recognition in an analytical and indirect manner, and in that sense they are on the same page as Honneth on this issue. When addressing the dynamics of processes of learning, they conclude from their studies of apprenticeship:

Notions like those of "intrinsic rewards" in empirical studies of apprenticeship focus quite narrowly on task knowledge and skill as the activities to be learned. Such knowledge is of course important; but a deeper sense of the value of participation to the community and the learner lies in becoming part of the community. Thus, making a hat reasonably well is seen as evidence that an apprentice tailor is becoming "a masterful practitioner", though it may be perceived in a more utilitarian vein in terms of reward or even value. Similarly, telling one's life story or making a Twelfth Step call confers a sense of belonging. Moving toward full participation in practice involves not just a greater commitment of time, intensified effort, more and broader responsibilities within the community, and more difficult and risky tasks, but, more significantly, an increasing sense of identity as a master practitioner. (Lave & Wenger 1991, p. 111)

In my interpretation of Lave and Wenger's description of processes of recognition, they have the important insight that processes of recognitions are always embedded in processes of everyday participation. In this case, to become recognized as a master practitioner involves also recognizing the products that the master practitioner is able to produce. Producing a high-quality hat is intertwined with processes of social recognition. It is not two different processes; they are part of the same process.

## More on Learning

Lave and Wenger (1991) are not merely confirming Honneth's theories, but they are also adding to an understanding of learning from a social-ontological perspective being the central project of this chapter. I will briefly outline some of the fundamental insights they have to offer when addressing issues of learning from a social-ontological perspective.

Firstly, as analyzed by Lave and Wenger (1991), processes of learning are closely related to ongoing participation in various communities of practices. As suggested by Lave and Wenger with their concept of legitimate peripheral participation, processes of learning are nourished by a continuity of what I will interpret as ongoing struggles for recognition (see p. 110-117). The central point, based on studies of learning in apprenticeship and learning in everyday practice, is that learning is closely related to changing social positions, social relations, and tasks often related to a growing social significance of what the individual is doing in relation to the other participants in the community of practice. In this sense, the understanding of learning related to legitimate peripheral participation allows us to understand learning in two ways. First of all, matters of learning are related to a growing insight into what others are doing and why. Moreover, matters of learning are related to processes of growing social recognition and hence a change in social positions and a change in a person's self-evaluation in a positive direction.

Second, as underlined by both Lave and Wenger (1991) and Honneth (1996), processes of recognition and learning have an identity-constituting dimension. As suggested by Honneth (1996), processes of recognition are closely related to the values dominating the everyday practices people participate in. According to Honneth (1996), this value-dimension manifests itself in a struggle for status or social respect within the communities of practice that people participate in. In Lave and Wenger's outline of legitimate peripheral participation as a central way to understand learning, they describe how it is possible for the participants, through taking part in different parts of practice, to become recognized and in that sense develop a sense of social esteem.

Third, in a social-ontological perspective, learning is part of everyday practice. It is not reserved for specific institutions, and in that sense, processes of learning are not necessarily a part of an educational practice or closely related to processes of teaching. Processes of recognition happen in a variety of contexts (e.g., among family members, friends, peers, colleagues), and this suggests that we need to understand more formalized school activities as part of other activities and not the other around.

Fourth, processes of learning involve both a social and an individual dimension. As suggested by both Lave and Wenger (1991) and Honneth, the social and individual dimensions of human existence are inseparable. This means that we need to understand learning as within the frames of developing a specific identity and at the same time maintaining and changing communities of practices. By focusing on struggles of recognition and identity as a central part of learning processes, both Lave and Wenger and Honneth are calling attention to the importance of reformulating the cognitive-inspired educational agenda, where processes of learning are equivalent to processes of knowledge acquisition.

## The Critical Dimension of a Social-Ontological Learning Theory

Addressing issues of learning from a social-ontological perspective makes it possible to ask critical questions about societal learning practices in general. It is important to be aware of the negativistic approach Honneth is introducing. We can argue that if we take the considerations of a social-ontological approach to learning seriously, we have the opportunity to develop a way of critically approaching situations where mutual recognition is failing. This leads us to identify disrespect and social struggles for recognition when approaching issues of learning.

This means, more precisely, that we can understand problems with learning as more than individual problems. It is possible to analyze them as problems constituted by social practice and lack of mutual recognition. As outlined above, the impetus for writing this chapter was the growing individualization and instrumentalization we are experiencing today and the lack of potential in mainstream learning theory for developing a critical stance to this mindset. Rather, mainstream theories of learning seem to fit nicely, with their focus on means–end thinking, technology, and control, into the regime of homo economicus.

If we accept the premises laid out in the social-ontological approach to learning outlined above, it can be argued that mainstream theories of learning do not really add to our understanding of what constitute processes of change in everyday life. Inspired by Kvale's analysis (1977), it can be claimed that mainstream theories of learning lead us to misrecognize where the potential for real change lies. Faced with issues of gender, ethnicity, and social class, there is a strong tendency to turn these issues into distinct problems of learning deficits (Reid & Valle 2004) rather than seeing them as struggles for recognition calling for the presence of an open, pluralistic, evaluative framework within which social esteem is ascribed. One of the ways that a social-ontological perspective to learning would approach the problems that schools are faced with is by analyzing struggles for recognition within the frames of processes of social disrespect and lack of social recognition. Rather than seeing problems as the results of cognitive malfunctions like lack of intelligence, lack of appropriate proschool behavior, and lack of motivation (Reid & Valle 2004), problems should be thematized within a social-ontological frame as problems of communication and misrecognition.

As mentioned in the introduction, in mainstream theories of learning there is a strong focus on control, input and output variables, and the processing, storing, and retrieving of knowledge, leading to a strong focus on the formal processes of learning. However, little attention is paid to the content or the subject matter of the learning process. By introducing a stronger focus on participation and processes of recognition, it becomes important to address what is being recognized in processes of learning and why. In everyday life, it is often more transparent why students are learning what they are learning and why it might be important. This division between processes of recognition and processes of learning tends to exclude aspects of meaning and understanding, making mainstream theories of learning redundant.

Finally, one of the main problems with the educational organizational structure following the logic of homo economicus is that processes of recognition is kept at a minimum. As mentioned above, there is a strong focus on tests, examinations and grades as central but formalized ways of receiving a technical version of recognition. As indicated by Honneth (1996) recognition is in many cases a very practical endeavor and as suggested by Lave and Wenger (1991) a presupposition for being part of recognitional interactions is to participate in a shared social practice. If we take these considerations seriously when addressing issues of learning, we need to develop possibilities of shared participation in communities of practices as a central presupposition for nourishing processes of recognition.

## Conclusion

Based on situated learning and Honneth's work, I have tried to develop a social-ontological approach to learning in which Honneth's focus on the struggle for recognition was central. I read Honneth and Lave and Wenger's work in line with a tradition from humanistic psychology in which ontology was considered important when addressing issues of learning. In this context, the notion of a social-ontological approach to issues of learning was used to formulate a critique of the tendencies both in the current regime of homo economicus and in the mainstream theories of learning that seem to fit nicely into the regime of homo economicus, with its strong focus on technology and instrumentality. The main idea of the chapter and the main idea in formulating a social-ontological perspective on how we comprehend processes of learning was to make it possible to formulate a critique of the image of the homo economicus. A few words of reservation are warranted: even though I claim that the situated learning perspective as developed by Lave and Wenger shares concerns with Honneth's work, there are number of differences that I did not have the time or space to elaborate on. Another issue that I would like to make clear is that even though a social-ontological perspective has been central in the last part of the chapter, I have not meant to develop a new kind of dualism in relation to, for example, cognitive processes. Cognitive processes are important parts of our being-in-the-world with other persons and hence needs to be understood as an important part of social ontology. As mentioned above, it becomes problematic when issues of cognition are what define man and when issues of cognition become decontextualized and reified (see Honneth 2008, for an elaboration).

## Notes

1   For critiques of homo economicus within educational theory see Read 2009; Olssen & Peters 2005.
2   It must be underlined that my presentation of behavioral psychology and information processing theory is a brief summary and does not claim to be theoretically adequate, due to my aim of outlining a theory of learning related to the social-ontological dimension.
3   Only Bandura's theory of social learning is often mentioned.
4   According to Heidegger, there is a significant difference between the ontical and the ontological: "Ontological inquiry is concerned primarily with Being; ontical inquiry is concerned primarily with entities and the facts about them" (Heidegger 1988, p. 31). In my understanding of Heidgger, an ontical inquiry is one in which we try to understand something (e.g., a human being) as an entity, a product of biological or sociological processes. In one respect, this is not wrong, but it is not the whole story about what it means to be a human being. There is an ontological question focusing on meaning and understanding that is more essential when trying to understand what a human being is.
5   For an elaboration of this critique, see Honneth's discussion of Sartre's understanding of recognition (Honneth 1996, p. 156).
6   See Dreyfus and Dreyfus's defence of an ontological understanding of learning and their critique of a social-ontological perspective on learning (Dreyfus & Dreyfus 1999, p. 71–74).

7   Even though Honneth does not develop a theory of learning, he uses the notion of learning quite frequently throughout his texts.
8   Honneth replaces Heidegger's care with Hegel's recognition as the privileged stance in man's relation to self and world (Honneth 2008, p. 36).
9   Autonomy is different from processes of individualization (see Honneth 2014, for an elaboration).

## References

Anderson, J. R. (1999). *Learning and memory: An integrated approach*. New York, NY: John Wiley & Sons.
Anderson, J. (1996). Translator's Introduction. In: A. Honneth, *Struggle for recognition: The moral grammar of social conflicts*. Cambridge University Press.
Brinkmann, S. (2005). *Selvrealisering: Kritiske diskussioner af en grænseudviklingskultur*. Aarhus: Klim.
Carleheden, M., Heidegren, C., & Willig, R. (2012). Recognition, social invisibility, and disrespect. *Distinktion: Scandinavian Journal of Social Theory, 13*(1), p. 1–3.
Colaizzi, P. (1978). Learning and existence. In: R. S. Valled and M. King (Eds.), *Existential-phenomenological alternatives for psychology*. New York, NY: Oxford Press.
Deese, J., and Hulse, S. H. (1975). *The psychology of learning*. New York: McGraw-Hill.
Deranty, J.-P. (2009). *Beyond communication. A critical study of Axel Honneth's social philosophy*. Leiden: Brill.
Dreyfus, H. (1995). *Being-in-the-world: A commentary on Heidegger's Being and Time/Division I*. Cambridge, MA: MIT Press.
Dreyfus, H., & Dreyfus, S. (1999). Mesterlære og eksperters læring. In: K. Nielsen & S. Kvale (red): *Mesterlære: Læring som social praksis*. København: Hans Reitzels Forlag.
Driscoll, M. P. (2005). *Psychology of learning for instruction*. Boston: Pearson Allyn and Bacon.
Fraser, N., & Honneth, A. (2003). *Redistribution or recognition? A political-philosophical exchange*. London: Verso.
Ferguson, I. (2007). Increasing user choice or privatizing risk? The antinomies of personalization. *British Journal of Social Work, 37*, p. 387–403.
Gadamer, H. (1975). *Truth and Method*. New York, NY: The Seabury Press.
Hegel, G. W. F. (1998). *The phenomenology of mind*. New York, NY: Harper & Row.
Heidegger, M. (1988). *Being and time*. Oxford, England: Basil Blackwell.
Hattie, J., & Timperley, H. (2007). The power of feedback. *Review of Educational Research, 77*(1), p. 81–112.
Honneth, A. (1996). *Struggle for recognition: The moral grammar of social conflicts*. Cambridge University Press.
Honneth, A. (2008). *Reification and recognition: A new look at an old idea*. Oxford University Press.
Honneth, A., & Joas, H. (1988). *Social action and human nature*. Cambridge University Press

Honneth, A., & Margalit, A. (2001). Recognition. *Aristotelian Society Proceedings, 75*, p. 111-139.
Houston, S. (2010). Beyond homo economicus: Recognition, self-realization and social work. *British Journal of Social Work, 40*, p. 841-857.
Islam, G. (2012). Recognition, reification, and practices of forgetting: Ethical implications of human resource management. *Journal of Business Ethics, 111*, p. 37-48.
Kvale, S. (1976). The psychology of learning as ideology and technology. *Behaviorism, 4*, p. 97-116.
Kvale, S. (1977). Dialectics of remembering. In: N. Datan & H.W. Reese (Eds.), *Life-span developmental psychology: Dialectical perspectives on experimental research*. New York, NY: Academic Press.
Lave, J. (1992, April). *Learning as participation in communities of practice*. Paper presented at the annual meeting of the American Educational Research Association, San Francisco, CA.
Lave, J. (1997). Learning, apprenticeship, social practice. *Nordisk Pedagogik, 17*, p. 140-152.
Lave, J., & Wenger, E. (1991). *Situated learning: Legitimate peripheral participation*. Cambridge University Press.
Lave, J., & Packer, M. (1991). *Towards a social ontology of learning*. First draft for Wenner-Gren Conference.
Lave, J. & Packer, M. (2008). Towards a social ontology of learning. In: K. Nielsen, S. Brinkmann, C. Elmholdt, L. Tanggaard, P. Museaus, & G. Kraft(Eds.), *A qualitative stance: Essays in honor of Steinar Kvale*. Aarhus: Aarhus Universitetsforlag.
Mead, G. H. (1997). *Mind, self and society from the standpoint of a social behaviorist*. Chicago University Press.
Merleau-Ponty, M. (1981). *Phenomenology of perception*. London, England: Routledge & Kegan Paul.
Miller, P. H. (1983). *Theories of developmental psychology*. San Francisco, CA: W.H. Freeman and Company.
Nielsen, K. (2005). Frelserpædagogik og selvrealisering: Moderne bekendelsesformer i dansk pædagogik. In: S. Brinkmann (Ed), *Selvrealisering: Kritiske diskussioner af en grænseudviklingskultur*. Aarhus: Klim.
Nielsen, K. (2008). Learning, trajectories of participation and social practice. *Outlines: Critical Social Studies, 1*, p. 22-36.
Norman, D. A. (1976). *Memory and attention: An introduction to human information processing* (2nd ed.). New York, NY: Wiley.
Olssen, M., & Peters, M. A. (2005). Neoliberalism, higher education and the knowledge economy: From the free market to knowledge capitalism, *Journal of Education Policy, 20*(3), p. 313-345.
Omrod, J. (2012). *Human learning*. Upper Saddle River, NJ: Prentice-Hall.
Packer, M. (1985). Hermeneutic inquiry in the study of human conduct. *American Psychologist, 40*(10), p. 1081-1093.
Packer, M. J., & Goicoechea, J. (2000). Sociocultural and constructivist theories of learning: Ontology, not just epistemology. *Educational Psychologist, 35*(4).

Read, J. (2009). A genealogy of homo-economicus: Neoliberalism and the production of subjectivity. *Foucault Studies*, 6, p. 25-36.

Reid, K. D., & Valle, J. W. (2004). The discursive practice of learning disability: Implications for instructions and parent-school relations. *Journal of Learning Disabilities, 37*(6), p. 466-481.

Rogers, C. R., & Freiberg, H. J. (1994). *Freedom to learn.* Columbus, OH: Merrill/Macmillan.

Solomon, R. C. (1983). *In the spirit of Hegel: A study of G. W. F. Hegel's Phenomenology of Spirit.* New York, NY: Oxford University Press.

# The mistake to mistake learning theory for didactics

*Ane Qvortrup & Tina Bering Keiding*

## The Methodification of Higher Education Didactics

Since the mid1980s, higher education has witnessed an enhanced focus on pedagogical and didactical professionalization (Murray 2008; Trigwell, Martin, Benjamin, & Prosser 2000). Initially it expressed itself as a nascent interest in teacher professionalism and formalized teacher qualification programs, but gradually a 'scholarship of teaching and learning' (SoTL) in higher education has emerged (Tight 2012; Trigwell et al., 2000). Based on the aim to offer research-based contributions to the practice of higher education, we might describe SoTL as a domain of didactics, understood as a body of knowledge that *"provides teachers with ways of considering the essential what, how, and why questions around their teaching of their students in their classrooms"* (Westbury 2000, p. 17). In line with this Künzli (1998, p. 42) describes didactics *"as theory of instruction and the embodiment of knowledge about instruction"* and Luhmann (2002b, p. 201) describes didactics as theories or programs for reflection.

In Keiding and Qvortrup (2015) we asked: What is the content of this new scholarship or didactic domain? What knowledge does it provide to teachers emerging professionalism? Inspired by Tights (2012) metaanalysis and Hopmann's (s.a) concept 'didactics of didactics', we conducted a meta-didactic analysis of the contributions in four journals, sharing a common aim of contributing to the theory, practice or research of higher education. The conclusion was that the SoTL journals share a number of distinctive characteristics (Keiding & Qvortrup 2015):

- a strong orientation towards methods; 40% of the contributions had a methodological question as its main topic
- the methods are characterized by a student-centred point of departure leading towards either dialogue-based methods (e.g. feed-back, peer-

assessment and co-operative learning) or various types of structured, student-centred activities (e.g. PBL and practice-based learning)
- "teaching as representation", e.g. various ways of lecturing and various ways of structuring the content are rare topics
- the categories "intention", i.e. learning objectives, and "assessment" receive only minor attention, and the category "subject matter" barely exists as research topic in its own right

Textbooks for higher education seem to mirror this pattern. For instance, Biggs & Tang (2011) do not at all address the question about selection of content. Ramsden (1992) acknowledges the relevance of the topic, but nor do we find a conceptual framework for systematic reflections on selection content here.

If one agrees with Tight (2008, p. 64) that one of the main purposes of research into higher education is to sharpen the educators' mind, one might argue that the strong focus on teaching methods makes SoTL a somewhat one-sided sharpening tool. In the "Lerntheoretische Didaktik", Heimann (1976) argues that a holistic reflection of teaching requires six didactic categories: aim, content, media, methods, students background and organizational context. Similar categories are found in newer didactic theories (e.g. Hiim & Hippe 2007) and, although less elaborated, in broad understandings of curriculum theory e.g. Dillon (2009). A common premise is that decisions within one category influence the space of decisions in other categories and that didactic practice must avoid contradictions between categories. The relevance of addressing the interdependence between categories is substantiated empirically by the fact that clarity and transparency are fundamental for quality teaching (Hattie 2009; Helmke 2009; Meyer 1994)

In this chapter, we expose the contributions on teaching methods to further inquiry by asking to the conceptual sources for these student-centred methods, or learning activities, as they are often called. A central aspect of didactic analysis has to do with reasoning the choices of teaching: "Why did you select this instead of something else?" is what didactics is all about (Hopmann n.d., p. 144; Heimann 1976, p. 151ff) and therefore, knowledge about the conditioning factors framing the articles seems to be essential in order to understand the scope of this new didactic domain. By doing this, we intend to come to a deeper understanding of the reason for the strong focus on student-centred methods or learning activities and, based on the fact that in great many of the contributions the argument for the focus on student centred methods or learning activities are found in learning theory, to discuss the interplay between theories or concepts of learning and practices of teaching.

## Analytic design

### The data

The empirical data comprises the contributions classified as student-centred methods in two of the four journals examined in Keiding & Qvortrup (2015): Higher Education Research & Development (HERD), and Dansk Universitetspædagogisk Tidsskrift/Danish Journal for Teaching and Learning in Higher Education (DUT). The criterion for selection of these two journals was that we wanted journals with background in the Didaktik tradition and the Curriculum tradition, respectively. See for instance Gundem and Hopmann (1998). Table 1 gives an overview of the data.

| Journal | Year | Number of contributions |
| --- | --- | --- |
| Higher Education Research & Development (HERD)[1] | 2013-2008 | 48 |
| Dansk Universitetspædagogisk Tidsskrift/ Danish Journal for Teaching and Learning in Higher Education[2] (DUT) | 2014-2016 | 49/47 |

Table 1. Selected journals and number of contributions dealing with student-centred methods. As the number of contributions per year in DUT is small compared to HERD, all available volumes are included. Two contributions in DUT based exclusively on the authors' experiences and without links to conceptual frameworks were excluded.

## Analytical strategy

The inquiry of the conceptual background for the student-centred teaching methods is based on Heimann's (1976, p.151ff) distinction between two levels of didactic reflection and analysis (Figure 1). The first level, "the structure analysis", deals with decisions and reflections on aim, content, media and methods. This level was the guiding framework for the classification in Keiding and Qvortrup (2015). The second level of didactic analysis examines conditioning and organizing factors, e.g. personal and organizational norms, values and beliefs, framing the horizon for the didactic decisions in the structure analysis. Heimann describes the inquiry of these organizing factors as "factor analysis". The factor analysis is the guiding framework in this article. It is operationalized in the guiding difference "**organizing and conditioning factors**|anything else", see for instance Andersen (2003), Luhmann (2002c), Keiding (2010).

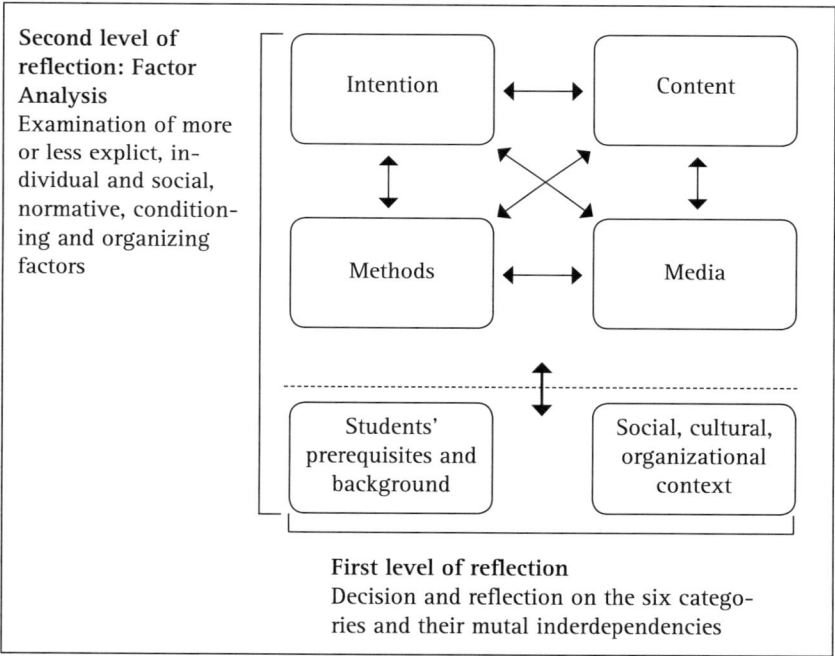

Figure 1. The Berliner-model: two levels of didactic analysis (Heimann, 1976, p. 151ff.; after Keiding 2013)

The organizing and conditioning factors were categorized in three groups: 'Learning theory', 'Didactics' and 'Various'. The categories 'Learning theory' and 'Didactics' includes contributions that find their arguments in theories of learning and theories of teaching and instructional design, respectively. Various includes articles drawing on for instance empirical data without explicit theoretical arguments for analytic categories (e.g. Cooper, 2009), philosophy (e.g. Hansen, 2008) or organizational theory (e.g. Adriansen & Ravn 2012). Several contributions draw on several sources. In this case, the categorization is based on the constituent approach. Table 2 shows examples of contributions from each of the three categories 'Learning theory', 'Didactics' and 'Various'.

| | DUT | HERD |
|---|---|---|
| Learning theory | We have developed a way of teaching the highly individual art and craft of speaking well in front of an audience by means of socio-cultural learning principles, group and project work stressing the importance of collective responsibility, and workshops in which students are teaching students. (Juel 2010, p. 23) | The basic principle of the pragmatic, social constructivist approach to teaching is that students learn most effectively by engaging in carefully selected collaborative problem-solving activities, under the close supervision and coaching of an educator. Hanson & Sinclair 2008, p. 170) |
| Didactics | Jank & Meyer argue that teaching can be described completely by the use of five basic categories related to the structure of aim, content, social dimension, actions and process (Thorp 2011, p. 33) | Problem-based learning is a teaching methodology that develops knowledge, abilities and skills through participation, collaborative investigation and the resolution of authentic problems. (Dickie & Jay 2010, p. 32) |
| Various | It is shown how Marx's concept of technology can be used to analyse IT-mediated learning. (Hansen 2008, p. 40) | Learning disabilities are generally defined as dysfunctions in cognitive and information processing that interfere with academic performance despite average to above average intelligence Reed et al. 2009, p. 385) |

Table 2. Examples of classification.

## Findings

Table 3 shows result of the classification.

| Journal | Learning theory | Didactics | Various |
|---|---|---|---|
| HERD (n = 48) | 11 (23%) | 21 (44%) | 16 (33%) |
| DUT (n = 47) | 19 (40%) | 20 (43%) | 8 (17%) |

Table 3. Number of contributions in the three categories. To ease comparison across categories within the sample, the brackets show number of contributions in the categories in percent of total number of contributions (n).

Given the subject, Scholarship of Teaching and Learning, we expected that many contributions would find their arguments for decisions in didactics, theories of instruction and empirical didactics. On one hand, the findings confirm this expectation. On the other hand, less than half of the contributions are founded in didactics, theories of instruction and empirical didactics. It is common to both journals that arguments for teaching methods are based on learning theory. This is even more distinctive in DUT (40%) than in HERD (23%). The category "Various" covers 33% of the contributions in HERD, compared to 17% in DUT. The difference between the numbers of contributions based on learning theory in DUT (40%) vs. HERD (23%) remains an open question. One explanation might be that SoTL in Higher Education is a young discipline in Denmark and, drawing on Tight (2004), the limited number of theoretical positions might be an expression of an immature field of research. The first number of DUT was published in 2006 as a "framework for the exchange of experiences between engaged teachers about didactic and university pedagogical issues and framework for the research that takes the form of studies of their own practice, and can be performed by teachers in all subjects" (Jensen 2006, p. 1). In contrast, the first issue of HERD was published in 1982.

If we subject the contributions to further classification we find that two-third of the contributions draw on various forms of social learning theories using concepts as "communities of practice" (Lave & Wenger), "dialogue-based learning" (Dysthe) and "collaboration" (Vygotsky). Common to these theories are that they use social interaction/practice as foreground for understanding and analysing learning. We might also describe this approach as "contextualism"[3]. Among the most influent concepts in the cognitively oriented category, we find for instance Schön's concept of the reflective practitioner (Schön) and Kolb's idea about experiential learning (Kolb). Here the cognitive processes of the learner – or more specifically the concepts of action and reflection – are used as foreground for interpretation of learning. Table 4 shows the distribution between learning theoretical approaches in the two journals.

|  | Learning theories | Social learning theories | Cognitive learning theories |
| --- | --- | --- | --- |
| HERD | 11 | 7 (64%) | 4 (36%) |
| DUT | 19 | 12 (63%) | 7 (37%) |

Table 4. Distribution of learning theoretical approaches

Figure 2 illustrates the overall distribution between the frequencies of the two learning theoretical approaches.

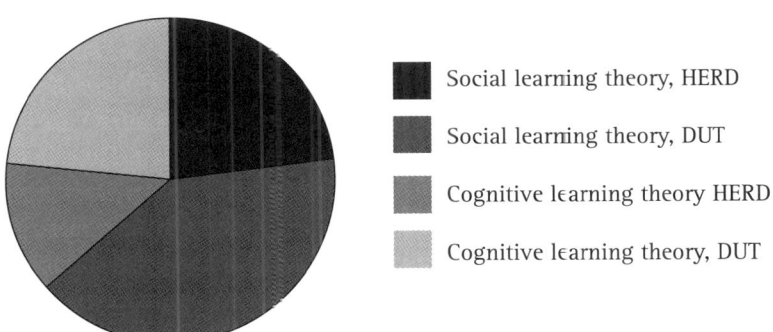

Figure 2. Distribution between the two learning theoretical approaches. Based on table 4.

Especially the contributions in DUT apply learning theories in a very general form. An example is Juel (2010, p. 23), who has *"developed a way of teaching [...] by means of socio-cultural learning principles, group and project work"*, but omits to describe which principles and concepts he refers to and how they are transposed into instructional design. Another example is found in Kobayashi, Grout and Rump (2013, p. 15) which *"is based on a socio-cultural understanding of learning as a human social activity conducted within institutional and cultural contexts"* and *"Learning opportunities were created through the diverging voices of the supervisors"* without explicit descriptions of the criteria used to describe voices as "diverging". In this sense, especially DUT mirrors the findings from the meta-analysis described by Tight (2004, p. 399), who based on the distinction explicit/implicit and evident/non-evident use of theory concludes that *"it is perfectly possible to write an article about, say, problem based learning, staff development or institutional change in higher education without ever mentioning or articulating any relevant theory at all".*

## Picturing why learning theories became so influential

The findings raise the question, why learning theories, and especially social learning theory, have become so influential in the scholarship of teaching in higher education? Our assumption is that it can be understood as an imprint of a general preoccupation with learning in the education system and a strong resonance with tendencies in the political system, describing the society through terms as "information or knowledge society" (Bell 1979; UNESCO, 2005), "complexity" (Luhmann 1995), "detraditionalization" and "individualization" (Giddens 1991). We will, however, restrain our focus to education system.

In 1985 the Australian "Project for Enhancing Effective Learning" (PEEL-project) was initiated *"by a group of teachers and academics who shared concerns about the prevalence of passive, unreflective dependent student learning, even in apparently successful lessons"* (Mitchell & Mitchell, 2008, p. 7). Some of the keywords in the PEEL-project were "independent learning", "metacognition" and *"change of attitudes to ones that promote such learning"* (Ibid.; see also Baird & Mitchel 1986). The PEEL-project's focus on meta-cognition origins from an observation that continuously learning and learn-to-learn is *"widely recognized as a necessary skill for the learners in the future"* [Mitchell & Mitchell 2008, p. 7) . This is in line with Luhmann (2002b) who argues an enhanced societal complexity and an enhanced uncertainty about the aim and content of education has transformed the overarching aim of education towards open-ended focuses such as learning-to-learn and innovation. See also Keiding and Qvortrup (2014, p. 91ff.).

A similar concern manifests itself in the "From teaching to learning" paradigm, formulated in Barr & Tagg's (1995) as well as the Scandinavian concept "Responsibility for own Learning" (Bjørgen, 1991). Common to these contributions is that *"the chief agent in the process is the learner. Thus students must be active discoverers and constructors of their own knowledge"* (Barr & Tagg 1995, p. 21).

At a first glance, this appears to be a didactic and empirical question: How can we teach students to become independent and proficient learners in relation to the demand for lifelong formalized and informal education both inside and outside the education system? What do they need to know and how can teaching be organized to render this type of learning? As illustrated in Figure 1, such didactic reflections involve four didactic categories (aim, content, methods and media). Nevertheless, the heavy focus on the students *as learners* tends to direct our attention towards how students' engage with the content and hence toward the axis of experience in the didactic triangle (Figure 3).

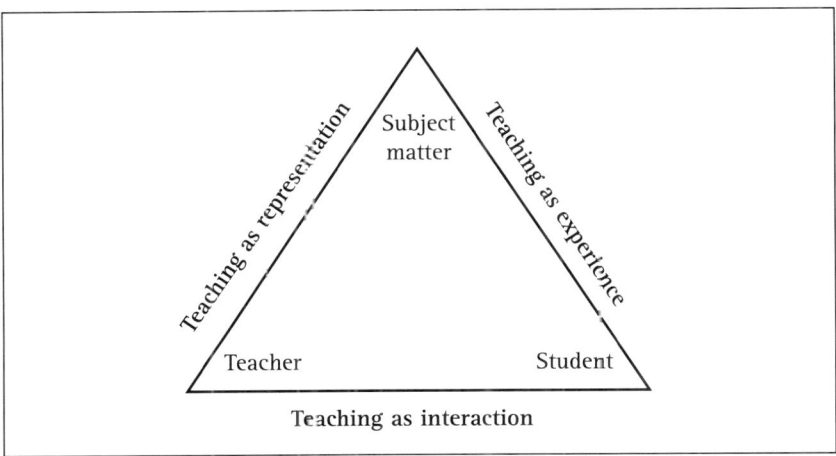

**Figure 3.** The didactic triangle. (Künzli 1998, 2000)

The question on how students (should) engage with content is a common topic in didactics, and does not necessarily lead us into the domain of learning theory. We find several examples of didactics with a strong displacement toward teaching methods and students engagement with content in for instance progressive pedagogy (Myhre 1971; Röhrs 1982), PBL (Uden & Beaumont 2006) and programmed teaching (König & Riedel 1973; Mager 1962; von Cube 1999). Nevertheless, the preoccupation with learning activities and concepts like "students as chief agents or constructors of their own learning" and "from teaching to learning" seem to have changed how we talk (and think?) about teaching. According to Biesta (2012, p. 37), we have witnessed a new language of learning in the education system and a shift from teaching to "teachingandlearning", which he deliberately writes as one word as this is, how many people nowadays seem to use it. The consequence is a "learnification" of the education system (Biesta 2010) Other researchers consent that the new orientations have guided the attention away from teaching, and consequently from didactics and theories of instruction, towards the learner and learning strategies, and placed activities referring to learning on the center stage (Haugsbakk & Nordkvelle 2007; Richardson 2003; Terhart 2003).

In this perspective, the strong preoccupation with learning theory appears understandable. Nevertheless, we will earmark the next sections to argue that learning theory cannot replace didactics and that the fact that it to some extend seems to be the case leave us behind with a restricted framework for reflection on teaching.

## The whole story: Learning theory and didactics

In this section, we will dig deeper into how the relation between learning theory and didactics can be conceptualized and discuss the use of learning theories in didactic settings.

## Learning theory

Learning theories help us to understand learning as phenomenon. They answer questions like: "What is learning?" and "What matters to learning?". Different theories offer different answers to these questions. Sociocultural learning theory emphasizes communities and practice

(Lave & Wenger 1991). To systems theory, differences and differences 'that make a difference' are some of the key concepts (Bateson 2000b; Luhmann 2002a). Behaviourism is occupied with systematic couplings between stimuli and response (Skinner 1974) and emancipatory learning as described by Mezirow (1991) focuses on personal meaning and transformation of identity.

Learning theories help us understand learning as phenomenon, but they do not support reflections on what, how and why something should be taught and learned in school. They are in other words empty with regard to aim and content of teaching. This can be illustrated with Mezirow's (1991) concept of "personal meaning". The concept emphasizes *that* the experience of meaningfulness is important for learning, but it does not say anything about *how* one makes something meaningful to the learner. Should teaching, for instance, relate to the student's former experiences as we see in some parts of progressive pedagogy (e.g. Dewey 1997; Kerschensteiner 1971), point to future applications as we see in for instance problem-based teaching (Frey 1984), or should we select a playful approach as it is suggested in one of the most child-centred pedagogies (Neill 1960)?

Another example can be taken from Lave and Wenger's (1991) idea of "trajectories of participation". The concept describes how a learner gradually becomes a full member of a community of practice, but it does not offer concepts for systematic reflection of valuable knowledge, skills and competence of the community, nor for reflection of the sequencing of the process: in which order must the single elements be taught (and learned).

Similar arguments can be directed towards for instance functionalist learning theories, e.g. Piaget, Bateson and Luhmann. These theories tell us, that learning is adaptive or meaningful seen from the perspective of the learner, but this does not tell us anything about what should be learned in school.

## Didactics

The questions about *what* to teach, *how* to teach it and *why* it should be taught in school is the domain of didactics: *"Didaktike techne or Didaktik would thus be the art of showing, of pointing and drawing attention, of allowing something which does not simply demonstrate itself, or cannot be understood, seen, perceived and recognized. In keeping with this original meaning of the word, Didaktik can be used to mean the science of such actions of demonstrating, or more specifically, as a science of instruction. Didaktik as theory of instruction and the embodiment of knowledge about instruction"* (Künzli 1998, p. 42)

Just as different learning theories reflect on different aspects of learning, didactics reflect on different aspects of teaching. Theories of Bildung (Education) ask to the fundamental aim and content of schooling (Klafki 1998, 2000, 2001). Progressive pedagogy offers different suggestions on why and how world life experiences should be integrated in the school (Blonskij 1971; Dewey 1997; Kerschensteiner 1971). Theories of supervisions offer conceptual frameworks for understanding and guiding decisions in relation to supervision (Handal and Lauvås 1987) And didactics founded in systems theory point towards either programmed teaching (König & Riedel 1973; Mager 1962; von Cube 1999) or process and reflection oriented approaches (Arnold 2007; Holtz 2008; Keiding & Qvortrup 2014).

Based on Luhmann, we might distinguish between three types of didactic knowledge: Experiential didactic knowledge, didactic theory and science of teaching, see Figure 4.

|  | Experiential didactic knowledge | Didactics | Science of teaching |
|---|---|---|---|
| Type of knowledge | Individual and collective knowledge based on experiences and tradition | Programs of reflection for teaching and instruction | Scientific knowledge about teaching and learning |
| Code of | Useful/not useful | Guiding/not guiding | True/false |

Figure 4. Three types of didactical knowledge and their knowledge codes (Keiding & Qvortrup 2014; Qvortrup & Keiding 2014)


With the term "experiential knowledge", we refer to the body of experience or practice-based knowledge about teaching and about what works in different situations that the single teacher, each team, each educational institution and the teacher profession as a whole possess. Experiental knowledge is closely linked to the context where it is produced. It is partly a result of a teacher's own teaching practice, and partly a result of social conventions and norms within the professional contexts outside the classroom (colleagues, teams, institutions and profession) (tradition) (Keiding & Qvortrup 2014; Qvortrup & Keiding 2014)

We have several times indicated how theories of didactic might guide decisions in relation to the fundamental didactic questions and categories. The field of didactics can be described as systematic descriptions of and reflections on teaching that teachers can use *to guide* the choices made in planning, conducting and evaluation of teaching. Didactics is not characterized by consensus about what good teaching is. As we have shown through the article, different didactic positions reflect and present teaching in different ways and accordingly tell different stories about what teaching is or should be. This variety of perspectives is useful and desirable, when teaching for some reason has to change direction, for instance when experience and tradition no longer suffice to meet new ideas or conditions. This is especially important when teaching does not go to plan; for example, if a selected approach or content proves inappropriate for those, who are going to use it (Hopmann, s.a, p. 142). In such a case, it would seem futile to simply repeat previous actions (ibid., p. 182).

During the latest years, the empirical teaching research has contributed with knowledge about, what seems to work or not work across contexts, in form of indicators of how different forms of didactic practice influence student's learning. The empirical teaching research has, at least in Denmark, been treated with skepticism. This skepticism seems to originate in an interpretation of pedagogical practice as a unique relation between two unique individuals, which means that it is not possible to generalize. Pedagogics is a normative and not empirical science, and decisions must be based on professional judgment (e.g. Moos, Krejsler, Hjort, Laursen, & Braad 2008).

However, the empirical teaching research does not question that pedagogics and didactics are normative sciences and that concrete practices and actions are contextually rooted (Johannsen 2011). It simply looks for another kind of knowledge than didactics and pedagogics. The empirical teaching research provides knowledge about correlations between single elements and students' learning, but *"does not supply us with rules for action but only with hypotheses for intelligent problem solving, and for making inquiries about our ends in education"* (Hattie 2009, p. 247).

The three types of knowledge on one hand increase complexity of didactic practice by means of a wider horizon of opportunities. On the other hand, they reduce complexity by offering new perspectives. What they can do is to offer knowledge, which teachers can use to narrow and reflect on the horizon of possibilities and hereby guide the selections in a given situation. Neither of these knowledge domains, nor the collection as a whole, prescribes actions. The micro-diversity and complexity of teaching as interaction are simply too high. It always contains an aspect of unpredictability. Therefore, no matter how closely we read empirical teaching research and/or didactics, it is the teacher, who makes the concrete didactical selections in a given situation based on his/her professional knowledge and judgment.

## The form "didactics"

Learning (in the broadest meaning of the word, i.e. containing concepts of Bildung as well as concepts of knowledge, skills and competences) is the purpose of teaching. *"There cannot be taught or learned either language or science, either history or mathematics on the assumption that it does not matter how the learner deals with the content"* (Luhmann 2002b, p. 63). Schooling and education is not just about learning, but about *learning something specific*. In this sense, the distinction between better and worse learning is fundamental for the education system and teachers use both concepts of learning and conceptualizations of learning processes to reflect the quality of their teaching.

In Keiding and Qvortrup (2014) we have used Luhmann's concept of observation to illustrate how learning serves as concept for didactical reflection. Luhmann describes observation as the unity of distinction and indication: *"Observations are asymmetric (or symmetry-breaking) operations. They use distinctions as forms and take forms as boundaries, separating an inner side (the Gestalt) and an outer side. The inner side is the indicated side, the marked side. From here, one has to start the next operation. The inner side has connective value"* (Luhmann 2002c, p. 101). *"But normally our indications will frame our observations with the effect that the other side implicitly will receive a corresponding specification"* (Luhmann 2002d, p. 85).

Drawing on Spencer-Browns form-notation, the didactics as theories *about* teaching *aiming* to stimulate not-random learning can be expressed as showed in figure 5.

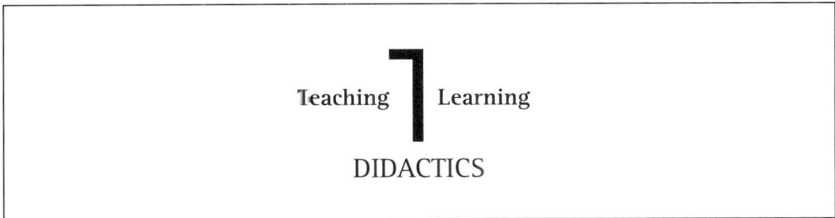

Figure 5. The form didactics

The form notation illustrates the previous stated points that didactics are theories of teaching, and that learning serves as the fundamental concept of reflection.

But what happens to our reflections on teaching if we replace didactics with learning theories as program of reflections? As learning theories deal with learning processes in the sense "what matters to learning", the concept of teaching is replaced by learning processes (Figure 6).

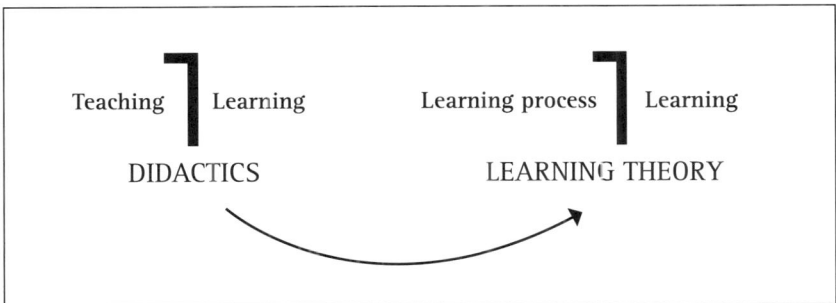

Figure 6. Transformation of the form Didactics into the form of Learning

The transformation means that learning no longer serves as concept of reflection of students achievement in relation to the intended learning objectives embedded in teaching. Learning becomes the concept of reflection in relation to a learning theory's conceptualization of the learning process (e.g. participation, shared repertoire, existentially meaningfulness or differences that make a difference). This means, that the normativity of a description of a learning process replaces the normativity of teaching, defined by the intention to teach someone something specific. Learning processes in themselves become the success criteria of the social interaction.

We find several examples in HERD and DUT that may serve to illustrate how the learning process itself replaces intended learning. One example is found in Hanson and Sinclair (2008) (Table 2). Another in Durey, Lin, and Thompson (2013, p. 722) who state that the methodological design is based on *"situated learning theory [...], which prioritised context and participation in the construction of knowledge:"*. An example from DUT is found in Dalsgaard (2011, p. 11), who argues that: *"a socio-cultural perspective, learning requires active participation in socio cultural contexts [...]. The consequence is a motion from the idea of a fixed syllabus"*. See also Thøgersen (2011) and Thomsen and Nordentoft (2012)

In this sense, the form notation brings us closer to an understanding of what happens when Biesta (2012, p. 38) claims that, if learning *"is indeed the only language available, then teachers end up being a kind of process-managers of empty and in themselves directionless learning processes"*

## Didactic analysis in the center of teacher professionalism

In the previous sections, we discussed the relation between learning theory and didactics, and we argued that learning theories cannot replace didactics. Learning theories help us to understand learning as phenomenon and hereby offer insights, which are able to qualify didactic analysis. In this section, we will elaborate on this perspective.

As argued above, learning serves as the fundamental concept for reflection of teaching. In line with this Luhmann (2002b, p. 59; 143) describes intention as the central symbol of education. In contrast, learning – as the outer side of the form – has no connective value (Luhmann 2002c, p. 101). Teaching cannot promote and observe learning directly, but must produce its own observation strategies, which align with teaching as social interaction. It must, in other words, look for "signs of learning" based on changes in communication and behavior. In this sense, learning as it is conceptualized in teaching can be described as a semantic construction that *"indicates that one cannot observe how information triggers far reaching consequences by bringing about partial structural changes in a system without interrupting its self-identification."* (Luhmann 1995, p. 111)

When teaching produces its *own opportunities* for observation of learning, we might say that learning as outer side of the form teaching/learning *reenters* on the inner side of the form. Using the form notation, we might expressed this as illustrated in figure 7.

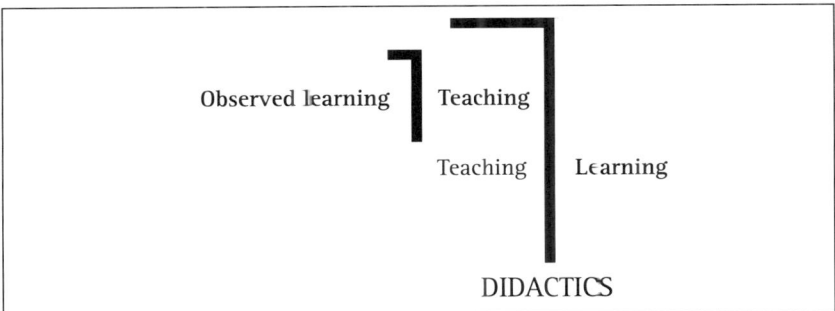

Figure 7. Teaching's observation of learning takes place from the inner side of the form

## Learning observed from didactics

Teaching is interested in learning in three dimensions of time: Before, now, after (Luhmann 1990). The dimensions relate to three didactic questions: What should student learn and what do they know beforehand? How is learning observed procedurally and used for conformation and/or correcting of teaching as interaction? And how is learning assessed after the lesson/course?

The three questions are themes in different theories of didactics. For instance, learning outcomes and the operationalization of learning outcomes into learning objectives as described in for instance study regulations and syllabi/lesson plans is the key topic in Möller (1973) and Mager (1962). Also various learning taxonomies Bloom (1956) and Krathwohl, Bloom, and Masia (1964) contribute to the field. And the shift from content-based to outcome-based curricula, that we have witnessed during the last 10 years, has revitalized a dormant empirical interest in how learning outcomes are described (Biggs & Tang 2011; Guskey 2013).

Formative and process-related assessment and *"seeing teaching through the eyes of the student"* is one of the cornerstones of quality teaching (Hattie 2009; see also Helmke 2009; Meyer 1994; Nordenbo, Larsen, Tiftikçi, Wendt, & Østergaard 2008; Weinert 2000). In Keiding and Qvortrup (2014) we argue for an intimate link between process-related observation of learning and didactic rationality. But so far, research and didactics have primarily been concerned with the observation of learning based on planned procedures and technologies (Biggs 1998; Knight 2004; Ruiz-Primo & Furtal 2006; Rust 2002). This means that enhanced research in informal process-related observation and interpretation of learning and how it influence teaching as interaction is vital.

## Didactic sight points in learning theories

As mentioned, the different learning theories offer concepts that help us to understand and conceptualize the unobservable and inaccessible outer side for the form: learning as process and result. One example concerns the conceptualization of prerequisites for learning. Behaviorism talks about the necessity of appropriate couplings between stimuli, response and reinforcement (Skinner, 1974). The cogntive approaches that we meet in for instance Piaget (1970) and Bateson (2000a) suggests that we understand learning as more or less radical reconstruction of cognitive schema and Lave and Wengers theory about communities of practice points at 'legitimate peripheral partication' as a prerequisite for learning in communities of practice (Lave & Wenger 1991). These various descriptions of learning conditions can be used to identify didactical awareness and to guide the didactical choices in the planning of teaching strategies and activies.

Figure 8 offers a non-exhaustive example on which concepts didactics and learning theories offer for description of the three dimensions of learning.

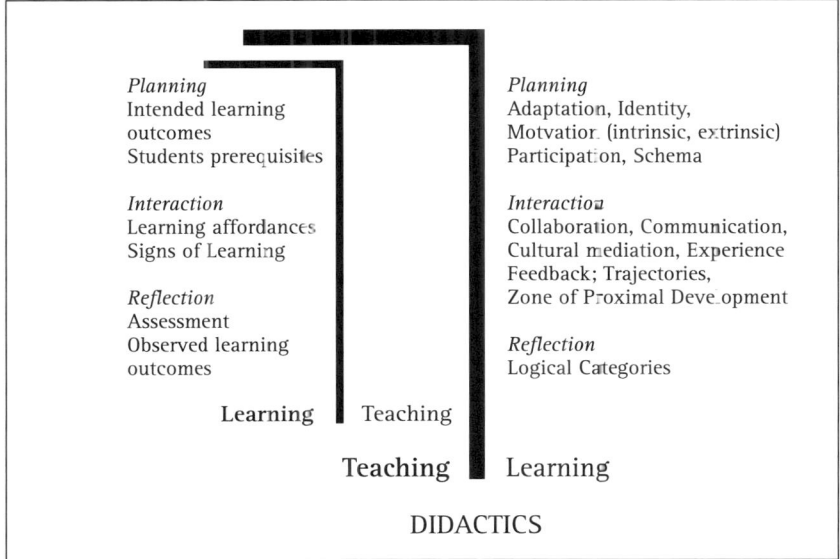

Figure 8. Examples on how learning is observed in didactics and learning theories, respectively.

## Conclusion

In the article, we have shown how, especially in Denmark, broad concepts of constructivism and socio-cultural learning theories seem to have replaced education theory and didactics as conceptual framework reasoning on teaching and choices of design in the Scholarship of Teaching and Learning in Higher Education. We have illustrated how and why didactic theory and practice cannot be deduced from learning theoretical concepts and have discussed possible consequences of the displacement towards learning theory. Finally, we have argued that both learning theories and didactics are fundamental for systematic reflection of teaching and learning and cannot be replaced by each other.

Empirical research gives strong arguments for a variety of methods and a clear eye for the students' learning process as a whole, and we do not question the relevance of a student-oriented approach in the sense that teaching is planned and carried out with a clear focus on the pedagogical significance and students learning.

But we do question student-oriented approaches as the only methodological dimension in teaching. In line with Barr & Tagg (1995,

p. 14) our credo is that teachers must chose *"whatever approaches serves best to prompt learning of particular knowledge by particular students"*.

Furthermore, we do question the idea that learning theory can replace didactics and that the education system benefits from the current learnification. The exchange of the language of teaching with the language of learning is not just a simple replacement of one word with another without significance of the meaning. On the contrary, it deprives us a systematic framework for reflection on teaching, at the risk of becoming blind for the many didactic decisions that we make whenever we try to design "learning environments" and "learning activities". The risk points in two directions: Either we forget the role of schooling and teaching and leaves the student with the responsibly of designing educational relevant activities. In this case, students become responsible not only for their own learning but for *own teaching*. Or we might be seduced to think that we as teachers actually plan – or even steer and observe – students learning and risk to neglect *"the educative difference of matter and meaning and a strong conviction that teaching and learning are necessarily autonomous activities"* (Hopmann 2007, p. 121).

We will designate the first risk as "the students as his/hers own didactician" (Keiding 2008) and the second as "trivialization" (Luhmann 2002b, p. 77ff) and in line with Keiding and Qvortrup (2014) uphold that neither is compatible with quality teaching and hence not with the function of a Scholarship in Teaching and Learning in Higher Education.

## Notes
1   http://www.tandfonline.com/toc/cher20/current#.UlfD-1DIaCq
2   http://www.dun-net.dk/tidsskrift/
3   We thank Gerd Christensen for proposing the term contextualism.

## References
Adriansen, H. K., & Ravn, I. (2012). Det er blevet et socialt netværk - forbedring af studiemiljøet gennem studiefacilitering *Dansk Universitetspædagogisk Tidsskrift, 7*(13), p. 14-26.

Andersen, N. Å. (2003). *Discursive analytical strategies: Understanding Foucault, Koselleck, Laclau, Luhmann*. Bristol: Policy Press.
Arnold, R. (2007). *Ich lerne, also bin ich. Eine systemisch-konstruktivistische Didaktik*. Heidelberg: Carl-Auer-Systeme.
Baird, J. R., & Mitchel, I. J. (Eds.). (1986). *Improving the Quality of Teaching and Learning: An Australian Case Study — The PEEL Project*. Melbourne: The PEEL Group, Monash University.
Barr, R. B., & Tagg, J. (1995) From Teaching to Learning - A new paradigm for Undergraduate Education. *Change, 27*(6), p. 13-25.
Bateson, G. (2000a). The Logical Categories of Learning and Communication. In: G. Bateson (Ed.), *Steps to an Ecology of Mind* (pp. 279-308). Chicago: Chicago University Press.
Bateson, G. (2000b). *Steps to an Ecology of Mind*. Chicago: Chicago University Press.
Bell, D. (1979). Social Framework of the Information Society. In: M. L. Dertoozos & J. Moses (Eds.), *The Computer Age: A 20 Year View* (p. 500-549.). Cambridge, MA: MIT Press.
Biesta, G. (2010). *Good education in an age of measurement: Ethics, politics, democracy.* . Boulder, Co: Paradigm Publishers.
Biesta, G. (2012). Giving Teaching Back to Education: Responding to the Disappearance of the Teacher. *Phenomenology & Practice, 6*(2), p. 35-49.
Biggs, J. (1998). Assessment and Classroom Learning: a role for summative assessment? *Assessment in Education: Principles, Policy & Practice, 5*(1), p. 103-110. doi: 10.1080/0969595980050106
Biggs, J., & Tang, C. (2011). *Teaching for Quality Learning at University: What the Student Does* (4. ed.). Berkshire: Open University Press.
Bjørgen, I. (1991). *Ansvar for egen læring*. Trondheim: Tapir.
Blonskij, P. P. (1971). Hvad er en 'arbeidsskole'? In: R. Myhre (Ed.), *Store pedagoger i egne skrifter. V. Europeisk reformpedagogik i det 20. århundre* (p. 105-111). Oslo: Fabritius & sønner.
Bloom, B. S. (Ed.). (1956). *Taxonomy of Educational Objectives. The Classification of Educational Goals. Handbook I: Cognitive Domain*. New York: David McKay.
Cooper, V. A. (2009). Intercultural student interaction in post-graduate business and information technology programs: the potentialities of global study tours. *Higher Education Research & Development, 28*(6), p. 557-570. doi: 10.1080/07294360903208112
Dalsgaard, C. (2011). Personlige læringsmiljøer: Universitetsuddannelse på internettet. *Dansk Universitetspædagogisk Tidsskrift, 6*(11), p. 9-13.
Dewey, J. (1997). *Experience and Education*. New York: Touchstone.
Dickie, C., & Jay, L. (2010). Innovation in postgraduate teaching: mixed methods to enhance learning and learning about learning. *Higher Education Research & Development, 29*(1), p. 29-43. doi: 10.1080/07294360903421376
Dillon, J. T. (2009). The questions of curriculum. *Journal of Curriculum Studies, 41*(3), p. 343-359. doi: 10.1080/00220270802433261
Durey, A., Lin, I., & Thompson, D. (2013). 'It's a different world out there': improving how academics prepare health science students for rural and Indigenous

practice in Australia. *Higher Education Research & Development, 32*(5), p. 722-733. doi: 10.1080/07294360.2013.777035

Frey, K. (1984). *Die Projektmethode*. Weinheim: Beltz.

Giddens, A. (1991). *Modernity and Self-Identify*. Cambridge: Polity.

Gundem, B. B., & Hopmann, S. (Eds.). (1998). *Didaktik and/or curriculum: an international dialogue*. New York: P. Lang.

Guskey, T. R. (2013). Defining Student Achievement. In J. Hattie & E. M. Anderman (Eds.), *International Guide to Student Achievement* (p. 3-6). London: Pouthledge.

Handal, G., & Lauvås, P. (1987). *Promoting Reflective Teaching: Supervision in Practice*. Milton Keynes: Open University Press.

Hansen, S. B. (2008). Asynkron e-læring: Skriften på nettet? *Dansk Universitetspædagogisk Tidsskrift, 3*(6), p. 40-44.

Hanson, J. M., & Sinclair, K. E. (2008). Social constructivist teaching methods in Australian universities – reported uptake and perceived learning effects: a survey of lecturers. *Higher Education Research & Development, 27*(3), p. 169-186. doi: 10.1080/07294360802183754

Hattie, J. (2009). *Visible Learning. A synthesis of over 800 meta-analyses related to achievement*. London: Routledge.

Haugsbakk, G., & Nordkvelle, Y. (2007). The Rhetoric of ICT and the New Language of Learning: a critical analysis of the use of ICT in the curricular field. *European Educational Research Journal, 6*(1), p. 1-12. doi: http://dx.doi.org/10.2304/eerj.2007.6.1.1

Heimann, P. (1976). *Didaktik als Unterrichtswissenschaft*. Stuttgart: Klett.

Helmke, A. (2009). *Unterrichsqualität und Lehrerprofessionalität. Diagnose, Evaluation und Verbesserung*. Seelze-Velber: Klett-Kallmeyer.

Hiim, H., & Hippe, E. (2007). *Læring gennem oplevelse, forståelse og handling: En studiebog i didaktik*. København: Nordisk.

Holtz, K. L. (2008). *Einführung in die systemische Pädagogik*. Heidelberg: Carl-Auer-Systeme.

Hopmann, S. T. (2007). Restrained Teaching: the common core of Didaktik. *European Educational Research Journal, 6*(2), p. 109-124.

Jensen, T. (2006). Dansk Universitetspædagogisk Tidsskrift – derfor! *Dansk Universitetspædagogisk Tidsskrift, 1*(1), p. 1-3.

Johannsen, C. G. (2011). Kritik af evidensbevægelsen. http://www.danskbiblioteksforskning.dk/2010/nr2-3/johannsen.pdf

Juel, H. (2010). The Individual Art of Speaking Well – teaching it by means of group and project work. *Dansk Universitetspædagogisk Tidsskrift, 5*(8), p. 23-28.

Keiding, T. B. (2008). Projektmetoden - en systemteoretisk genbeskrivelse. *Dansk Universitetspædagogisk Tidsskrift, 3*(5), p. 22-29.

Keiding, T. B. (2010). Observing Participating Observation - A Redescription Based on Systems Theory. *Forum: Qualitative Social Research, 11*(3), Art 11. http://www.qualitative-research.net/index.php/fqs/article/view/1538/3041

Keiding, T. B. (2013). Læreteoretisk didaktik. In A. Qvortrup & M. Wiberg (Eds.), *Læringsteori og didaktik* (p. 353-373). København: Hans Reitzels.

Keiding, T. B., & Qvortrup, A. (2014). *Systemteori og didaktik*. København: Hans Reitzels.
Keiding, T. B., & Qvortrup, A (2015). The didactics of higher education didactics. *Teaching in Higher Education (Submitted)*.
Kerschensteiner, G. (1971). Kritikk av den herbartianske metode og det produktive arbeid som nyt metodisk princip. In: R. Myhre (Ed.), *Store pedagoger i egne skifter. V. Europeisk reformpedagogikk i det 20. århundre*. Oslo: Fabritius & sønner
Klafki, W. (1998). Characteristics of critical constructive didaktik. In: B. B. Gundem & S. T. Hopmann (Eds.), *Didaktik and/or Curriculum. An International Dialogue* (p. 307-330). New York: Peter Lang.
Klafki, W. (2000). Didaktik analysis as the core of Preparation of Instruction. In: I. Westbury, S. T. Hopmann, & K. Riquarts (Eds.), *Teaching as Reflective Practice. Ther German Didaktik Tradition* (p. 139-159). London: Lawrence Erlbaum.
Klafki, W. (2001). *Dannelsesteori og Didaktik – nye studier*. Aarhus: Klim.
Knight, P. (Ed.). (2004). *Assessment for Learning in Higher Education*. Oxon: RouthledgeFalmer.
Kobayashi, S., Grout, B., & Rump, C. (2013). Interaction and learning in PhD supervision – a qualitative study of supervision with multiple supervisors *Dansk Universitetspædagogisk Tidsskrift, 8*(14), p. 13-25.
Krathwohl, D. R., Bloom, B. S., & Masia, B. B. (Eds.). (1964). *Taxonomy of Educational Objectives. The Classification of Educational Goals. Handbook II: Affective Domain*. New York: David McKay.
Künzli, R. (1998). The Common Frame and the Places of Didaktik. In: B. B. Gundem & S. T. Hopmann (Eds.), *Didaktik and/or Curriculum*. New York: Peter Lang.
Künzli, R. (2000). German Didaktik: Models of Re-presentation, of Intercourse, and of Experience. In: I. Westbury, S. Hopmann, & K. Riquarts (Eds.), *Teaching as a reflective practice : the German Didaktik tradition*. Mahwah: Lawrence Erlbaum.
König, E., & Riedel, H. (1973). *Systemtheoretische Didaktik* (3 ed.). Weinheim und Basel: Beltz.
Lave, J., & Wenger, E. (1991). *Situated Learning: Legitimate Peripheral Participation*. Cambridge: Cambridge University Press.
Luhmann, N. (1990). Anfang und Ende: Probleme einer Unterscheidung In N. Luhmann & K. E. Schorr (Eds.), *Zwischen Anfang und Ende. Fragen an die Pädagogik* (p. 11-23). Frankfurt am Main: Suhrkamp.
Luhmann, N. (1995). *Social Systems*. Stanford: Stanford University Press.
Luhmann, N. (2002a). The Cognitive Program of Constructivism and the Reality That Remains Unknown. In: W. Rasch (Ed.), *Theories of Distinction. Redescribing the Descriptions of Modernity* (p. 128-152). Stanford: Stanford University Press.
Luhmann, N. (2002b). *Das Erziehungssystem der Gesellschaft*. Frankfurt am Main: Suhrkamp.
Luhmann, N. (2002c). Deconstruction as Second-Order Observing. In: W. Rasch (Ed.), *Theories of Distinction. Redescribing the Descriptions of Modernity* (p. 94-112). Stanford: Stanford University Press.

Luhmann, N. (2002d). The Paradox of Observing Systems. In: W. Rasch (Ed.), *Theories of Distinction. Redescribing the Descriptions of Modernity* (p. 79-93). Stanford: Stanford University Press.
Mager, R. F. (1962). *Preparing Instructional Objectives*. Palo Alto: Fearon.
Meyer, H. (1994). *Was its guter Unterricht?* Berlin: Cornelsen Scriptor.
Mezirow, J. (1991). *Transformative Dimensions of Adult Learning*. San Francisco: Jossey-Bass.
Mitchell, I., & Mitchell, J. (2008). The Project for Enhancing Effective Learning (PEEL): 22 Years of Praxis ... In: A. P. Samaras, A. R. Freese, C. Kosnik, & C. Beck (Eds.), *Learning Communities In Practice*. n.p.: Springer.
Moos, L., Krejsler, J., Hjort, K., Laursen, P. F., & Braad, K. B. (Eds.). (2008). *Evidens i uddannelse?* København: Danmarks Pædagogiske Universitetsforlag.
Murray, R. (Ed.). (2008). *The Scholarship of Teaching and Learning in Higher Education*. Maidenhead: Open University Press & McGraw-Hill.
Myhre, R. (Ed.). (1971). *Store pedagoger i egne skifter. V. Europeisk reformpedagogikk i det 20. århundre*. Oslo: Fabritius.
Möller, C. (1973). *Technik der Lernplanung*. Weinheim Beltz.
Neill, A. S. (1960). *Summerhill: A Radical Approach to Child Rearing*. New York: Hart Publishing Company.
Nordenbo, S. E., Larsen, M. S., Tiftikçi, N., Wendt, R. E., & Østergaard, S. (2008). Lærerkompetanser og elevers læring i barnehage og skole – Et systematisk review utført for Kunnskapsdepartementet, Oslo. København: Danmarks Pædagogiske Universitetsforlag og Dansk Clearinghouse for Uddannelsesforskning.
Piaget, J. (1970). Piaget's theory. In: P. H. Mussen (Ed.), *Carmichael's manual of child psychology, Vol. 1*. New York: Wiley.
Qvortrup, A., & Keiding, T. B. (2014). Undervisningens vidensdomæner: erfaring, didaktik og uddannelsesvidenskab *Dansk Universitetspædagogisk Tidsskrift, 9*(17), p. 6-19.
Ramsden, P. (1992). *Learning to teach in higher education*. London: Routledge.
Reed, M. J., Kennett, D. J., Lewis, T., Lund-Lucas, E., Stallberg, C., & Newbold, I. L. (2009). The relative effects of university success courses and individualized interventions for students with learning disabilities. *Higher Education Research & Development, 28*(4), p. 385-400. doi: 10.1080/07294360903067013
Richardson, V. (2003). Constructivist Pedagogy. *Teachers College Record, 105*(9), p. 1626-1640.
Ruiz-Primo, M. A., & Furtal, E. M. (2006). Informal Formative Assessment and Scientific Inquiry: Exploring Teachers' Practices and Student Learning. *Educational Assessment, 11*(3-4), p. 205-235.
Rust, C. (2002). The impact of assessment on student learning *Active learning in higher education, 3*(2), p. 145-158.
Röhrs, H. (Ed.). (1982). *Die Reformpädagogik des Auslands*. Stuttgart: Klett-Cotta.
Skinner, B. F. (1974). *About behaviorism* New York: Knopf.
Terhart, E. (2003). Constructivism and teaching: A new paradigm in general didactics? *Journal of Curriculum Studies, 35*(1), p. 25-44. doi: 10.1080/00220270210163653
Thomsen, R., & Nordentoft, H. M. (2012). Kollektiv Akademisk Vejledning - et

bud på en ændret organisering af vejledningen på universitetet. *Dansk Universitetspædagogisk Tidsskrift, 7*(12), p. 106-116.
Thorp, H. C. (2011). Udvikling af kursus i konceptsyntese for forskellige ingeniørstuderende. *Dansk Universitetspædagogisk Tidsskrift, 6*(11), p. 32-38.
Thøgersen, U. (2011). Samskabelse af engagement – om fastholdelse af de studerendes deltagelse i undervisning. *Dansk Universitetspædagogisk Tidsskrift, 6*(10), p. 45-51.
Tight, M. (2004). Research into higher education: an a-theoretical community of practice? *Higher Education Research & Development, 23*(4), p. 395-411. doi: 10.1080/0729436042000276431
Tight, M. (2008). What's the point of it all? Researching and writing higher education. *Uniped, 31*(4), p. 61-69.
Tight, M. (2012). *Researching Higher Education*. Maidenhead: McGraw-Hill.
Trigwell, K., Martin, E., Benjamin, J., & Prosser, M. (2000). Scholarship of Teaching: A model. *Higher Education Research & Development, 19*(2), p. 155-168.
Uden, L., & Beaumont, C. (2005). *Technology and Problem-Based Learning*. London: Information Science Publishing.
UNESCO. (2005). Toward knowledge societies: UNESCO World Report. Conde-sur-Noireau, France: United Nations Educational, Scientific and Cultural Organization.
von Cube, F. (1999). Die kybernetisch-informationstheoretische Didaktik. In: H. Gudjons & R. Winkel (Eds.), *Didaktische Theorien* (p. 57-74). Hamburg: Bergmann+Helbig.
Weinert, F. E. (2000). Lehren und Lernen für die Zukunft - Ansprüche an das Lernen in der Schule. *Pädagogische Nachrichten Rheinland-Pfalz, Heft 2/00 - Schulleben Schulkultur, 2,* p. 1-16.
Westbury, I. (2000). Teaching as a Reflective Practice: What might Didaktik Teach Curriculum. In: I. Westbury, S. Hopmann, & K. Riquarts (Eds.), *Didaktik as a Reflective Practive. The German Didaktik Tradition* (p. 15-39). London: Lawrence Erlbaum.

# Student notes as a mediating tool for learning in school subjects

*Torben Spanget Christensen*

## Student notes - a mediating tool and a tool for identity shifts[1]

How do fifteen year-old students approach learning when they begin upper secondary school? And how is this approach connected to their demonstration of maturity and willingness to assume responsibility for their own education? This kind of questions kept emerging during a four-year longitudinal and ethnographic study that followed two students in their transition from Danish lower to upper secondary school[2] and they constitute the focus of the sub study presented in this chapter. During this sub study, one observation continued to surface: students approach learning by writing notes. However, upon observing the notes, I discovered a disparity between the significance the students attach to them and their perception of them as their own making on the one hand and their reliance on teaching and textbook examples and wording on the other hand. This disparity fuelled my interest in what roles student notes play and represent an underlying source of curiosity throughout the analysis. Two learning functions of note-writing appeared relevant to focus, one relating to a shift in identity, and one on learning particular contents in the disciplines. The two are probably closely linked; learning a subject can be viewed as a process of gradually becoming part of a new disciplinary community which involves a gradual enculturation into the disciplinary discourse and thereby imply identity changes. In the chapter focus is on the interconnectedness of learning particular contents in the disciplines and identity changes. When focusing on learning contents identity changes is constantly implied and when focusing on identity changes the character of learning content is the underlying premise.

## Analytical concepts

The notes I examined generally resembled information on the blackboard or transcripts of the teacher's words during the lessons. For this reason, it seemed reasonable to question whether the students were creating or simply copying their notes (cf Danielsson 2010). A recent study of university students (Castelló et al. 2005) identifies two approaches to note-writing – the copying and the strategic approach – and claims that, on average, students are situated halfway between the two. This suggests that there is more to note-writing than mere copying. We can also ask the following question: what level of literacy is required to write independent notes that can be recognised as relevant and adequate within a subject community? When learning a new subject, a student will most likely make more primitive notes than when writing about a subject he/she knows well. If independence is defined as critique, it could prove unattainable for some students. Macken-Horarik establishes a continuum that ranges from 'personal growth literacy' to 'skill literacy', 'specialized literacy' and ultimately to 'critical literacy' (Macken-Horarik 1998, p. 78). She argues that, within school, critical literacy must be approached through the three previous mainstream literacies. According to this theory, the 'independence' of student notes must be measured in light of the student's placement on the continuum. We could therefore speak of critical note-writing literacy as the goal of note-writing literacy, and not as a precondition. To some extent, this accords with the social-cognitive approach, which views note-writing as self-regulated learning (SRL) (Moss 2009). From a SRL perspective, independent note-writing comprises a series of skills—planning and goal setting; metacognitive awareness and monitoring of cognition; selection of cognitive strategies; cognitive judgments and reflections—that students are either able or unable to master.

According to Gunther Kress, we should reject the idea of copying altogether: "when we make our signs we make them as (relatively) new combinations of form and meaning. This goes right against the common sense of most theorists as much as of the man and woman in the street, who assume that we *use* language, not that we *make it*. By complete contrast I wish to insist that we always make new signs – often imperceptibly different, even to the maker, and rare conscious, even to the maker" (Kress 1997, p. 7) [Italics in original]. When students write notes, they make language. They do not simply take the teacher's language; even if they use the teacher's sentences, they select appropriate sentences and re-contextualise them into their own notes. From Kress' socio-semiotic perspective, note-writing—like all writing—is always independent in the sense that it is a product of the writer's own selection and making. But it is also dependent insofar as the selection and making are miming already existing linguistic conventions. As Kress puts it: "... we make our always new signs in the environment of our constant interactions; but we make them out of the old, available stuff." (p. 7-8). In this sense note-writing is an interaction or a mediating tool between the writers' language and the linguistic conventions already in place.

The mediating tool is a socio-cultural concept that dates back to Vygotsky and Luria's concept of symbolic tools. Vygotsky and Luria believe that learning is mediated either by human mediators (for example, adults and teachers) or by symbolic tools. Symbolic tools are culturally transmitted tools which, according to Vygotsky and Luria, change the entire system of the learner's cognitive processes (Kozulin 2003, p. 24). Examples of higher-order symbolic tools are numbers, letters and graphs, but also more complex tools such as formal education and other organised learning activities (p. 17). The learner's interaction with the environment does not occur by itself but is necessarily mediated, and the use of symbolic tools serves as media for this process. Note-writing can be understood as such a tool that mediates between the school subjects and learners.

## Method

This chapter explores the role of note-writing by examining the practices and attitudes of two male students, Michael and Rasmus, whom I observed and interviewed in their educational contexts over a four-year period. This study focuses specifically on their transition from lower secondary school (folkeskole) to upper secondary school (gymnasium) in Denmark.[3] Michael attended the General Upper Secondary Programme and Rasmus attended the Higher Commercial Examination Programme. Michael is fairly communicative, and it was he who first alerted me to the note-writing disparity when describing the significance he attached to his notes. Rasmus was less forthcoming, and he gave me no reason to assume a disparity existed. For this reason,

I decided to develop a note-writing hypothesis based on Michael and to test it on Rasmus.

Focus for the overall study was writing of all kinds in all subjects. Data was generated by ethnographic methods, i.e. classroom observations, ongoing interview with students (meaning conversation-like interviews conducted sometimes monthly), collection of prompts, student texts and teacher responses. Also general observations at the schools and talks with teachers etc. were included. Observations in classroom were fixed to an observation scheme and general observations at the schools were maintained in field reports. All data were shared in a group of four researchers, who each generated data at various schools following other students. Data was continuously discussed among the researchers. Field reports were shared and often commented instantly by the researchers. Each researcher followed two (three) students from year nine till the end of upper secondary school (four years all together). Three lower secondary and eight upper secondary schools were included in the project.

In this sub study two students are analysed. Both followed in the four year period by the author of this article. Data used for this sub study are primarily from their first half year of upper secondary school. In the case of Michael the data set used consists of 14 classroom observations in various subjects, 5 interviews, 75 student notes from various subjects and 4 field reports. In the case of Rasmus the data set consists of 13 classroom observations in various subjects, 3 interviews, 38 student notes from various subjects and 9 field reports. In both cases some data from year nine is also included.

It is very demanding for the students and for the researcher to conduct such a study, and it is inevitable that students to some extent will have a role as co-researchers - or at least co-analysts. In the research group we referred to the students as participants – not as informants.

## Danish institutional context

The transition from lower to upper secondary school is viewed as particularly important for the student's self-understanding. This is because it involves a significant (and arguably a cultural) change; for the first time students encounter subject teachers holding a master degree, they face the prospect of exams, and they make their first crucial decisions regarding their future education. Upper secondary school demands more independent student behaviour due to a somewhat stronger academic focus in teaching. For this reason, the transition represents a serious and potentially daunting prospect for a fifteen year-old student.

In a similar longitudinal study that observed the transition of four American students from high school to college, Linda Harklau (2001, p. 45f) suggests that the most salient difference in literacy practices and cultural assumptions between the two educational levels are lecture and note-writing conventions. However, Harclau's discussion of note-writing practices in US high school reveals a marked difference from note-writing practices in Danish upper secondary school. In US high schools, note-writing practices are more teacher-controlled through the use of scaffolding note-writing methods. Danielsson (2010, p. 4) describes two enculturation methods to writing genres. One is implicit and the other is explicit *"[Students] participate in a rich textual and linguistic environment, thus being given various opportunities to learn genres inductively. Or it could involve more explicit teaching"*. The predominant method with respect to note-writing in Danish upper secondary school tends to be implicit. Students are thus encouraged to initiate and develop their own note-writing style. Although Danish student advisors provide note-writing courses, these are rarely directly linked to practices in specific subjects. Moreover, teachers seem reluctant to demand note-writing, since their expectation is that student development is connected to the student's ability to initiate note-writing independently. In educational research, it is therefore assumed that the importance of the transition from lower to upper secondary school is characterised by shift in school writing culture (Christensen et al. 2014, Harklau 2001, p. 51f) rather than shift in educational level per se.

For the students, a central question is how to respond adequately to this new and implicit expectation of note-writing. Their answer involves a change in study behaviour that implies a change in how they perceive themselves and how they wish to be perceived; in other words, it involves issues of identity (Sfard et al. 2005, Ivanič, R. 1998, Christensen 2015).

## Research questions
The above mentioned disparity between the significance the students attach to their note-writing and their reliance on teaching and textbook examples and wording is based on empirical data which showed that, although student notes do not look independent and although institutional factors support—and implicitly insist on—note-writing, students still attach great importance to their notes and claim to write them on their own initiative. This suggests that, with the move to a more academic education, there is a pressure on students to meet increasingly challenging demands with regard to literacy competencies and note-writing; this is not immediately apparent upon a first examination of the notes themselves. In order to explain why students attach so much value to their notes, two central research questions are addressed:

- Can note-writing serve as a mediating tool between everyday language and subject discourse language?
- Can note-writing function as a tool for a shift in identity from school child to student?

## Hypothesis
I would like to put forward the hypothesis that, in the transition from a less academic education to a more academic education, student notes represent the first attempts to capture the rhetorics and conventions of new disciplinary and genre challenges. This hypothesis suggests that two related aspects or learning strategies are at stake, which may jointly explain that student notes seems to be of great importance to the student (process of writing) but do not look like much (product of writing). One could be labelled an *acquisition strategy* and the other a *participation strategy* (Sfard 1998). The two strategies imply one another.

## Research on note-writing
Current research on student notes attempts to understand note-writing from either a cognitive position or a socio-cultural position, and it can be divided into at least four partly overlapping traditions. The first

tradition focuses on *cognitive variables;* for example, encoding, storage and recall of lecture information (Moss 2009, Kobayashi 2005, Boch and Piolat 2005, Santa et al. 1979, Rickards et al. 1978); the second tradition focuses on the *quality of notes*; for example, the degree of accordance between what is taught and what is represented in the notes, either as investigations into experimental teacher-led efforts to improve note-writing skills (Çetingöza 2010, Eskritt et al. 2008, Boch and Piolat 2005, Castelló et al. 2005, Dezure et al. 2001, Anderson et al. 1981) or investigations of authentic student notes written under non-teacher-led naturalistic conditions (Clerehan 1995); the third tradition focuses on *roles and strategies of note-writing*; in other words, whether note-writing is a way to organise the content taught, a direct tool for better understanding and retention of the content taught, or a more indirect way to approach content and subjects (Teng 2011, Castelló et al. 2005, Badger et al. 2001); and the fourth tradition—found in new literacy studies—focuses on *writing as text production in a social context* (Gee 2008, 2009, Blåsjö 2010, Danielsson 2010, Harklau 2001, Ivanič, R. 1998,) and *writing as multimodal communication* (Kress 1997, Jewitt ed. 2011), which allows us to consider other functions of note-writing than those related to a specific content to be learned, such as student positioning towards academic genres and subjects and the use of various modalities. This study takes its theoretical point of departure in the new literacy tradition, viewing note-writing as imbedded in school writing cultures, subject writing cultures and student writing cultures (Christensen et al. 2014); however, it is also interested in specific functions of note-writing, including knowledge-transforming (Castelló et al. 2005) and concept-forming (Vygotsky 1986).

## Student attitudes towards notes – the case of Michael

As mentioned I followed Michael for four years, from year nine and all the way through upper secondary school. In an interview a few weeks after he started upper secondary, it became clear to me that note-writing played an important role in his transition. Michael was enthusiastic about his notes and, according to him, he wrote them on his own initiative. He spoke about them with pride. From the very outset of the interview, Michael was keen to tell me about his notes, even though I had not prompted this discussion (in fact, I had to ask him to wait until I had switched on the recorder). This eagerness demonstrated the importance he attached to his notes. However, as Michael already knew me well from year nine it is likely that he viewed me as an acquaintance from lower secondary school now visiting him in upper secondary school, a fact that could account for some of his eagerness. Anyway, Michael had a great deal to say. The first sentences I recorded are transcribed below:

> I: You were telling about OneNote- can you repeat what you said?
> M: Yeah, okay. So - to summarise. This program, Microsoft OneNote, has been out since 2007. And it is simply brilliant to write notes in. It allows me to keep overall control over school, home and everything. (...) It has also allowed me to set up various subjects under different tabs and onto these tabs I can draw an infinite number of sites, where I can draw all over, and write, and just throw images in and out, and move everything around. So it is simply so easy and so convenient when you have to sit and write many notes as I have to here [in upper secondary school].
> (Interview, Michael 26.08.10)

Michael is enthusiastic about OneNote, but his underlying message is that it is imperative for him *to write lots of notes*. When asked if he wrote notes because the teachers demanded it or because he found it necessary, he answered promptly: "It's necessary!" (Interview, Michael 26.08.10). And, when I later concluded that note-writing in upper secondary school is more demanding than in year nine, that his approach to notes seems to have changed from year nine, and that the attitude and climate in the classroom towards notes had significantly changed from year nine, he agreed and added his support:

> M: That's it. It's a totally different world.
> I: Yes
> M: And I like it.
> (Interview, Michael 26.08.10)

Michael's enthusiasm indicates that note-writing represents a way to deal with his new position as an upper secondary school student, a way to respond adequately to the challenge of showing maturity and willingness to assume responsibility, and therefore a way of handling the identity work involved in the transition from lower to upper secondary school. When asked about this, he explained:

> M: No, in fact they [the teachers/TSC] don't demand [that we write notes/TSC], and there are also some students in the class who don't write many notes (...) [but] I can see that it is simply necessary. (...), only in the last three weeks we have received so much information (...) about how the school works and about the fact that we have started upper secondary school (...). There are so many things you constantly need to think through, and then it helps if you can write them down. (Interview, Michael 26.08.10)

In this quotation, Michael reveals that he is aware of the actions of his fellow students, and he uses their behaviour to support his own; in other words, he generalises his own behaviour as the common and the sensible. According to him, the majority of his classmates write notes. His attention to this indicates that note-writing is not simply a way to learn or retain knowledge in pursuit of other purposes directly related to teaching and learning, but also a way to signal (and try out) the transformation from school child (in lower secondary school) to student (in upper secondary school). This suggests there is a strong identification and positioning element at stake.

I also asked Michael an open question about his most significant writing experience since starting upper secondary school (less than three weeks prior to the interview). His answer was insightful. He began by stating that, since the class had not yet begun to write assignments, his most significant writing experience had been taking extensive notes.

> I: Is that new compared with year nine? (...)
> M: (...) that you have to write notes? You simply need to write notes (...). These three weeks I've written more notes than I did in two months in year nine. In fact, you rarely had to write notes then. (...). Let's take maths; you don't sit and write notes in maths in year nine (...), but you do in upper secondary school, because there are just a few more things to keep track of. Even [in] music you write notes from time to time, although not quite as much, because I am studying music at level C. But I can imagine that if you are studying at level A, then much of it will be theory ...
> (Interview, Michael 26.08.10)

When I later investigated Michael's claim, it appeared that the increase in note-writing was not as dramatic as he perceived it (Interview, 26.08.10). An examination of his notes revealed that Michael had written far fewer notes in his first three weeks of upper secondary school than he suggested. Contrary to his recollections, Michael wrote many notes in year nine. He wrote handwritten notes for German (46 pages), Danish (39 pages), history (31 pages), biology (4 pages) and English (4 pages). In addition to these, Michael wrote notes on pre-printed forms—such as gap-fill, multiple choice and short answer exercises—in biology, geography and social science (and most likely also in science, but these were not included in the data). He also wrote provisional computer notes in the form of a retrieval of information and preparation for presentations in various subjects, including an interdisciplinary project.

An interview with Michael in year nine shows that, even at this stage, he already had a relatively developed view on notes.

> M: It's something I do myself. We used to have a terrible history teacher. She had all notes [written] before we started, and wrote them on the blackboard, and then we had to sit and write it down.
> And it worked terribly, I think, because, even if I have all these sentences, it doesn't make me better. I still have to read the whole chapter again, because it wasn't what I thought when I heard or read it, and it is not what I would focus on.
> (Interview, Michael 25.02.10 - Folkeskole)

As early as year nine, Michael perceives note-writing as an act of his own and associates learning effects with independent note-writing. This suggests that even highly reflective students experience a cultural shift from lower to upper secondary school and an associated increased demand for independent note-writing.

## Actual and perceived note-writing - the case of Rasmus

It is also possible to identify a disparity between actual and perceived note-writing in the case of Rasmus. Like Michael, Rasmus also claims to write notes on his own initiative:

> I: Do the teachers tell you to write notes, or is it something you do by yourself?
> R: It's something you definitely choose yourself.
> (Interview Rasmus 29.09.10)

Rasmus' perception can be contested by the local school writing culture. Students are permitted to bring their notes to the oral exam, which suggests an institutionalised and expected note-writing practice (as illustrated below). But, despite this, Rasmus still perceives note-writing as an act of his own.

> I: What is the exam going to be like?
> R: We have to talk about what we learned in this period and then present our business ......... economic project.
> I: Is it an individual exam?
> R: Yes. It is individual, but we prepared it [the project] in groups, and then we are examined ......... individually.
> I: And you have prepared some notes, I understand. What if you didn't have any notes but had only read the textbook?
> R: Then I don't quite know what I would say at the presentation.
> (Interview Rasmus 14.10.10)

The subject writing culture also supported note-writing through the organisation of classroom instruction and the explicit recommendation that students bring their computers to class. During a conversation about tests in one of our interviews, Rasmus corrected my misapprehension that students were forbidden to bring their notes to the relatively frequent tests carried out in different subjects (Interview Rasmus 14.12.10). In the course plan for one of Rasmus' major subjects, business economics, students are advised to bring a computer. As such, the expectation that students write notes is so deeply embedded in upper secondary school culture that it does not receive explicit explanation. It is perhaps for this reason that I did not at first focus on note-writing during my observations. It appeared so obvious to me that I only occasionally noticed it. At one observation in marketing, Rasmus' second major subject, I wrote:

> Whenever a student is asked [by the teacher], he/she consults his/her notes on the computer.
> (Observation Rasmus 11.11.10)

It is clear that, even though the school writing culture and the subject writing cultures heavily support note-writing, Michael and Rasmus confidently state that note-writing is their own responsibility. They both present themselves as keen note-writers, which indicate that note-writing serves as an identification marker for their new status as upper secondary school students.

## Writing – Identification and positioning

To write is to express oneself about something in a context, and note-writing is no exception. Writing is an utterance, an answer to something, and a positioning of the writer socially (Smidt 2002). In business-economics, Rasmus cannot avoid positioning himself as a student, but he also strives to position himself as an economist, or at least a potential economist.

Roz Ivanič (1998) distinguishes between the writer's autobiographical self, discoursal self and authorial self (the self as author) as "aspects of the identity of an actual writer writing a particular text" (p. 23). By this, Ivanič means that nobody can write anything without these aspects being present. The autobiographical aspect refers to what the author contributes in terms of experience, values, perceptions and self-understanding (among other things) to the writing event. The discoursal self refers to how the writer wishes to appear (sound) in a text, and the authorial self refers to whether the writer assumes authority in the text or if he/she attributes authority to others. Ivanič also writes about possibilities for self-hood, which are "identities available in the socio-cultural context of writing" (p. 23). In school writing, these are normally offered in writing prompts. However, student notes have no prompts as such, so, instead, it is the students' responsibility to define the possibilities, to pose the questions their notes should answer, and to decide which genre their notes should live up to.

In Rasmus' third year in upper secondary school, we discussed what he liked about business economics. He mentioned that his history teacher once described history as a reductionist subject compared to

Danish, and he also considered this description very appropriate for business economics and marketing. He said:

> R: That's what I like, because somehow there cannot be much doubt whether my arguments hold true. You can say, in Danish, you hold a broader view and there may be some disagreements about how to judge something.
> I: And this reductionism suits you well?
> R: Certainly, yes.
> (Rasmus Interview 08.03.13)

What Rasmus expresses in this quotation corresponds to the picture I formed of him throughout the years of observation. This is something he contributes as part of his autobiographical self. But it is also how he strives to present himself, at least in economic subjects. When Rasmus writes, he tries to approach the economic discourse. An economic text should be brief, factual and precise – verbally reductionist, we could say. Viewed in this way, his minimalistic student notes from business economics (see below) correspond to his autobiographical self, but they are also an expression of his discoursal self (how he wishes to present himself) and, ultimately, they are how he positions himself with authority as 'an economist writer'.

## Student notes as discursive learning

As part of this study, I investigated Rasmus' business economics notes from the first half-year of upper secondary school. Business economics is a discipline Rasmus appreciates highly. From his first half-year, I collected 26 examples of handwritten notes from business economics (more than half the notes I collected); each example represented one lesson, so I had close to a complete set of notes in business economics. 20 out of the 26 examples contained the word 'opgave' (meaning 'task' or 'problem') in the title, indicating that students should solve a task given by the teacher or the textbook. In an interview conducted a few weeks after starting upper secondary school, Rasmus and I discussed the differences between lower and upper secondary school; just as I was beginning to conclude, Rasmus reminded me that, apparently, I had forgotten to discuss the new subjects in upper secondary school.

> I: New subjects, of course, what about the new subjects?
> R: They are incredibly exciting
> I: Can you mention some?
> R: Business economics, marketing and ICT
> I: These are the ones you like the best?
> R: Yes, and we also learn a different kind of mathematics
> I: Different, how?
> R: It is not so much with fractions, but more algebra.
> (Interview Rasmus 26.08.10)

On the basis of his interest in economics—an interest he already expressed in lower secondary school—and his particular enthusiasm for business economics, there is reason to believe that his business economics notes will display clear signs of note-making (independent construction of notes). In the quotation below, Rasmus refers to his notes as self-made. In his first interview after starting upper secondary school, he mentioned that he used to find it difficult to use his own words and that he was improving in this respect. He repeats this statement in this second interview, where he specifically addresses business economics. However, he states that he takes more notes from the textbook in business economics than in marketing, because the textbook in business economics is easier to understand and, therefore, he can select the 'best bets', which he finds tempting but realises is not his ultimate goal.

> I: Do you pick from the text and write it ...?
> R: Some things – and then I use my own words. It's more of a mixture when I write
> I: A mixture of the words from the textbook and your own words?
> R: Yes
> I: Why do you mix?
> R: Because it can be difficult, at times, to reformulate a good sentence.
> I: I understand, but why don't you use the good sentence, then? Why don't you just take it?
> R: Well... maybe I want to clarify something – something the teacher has said. Besides, if we (...) have something specific, then I clarify it a bit. Then I write it with my own words.
> (Interview Rasmus 29.09.10)

In an interview from year nine, Rasmus claimed that he sometimes copied from the blackboard "because (...) what is written on the blackboard is pretty good" (Interview Rasmus 07.04.10 - Folkeskole). Apart from demonstrating that Rasmus (just like Michael) was a relatively reflective student in year nine, this also shows that, even when copying from the blackboard, he copied for a reason; we could therefore argue that this was not mere 'copying' at all. Rasmus only copies from the blackboard when he finds the blackboard worth copying.

In general, Rasmus struggles to write independent notes, but this is something he is striving to master. Rasmus finds it difficult to express his selfhood and take authority in his notes. We could also claim that he is trying to capture and participate in the economic discourse. This is a way of expressing his self, a process which can be called discursive learning.

The discursive learning strategy reveals itself as a shift that oscillates between the language he already has and the language of the subject discourse in which he develops his pre-scientific concepts (Vygotsky 1986) and transforms knowledge (Castelló et al. 2005). Note-writing functions as a mediating tool for this process (Kozulin 2003).

## Student notes as identification

The student notes I analysed can be described as oddly disjointed and minimalistic; they were lacking in words (some of them were almost wordless), half written, without narratives, broken in composition and contained other characteristics that rendered them utterly uninteresting and often meaningless to an outside reader. And it is clear that they were not written in order to communicate with anybody but the note-writer. They are in-text (Liberg 2008) and not designed for the teacher or anybody else to read.

Below are two sets of notes from the same lesson. The first example is of a task from the textbook with Rasmus' handwritten notes in the margins and below the text. The second consists of two handwritten graphs.

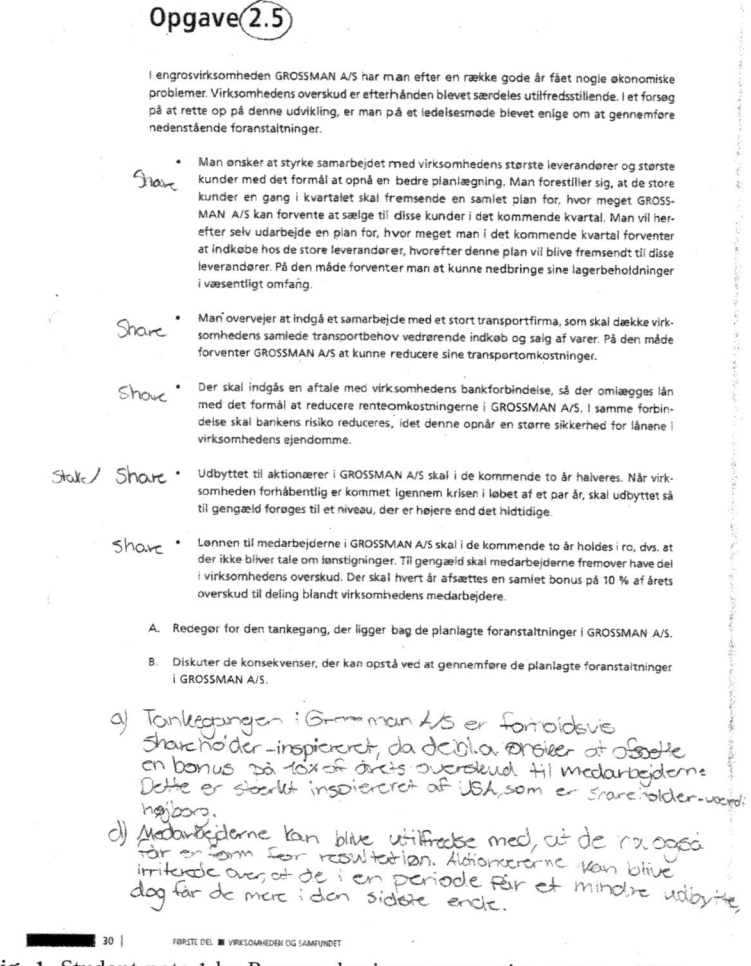

Fig. 1. Student note 1 by Rasmus, business economics, autumn 2010

The circle around "2.5" at the top of the page illustrates that Rasmus has marked the task as one to prepare for the coming lesson. In the margin, he has written 'Share' in connection with four of the bullet points and 'stake/share' in connection with one bullet point. It is unclear whether Rasmus wrote these notes while preparing for class or during class. Perhaps the handwritten 'share' and 'stake/share' suggest Rasmus' first step towards note-making and building an argument. We can only speculate. However, in any case, Rasmus found the information worth noting.

The two points *a* and *d* (most likely d is a mistake for b) are answers to the two questions that complete the task. In translation, they read:

a) The philosophy of Grossman Ltd is relatively shareholder-inspired, since it wants to allocate a bonus of 10% of its profits to employees. This is strongly inspired by the USA as the share-holder-value stronghold
d) Employees may be unhappy that they now receive some form of performance pay. Shareholders may be annoyed that in a period they receive a lower yield, but they get more in the end.

In this translation, I attempt to remain as faithful as possible to the Danish wording whilst disclosing the linguistic impression given by the Danish sentences. The wording of the two points is relatively close to the subject discourse in business economics. However, the word '*wants*' in the first point and the word '*annoyed*' in the second point are unlikely to appear in an economics textbook or on the classroom blackboard. Instead, the words '*wishes to* ' or 'dissatisfied with' would most likely appear in their place. Perhaps we can view Rasmus' wording here as a relatively successful attempt to participate in the subject discourse with a few remnants of an everyday linguistic discourse. The bullet list and his points "a" and "d" can be seen as his use of a writing practice in economics; in other words, making lists rather than formulating coherent texts.

On the back of the paper, Rasmus has hand-drawn two graphs that refer to another task (task 3.18)

206 · ON THE DEFINITION OF LEARNING

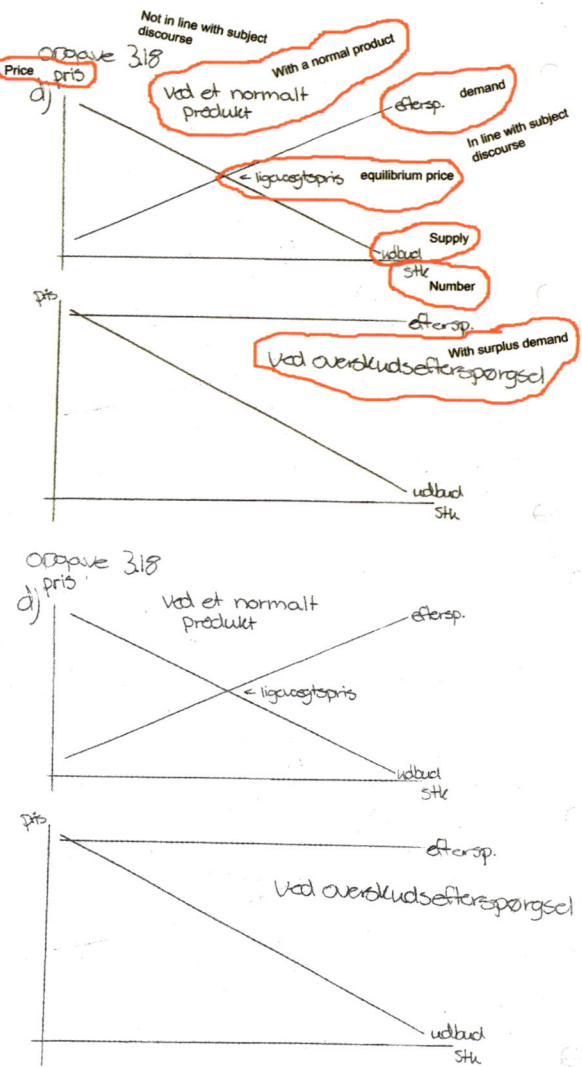

Fig. 2. Student note 2 by Rasmus, business-economics, autumn 2010

The graphs illustrate relations between supply and demand: price, quantity and equilibrium *'with a normal product'*, and *'with surplus demand'*. Graphs of this sort are what we would expect the teacher to draw on the blackboard; they are not something a student would devise by himself. However, in the subject discourse, we would not speak of a '*normal product*'. Instead, we would speak of '*perfect competition*', which is by no means 'normal' in the sense of frequently found or occurring, but refers to a theoretical ideal situation. For this reason, we may assume that these words represent Rasmus' more mundane reformulation (either intended or unintended). The expression '*with surplus demand*' written next to the second graph is in line with the subject discourse. Rasmus believes that his business economics notes can be categorised into *results and final answers*; unlike his Danish notes which, according to him, have a more reflective character.

> R: In socioeconomic subjects you could say there is a kind of result or final answer, and that's what I need to [jot down] and then come up with an interpretation of some of the things.
> (Interview Rasmus 14.12.10)

Considering these two note samples from business economics (note 1 and 2), we could initially conclude that Rasmus' notes resemble copying. However, a closer analysis reveals that they do not. Although Rasmus' notes resemble information from the textbook and at the teacher's blackboard, I would like to argue that they are still of his own making.

According to Rasmus' interview and my observations[4], the teacher talked a great deal during lessons and provided ample opportunity to make notes about arguments put forward or meta-notes about the student's own understanding. However, in his notes, Rasmus does not refer to any discussions or disagreements in class and he does not provide an insight into his own understanding. His notes are answers to questions (the two points a and d in note 1) and what he views as facts (the two graphs in note 2). He sticks to results and final answers.

It is also worth considering that Rasmus selected the mode 'graph' for his notes (Kress 1997, 2011). The primary modes employed by the teacher during the lesson were 'speech' and 'verbal writing'; however, of course, in business economics, 'graph' is also a prominent mode. From all these options, Rasmus selected the mode 'graph' for his notes, which is a distinctive mode of business economics. It is impossible to not interpret this selection as an act of note-making. By seeking the discourse of business economics in his note-writing (facts, final answers and graphs), Rasmus attempts to identify with (Ivanič 1998) and participate in (Sfard 1998) the academic and disciplinary community of his class and school.

## Conclusions

Rasmus struggles to make notes using his own words and therefore oscillates between his everyday language and the subject discourse language. It is difficult to remain within the subject discourse language, and arguably more difficult in subjects like business economics, which employ a minimalistic approach to the use of verbal text, as opposed to subjects like Danish, which create more space for notes of a reflective character. This demonstrates how Rasmus uses note-writing as a mediation tool in his effort to acquire subject content.

According to Rasmus and confirmed by observations, the students listen a lot to the teacher. Regardless of the origin of Rasmus' notes (textbook, teacher, class discussion, Rasmus) or whether the teaching encourages a certain type of (narrow) note-writing, Rasmus' notes are the result of what he has chosen to record from a large amount of textbook text, teacher presentation, blackboard information and class discussion. And it is clear that he has chosen to record 'results and final answers' using a graphical mode. His choice is important, because it is an expression of what *he* finds important to record, and he believes that 'results and final answers' and the graphical mode is important in business economics. In his notes, Rasmus writes as closely as possible to the subject discourse; he minimises his verbal language and embraces the graphical mode. This can be understood as an act of identification and participation.

For Rasmus, note-writing in business economics fulfills a learning function. Note-writing appears to be Rasmus' way to align everyday language with the language of the subject and a way to identify with and participate in the academic and disciplinary community of his class and school. In this way, Rasmus makes use of note-writing as a discoursal learning strategy, and he employs note-writing as a mediating tool in this endeavour.

It is also clear that Rasmus has not yet appropriated note-writing to a level that can be characterised as critical note-writing literacy. Note-writing is difficult for him because he needs to develop note-writing-literacy during the note-writing process.

One focus in the article is note writing functioning as a mediating tool between the students' everyday language and the language of the subject discourse. By looking for specific elements you always run a risk to over-emphasize them when you find them. And by observing writing in classrooms you encounter much writing, on which you can think: is it worth checking for independence and reflexivity let alone mediating functions. But our focus should not be blurred by the fact that students occasionally write notes that are less reflective, because they don't know what else to do – note-writing as something they more or less are expected to do and not as something they do in an effort to learn something new. If that's the case nothing or very little is mediated, you can argue. But a student might start with unreflective note-writing (writing because that's what you do – writing without any intention to learn) that at a given point turns into a more reflective process (writing because something catches your attention – writing with an intention to learn). The unreflective and the reflective parts must thus be seen as elements of one continuous process with varying mediating intensity at different time points. It makes no sense to split the two into separate processes, one infertile and one fertile. What thus may appear as ritualized and unreflective note writing may prove to contain non-ritualized and reflective moments which actually mediate between everyday language and subject discourse.

Compared to the two Sfard-inspired learning strategies acquisition and participation we are now able to characterize students' note-writing as the use of both. Note writing can be understood as an attempt to identify with and act as a member of the academic and disciplinary social community of the class and school, and note-writing can also – at least occasionally be seen as an attempt to align everyday language with the language of the subject discourse and thereby to capture and acquire the subject discourse.

We will now turn the attention back to Michael and his enthusiasm for writing notes himself and his awareness of the prevalence of his classmates note-writing. Although primarily used as an impetus for the analysis of the Rasmus-case, and therefore not analysed as thoroughly, the analysis still documents that an identity shift is at stake in the case of Michael, but also for Rasmus. In this sense the analysis shows that students' note-writing in general is (or can be) a way of constituting an identity shift: by writing notes and by showing others that I do write notes, I tell a narrative of myself as a competent or responsible student.

## Notes
1   The anthology as a whole has three foci; 1)Theory building within the field of learning theory, 2) the interplay between theories of learning and practices of teaching and 3) the relation between learning theory and empirical research. This chapter deals with issue 2. It does so by investigating the impact on learning of a little explored and often neglected student activity; note-writing, and it circles around the question of the role of note-writing in the learning process.
2   This study is part of a larger, four-year longitudinal and ethnographic study of student writer development: 'Writing to Learn and Learning to Write' (WLLW). This study was carried out by a number of researchers at the University of Southern Denmark and supported by the Danish Council for Independent Research (Christensen et al. 2014).
3   In this chapter, I refer to the Danish *folkeskole* as lower secondary school and the Danish *gymnasium* as upper secondary school.
4   Unfortunately I didn't observe this particular lesson.

## References
Anderson, Terrence N. & Glover, John A. (1981). Active Response Modes: Comprehension "Aids" in Need of a Theory. *Journal of Literacy Research* 13: 99 DOI: 10.1080/10862968109547399 http://jlr.sagepub.com/content/13/2/99.

Badger, R., White, G., Sutherland, P. & Haggis, T. (2001). Note perfect: an investigation of how students view taking notes in lectures. *System 29*, p. 405-417.

Boch, F., & Piolat, A. (2005). Note-taking and Learning: A Summary of Research. *The WAC Journal, Vol 16*.

Berge, K.L. (1988). *Skolestilen som genre. Med påtvungen penn*. Oslo: LNU/Cappelen.

Blåsjö, Mona (2010). *Skrivteori och skrivforskning – En forskningsoversigt*. MINS 56. Institutionen för nordiska språk. Stockholms Universitet.

Castelló, Montserrat and Monereo, Carles (2005). Students' Note-Taking as a Knowledge-Construction Tool *L1-Educational Studies in Language and Literature Volume 5, Issue* 3, p. 265-285.

Çetingöza, Duygu (2010). University students' learning processes of note-taking strategies. *Procedia Social and Behavioral Sciences 2* p. 4098-4108.

Christensen, Torben Spanget (2015). Susan – identitet og skriverudvikling i overgangen mellem folkeskole og gymnasium. Krogh, E. Christensen, T.S. & Jacobsen, K.S. red (2015). *Elevskrivere i gymnasiefag*. Odense: Syddansk Universitetsforlag.

Christensen, T.S., Elf, N.F. og Krogh, E. (2014). *Skrivekulturer i folkeskolens niende klasse*. Odense: Syddansk Universitetsforlag

Clerehan, Rosemary (1995). Taking it Down: Notetaking Practices of L1 and L2 Students. *Pergamon. English for Specific Purposes, Vol. 14, No. 2*, p. 137-155.

Danielsson, Kristina (2010). Learning Chemistry: Text Use and Text Talk in a Finland-Swedish Chemistry. *IARTEM e-Journal 2010* Volume 3 No p. 21-28

DeZure, Deborah, Kaplan, Matthew, and Deerman, Martha A. (2001). Research on Student Note-taking: Implications for Faculty and Graduate Student Instructors. N.p., n.d. Web. *Center for Research on Learning and Teaching (CRLT) Occasional Papers no 16*, University of Michigan.

Eskritt, Michelle, McLeod Kelle (2008). Children's note taking as a mnemonic tool. *Journal of Experimental Child Psychology 101* p. 52-74.

Evensen, L.S. (2010). En gyldig vurdering av elevers skrivekompetanse? Smidt, J., Folkvord, I., Aasen, A.J. (red.) (2010). *Rammer for skriving. Om skriveutvikling i skole og yrkesliv* p. 13-32. Trondheim: Tapir Akademisk Forlag.

Gee, J. P (2008). *Social Linguistics and Literacies – Ideology in Discourses.* 3rd edition. London and New York: Routledge Taylor & Francis Group.

Gee, J.P. (2009). Identity without identification. Carter, A., Lillis, T., Parkin, S. (eds.) *Why Writing Matters. Issues of access and identity in writing research and pedagogy* p. 45-46 Amsterdam, Philadelphia: John Benjamins..

Harklau, Linda (2001). From High School to College: Student Perspectives on Literacy Practices. *Journal of Literacy Research 2001 vol 33 no 1*, p. 33-70. DOI: 10.1080/10862960109548102.

Ivanič, R. (1998). *Writing and Identity. The Discoursal Construction of Identity in Academic Writing.* Amsterdam/Philadelphia: John Benjamins Publishing Company.

Jewitt, Carey (ed.) (2011). *The Routledge Handbook of Multimodal Analysis.* London and New York: Routledge Taylor & Francis Group.

Kobayashi, Keiichi (2005). What limits the encoding effect of note-taking? - A meta-analytic examination. *Contemporary Educational Psychology* 30 p. 242-262 doi:10.1016/j.cedpsych.2004.10.001.

Kress, Gunther (1997). *Before writing - Rethinking the paths to literacy.* London and New York: Routledge.

Kress, Gunther (2011). What is mode? Jewitt. Carey (ed.) *The Routledge Handbook of Multimodal Analysis* p. 54-67. London and New York: Routledge Taylor & Francis Group.

Kuzulin, Alex (2003). Psychological Tools and Mediated Learning. In: Kuzulin, Alex, Gindis, Boris. Ageyev. Vladimir S. and Miller, Suzanne M. (eds.) *Vygotsky's Educational Theory in Cultural Context* p. 15-38. Cambridge University Press.

Liberg, C. (2008). Skrivande i olika ämnen – lärares textkompetens. Lorentsen, R.T. & Smidt, J. (red.). *Å skrive i alle fag* p. 51-61. Oslo: Universitetsforlaget.

Macken-Horarik, Mary (1998). Exploring the requirements of critical school literacy – A view from two classrooms. In Christie, Frances and Misson, Ray (eds.) *Literacy and Schooling* p. 74-103. New York/London – Routledge.

Moos, Daniel C. (2009). Note-taking while learning hypermedia: Cognitive and motivational considerations. *Computers in Human Behavior 25.* p. 1120-1128.

Rickards, John R. and Friedman, Frank (1978).The Encoding Versus the External

Storage Hypothesis in Note-taking. Contemporary Educational Psychology 3. p. 136- 143.

Santa, Carol Minnick, Abrams, Lindsay and Santa, John L. (1979). Effects of Notetaking and Studying on the Retention of Prose. *Journal of Reading Behavior Vol. XI, No. 3*.

Sfard, Anna (1998). On Two Metaphors for Learning and the Dangers of Choosing Just One. *Educational Researcher 1998 27: 4*. DOI: 10.3102/0013189X027002004 (http://edr.sagepub.com/content/27/2/4).

Sfard, Anna and Prusak, Anna (2005).Telling Identities: In Search of an Analytic Tool for Investigating Learning as a Culturally Shaped Activity. *Educational Researcher Vol. 34*, No. 4, p. 14-22.

Smidt, Jon (2008). Skriving og skriveformål – barns og unges veier til ulike fag. Lorentzen, R. T. & Smidt, J. (red.) (2008). *Å skrive i alle fag* p. 22-36. Oslo: Universitetsforlaget.

Smidt Jon (2002). Double Histories in Multivocal Classrooms: Notes Toward an Ecological Account of Writing *Written Communication* 2002 19: 414 DOI: 10.1177/074108802237753.

Teng, Huei-Chun (2011). Exploring Note-taking Strategies of EFL Listeners. *Procedia Social and Behavioral Sciences 15*. p. 480–484.

Vygotsky, Lev (1986). *Thought and Language.* (revised and edited by Alex Kozulin). Massachusetts Institute of Technology.

# What's space to learning?
Exploring ways of investigating learning from a spatial perspective

*Rie Troelsen*

## Introduction - what do we know so far on the interplay between space and learning?

Churchill once said: "We shape the buildings, and then the buildings shape us", indicating the interplay between space and its occupants. In an educational setting this means that both students and teachers are influenced by the physical contexts in which learning occurs. Nevertheless, so far there hasn't been an overwhelming focus on the furnishing of classrooms (and built environment as a whole) in universities as being of importance to the student learning experience (Temple 2008). In this chapter preliminary findings from a small-scale research project are presented aiming at exploring ways of investigating learning from a spatial perspective. The research project focuses on teachers' perceptions of the impact of space on their personal experiences of learning – that is, how teachers shape the room and how the room then shapes their teaching.

All though the spatial conditions for learning in university settings is an under-researched topic there has been a lot of interest into designing learning spaces at primary and secondary school level. Research demonstrates that quality in school buildings can have a positive impact on achievement and, in particular, on teacher and pupil behaviour (Clark 2002). Most of this research, however, is less likely to establish direct causal between spatial features and educational outcomes than to show how physical conditions indirectly affect pupil outcomes. In a higher education setting the little focus on learning spaces there so far has been, concentrates on designing spaces for a new generation of students and according to "new" views on learning (Bennett 2006; Grummon 2009; Jamieson 2003; Villano 2010). It is argued that the traditional lecture theatre manifests particular power relations between teacher and students and that interactive or group-based learning cannot occur in lecture halls (Jamieson 2003). New learning spaces, on the contrary, should be designed as adaptable, flexible, multi-dimensional, accesible and secure in order to meet the needs of students learning in a collaborative, active and problem-based way (Jamieson, Dane, & Lippman 2005).

Recently, the focus of literature on learning spaces in higher education is not just on designing them, but also on evaluating them. Reviews on evaluations (Pearshouse et al. 2009; Temple & Barnett 2007) reveal that even though evaluations focus on student experiences as a means to understand the effectiveness of a particular learning space, they lack any theoretical background from research on the interplay between space and learning. Hence, many evaluations can still be described as conventional post-occupancy evaluations, such as surveys on students' experience of comfortable chairs, appropriate brightness and temperature in the room or visibility between desk and blackboard (Bligh & Pearshouse 2011).

This chapter strives at creating ways of investigating the impact of space on learning by exploring how teachers perceive the kind of learning possible in a particular space. The interplay between space and learning has in this way the teacher as the intermediate given that the teacher – in the learning space of this project at least - is the planner and facilitator of learning activities.

## Methods – how can space be analysed?

The relation between space and the activity taking place in the space is often regarded as binary; either the space "works" for the social activity planned to take place or it doesn't work. However, the relation is much more complex and it is naïve to imagine that any specific architectural design should work at all times, for everybody or for every reason. One way of analysing the complex relationship between space and its occupation is proposed by Lefebvre (1991) in his famous "spatial triad". The first aspect of the triad is the *spatial practices*; the routines and unconsidered actions that both are formed by and constitute the space – what you do and are able to do in for example a public swimming pool's changing room. The second aspect is *representations of space*; the conceptualisations of space done by architects, city planners or engineers through maps, plans, models or designs. Lefebvre's third aspect is *representational space*; the way people intervene with and try to adapt space to their own purposes using the symbols and images of the space. Lefebvre also calls this triad the *lived*, the *conceived* and the *perceived* space and he argues that the production of space is a "trialectical" negotiation between these three aspects – space is not only decided on by architects or city planners, but space is also produced by the way people use it and by the meaning they inscribe on to it.

The meaning-making of space requires some form of visual literacy. The signs, symbols, images, affordances (Gibson 1977) of a given space all communicate meaning to the user. To focus on the grammar of visual design is hence also important in order to understand how space influences its occupants. Kress and van Leeuwen have worked with visual grammar as a means to understand how meaning is communicated through spatial configurations (Kress & Leeuwen 1996). In this context the concept of visual grammar is interesting, not only as the tool of designers of learning spaces, but also as a way for the users of a learning space to describe their perception of the space – their *representational space*. When describing an object, physical or semiotic, Kress and van Leeuwen label this act as sign-making, and they see "representation as a process in which the makers of signs [...] seek to make a representation of some object or entity [...] and in which their interest in the object, at the point of making the representation, is a complex one arising out of the cultural, social and psychological history of the sign-maker and focused by the specific context in which the sign is produced."(Kress & Leeuwen 1996, p. 6)

Building on both Lefebvre and Kress I suggest a three-fold methodological framework for investigating the relation between space and teachers' view of learning:

- Lived space – observational studies of how teaching proceeds focusing on how teachers and students use the learning space in a teaching situation
- Conceived space – teachers' sketching their perception of the learning space and analyses of these sketches as to which elements are drawn and in which order
- Perceived space – interviews with teachers describing actions and activities that can and will take place in the learning space

Four teachers were interviewed in semi-structured sessions of approximately 45 minutes. The interview guide consisted of four themes:

- How does the space look like – make a sketch
- How do you usually teach in this space?
- How are you going to teach in this space next time?
- Could you teach in the same way in another space?

Furthermore, two of the teachers' teaching sessions in the space were observed. Due to time constraints, it was impossible to observe the teaching sessions of the remaining two teachers.

## Results – what's space to learning?

All four teachers (Kathryn, Alan, Daniel and Andrew – anonymised names) taught in the same space (fig. 1).

In the centre of the space a table is placed with a main computer that is connected with several screens on the walls. Along the walls eight oval tables with computers are placed. Four to eight chairs are placed around each table. In the back of the room, there is an open space with no tables or chairs. Here, some of the teachers put up catapults and other experimental designs to use in their teaching. Other teachers leave the space empty. On the carpet there is three squares made of masking tape. The room has windows on two sides and the remaining walls are painted in a green colour. The chairs are also green.

All the teachers identify the group tables, the electronic equipment and the open space as distinct features of the learning space. In the following, data from the interviews and observational studies are presented and analysed according to these three features with significant implications for the teaching and learning processes in the space. Quotations from the teachers are in italic.

Fig. 1. The learning space where all four teachers taught.

## Group tables

The tables placed around the room are for students. One teacher, Kathryn, describes these tables as places where "*students work*" (not sit), and another teacher, Andrew, highlights the group tables as working stations where he "*just gets everyone working and kind of walk around just helping people on the spot*" instead of a "*lecture-type teaching*". These two teachers use the group tables as vehicles for student-centred learning processes. Kathryn is a firm believer of problem-based learning and project-based teaching and her entire course is designed with that in mind. The students work in groups on a project formulated by them but within a framework introduced by the teacher. During the course Kathryn asks the students to participate in exercises and games to help them onwards in their projects or to give them subject input. She uses brown paper and wooden bricks to make the students visualize their thoughts and knowledge and is very conscious about creating an atmosphere of safety and trust among the students in order for the group work aspect of her teaching to succeed. The tables make group work possible and ensure and prompt students and teacher to use movement as part of the teaching and learning. At the time of the observation the students are working in groups on their project (fig. 2)

Fig. 2. Students discussing their project in Kathryn's class.

and Kathryn and a teaching assistant are present to answer questions from the groups. It is a very informal teaching session running for three hours where the students work at own pace and with different media; some type on a computer, some draw concept maps on brown paper and some students just talk. If the groups have any questions the teacher and the teaching assistant discuss with them, sometimes for 30 minutes and sometimes just for two minutes. The students and teachers seem comfortable and trusting in each other's company in the physical setting. In Andrew's class the students partly work on questions set out for them beforehand and partly do small computer-based experiments together. If he thinks that a question is very important he'll *"stop and hop on the screens, perhaps grab a mike and tell everyone."* He prefers, however, to have the students work on the questions in a *"self-directed"* way. At the time of the observation the students sit in groups around a computer and a screen (fig. 3). There is a very informal atmosphere and students are talking and laughing and moving in and out of the room during the session. Andrew and the teaching assistant also move

Fig. 3. Students discussing an assignment in Andrew's class.

around the groups both to answer questions and to ask if there are any questions.

The two other teachers also point to the group tables as distinct features of the room. Alan points to the informal settings as being connected with his teacher role as not the expert providing students with the answers but the facilitator in the process of teaching the students how to learn and think for themselves. He sees the group tables as important for his philosophy of "*sharing not teaching*". However, the electronic equipment in the space makes Alan uncomfortable and prohibits his use of the group tables to enhance independent learning processes because this, in his view, requires him to use the computer at the lecturer desk. Daniel also recognizes the group tables as the main reason for the space being flexible, enabling teachers and students to walk around and probably being designed for students to work in groups, but he hasn't been introduced to teaching methods relevant to the space. Daniel would like "*to really adapt to the room*" but doesn't know how.

In all, the shape of the group tables, the moveable chairs around them and the in-built computers all signal student-centred, interactive and collaborative learning. The room is pointing to no particular spot for the teacher to be located and is signalling to the students that they are not there just to listen. The spaces for students being at the same level as the desk of the teacher point to a more equal distribution of the "right answers" and learning activity as opposed to the traditional lecture hall with its one-dimensional view on the active performer and the passive audience. All though the group tables is recognized by all teachers to correspond to interactive and collaborative learning processes, not all teachers respond in the same way to these spatial settings. In the cases of Alan and Daniel, the potential impact of the group tables on interactive learning processes are acknowledged, but the teachers feel intimidated by the electronic equipment in Alan's case and the perceived necessary new teaching methods in Daniel's case – an intimidation that also affects the learning processes.

### The electronic equipment

The main computer at the desk in the center of the room is connected to several screens along the walls. This is for every student at the group tables to see what the teacher chooses to show on the main computer. At every group table there are also several computers with screens for the students to work on, individually or in groups. Teachers mention that the students can *"see things you put up, and they can also do things themselves on the screens in front of them."* The desk in the centre – the teacher's desk – contains various electronic equipment; different kinds of computers, document cams, audio techniques and microphones. Andrew uses these tools without hesitation as they help him creating an atmosphere of sharing and having fun. The students work on small exercises and the results from the exercises are projected on the screens for everybody to see. The exercises are *"meant to be fun, not particularly difficult. This is straight out of high school, so there is a big knowledge gap. Some students are very strong in math and physics and others are very weak."* The electronic equipment in the room makes it possible for Andrew and his students to coordinate and cooperate in their learning processes. Quite the opposite is true for Alan. He uses an OH projector with a camera that captures what he's writing and projects his problem solving on to the screens on the wall. At too many occasions he has experienced that the electronic devices in the room didn't work and with too few whiteboards located where all students could see them, he has come up with the OH-solutions as a safe, dependable way of communicating. Alan is not comfortable in this room because of its electronic dependency and has actually asked to teach next semester's tutorials in another room with only whiteboards. Alan describes himself as "*not that reliant on electronics*" and prefers to teach in a room with no screens even though the room is considerably smaller – he will just have "*to stuff the students in*". The most important aspect of teaching to Alan is the ability to "*bond with the students*" so that they are encouraged to ask and answer questions. It seems that the electronic equipment of the given space somehow comes in the way for Alan to create that bond.

Again, the spatial conditions are not deterministic as to which learning processes take place. Andrew feels comfortable using all kinds of electronic aids to enhance the collaboration between the learners, Alan would rather teach in a smaller and darker room in order to get rid of the intimidating electronic equipment and be able to pursue interactive and bonding learning processes.

## The open space

The open space in the back of the room is recognized by all four teachers as a significant part of the learning space but only used by two of the teachers. Kathryn uses the floor to do exercises where students must position themselves according to their beliefs and feelings towards e.g. sustainability. She includes games in her teaching to "*make it fun and surprising*". The same "fun factor" is also important to Andrew. The workshop Andrew teaches consists of two parts; a computer exercise part and a "*lab component*". In the second part of the workshop he and his teaching assistant will set up a little catapult and a target plate in one end of the room. The students have in groups been asked to model the process of a ball hitting the target plate using the catapult, and Andrew will set up the catapult according to the students' settings. The students "*get marked if they hit the target or not.*" The workshop is divided into two because "*it's kind of a long roll – if you keep asking questions they'll get bored.*" The lab component is simply more fun. And fun is important "*to keep them motivated.*" At the time of the observation the students either stand around the catapult watching the process or sitting by their computers to prepare or refine their model used in the catapult exercise. Students who have come up with answers to the model exercise quickly, start by the catapult while other students still work on the modelling at their computer. In this way, the space and the exercise that make students stand up and move to other parts of the space lend itself to an informal and unofficial assessment; by noticing which group of students changing position in the room you can de-code which students understand/learned the theoretical concepts connected to the exercise and which students don't (yet). Andrew needs the floor space – not just for the catapult experiment but also for other experiments during the semester that require floor space (Lego robots following masking tape tracks). The two remaining teachers acknowledge the open space but do not use it. Daniel is aware of the space he is teaching in but mostly as an awareness of the possibilities that the space provides that he as a teacher doesn't take advantage of; *"We're not using the room's full potential; we're doing a standard tutorial workshop and this room is not designed for that."* What it is the space is designed for, he's not sure, he just *"knows that something's missing."*

Both Andrew and Kathryn use the open space to create variation in their teaching methods and hence also in the learning processes involved. Exercises and hands-on experiments in the open space require movement and the students to be physical active and thereby boost motivation and concentration. The open space being such a prominent element of the learning space without being able to take advantage of it frustrates both Daniel and Alan. The very flexible learning space points to new and different ways of learning, but Daniel and Alan has lost their sense of ownership of the space. This lead them to plan and conduct teaching in this *new* learning spaces on the grounds of learning views more relevant for teaching in *traditional* spaces. Or like Daniel puts it: *"We teach with old paradigms in new learning spaces".* In this way space in itself becomes a hindrance for learning.

## Discussion – views on space as views on learning?

In the above, the spatial practices of learning are described through exploring how teachers act in and perceive the impact of space on learning. The third part of the methodological framework was to explore

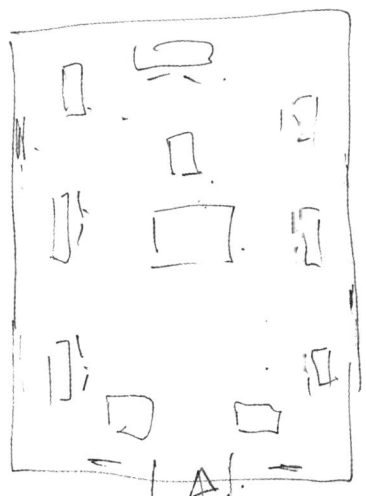 

Fig. 4. Daniel's sketch of the learning space. Numbers indicate the order in which elements are drawn.

Fig. 5. Andrew's sketch of the learning space. Numbers indicate the order in which elements are drawn.

the conceived space, that is to have teachers sketch their perception of the learning space as the method enables other expressions of meaning than talking or writing about learning spaces (Mavers, 2011). It is interesting to note that the four teachers sketch the same space in different ways and the components of the space in different orders. Andrew draws masking tape on the floor in his sketch of the space (fig. 5), but Daniel doesn't (fig. 4). The conceived space is thereby a visualisation of the components in the space that is important in the planning of learning processes – Daniel doesn't use the masking tape, so he doesn't draw it. Likewise, the teachers differ by the order in which they draw components of the space. Alan starts by drawing the windows and the teacher's desk (fig. 7), but Kathryn starts by drawing where the students are placed (fig. 6) which could be indications of teacher-focused and student-centred approaches to learning, respectively. In this way the sketches of learning spaces triangulates the data from the interviews and observations.

Bringing information together from how teachers use learning spaces, how they sketch the learning space and how they describe their intentional use of a learning space in a Lefebvrian sense the production

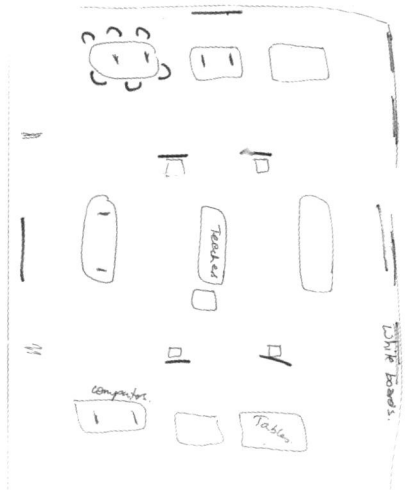 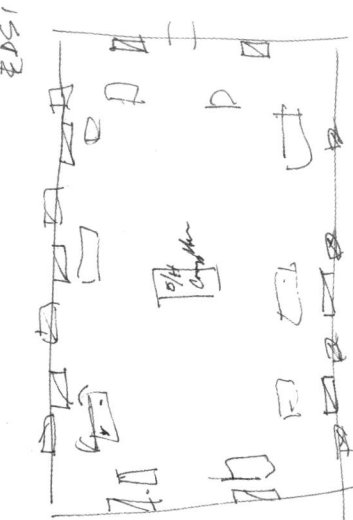

Fig. 6. Kathryn's sketch of the learning space. Numbers indicate the order in which elements are drawn.

Fig. 7. Alan's sketch of the learning space. Numbers indicate the order in which elements are drawn.

of a mental learning space comes to life which mimics the production of the physical learning space. By exploring the spatial practices of learning in this threefold way we might add to our knowledge of the kinds of learning taking place – at least from a teacher's perspective. A next step would be to apply the method on students; ask students to sketch and describe their learning space together with observations on the actual use of the learning space.

Taking the results on the interplay between space and learning further on to the didactical implications, the results show teachers including considerations on space in their planning and conducting of teaching as they consider (and try out) possible and impossible teaching methods in the given space. The four teachers interpret, however, the possibilities and limitations of the same space in very different ways. Some focus on the distribution between floor space and tables in the learning space while others focus on the space's technical devices as opposed to its whiteboards. Some teachers focus on how colours, light and non-hierarchical furnishing in the space create an informal and safe atmosphere, while electronic equipment in the space creates a scary and unsafe atmosphere for other teachers. Seen through the lens of the didactical relation model (Hiim & Hippe 2007), space is a framing factor in understanding what happens in a teaching situation and why. Framing factors are given conditions that either limit teaching or make teaching possible and can be rules and regulations, time of day, number of students – or the physical space in which teaching takes place. As with all framing factors, space as a didactical category is related to the prerequisites of the students, the learning objectives, the content, the learning process and the evaluation. In this project it is clear that teachers' perceptions of space are related to their former experiences and views of learning. Alan has had experiences of electronic equipment breaking down and hence prefers a space without technical solutions even if it means less room for the students and for him as a teacher to act out his teaching philosophy of creating relationships with the students as a prerequisite for learning. Kathryn describes the space with its group tables and no obvious place for the teacher to stand as underpinning her teaching philosophy of learning as a social practice. Hence, the physical space either inhibits or enhances the didactical space of action for the teachers to plan and conduct activities that produces student learning.

The findings also point to recommendations of creating ownership for teachers and students of a learning space and its resources in order to enhance teaching that uses the full potential of a given learning space. The need for ownership is seen as crucial for teachers to accept and embrace (new) learning spaces (Melhuish 2010; Pearshouse et al. 2009) and recommendations are to include teachers in the design process of new learning spaces (Grummon 2009; Lippincott 2009). One might argue that the lack of ownership leads to an annulment of the interplay between space and learning. In this project, the learning space in question is not a *new* learning space, where teachers have had (or haven't had) the opportunity to get involved in the design process. Even so, the cases of Daniel and Alan show that ownership perhaps also can be established by providing teachers with instructions on how to use the space through courses, hands-on workshops, videos or pamphlets.

## Conclusion

This small-scale project has strived at exploring ways of investigating learning from a spatial perspective. By using a threefold method consisting of investigations of how teachers act in, conceive and perceive the impact of space on learning our understanding of the spatial practices of learning can be enriched. The method, however, does not only have the potential to enrich our/researchers' understanding of the impact of space on learning. Sketching and describing your learning space could also support the individual teacher in his/her reflection on views on and use of space and thereby expand teachers' didactical space for action. The results from the project indicate that teachers include space as a didactical category in their planning and conducting of learning activities, but that it is important for the teachers to feel some kind of ownership of the learning space in order not to teach despite of space. In a time where many learning spaces at university are rebuilt, renovated and redesigned this is an important point. Moving from traditional spaces, like the lecture theatre, recognisable to most teachers to more flexible learning spaces, like the space in this project, which point to new and different ways of learning, many teachers might become uncertain and lose their sense of ownership of the space. This might lead to teachers planning and conducting teaching in new learning spaces on the grounds of learning views more relevant for teaching in traditional spaces. In this way space in itself becomes a hindrance for good teaching and learning.

This chapter aimed at investigating the relationship between space and its occupants. Even though not traditionally acknowledged in higher education, space do play a role in teaching and learning, and the interplay between space and learning becomes clearer as learning spaces in higher education change. To rephrase Churchill, if we re-shape the buildings, then how do we shape up?

## References

Bennett, S. (2006). First questions for designing higher education learning spaces. *The Journal of Academic Librarianship, 33*(1), p. 14-26.

Bligh, B., & Pearshouse, I. (2011). Doing learning space evaluations. In: A. Boddington & J. Boys (Eds.), *Re-shaping learning: A critical reader. The future of learning spaces in post-complusory education* (p. 3-18). Rotterdam: Sense Publishers.

Clark, H. (2002). Building Education: The role of the physical environment in enhancing teaching and research. *Issues in pratice.* London: Institute of Education, University of London.

Gibson, J. J. (1977). The Theory of Affordances. In: R. Shaw & J. Bransford (Eds.), *Perceiving, Acting, and Knowing: Toward an Ecological Psycology*.

Grummon, P. T. H. (2009). Best practices in learning space design: Engaging Users. *EDUCAUSE Quarterly, 32*(1).

Jamieson, P. (2003). Designing more effective on-campus teaching and learning spaces: a role for academic developers. *International Journal for Academic Development, 8*(1/2), p. 119-133.

Jamieson, P., Dane, J., & Lippman, P. (2005). *Moving beyond the classroom: Accomodating the changing pedagogy of higher education*. Paper presented at the Forum of the Ausatralasian Association for Institutional Research.

Kress, G., & Leeuwen, T. v. (1996). *Reading images. The grammar of visual design*. London: Routledge.

Lefebvre, H. (1991). *The production of space* (D. Nicholson-Smith, Trans.). Padstow, Cornwall: Blackwell.

Lippincott, J. K. (2009). Learning spaces. Involving faculty to improve pedagogy. *EDUCAUSE review, March/April*, p. 17-25.

Mavers, D. (2011). Image in the multimodal ensemble. In: C. Jewitt (Ed.), *The Routledge Handbook of Multimodal Analysis* (p. 263-271). London: Routledge.

Melhuish, C. (2010). Ethnographic case study: perceptions of three new learning spaces and their impact on the learning and teaching process at the University of Sussex and Brighton. CETLD, Universities of Sussex and Brighton, and CETLD, School of Arts and Architecture, University of Brighton.

Pearshouse, I., Bligh, B., Brown, E., Lewthwaite, S., Graber, R., Hartnell-Young, E., & Sharples, M. (2009). A study of effective evaluation models and practices for technology supported physical learning spaces (JELS). Learning Sciences Research Institute at Nottingham University.

Temple, P. (2008). Learning spaces in higher education: an under-researched topic. *London Review of Education, 6*(3), p. 229-241.

Temple, P., & Barnett, R. (2007). Higher Education Space: Future Directions. *Planning for higher education, 36*(1), p. 5-15.

Villano, M. (2010). 7 tips for building collaborative learning spaces. *Campus Technology, 6*(1).

# Learning from a social practice theoretical perspective

*Maj Sofie Rasmussen*

## Introduction

With an outset in social practice theory (Holland & Lave 2009; Lave 2011) and substantialized by empirical research from *Fryshuset*,[1] the chapter offers an approach to the educational field that allows us to examine learning processes in their constitutive relations between persons, materiality, and social, historical, and political conditions. It is argued that this way of exploring learning may facilitate the conceptualization of expansive mo(ve)ments[2] (Mørck 2014) and the processes of becoming a legitimate member of the varied communities of practice at *Fryshuset* (Lave & Wenger 1991; Wenger 2004). Embedded in this conceptualization of learning lies a critique of conventional learning theories, which are understood as theories that enhance behavioral and cognitive dimensions of learning, e.g. empiristic and rationalistic schools of thought (Packer 1985), and seem to originate in dualistic views of the world-subject relationship (Nielsen 1999). These theories will, however, only be shortly touched upon throughout this chapter, since the aim is to discuss, illustrate and suggest how a social practice theoretical approach may contribute to the educational field, rather than giving a complete account of the learning theories that it challenges.[3] One point of criticism worth addressing here, though, is that conventional learning theories seem to ignore the historical, political contexts in and across which learning takes place, thereby separating learning processes from social life. As Lave argues (2011, 152f.):

> "...social life is not reducible to knowledge or even to knowing, but to collective doing, as what being is, as part of the lived-in world. Reducing activity to mental activity – acquiring, transferring, creating, transmitting, internalizing knowledge is not inclusive enough to identify where, how, or with what meaning the stuff we call 'knowledge' is part of social life. Knowledgeability is always part of situated social, historical being".

With this implicit critique of information processing theory and learning transfer, Lave introduces an understanding of learning that emphasizes collective, situational, and social dimensions, where learning 'something' is to change one's social existence towards becoming a member of different communities of practice (Lave & Wenger, 1991).

Before elaborating further on social practice theory, the following section will provide a short presentation of the empirical outset for this chapter, *Fryshuset*.

## Fryshuset – different ways of 'doing' school?

*Fryshuset,* which is often referred to as the largest youth center in the world, was founded in 1984 by Anders Carlberg among others. Initially it was a place where young people met to do sports and music, and gradually different social projects and educational programs were added to the agenda. Today *Fryshuset* runs both a high school and a lower-secondary school (as well as various other educational programs), and is the initiator of two exit programs (*Exit* and *Passus*). Common to both the educational programs and the many social projects is a conviction that in order to enable young people to explore their passions and find their way into society, values such as encouragement, confidence, responsibility and understanding are crucial (see www.fryshuset.se).

At *Fryshuset* the pupils' passionate interests[4] (basketball, dancing, music, skateboarding, and art) are part of the schedule three times a week (approx. 6 hours per week), and according to the head of the school they are considered just as necessary for the pupils' learning and development as the more academic subjects. However, being passionate is not exclusively linked to organized 'non-academic' activities: "reading books may also be a passionate interest" – as the head of the school emphasizes in an interview – but "developing your personality and your social competences is just as important for the students". According to her, this way of doing school and organizing learning environments attracts pupils who have previously experienced school from marginal positions and felt that they did not fit in. A considerable number of them come from socioeconomically disadvantaged families and may not get the necessary support from their parents. To many of these pupils the passionate interests and the communities around them are what motivate them to come to school and stay there as well:

> "One thing is that even if you're tired in the morning and don't want to go school, you go anyway because you want to skate, and then you stay... You stay and do your schoolwork even though you are not up for it" (Johan, 9th grade).

On the other hand, *Fryshuset* also attracts pupils from more privileged families, who deliberately choose *Fryshuset* because they have the opportunity to start pursuing a dream of becoming e.g. a professional dancer or basketball player while attending school and taking their exams.

As the American professor Ken Robinson points out, today's educational systems are marked by a so-called 'academic inflation' (Robinson 2012), and he requests that the students' creativity and 'non-academic' interests and passions are brought into focus to a much greater extent – both to avoid (further) marginalization of many students and to improve the educational system in general. Offhand, this is what *Fryshuset* is trying to do – but the question remains: how do the students experience this way of doing school, and how does it influence their possibilities for learning and participation across different contexts in and out of school? To explore these questions, this chapter proposes a social practice theoretical framework of learning, which will be elaborated in the following section.

## A social practice theory of learning

This paper draws on a social practice theoretical framework (Holland & Lave 2009; Lave 2011) that emphasizes the historical and material productions of persons in changing social practices and integrates concepts from Danish/German critical psychology (e.g. Dreier 2008; Mørck 2006; Holzkamp 1979) and situated learning theory (Lave & Wenger 1991). It originates in a Marxist understanding of 'praxis' (Lave 2011), which implicates that persons are understood as always material and embodied in the local practices in which they participate, and in their relations with other persons, things, and institutional arrangements. From a Marxist perspective, man is, thus, what he *does* [Bernstein

1971), and consequently, knowledge is regarded as inseparable from engagement in practice (Lave 2011, p. 152).

The notion of situated activity points to the assumption of how subjects, objects, and lives are made in relation to each other, and as Lave (2011, p. 152) writes: "..the contexts of people's lives aren't merely containers or backdrops, nor are they simply whatever seems salient to immediate experience".

'Praxis' or 'practice' is to be understood as "the encounter between people as they address and respond to each other while enacting cultural activities under conditions of political-economic and cultural-historical conjuncture" (Holland & Lave 2009, p. 3). In other words, practice is constituted by the actions of persons, who (re)produce and change the practice self-constituently through participation (Dreier 2008). The historically and politically produced relations thus create the conditions for how persons can participate in a specific practice.

Consequently, in a social practice theoretical understanding, learning is closely connected to the learner's participation in changing social practices and cannot be reduced to the accumulation of knowledge or a measurable outcome of teaching. Both the situational and relational character of social life are thus emphasized, and to understand social life – or, more specifically, understand and conceptualize learning – we cannot ignore the political and historical dimensions of these practices. Thus, in order to understand how and under which conditions possibilities for learning are produced in and across contexts within *Fryshuset*'s lower-secondary school, it is crucial to examine the school's historical, political-economic, and cultural-institutional position and how this may have changed and changes over time (Lave & Packer 2008). Through the politically and historically produced relations that Lave refers to above, possibilities and limitations for action and participation are created.

In the educational field this means that in order to understand and conceptualize learning we need to bring into focus the conditions under which learning is both made possible and/or limited, i.e. the relations between the institutional arrangements, political agendas, (non-)academic subjects, teachers, leaders, and the students themselves.

Woven into the core of the social practice theory presented here, Danish-German critical psychology (e.g. Dreier 2008; Mørck 2006; Holzkamp 1979) stresses the dialectical and mutually constitutive relation between the subject and the world. This chapter thus argues that learning is understood within a dialectical framework that does not oppose or separate subject and world, unlike some cognitive learning theories that rest on dualistic accounts and define learning as a matter of achieving better knowledge about the world and transforming knowledge into memory (Nielsen 2008b). Moreover, cognitive approaches tend to primarily study the learner's 'inner landscape', metaphorically speaking, and regard learning as a predominantly epistemological question. According to Nielsen (2006), Descartes' understanding of epistemology influences the way educational arrangements and situations are organized, i.e. on principles of moving from analysis of basic elements of a specific subject matter to a more complex recognition or synthesis. This process of achieving knowledge about the world is problematic, Nielsen argues (ibid. p. 211), since it decontextualizes the problems we encounter in order to reduce complexity.

From a social practice theoretical perspective, learning is studied and analyzed with an outset in the learner's perspectives on participation and (reasons for) action in and across different contexts, a so-called first-person perspective (Holzkamp 1983; Mørck 2006: 257).[5] When conducting empirical research, this means that trajectories of change and the ways in which we shape/are shaped into the persons we are and become through (more or less) participation in changing social practices over time are pivotal. If one accepts this position, the learner's perspectives on possibilities (and limitations) for action and learning, on meaningful mo(ve)ments, and on his or her changing participation in and across different social contexts are crucial in order to study learning at all.

In the following section two cases from my empirical study at *Fryshuset* will be presented in order to ground my theoretical arguments and illustrate what a social practice theoretical understanding of learning may allow us to capture when we move into the educational field. The cases are situated in the skater park and the classroom, respectively, and we follow a group of four male students, who are all skaters.

## Empirical cases: The skater park and the classroom

The cases below have been chosen because they illustrate how following students across learning communities within the school allows us to gain insight into how the students' participation changes and, thus, how different social and material arrangements constitute possibilities and/or limitations in relation to learning and participation. The cases derive from field notes conducted during observations.

*Case 1: The skater park*

> When I enter the skater park, a group of boys from 9th grade are waiting on the staircase and cheering on the 7th graders, who are about to finish their skating lesson. Instead of shouting or clapping, the 9th graders slam their boards onto the concrete floor to make loud noises. As soon as the 7th graders have left the skater park, the 9th graders jump onto their boards. The four boys from 9.X are all there. At first there are 12 boys skating, but eventually a few more arrive. They are all wearing helmets, and most of them are in baggy pants and a loose t-shirt. From the speakers loud jazz music is floating and mixing with the sounds of the skateboards. The skater park is spacious with several ramps and obstacles for the skaters to challenge themselves – but not once do the boys collide or get in each other's way. Watching the four boys from 9.X, I notice how engaged, focused and persistent they all are when practicing a trick on the board. They keep trying, and every time they fall on the ground they jump right up with a smile on their faces to give it another try. For an outsider like me, skating seems to be a rather individual activity at first glance, but I soon come to realize how interdependent the boys are – both in order to navigate among each other in a space which is unpredictable and possibly dangerous, and in order to be able to learn new tricks. (field notes)

*Case 2: The classroom*

> The subject is religion, and the students in 9.X are to work on questions relating to Buddhism. Prior to this class they have read a text about Buddhism, which will be the outset for the task. They are divided into groups by the teacher, and the four skater boys end up in the same group, because they already sit together. A fifth boy, Jason, whose passionate interest is basketball, arrives late and is asked by the teacher to join the skaters. Another group of three girls and a boy starts discussing the task. The other students leave to sit outside the classroom. The teacher follows

them, and the four skater boys start chatting to each other. Facing each other and turning their backs on the fifth boy, they stare at one of their phones, where – judging by the sound – a video is playing. With the textbook on his lap, Jason seems to be reading the text on Buddhism. He looks up at the skater boys several times as if to say, "let's start working on the questions", but he doesn't utter a word, and the four boys never pay him any attention. Not until the teacher arrives do the skater boys look up from the phone and turn to the book, but as soon as she leaves again, they are busy discussing the video. When the class ends they have barely done anything in relation to the task demanded by the teacher. (field notes)

In the following sections, the cases will be used to discuss the theoretical framework presented above in relation to how a social practice theoretical approach may contribute to our understanding of the empirical field when conducting educational research, as well as challenging more conventional theories.

## Participation and learning in and across socio-material arrangements

As argued above, persons engage in practices constituted by their social interactions, by structural arrangements, and by material objects (Lave 2011). This means that different arrangements offer different possibilities or conditions for learning and participation for different persons. Thus, the way persons participate may change across contexts, but their participation in one context will always be related to their participation in other contexts in some way. If we look at the two cases, there does not necessarily – at first glance – seem to be a link between how the boys participate in the classroom and the skater park, respectively. However, this assumption changes as I learn more about the skater culture in *Fryshuset*.

The skater teacher explains that when you are a skater, you can barely think of anything else. Skating is "the only thing on your mind", and the switch to e.g. an 'ordinary' lesson can be very difficult, because you are focused on the tricks you just managed (or failed to manage), and the embodied feelings connected to this leave you uneasy and restless. I later learn that this was exactly the case with the boys in the classroom, and that their attention was directed towards skater videos on YouTube. Their way of participating within the classroom, though it may be regarded as disengagement or laziness from a teacher's point of view, is therefore not necessarily an expression of 'participation in opposition' (Willis 2000) to school or academic subjects, and cannot be understood in isolation from their participation and engagement in the skater park (and other contexts). According to Dreier (2008, p. 90f), the socio-material arrangements that form educational institutions decide what is considered acceptable or appropriate, and consequently influence learning processes within e.g. a classroom:

> "The socio-material arrangements of ordinary classrooms affect the course and dynamics of learning processes in them [...] This arrangement [...] conjures up a special way of engaging with these abstractions that we call 'concentration', and which turns engaging in anything else, even in various contextual connections of the learning issue, into disturbances of the learning process thus arranged"

Having observed the same boys in the skater park, their participation within the classroom is more likely an example of what it means to be passionate about or truly engaged in *something*. As the skater teacher stresses, "skating is an addiction". Considering their participation unambiguously as a 'disturbance' is therefore a rather restrictive understanding that does not recognize or capture the fact that these students are actually engaged in 'something' that is meaningful to them and may be part of important learning trajectories – an understanding where so-called 'school learning' is considered the paradigm case of learning (Dreier 2008), and where learning does not reach beyond the structural arrangements of the classroom.

Exploring this further in practice, it turns out that the skater teacher and the other teachers do not share their different perspectives on the skater students with each other. Moreover, there seems to be a tendency among the academic teachers to categorize the skater students and explain their relatively passive way of participation in other subjects with an outset in what (from the skater teachers' point of view) seems to be a narrow understanding of what it means to be a skater – they are skaters, consequently they are lazy and disengaged. Paying attention to historical dimensions, as argued above, skateboarding is known to be a culture of oppositional character, and the skaters are often looked upon as outsiders, which may help us to understand the teachers' perspectives. The fact that the students *seem* passive and unfocused from a teacher's perspective only enhances the categorization. At the same time, this understanding of skateboarding as a so-called counterculture (Willis 2000) may prevent us from discovering how being a skater is not necessarily about acting in an anti-school manner and being unwilling to learn – on the contrary, it seems to be linked with high levels of engagement, success, and, as will be argued below, certain academic skills. In other words, the skater park seems to constitute an important but complex learning environment that, on the one hand, allows the students to immerse themselves in and participate actively in something they really enjoy – but on the other hand seems to influence their participation in other subjects, as the empirical examples suggest.

This complexity demands further attention and points to critical issues in the educational field: Which ways of participation are supported and/or limited in the classroom and, in this case, the skater park, respectively – and how/why? How do these different socio-material arrangements enhance or undermine each other in relation to the students' possibilities for learning and participation? Which understandings/categorizations of what it means to an 'appropriate' student are (re)produced across the different contexts, and how does this influence the students' possibilities for participation?

The empirical cases underpin the notion that in order to grasp and understand participation and learning we need to focus our attention on both the differences and the interrelatedness between learning situations which influence possibilities of participation and learning and the way we understand the students' participation. This means paying attention to how such situations are arranged structurally, socially, and materially, and following persons as they move and change within and across them. As Dreier (2008, p. 94) argues, "no context can then be grasped on its own, as an island, but must be analysed as being involved somehow in structural arrangements of social practice".

## Learning as expansive mo(ve)ments and social self-understanding

Mørck (2014) introduces the notion of learning as meaningful, expansive mo(ve)ments in and across different social contexts. This means that learning is analyzed through mo(ve)ments significant to the pupil's processes towards becoming more (or less) of a legitimate member in different communities of practice (Lave & Wenger 1991). A significant or meaningful mo(ve)ment could be the experience of actually 'being able' to contribute to and be recognized as a legitimate member of a community, e.g. the skaters, the basketball team, or the dance group – a position that may change the student's social self-understanding (Holzkamp 2013b) of himself or herself as a 'capable learner' and support learning processes in other contexts. The concept of *expansive learning* (Mørck 2010; Kristensen & Mørck 2014) is inspired by Engeström (1987) and Holzkamp (2013a). Engeström (1987) enhances the collective character of learning, whereas Holzkamp (2013a) distinguishes *expansive learning* from *defensive learning* – the former being in line with the student's interests – i.e. their orientations and personal trajectories (Dreier 1999) – and increasing his or her influence upon personal life conditions/quality, while *defensive learning* involves coping with particular external demands by demonstrating learning results (Holzkamp 2013a). According to Holzkamp (ibid. p. 124), *defensive learning* leaves the student "cut off from the perspective of a joint control over the living conditions" and without personal motives to learn. Holzkamp thereby creates an analytical dichotomy in order to stress that learning cannot be conceived as a direct result of teaching. As Nielsen (2008a, p. 178) puts it: "even the most perfect teacher cannot ensure that expansive learning takes place".

## Trajectories of learning

To some degree the two cases illustrate the distinction made by Holzkamp (ibid.). The students' personal trajectories (Dreier 2003) are clearly oriented towards skating (they also skate when not in school), and this influences their way of participation in the classroom and the skater park. In the skater park, the personal motives to learn are evident, though the object of learning, i.e. mastering different moves and tricks, is demanding and at times intangible. I realized this when I decided to learn the most basic skating skills myself, supported by one of the boys, Lukas. Besides the bodily challenges, e.g. keeping your balance, skating requires both mathematical and physical skills to move, turn, and make the board jump – both on the ground and on the ramps.

Furthermore, it takes a great deal of courage and patience. So learning to skate requires the students to engage fully in the processes involved. The more you engage in learning to skate, the more you want to learn, as one of the students underlines: "When I succeed in doing a new trick, I go 'yes, I did it', and then I want more challenge" (Victor, 9.Y). For him, mastering a trick constitutes an expansive moment or movement that not only increases his engagement in learning more and on a higher level – it also *moves* him towards becoming more of a legitimate member of the skater community, towards a feeling of belonging (Rabøl Hansen, 2011). Victor reports that: "The students, we are all friends, so we just skate, and when you miss a trick, the others cheer, and when you succeed, they also cheer, and you get happy". Moving into (and not away from) the community and the mutual support herein seems to influence the students' confidence and increase their independence when they move in and across the different social contexts within (and outside) *Fryshuset*.

Conceptualizing learning as expansive mo(ve)ments does not only contribute to the notion of learning being situated and not an abstract phenomenon – it also allows us to recognize that learning has a direction or a certain *telos,* as Lave puts it (Lave 1997). A direction that is linked to processes of *becoming* a person in the world instead of being oriented towards societally determined educational goals – and to the students' social self-understanding (Holzkamp 2013b), as unfolded in the next section.

## Understanding yourself and others

The notion of learning as processes of *becoming*-a-person, for instance in communities of practice, is inspired by Lave & Wenger (1991), and may be linked to Holzkamp's conceptualization of social self-understanding (2013b) as "meaning-making processes of coming to understand oneself and others in relation to participation in and conduct of everyday life" (Kristensen & Mørck 2014, p. 4). As presented in the section on *Fryshuset,* for some students being able to skate within the school plays a crucial role in their understanding of themselves as people who 'stay in school' and engage in school work. As argued above, becoming and being part of the skater community is in line with the students' personal trajectories, and this seems to have a significant impact on the way the students participate and engage, as the cases illustrate. So far I have argued that the skater students' way of participating in the classroom may be understood in terms of their embodied and cognitive engagement in skating, which to some extent may be considered addictive, according to the skater teacher. In other words, their (lack of) participation in class is 'excused' because they are so engaged in skating and have a hard time shifting their focus away from it. The question still remains, though, whether an understanding of oneself as 'a skater' and being part of the skater culture also connotes being 'disengaged', which tends to be the conclusion drawn by some of the academic teachers. Are the students perhaps reproducing an 'attitude of disengagement' because they are used to being considered lazy or unwilling? Or is their way of participating in the classroom to be understood as part of the process of becoming a skater?

A social practice theory of learning allows us to ask such questions in the empirical field and, thereby, capture how learning is connected not only to a sense of belonging and being part of 'something' meaningful, but also to the students' (social) understanding of themselves as *learners*.

## Concluding remarks

Throughout the chapter several questions have been posed. It is not within the scope of this chapter to answer every one of them, though. Instead, the purpose has been to illustrate how a social practice theory of learning may focus our attention in the empirical field, help us question what may seem obvious, and raise our awareness of the 'doings of learners learning' (Lave 2011, p. 89) in different social contexts, instead of focusing on individual, mental processes and teaching. But why is this important?

The chapter argues that the importance of the socio-material arrangements in which learning processes are both limited and made possible seems to be disregarded within conventional learning theories. Moreover, it is argued that an unambiguous focus on mental, decontextualized processes undermines the fact that different contexts offer different possibilities for participation and learning, and it overlooks how educational circumstances are interwoven with other aspects of life, such as the students' personal trajectories. Moving beyond binary distinctions that separate subject and world will allow us to gain insight into how learning is embedded in social practices, such as skating; and that in order to understand why students participate as they do in one context, the complexity of different learning activities needs to be examined. This has not been done sufficiently in this chapter, though.

Studying students' ways of participation in one context, in this case the skater park, may help us to understand how, why, and under which conditions they participate as they do in the classroom (and vice versa). Their positions, possibilities, and action potency change as they move across contexts, and the structural, socio-material arrangements vary from one context to another as well.

Throughout the chapter, the historical and material production of persons and their embodied participation in socially, historically, and politically structured institutional arrangements has been enhanced in order to stress the situational and relational character of learning and to articulate the dialectical relation between personal learning and social practice. The chapter argues that in order to understand and conceptualize learning, we need to understand how persons move and participate in and across various contexts. The empirical examples illustrate and underpin the importance of studying different socio-material arrangements and their interrelatedness – how do they support and/or undermine each other in relation to the students' participation and learning? The empirical cases moreover focus our attention on a notion of learning as expansive mo(ve)ments that support processes of becoming more (or less) a member of different learning communities. In the example presented above, being able to skate when *in* school and pursue what is most meaningful to them changes the students' understanding of 'school' as a social context in which they belong to different communities and engage in skating as well as staying in school to do school work instead of staying at home.

When moving into the educational field from a social practice theoretical perspective, it is worth stressing the importance of the learners' perspective, i.e. the above-mentioned first-person perspective (Holzkamp 1983). Conventional learning theories seem to ignore this perspective and thereby undermine both the socio-cultural, historical contexts as well as issues of meaning. Moreover, a theory of learning that enhances social and contextual dimensions will allow us to approach the educational field with a practice-oriented and less school-centric understanding, thereby capturing learning processes not only among dominant groups of social practice but also 'from the margins' (Mørck 2014).

## Notes

1. I have conducted participative observations and semi-structured interviews (12 students, 4 teachers, and the head of the school) and engaged in informal conversations with students in 9th grade, teachers, and the head of the school.
2. The concept of mo(ve)ments will be elaborated further.
3. See e.g. Nielsen (1999, 2008b) for a discussion of shortcomings in rationalistic and empiristic conceptions of learning and e.g. Anderson, Reder & Simon (1997) and Anderson, Greeno, Reder & Simon (2000) for further discussions on situated versus cognitive perspectives in learning.
4. The term *'passionate interests'* is *Fryshuset's* translation of the Swedish word 'passion'.
5. The students' first-person perspectives were pursued through observations, informal talks, and semi-structured interviews with both students and teachers.

## References

Anderson, Reder & Simon (1997). Situative Versus Cognitive Perspectives: Form Versus Substance. In: *Educational Researcher,* 1997, vol. 26, No. 1, p. 18-21.

Anderson, Greeno, Reder & Simon (2000). Perspectives on learning, Thinking, and Activity. In: *Educational Researcher,* vol. 29, No. 4 (May, 2000), p. 11-13.

Bernstein, R.J. (1971). *Praxis and Action.* Pennsylvania: University of Pennsylvania Press.

Dreier, O. (1999). Læring som ændring af personlig deltagelse i sociale kontekster. In: Nielsen, K. & Kvale, S. (red.). *Mesterlære. Læring som social praksis.* København, Hans Reitzels Forlag, p. 76-79.

Dreier, O. (2003). Learning in Personal Trajectories of Participation. In: Stephenson, N., Radtke, H., Jorna, R.J., & Stam, H.J. (eds). *Theoretical Psychology. Critical Contributions.* Corcord, Canada: Captus University Publications, p. 20-29.

Dreier, O. (2008). Learning in structures of social practice. In: Nielsen, Brinkmann, Elmholdt, Tanggaard, Musaeus, Kraft (Ed.). *A Qualitative Stance.* Aarhus University Press.

Engeström, Y. (1987). *Learning by expanding: an activity-theoretical approach to developmental research.* Helsinki: Orienta-Konsultit.

Holland, D. & Lave, J. (2009). Social practice Theory and the Historical production of Persons. In: *Actio: An International Journal of Human Activity Theory,* No.2, p. 1-15.

Holzkamp, K. (1979). Den kritiske psykologis overvindelse af psykologiske teoriers vilkårlighed. In: Dreier, O. (Ed.). *Den kritiske psykologi.* Copehagen: Rhodos.

Holzkamp, K. (1983). *Grundlegung der Psychologie*. Frankfurt/Main: Campus Verlag GmbH.
Holzkamp, K. (2013a). The Fiction of Learning as Administratively Plannable. In: Schraube & Osterkamp (Eds.). *Psychology from the standpoint of the subject. Selected writings of Klaus Holzkamp.* p. 115-132. Basingstoke: Palgrave Macmillan.
Holzkamp, K. (2013b). Psychology: Social Self-Understanding on the Reasons for Action in the Conduct of Everyday Life. In: Schraube & Osterkamp (Eds.). *Psychology from the standpoint of the subject. Selected writings of Klaus Holzkamp.* p. 115-132. Basingstoke: Palgrave Macmillan.
Kristensen, K. & Mørck, L.L. (2014). ADHD Medication and Social Self-Understanding in a Danish Primary School. In: *The European Journal of Psychology of Education* (special issue): *From the Personal to the Collective and Back: Exploring Learning as a Collective Process in and beyond the Classroom*, p. 1-8.
Lave, J. (1997). Learning, Apprenticeship, Social Practice. In: *Journal of Nordic Educational Research*, 17(3), p. 140-151.
Lave, J. (2011). *Apprenticeship in Critical Ethnographic Practice*. The University of Chicago Press, Chicago.
Lave, J. & Packer, M. (2008). An Ontology of Learning. In: Nielsen, K., Brinkmann, S., Elmholdt, C., Tanggaard. L., Musaeus, P., Kraft, G., (ed.). *A Qualitative Stance*, Aarhus University Press, Aarhus, p. 17-46.
Lave, J. & Wenger, E. (1991). *Situated Learning. Legitimate Peripheral Participation.* New York: Cambridge University Press.
Mørck, L.L. (2006). *Grænsefællesskaber – læring og overskridelse af marginalisering.* Roskilde Universitetsforlag. 1. udgave.
Mørck, L.L. (2010). Expansive Learning as Production of Community. In: Penuel & O'Connor (ed.). *Learning Research as a Human Science*, Vol. 109, Issue 1, p. 176-191, National Society for the Study of Education, Columbia University.
Mørck, L.L. (2014, in press). *'Learning to live'. Expansive learning and mo(ve)ments beyond 'gang exit'.* Full paper, 11th International Conference of the Learning Sciences (ICLS), Boulder, Colorado, USA, 23-27th June, 2014.
Nielsen, K. (1999). *Musical Apprenticeship. Learning at The Academy of Music as Socially Situated*, vol. 24, No. 2, Psykologisk Institut 1999.
Nielsen, K. (2006). Learning to do things with things: Apprenticeship learning in bakery as economy and social practice. In: Costall, A., Dreier, O. (red.). *Doing things with things.* Ashgate Publishing, Aldershot, p. 209-224.
Nielsen, K. (2008a). Gender, learning, and social practice. In: *Vocations and Learning*, vol. 3, nr. 1, p. 173-190.
Nielsen, K. (2008b). Learning, Trajectories of Participation and Social Practice. In: *Outlines: Critical Social Studies*, vol. 10, nr. 1, p. 22-36.
Nissen, M. (2012). *The Subjectivity of Participation: Articulating Social Work Practice with Youth in Copenhagen*, Palgrave Macmillan.
Packer, M. (1985). Hermeneutic Inquiry in the Study of Human Conduct. In: *American Psychologist*, Vol 40, No. 10, p. 1081-1093.
Rabøl Hansen, H. (2011). (Be)longing. In: *Psyke & Logos*, årg. 32, nr. 2, p. 480-495.
Robinson, K. (2012). Do Schools Kill Creativity? In: *Huffington Post*, 12/7/2012.

Wenger, E. (2004). *Praksisfællesskaber.* Hans Reitzels Forlag, København.
Willis, P. (2000). *Learning to Labour. How working class kids get working class jobs.*
    Aldershot: Ashgate, 2000.
www.fryshuset.se.

# An interview with Paul Cobb

*Interviewed by Ane Qvortrup, Merete Wiberg and Peder Holm-Pedersen*

Paul Cobb is Professor in mathematics education in the Department of Teaching & Learning at Vanderbilt University Peabody College. He is the author of several articles and books and has received a large number of awards for his contributions to the educational research field.

Paul's work is interesting for different reasons in our work in the network On the Definition of Learning. During his career, Paul Cobb has travelled along a conceptual and methodological pathway and has modified, more than once, his theoretical position (Yackel, Gravemeijer & Sfard 2011) from radical constructivism over social constructivism, to his current work with the large MIST project (Middle-school Mathematics and the Institutional Setting of Teaching) based on a design research approach with a pragmatic approach to theory (Skott 2008)[1]. Both through his theoretical modifications and his pragmatic approach in the MIST project, he exemplifies on the one hand the use of different learning theories and learning concepts, and on the other hand different approaches to- and important development trends in educational research and practice. This is central to the work of the network. Furthermore it was the reading of the well-reputed article "Putting Philosophy to work – Coping with multiple theoretical perspectives" that inspired us to investigate the relation between learning theory and teaching theory and to combine different theoretical perspectives in order to describe learning, taking into account aspects of interaction and participation in classroom practices. Paul Cobb suggests characterizing teaching and teacher development as design sciences involving developing, testing and revising designs for supporting learning processes. This way of describing the relation between teaching and learning has been a great inspiration for us in our work and still is, together with Cobb's reflections over methods that provide empirical information to constrain explanatory theories. Therefore, it is a great pleasure to include this interview with him in this first contribution from the network On the Definition of Learning.

In the interview, he talks about his MIST project and their way of working with professional development, while he reflects on the development he has undergone during his research career.

The interview took place at Vanderbilt University December 2014.

## Support of learning – a question of organizational learning

Interviewer A: *What is the background for, and the idea behind the MIST project?*

Paul Cobb: The guiding question for the project is: What does it take to support improvement in the quality of math teaching and student learning on a large scale? And in the context of what current US math teaching looks like, and also of what we ourselves value in kids math learning, we think of improvement in terms of teachers not just extending or elaborating what they already doing and reorganizing in their current practice, but rethinking their answers to fundamental questions such as: What does it mean to know and do math? What should the goals for student learning be? How do students learn? The whole bit. It would involve a fundamental reorganization of current practice. Not just an elaboration or extension. So that is the challenge.

So how would you do that? I have done it and a lot of (other) people have done it. A group of researchers going camp out on one or two schools and work very closely with teachers. You can really support their learning if you stay there for an extended period of time, so that is not the question. The question is: How can this be done on a large scale? And the way we think about it is: How can we support the development of school and district capacity to support teachers learning? And when you frame that question, you will be getting into principle's learning, coaching of learning, development of tools, reorganization of routines, the whole bit. So it is also for us a question of organizational learning. It is not either-or. It is not just teachers learning. If you have to support the learning of a large number of teachers, the organization has to learn how to do that. So it is viewing teachers' practices, which are very much influenced by organizational niches, the school context in which they work. So that is the kind of questions we have been interested in. For many years I worked at the classroom level doing design experiments where we would be responsible for the learning of a group of kids for fifteen weeks or something. And a lot came out of that, not just from my work, but from a lot of other people's work. We made a lot of progress at least in math and science in developing long term trajectories, not just of learning and how to support that learning, but to do so, requires fundamental change for teachers and groups of teachers. And we learned a lot about professional development. But that work had very little impact on US classrooms. If you go into most US math classrooms, you will see very little impact of any of that research. Hence this focus on the sort of broader level or broader scale, so it does fit with this sort of concern with practice. So, that is the basic idea. And also the last thing I did before this was a long-term partnership with two groups of middle school teachers, meaning lower secondary school, teaching kids age 12 to 14, in two districts, where we were working to support their learning. And they did make a lot of progress. These were math teachers and we worked with them for five years. But also in the context of that work we realized ahead of time, that in order to do that work we had to understand the settings in which the teachers were working. So we also collected data about the school and district contexts, and that was critical to us, it actually influenced the design in the group I worked with. So we ended up actually feeding back some of what we were finding about their school leaders without naming them to the teachers and it influenced our work with the teachers as well, because they then formed an agenda to try to influence the settings, in which they worked, so they could be more productive. And so, based on that work, we realized it would be really critical to attend to the whole system, and system as far as we go is the district from kindergarten through the end of high school.

## Supporting learning on the whole system level

Interviewer A: *What does it take to support improvement across the system?*

Paul Cobb: We worked with four districts for four years and they ranged from 35,000 to 140,000 students. And then, we continued on for another four years with two more districts, the one with 85,000 students and the other with 100,000 students. Now, we did try to recruit districts, which were atypical in the US at that time, because they were aiming high in terms of their goals for student learning. They were not just aiming at kids getting through the low level test. They also had higher goals for the kids developing conceptual understanding. And they had teachers with a pretty sophisticated inquiry oriented set of instruction practices.

What we did initially was to go to the district to interview a bunch of district leaders. And if we look at the central offices, there are a number of different departments. So, we interviewed people mainly from two departments initially, which is curriculum instruction and includes the math specialists, and leadership, which is responsible for hiring, moving around and monitoring school leaders. And what we were trying to find out in the initial interviews was: what are the plans, strategies and policies for trying to support improvement. Then we wrote up about five pages on these audio-recorded interviews and we said: Here is what we see as your major strategies. And we actually send that to them saying: Did we get this right? We have to make sure, that from their point of view we understand what they are trying to do. So in other words, our initial points of reference are their strategies. We call these district theories of action. Then we carried out large data collection from January through to March each year, where we collected data to try and document how these policies and strategies are actually playing out in schools and classrooms. We can tell you about some of the data we collect. In the first four years we focused on six schools in each district, and we selected them in consultation with the districts locals: Here, we want a representative group of schools. We wanted to be representative in terms of capacity for improvement. So we did not want the weakest schools and we did not want the strongest schools. We do not want to tell a story about successful schools in the district. We want to be representative. And then, within that we randomly selected a total of 30 teachers in each district, so we have 120 teachers altogether. We organize getting two consecutive lessons video-recorded in each of their classrooms. The success of that is near to 100 % in every district, every year. Then we went to each district for a week, and we do 50 audio-recorded interviews with teachers, school leaders and coaches. Then the coaches, the principles and the teachers do online surveys complementing the interviews. And what we are trying to get at is: What is it like to be a teacher, or a principal or a coach in this district? What are the supports, both formal and informal, improving teaching? What do you perceive yourself accountable for? To whom are you accountable? What tools do you use as part of your practice? That sort of thing. What is happening on the ground? And there is a measure developed at the University of Michigan on mathematical knowledge for teaching, which has been shown to be related to student achievement. The teachers and the coaches use this measure. We are also videoing professional development. And when teachers meet in collaboration, they audio-recorded their own meetings and then sent us the tapes. And then, as we are also interested in teachers' informal networks, we have an online network survey: Who do you turn to when you have an issue or a question? What did you talk to them about? And so on. That was online. And for that, it is not just 120, for network data you have to get everybody in a school, 300 teachers. And then the schools provide all of their student achievement data so we can link teachers and kids participating in the teachers' classroom. So we get all of that every year. So to give you an idea of the scale, as of now, because we have done this for a large number of years, we now have 1,700 fully coded videos, so it is a big longitudinal database. And they are all coded and we do that every summer.

What we have to do between the January interviews and May is analyze the 200 interviews and write a feedback report for each district, and these are separate. They do not just look alike. Each one is specific to each district. And the reason that we have to do that by May is because it is the beginning of the summer. School leaders and district leaders in this country typically make plans for the following year over the summer, so we do that and then we send these back to them and then we go a week later to each district, and then we meet with senior district leaders to talk it through and discuss implications for the coming year and I should just explain. We did this for four districts for four years and then we went down to two districts and we worked with them even more closely by jointly designing and leading professional development work. We doubled the number of teachers to have adequate statistical power. And doubled the number of schools as well, so we had 25 schools. In total about 200 participants.

## Different measures

Interviewer A: *Can you talk a little bit more about your measures?*

Paul Cobb: There is a real shortage with measures. We had a conference or a meeting last week which we called small measures and I will clarify why. We had to develop – and this was part of our research proposal – what we call big measures, and big does not mean grand, it means it is quite demanding to get the data and to analyze it. So we have this measure from University of Michigan of mathematical knowledge for teaching. That is not straight math knowledge, it is a good measure, because it is mathematical knowledge specific to the practice of teaching and I read these initial questions and I know the people who have developed them and know, it has got face validity. Some of the things we ask would be: Here is a kid's solution to a problem. Is this going to always work? Is it trying to get the sort of decisions arising either when you are planning for instruction or when you are teaching that actually come up? And my guess is that most teachers are actually thinking about teaching when they are responding to these items. And that is why it is a good measure. In addition, we got the coding scheme for the videos. So many coding schemes just code teacher performance and that is really unhelpful, rather than coding what goes on between teachers and students to try to get at, in some way, student learning opportunities. We adopted a coding scheme developed at the University of Pittsburgh called Instruction Quality Assessment and the basics or the logic of it, is as follows. First of all, it looks at, or codes the level of rigor and cognitive challenge of the task. What task the teacher selected to use today. Then basically it looks at the extent to which the teacher maintains that level of challenge throughout the lesson. The reason for that is, that the default case in this country is teachers show kids how to solve a problem. They procedualise it. So they take a high level task and convert it into a low level task, which then reduces the learning opportunities. Another thing we are interested in is the concluding whole class discussion. To what extend are kids pressed to explain and justify their thinking? To what extend is a connection made between solutions? Who are making those connections, the teacher or the students? And so forth. We developed initial rubrics because the original things that the Pittsburgh people did, did not look at how tasks are introduced. And, we noticed that that is were a lot of things went wrong. You watch the first five minutes and a lot of these kids are screwed, either because of the level of challenge that is introduced or because of the way it is introduced, because of this incredible diversity of students in the class in two of our districts, I am trying to think about the percentage of English language learners across these districts, maybe 30 percent of the kids' first language is not English, and no attention is made to language, the context of the task, the story, the scenario around the task might be unfamiliar to kids and this is not addressed in any way in the introduction. There might be some key mathematical ideas that kids need, not to solve it (mathematical problems), but just to understand what is being asked, and they do not address this at all. So we developed some rubrics for the launch in collaboration with the original rubric developers. And we added those. So that is one big measure. The second one is developed by a doctoral student. He is now a faculty member, at the University of Pittsburgh, and in all of the interviews, not just with teachers, we have this little script in our interviews, where we say to whoever: Suppose that you could go into a math class, where you can stay as long you like. What would you look for to find out if it is high quality instruction? And then there is a series of probes, and what we probe on – at first let them talk and see what they say – but if they don't bring it up, and often they don't, we then want to know: If it is high quality math instruction, what would the task look like? And because we do not have a good language in math, a common technical language, they might say that they want to be problem solving. Then we ask: Could you give us an example? Because what they mean by problem solving might be different from what we mean by problem solving, so we try to get to examples. So we focus on the task, we focus on the concluding whole class discussion, which we expect to be a summary or concluding discussion. If yes, we then try to probe on, who is doing the talking of the discussion and what they are talking about?

## The coding of data

Interviewer A: *How do you handle all this data? How do you use them?*

Paul Cobb: All of our data gets formally coded, and we now have reliability on this and retrospectively have gone back and coded all of the interviews. What we did to develop the rubrics was to start coding. In the beginning we had eight or nine colors, and we then reduced it to three to make it feasible. The first rubrics only focused on the top level, you know they were based on case studies of really accomplished math teachers and then we filled in what current math teaching looks like, so we have the top and the bottom and a few cases from research reports. We then focused on some of the gaps and went to our interviews, because we already had interview data filling in some of the gaps. So we coded levels of tasks, it would be like four levels, I think, if it is the vision of what a discussion looks like, we have four levels, which are based on published empirical studies. So there is some empirical grounding. That is where the coding schemes came from. And then the other additional big measure. We are also very interested in issues of equity and we have a particular operationalization, which are not very fashionable, because for a lot of people they think of equity in terms of relations between home and school, and the answer is you have to realign what goes on in school with what goes on at home and then everything is wonderful. I would say that this is the default position and that *was* my position, but when I had the opportunity to really think about these issues and I began to think about it in the late 1990'es, that is about 15 years ago, as I happened to work with a doctoral student, Lynn Hodge, and worked through this. Over time we came to see the limitations of that position, I think it is very nice and comforting from wide liberal point of view, because it means, we are all different. It is all about difference and it ignores relations of power and authority and identity and so forth. We have come to think of it much more, if we look at what goes on in the math classroom, in terms of who is able and wants to participate substantially, and what is happening in that math classroom. For example, our launch rubric I just told you about, we look at the first five minutes of those math lessons and I said the kids are screwed. What that means is, because of the way the teacher introduces that task, a very large segment of those students are unable

– and it is not their fault – to participate substantially in the rest of the math lesson. That is inequitable. It might be because of language issues, it might be because task context is unfamiliar to them, because of their home backgrounds is without school experiences, but it is familiar to other people, it might be because those things to help them visualize what is happening in the task, was not clarified, whatever it is. So we would define equity and inequity in terms of the extent to which kids are able to participate substantially, and it is not the participating in the same way, but in participating substantially in what is going on. So that is the definition we take. And again from the interviews, we realize that there are always kids struggling in the class. And we take the view, there are always kids struggling, so it is not bad, it is what you do about it that is the issue. So: Who are these kids? It may be language learners, it might be poor kids, whatever, who are they? Then the key thing they code on is first of all, asking the reasons why the teacher or whoever it is thinks those kids are struggling and how do they count for it? And basically, an unproductive response would be that it is something to do inherent to the kids, it is something inherent to the kids families, it is something inherent to the kids communities. And the reason why we code that as unproductive is it implies, there is nothing I can do about it, that is the way it is. These kids parents do not care, these kids are lazy, whatever it is. And then a more productive response would be accounting for these kids who are struggling in the relation between student and current or prior instruction. You know: they missed a lot of school, they changed schools and they missed these topics. Because this is implicitly saying that there is something you can do about it. So that is the first thing that gets coded. Then the second thing that gets coded, having asked these kids are they struggling and why, is: What are you doing about it? And we code that response. Unproductive would be, oh I break the math into little pieces, I lower it and get rid of the hard stuff. Productive would be forms of extra support to enable those kids to participate substantially in the challenge, which might be how you introduce the task, it might be helping them with stuff they missed, whatever. Right now we are looking at the relations between these different measures. It is seven or eight measures of aspects of practice and measures of three aspects of teacher knowledge: content knowledge, visions of high quality math instruction and also this last thing we call teachers views of student's capabilities. I have always had high hopes for this measure. These are big measures. The small measures mean we also need little measures where we can administer that practitioners will actually collect the data themselves and might actually also do the analysis or we would assist and so you can feed it back immediately. So it is a sort of thing you could imagine doing every week or every two weeks on a very specific aspect of the improvement effort. Suppose you came up with a small measure around launch tasks and it might be a little four item student survey, trying to get at: Can I as a student engage in this? Can I do it? Do I understand what is going on? It seems like, to get the data from the students would be the best thing. And the hope is, you would actually focus teachers' attention on an aspect that something is happening in their classroom that they are not attending to right now. We do not think these teachers are saying to hell with these kids, I do not care if half my kids have a chance or not. We think, they do not know it. So it is also a leaver for improvement as well as a measure. That is why we want to go in this direction. We do not have a lot of process measures, the actual mechanisms of change at the micro level, but we have longitudinal data of points.

Interviewer M: *When you say coding. Can you say a little bit more about how they code?*

Paul Cobb: It is qualitative data that gets quantified, and we have to do it, because before I did this large project, we could just do it by hand, but now we have 240 videos per year, so we had to. And it is like all methodologies are interesting. There are always tradeoffs. It is not that there is one right solution, so I would justify the tradeoff but I also acknowledge what we gave up to work at this level of scale. We also do in-depth qualitative analysis of interesting cases and we can use the quantitative data to identify the cases that are interesting outliers to do an in-depth qualitative analysis. So we are hardcore pragmatics when it comes to methodologies. We are not ideological at all, anybody who is, we are trying to stamp out. It is always the question that drives the choice of methodology, so it is really a small quantitative study and a ridiculously large qualitative study. It is both. The trick is: How do you get the data informing each other, so they are not going in different directions, and that is what we are interested in and working very hard on.

We have about five to eight coders in the summer. We hire these coders externally. They are not part of our team. The training process takes about a week and then it takes about another month to establish reliability. So we spend a lot of time making sure that like my number four is the same as his number four, if we would watch a video and code for the quality of discussion – and it is the same as number four was last year. So the numbers, it takes a lot of time to establish reliability across a large group like that. It ends up being over a month before we can actually start coding the real numbers. And then we have to check for drift, the coding drift, so we have to have continuing reliability checks throughout the process, where specific numbers are double coded by you know, very experienced coders, expert coders. That is the only way that we feel comfortable trusting our numbers. We have seen it go horrible wrong in a study where they were not very rigorous about establishing reliability. That is not good. The other thing I want to say about the quantitative thing, is – my background is as a qualitative researcher, so I have no interest in getting into the nitty-gritty of the statistical methods. The thing I care about is *what* you are trying to measure? Is it worth trying to measure? Does it matter? What does everything mean? It is not just numbers, they are actually measures of something, and it is never forgetting that. So that is where I press people. And then they go out and crunch the numbers fine and then they come back and we talk about what it means *in* reality teaching and learning or whatever it is. So it has been hard for us to develop these measures.

## Indicators of good teaching

Interviewer A: *You told us that for instance you are looking for how a task is introduced. Could you say a little bit more about: where does that come from? How do you decide on these focus points?*

Paul Cobb: Yes, how do we say this is what teachers should do? So, I was actually somewhat involved or physically present when they were doing that work, and it was quite clever. So we already by that point had quite a large database, so we looked through our quantitative data to identify the positive outliers. So how would you identify positive outliers? So we got the achievement data and the issues of equity. The launch was about equity from our point of view, it is all about equity, really. But first of all, just looking at achievement data: Which teachers are doing a good job to support everybody's learning or even narrowing these achievement gaps. That is one thing. But it is not enough. Because the teachers could be doing that by being very good at teaching lower level skills to children. So we got a coding of videos, which gets to the rigor of instruction. So we can then put two filters on. Do we have any teachers, where the data indicates the support of everybody's learning or of closing achievement gaps, including kids whose first language is not English and the two groups we are actually focusing on? We had to pick our points. Our African American students are currently struggling. Then, of the teachers who appear to be supporting everybody, are there any of these teachers also choosing high-level tasks and maintaining the rigor of those tasks all the way through, so they appear to be doing it by challenging everybody. There are not many, but there are some, and those are the interesting cases. And what they then did was to do an in-depth qualitative analysis of those teachers' videos - you remember what I said about the two methods – to see if there are any patterns or regularities to identify specific practices in those teachers' instruction. That is where the criteria came from that were put into rubrics. So they grew out of the data.

An example of what we do find is that the teachers' vision of high quality math instruction appears to be a leading indicator of improvement in practice. This appeared, looking at the relationship longitudinally between changes in their visions and the practice over time. In other words: Teachers view of what counts as high quality math instruction appears to be developing and it influences how they make sense of improvement and how they actually teach.

Interviewer M: *So, they are kind of exemplary teachers?*

Paul Cobb: Yes, or, so these are regular teachers in our data, there were not many of them, but there were some.

Interviewer A: *And can you maybe say a little bit more about what characterizes those teachers. What they were doing?*

Paul Cobb: Yes. We have a little paper and it was written for teachers. I actually use this in my teaching future teachers. And one of these teachers was very kind and gave us permission to use one of these video recordings in my class. And so, what I do in there, I can tell you the whole activity, although it is more than you need to know, but I think it is an eight grade class and he happens to have chosen a problem which he is using on the particular day, it is about a dance marathon, where people dance for a long time to earn money for charity or to raise funds or whatever. But you know, a lot of these kids had no idea what a dance marathon was, but the teacher sticks with this context. The math he is aiming for is linear equations, and he is particular interested in the relation between graphs equations and tables. And this is the first problem, these kids would have to hit with a non-zero y-intersect. So there is math in here as well as issues of context So what would an exemplary launch be? There are also issues of language? So what the teacher did first of all was to spend some time making what a dance marathon is, real for the kids. This particular fellow does not give the kids the problem. He actually projects an image or a whole bunch of images taken from google of people dancing, and he asks the kids what these are doing, and then they talk about what a dance marathon is. And he does it a lot from listening to the kids' ideas, having other kids reword and revoice, calling of kids he is not sure if they understand. So it is very interactive. Then, the other thing I felt was important – this is my contribution – was the math. What is happening in a dance marathon? It is not just that people dance for a long time. As time passes, money accumulates. And kids having that image is critical, if they can engage in the problem. This relationship between these changes in quantities, because that is what is going to get mathematized. And so if that also gets attended to explicitly and in the problem you get three kids with three plans, one just gets given five bucks or whatever, it is for participating in the marathon, somebody else gets two dollars up front and maybe a dollar for every hour they dance, and a third kid gets nothing up front and 15 cents per hour. Different graphs, different slopes. It is not teaching them or showing them how to solve it. It is focusing on how they interpret and understand the problem, so they can begin to engage with it. So the additional supports we would see important for all kids, is addressing or clarifying the context, clarifying mathematical ideas, explicitly talking about any terms or words that might not be relevant, sometimes by using a picture to help kids to understand those terms. And this came out in a very interactive way where you are drawing on kid's ideas and language, and these kids would explain it, you know, one kid said, that you have to work for it. So he recasts it in kids language. Notice, this does not mean you have to align tasks with kids out of school experiences. You do not have to. But what you have to do is to make whatever the context is, real for the students. Otherwise it is inequitable. So that is where it came from.

## Teacher professionalization

Interviewer A: *Could you maybe also say a little bit more about this professionalization? What characterizes a professional teacher? And how do you use your knowledge of good teaching to qualify teachers in other schools or districts?*

Paul Cobb: What we try to do, it did not entirely work in one of our districts, in addition to our two-hour feedback meetings, we also for three years organized and led day-and-a-half long district leadership institute with district leaders about 15 of them, from across all over the main unit and we could show them coding of what launches currently look like in their district. They are not pretty and also went through this sort of activity with them with the video. To have this as a focus, that would be good. What we then did, we had the main math people there and everybody was hot to trot. The idea was that they would work with their math coaches on the launch and they could work with teachers. Sadly what happened, which we could not believe, the math people assigned the people to work with the coaches who had not been at the session, so they had no idea what a launch was. So it got mistaken. But our plan was to make this a focus of work and also to work with principles on this. It is about the importance of coordination professional development across groups. For us the problem is not us going into a teacher professional development, we are arrogant enough to think we know how to do that, it is how can we support them in doing it. This is a challenge. It is how can you support others in supporting teachers? And so, what we did the following year, this was specifically on the launch, we ourselves worked with the coaches, as a design experiment, to explore conjectures about supporting coaches learning. So we are trying to work out an experiment with designs where we purposely avoid doing teacher professional development ourselves, because that is not what we think the problem is. We think it is about building their capacity to support teachers' learning.

Interviewer M: *And the coaches, are they teachers?*

Paul Cobb: There are different designs. Some of them are district based, some of them are school based. But these are people whose charge is to work with teachers in the school buildings to support their learning and get better on the job. And sometimes that involves working with groups of teachers, they might be, I do not know, the eighth grade math teachers, meeting twice a week, and they would lead and be in those meetings. Sometimes it means they go into individual teacher's classrooms and work with them in their classrooms

Interviewer M: *Are they trained teachers, these coaches?*

Paul Cobb: Ideally, they should be at minimum pretty sophisticated teachers themselves. But that is not enough, right? Because coaching is different from teaching. You do not just have to be good at supporting kids learning. You also have to be good at supporting teachers learning. And the literature on coaching is really astonishingly thin and awful. That is why we view it as we are having to experiment, because there are no really good designs on which to build. So we view it as probing around, trying to come up with tests, revise and prove designs for supporting coaches or school leaders' learning. So that is why we work more closely with two districts, so that we can do that.

Interviewer P: *How do you go about using knowledge on examples of good teaching in professional development of teachers, because sometimes the trainee teachers cannot see themselves in such examples.*

Paul Cobb: I see it as a trajectory. There have to be a lot of things as a basis before you get to that point. They read an article and then they have to do an assignment. I think you should plan for something, you should think about this, before you actually go into the classroom. So we then give them some other tasks. Suppose you are a fifth grade teacher and you are going to use these.

## Knowledge about learning

Interviewer M: *This instruction thing, could you say something about how we should understand instruction in terms of theories of learning.*

Paul Cobb: The best I can tell you is, I used to – I come from that background – but my position has evolved and to be honest I do not think so much about theories of learning anymore, but if you would have gone into my head: When I say instruction I do not mean teacher performance, I mean teacher's interacting with kids to support their learning, and if you ask me to think about this learning, the best thing I can say – and this is not an ideological point – I am more on a socio cultural orientation, not the broad activity theory, which I do not find helpful at all, but more at the level of practice and I think to address this I have to say something about how we think about the relation between knowledge and practice. And I think so often, or the default is to think of knowledge as prior to driving practice and we see that as a very problematic way of thinking about it, but I think it is quite common. Can I tell a story, give an example? Take this construct of mathematical knowledge for teaching. I know the people very well that developed that, and I am pretty sure that the way they go into it is from a background not in math but a teaching background, and they view their own math background as quite weak, and that is why that became a focus for them. What they did to develop that measure was to really reflect and think hard about their own practice, both the planning, the doing, the actual interacting with the kids in the classroom and the reflection back on it afterwards, and they were able to identify some key moments, where particular forms of math knowledge were important. The reason why I am saying this, is that I think it is a nice example if you want to use the term knowledge at all, and I used to get hung up on this. I usually do not want to use it, and I say, you have to talk about knowing. And I guess I have given up on those issues. I think they are part of the world of academia, but my position is: let us think about how we want to use the word. It is a form of knowledge that is operative in practice, it is an aspect. Practice is not something where you go in with an empty head. You are thinking and reasoning, and it is the reasoning that is in the practice. And what they then did up in Michigan – they are very clever people up there – they then developed this paper and pencil multiple choice assessment, which we think is a good assessment, precisely they are thinking about teaching when they respond to those items. That is why it is a good assessment. Then so many people, because it is a paper and pencil assessment, then one thinks about it, then we are just going to boost their mathematical knowledge for teachers, then their teaching will get better. No! You have now separated it out of practice. Teachers, when you are working with them on math and not doing that in the context of practice, they will not relate. It will be this separate, academic exercise I do in this college class or I do in this professional development session. It will not influence or affect. They have to be – from their point of view – working on the practice.

Interviewer M: *Then these teachers, they are instructing. Do you think that they should consider how the children do learn? And how should they conceptualize it?*

Paul Cobb: I think so. I want to take it even a step before that, as this is telling a story. This is from my prior life, where we were with this group of teachers. We worked with these teachers for about two years, and we were really trying to orient these teachers not to focus on learning but just to focus on the kids mathematical thinking, a step in the right direction, right. That does mean you have to de-center and look at what is going on from their point of view to figure out their thinking. So we had the teachers bring sets of student work from their own classrooms and they looked at it and they were quite happy to do this and to identify different types of solutions and sort them into levels of sophistication. The wheels came off, because the teachers saw this as pointless, as no relevance to planning on what they do next. Afterwards we actually went back to the schools and observed the teachers' instruction and started questioning them, did interviews immediately afterwards about what they had seen in their lesson, and what came out was that any time they looked at student work or anything, it was always to assess or to check: Did they get it? It was never prospective to plan for the future. And so when they were looking at student work, they were figuring out what the students got, not that this is going to inform my future plan. So once we figured this out, we came up with a whole new design, and we had a summer session, and we said let's start with something that is a real problem. And what was a real problem in their language was motivating students. And a lot of the students did not really care – and if you saw the instruction you could understand why – so we said: Let us focus on motivation, but we wanted to recast it in terms of supporting the development of kids mathematical interest. And we were able to do that. We had a design and we had a successful three days with them. The thing is, if you begin to understand, it is not just something inherent in your students, they are not just unmotivated people – they are not motivated because they do not understand what is happening in my class and therefore it is really boring and pointless from their point of view –an initial decentering. That was the first time and the first step and then we build from that over time to also focusing on mathematical reasoning. So the thing we learned from this story is that even for these teachers in the US who teach secondary, even decentering to focus on trying to figure out what their kids are thinking is a huge achievement.

Interviewer A: *Earlier, you talked about the difference between knowledge and knowing. And my question is related to the teachers: Can one say that it is not about teacher knowledge, but about changing their minds about their teaching? Because, what I hear is that they have to think about teaching in another way?*

Paul Cobb: I like that image, but they also have to change their knowledge. It is not this separate thing. It is knowledge *in* practice. And if they change their knowledge in practice, their practice changes. It is an aspect of practice. Practice is both knowing and doing. It is not one or the other.

The other thing I was going to say was, when you asked about learning – it is a thing I have thought about for a long time: I maybe talk about a specific aspect of teaching, so like – one of the things we now and then think about, is teachers' understanding of what kids might be learning in a whole class discussion. So, we think about very specific things. We do not think about learning by and large. What was interesting in that study was the default whole class discussion, then and also now looks like the following. The kids have worked in groups and the first group gets up and presents, and they just present, whatever they present, and the teachers say: Thank you very much. And then the kids sit down. We call it show and tell. And then the next group and the next group. If you analyze that from a kids learning opportunity point of view, there is very little going on. So my assumption was that the teachers did this because they have other goals like self-esteem or, whatever it is. So we actually asked the teachers about this, and yes they had those goals but they also thought their kids were learning. Somehow they had this theory that the kids were picking out the good mathematical pieces, all on their own. And they might ask: Does it involve a change in learning? I would say: Do we want to teach teachers learning theories in general? No. Do we want to profoundly influence, how teachers think about, how kids learn from each other in classrooms, whether it is in small groups or in whole classes? I believe it. But not first. As part of the process, not apart from practice. So, how we think about it. We think about what should be happening in a whole class discussion, and what are the teachers attempting to achieve is number one. Seeing how kids solve a problem, looking at the kids solution, we think it is really important that there has been a good launch, so that everybody is engaged in the problem, so that they have a basis from which to understand each other. If they haven't been engaged in the problem, then they are not going to keep up when the whole class discussion begins. A big part of the teacher's role is number one: to make sure that they are drawing on kids' solutions. And then they have to think about: if I am explaining, and you are a student, how might you be understanding me? And their role is then to mediate the communication between the kids on important issues, so they might be using alternative representations in presenting the picture or diagram of my solution to help you understand it. Because it is worth to understand mathematically.

Interviewer M: *In some of your papers, you write about cognitive constructivist theories of learning. My question is whether these theories contribute to teaching practice in mathematics?*

Paul Cobb: Let us say this. Yes and no is the decision I have come to over the years. What I take and still hang on to from those days is *the* central idea to focus on the individual kid for example, or it could be individual teachers and assume that what they do is rational, and our job is to figure out that rationality. A lot of people are willing to do that with students and we see an increasing will to do it with teachers. This was not the case twenty years ago. I always assume that they are doing their best, or what they think is best for their students. And I am just trying to figure out why they are doing what they are doing as a starting point, before we even develop the initial design or supporting their learning or whatever it is. And then: where I think that cognitive approaches are not useful is when you try to come up with models, cognitive models, schema theory, or whatever else it is. I see absolutely *no* pay off in that, at least in the work we do. It is not saying it is wrong. There might be other purposes, like knowledge engineers do that to develop computer systems that simulate human activity. It could be very useful for that, just for what *we* do, and I would say for profession developers in general, it is really not helpful. It does not help you develop better disciplines, whereas I gave you the example before, where we were in the class with the teachers we are working with, and it was absolutely critical we understood why they had the reaction they had when they were working with us. We did not know why they were doing what they were doing when they saw no point or even the relevance of looking at kids' work in order to plan future instruction. The golden rule to me is to always assume it is a design failure rather than a person failure. That is incredibly helpful for me and my crew when we use to work in the classroom with classroom design experiments – and the kids were doing some bizarre things – we think: How did we teach them to do that? Where did we go wrong? And we go back to the tapes every time and then you can improve the design and make a better choice. Do you see what I mean? So that is the golden rule.

Interviewer M: *Teachers should ask themselves that question very often. That would be nice.*

Paul Cobb: That's part of equity, if you think about it. Rather than saying there is something wrong with the students. I got stupid students or lazy students or their parents do not care. No, it is your problem as a teacher or instructional designer.

Interviewer P: *Can you talk a bit about, if we kind of transfer that way of thinking to the professional development discussions, because I see a lot of resistance from teachers to professional development or to the things they are taught at these courses we have. So I am interested in hearing if you, in these designs you make, have seen some kind of resistance, and maybe how come.*

Paul Cobb: We see it from the districts. And we try to learn from it. What we have been doing, the group of us, the last few months, we have had periodic meetings where we say: What would we do differently, if we should do this over again? If we were, what would we do differently? What are some of the epic mistakes? And I would say that one of them is not to attend to what some would talk about as motivation. I would prefer to renounce that in terms of development of personal identity, but without going down the black whole of identity, but just refer to the minimum we can get away with to come up with a reason for operationalisation of identity. It is, I would say, it has been very striking in all this work, there has never been an instance I can recall – I do not think there *have* been any – of any district level people attending in supporting developmental reason, motivation, will agency and that sort of terrain of the folks they are working with, whether they are teachers or whatever, someone put into work to change their practice. And it is a hell of a commitment. I work with practicing teachers, so that is my world, mainly, rather than preservice. But the person I am thinking about – it is usually a she, but that is because I am sexist, who is a really accomplished teacher, really well regarded by his or her peers, been teaching like, I would say, 15 years, highly regarded in the school, has very good classroom management, has very good test scores, teaches mainly procedures or whatever, regarded well by the school leader and so on. You are asking that person to change how they teach. Wow! That person has so much to give up. If you know what I mean? So much is invested in it. And so, that is the person I think about. And so, what would a design look like? You must not only focus on their practice, but on supporting them in developing reason and motivation or will agency to change. And it has to be *their* will and *their* agency. This has to go back to themselves. Ultimately they have to be the one investing the effort to make the change. You cannot do that for anybody. That is part of the design. And I would say that this is a limitation I see in what we have been doing. I want to say, I kind of understand why we did that. There is so much else to focus on, but what is bizarre is, we use to go and work with groups of teachers ourselves. We used to have any design attend to that. I do when I teach my classes here. It is problematic in some way, really problematic, they have no reason to want to change. And so going forward, that is one of the things we want to make an explicit focus on in our future work. Now, that is the best I can say. I wrote a little paper about this. Because that group of teachers we work with ourselves, this was a district, which was attempting to change math teaching and we were given the teachers who were resisting by the district. We did not know that. Initially it was very hard, but by the end of the first year we just met them three times this year in the summer session. By the end of the second year they were volunteering to work through their lunch breaks to keep going. And they ended up being designated leaders of their district. Charged with developing units supporting the other teachers learning. So we went back and said: How the hell did that happen? And that is what the paper is about: Their development of human agency to want to change their work. And it is identity, I think. They develop an image of a new form of practice, but it is not just about that. It is what they identify with. They want to become that kind of teacher. Then they were really willing to put in the extra effort. They were trying to set up teacher groups to work with other teachers in their schools on their own initiative. So, trying to understand that process. That is what we try to do.

Interviewer P: *But then, one of the starting points for a development like that, is that they are actually able to see the picture that you are giving them of another kind of teaching. That it is kind of relevant to them?*

Paul Cobb. Yes, that is right. But this is over a period of time. This was not day one: Here is an image of teaching, do you like it or not? The other thing we had to do was, they were used to professional development, where somebody goes in for two days and tells them what to do. And we had envisioned a different type of relationship, where it really was a collaboration. And you cannot tell people, what to do – or you can, but they will not understand. And they cannot. It is not their fault. They have to have those kinds of experiences. So we have a negotiated way of working.

Interviewer A: *Now we are talking a lot about this teacher development. Could you talk a little bit about teacher education? Teachers who are going teach?*

Paul Cobb: I do think about it. Let me tell you the context. I have to draw a circle, so I am not getting into organizing entire programs and we have people who are supposed to do that anyway and it is their specialties. So I can only tell you about my class and about what I try to do. In my class, many of the students are going to work soon and they say: I want to be an elementary teacher. A lot of these people, you know they are bright people, they are very articulated, they write well. But a lot of them had very bad experiences as math students to start with. I do not know if that is the same in Denmark, but it is here, they do not like math, they would rather not be with me. So the first thing is to get that out on the table and to try and convince them that it is not their fault, it is the way they were taught. And the initial thing I do is I have an old piece of video from back in the days where I had hair and everything. It is very representative of second graders. And basically, what it prints out for these kids is that there are two different worlds in math. There is the world of quantism and relationships between them. And there is the real world. And these kids know some math. They have dealt with quantism to some extent. And then there is the stuff they do in school, which is some kind of symbolic hieroglyph. And the two have no relations. And so you can show them. You switch from one class to the other, and you can flip them from one room to the other in the interview they are operating in. At that time when I did that work, I were a constructivist, so I would say different cognitive contexts, and I would now broaden that account. But it makes the point: this is very typical. And for most people in my class, this is also very undesirable, so there is a reason, a motivation to want to work to begin to develop an alternative way of teaching. And then I had some videos we put together, modules of kids that my students do serious assignments on, where we try to edit down just a few segments of classroom teaching experiment. We took it from one of those, where I got interviews before and after, and these kids get really, their thinking really develops in like three months. Quite dramatically. So we have to look at them before and after and analyze the kids thinking. And they analyze classroom clips to begin to figure out what the teacher did. Just as an initial entry. And they seem to want to do that. They seem to find that as a worthwhile activity. That is just the start of the class and then, if we are looking at particular content strands, we do not for instance just focus on it is a very good idea to have a discussion, but what is a key characteristic of productive discussions and what is the teacher's role in making that happen? One thing I have learned from this work is the phrase I now use: fighting our way up to the level of concrete practice. And I put it that way on purpose to be provocative, because in the academia we have abstracts up here and highfalutin language and concrete practice is down here. And if you actually read a lot of stuff it is always abstract stuff. It sounds very good until you actually think about doing it and realize, it does not achieve contact. And our fight is the struggle up to specific learnable practices. It is getting to the specifics. And the specific is not the same for us as the procedure. It always involves wisdom and judgement. Invokes forms of knowing. And so part of what we have been trying to do to achieve success, is to begin to try to identify what we think might be productive. The launch would be an example of a teacher practice but also interesting in coach practices and school leadership practices and district practices. And the criterion we have is that you can envision someone actually practicing practice. So if you asked about metaphors for learning I would say graduated series for apprenticeship experiences, at least for professional learning, whether it is with teachers work or with somebody who is already a pretty sophisticated teacher. So if I am trying to figure out how to launch a task, I have an image of what a launch might look like and then I might try launching a task perhaps with a small group of teachers playing students and you are the coach and you give me feedback on my launch or even if you were the coach, you ask a question or do something kids might do, and I should try to handle that. That sort of thing. We have been influenced by Pam Grossmanns' work and she makes a really important distinction in professional development between pedagogies of investigation and pedagogies of enactment. So pedagogies of investigation, that is what we do a lot in professional development, analyzing classroom videos, investigating it, looking at student's work, records of practice. And that is really important, but our argument is that it is not enough. We also need to be trying to enact these things ourselves with somebody who is more advanced and could scaffold. So that is the way I see apprenticeship. So when we did our coaching design, the coaches would actually go out and do professional development sessions. Ideally we should have been there, but we could not so that would be videos, we analyze with them. We have something to work on. I think we talk a lot about the complexity of things and the messiness and I think a lot of it is. It is swampy and it is complex.

Interviewer M: *And it should not be a swampy lowland?*

Paul Cobb: We just do not have a good way of conceptually handle it in a way that is productive for practice. I also think, this is a big issue for me. I have come to see most educational research as pretty irrelevant, at least in math education and particularly the learning sciences – this relates to the abstract-concrete issue – because I think what goes on in most educational research is groups of researchers in quite small cliques studying, I do not know, kids and discourse learning, and what counts as an important problem to study is defined by the other researchers. So I think of it as kind of this sort of hole of mirrors, just a group of researchers refracting each other and their views and there is no reality, there is no practice, no reality of school in it at all. And I think, we, to understand, at least in this country and in a research university like this one, to understand the institutional setting which encourages this pathological behavior in terms of what it rewards. If you are interested in actually, ultimately it is about the quality of kid's education, that is not there. So you have to be aware of the reward structures and the norms in the places where you work – it is in the water we swim every day – and to decide if you will play that game or not. So I have made the decision that I don't want to play that game.

Interviewer P: *Do you remember we talked about our thinking about these small measures that you were working on developing? And we also talked about this with the professional teacher who was a bit like you when you are doing these research designs where you always analyze a situation, then use that knowledge to improve practices. Is that really – of course in a minor scale – the picture of a good teacher?*

Paul Cobb: In part. In big part. There are a lot of analogies.

Interviewer P: *Am I right, when I see these small measures as a part of it?*

Paul Cobb: Surely, that would be part of what we want to feed them back on. The other thing I will say is the difference between research and teaching. They should be in contact right. For most teachers their work for improving, their practice if it is a group of teachers and what they do collectively together in their school, that is their focus. That is not only my focus. That is my focus – if I am not doing that, it is not ethical – but I am also interested in generating knowledge that is relevant to other people in other schools, but it is still about improving practice. That is the difference, I see that as a big part of the difference between design research and action research.

Interviewer P: *But could we also imagine it as the teacher, the way he is looking at his or her teaching?*

Paul Cobb: Yes. And I want to take it up a little bit through the system. So if we could dream: What becomes interesting in this country with its high stake accountability? For district leaders there is this huge sense of agency, so they keep coming up with ideas and want to roll it out across the system immediately, and it fails. It will fail. Your initial design is always broad. You are doing stuff that we do not know how to do. Otherwise you would not be working on it. If we knew, what to do, then why...? Do you see what I mean? So. Part of what I want to do when going forward is to see if it is possible – I do not know if it is – to negotiate a way of working at the district level parallel to this, where you start very small, suppose we were working with teachers, it will be one or two teachers, only, to have them as partners working out the design. And then maybe go to one school and then two. But no, you want to do it quickly, you know. Does that make sense?

Interviewer M: *All the methods you have developed, can they be transferred to other discipline areas?*

Paul Cobb: I think so. But you need people with that disciplinary expertise. Because they have to be adaptable. What we do is not generic. I should explain the position we have come to. It does not just matter that we work in math. It is not just math. It is what is the specific vision of high quality math instruction. We start in the classroom with kids and their learning and how do you support that learning and so on. And that has implications throughout the system. But rather than starting with the policy and seeing if it goes down, we try to create policy by starting with the kids and the teacher and going up. And if that is where you start, your visions of high quality math instruction have implications for the policy, and so it could be that the policy in English art would be different if you have a different vision in relation to teachers current practice. But I think the heuristics is probably transferable.

Interviewer M: *You talk in some papers about this emergent perspective. What is that? It is a theory or is it just to understand emergence?*

Paul Cobb: It is a way of looking at things. I don't want to use the word theory because that seems very grand. We have a phrase. "Self-made grand iceman". You're building yourself up and making yourself look important and that is what it smacks off for me. So, I would not call it a theory. It is a way of looking. It is a lens. It relates to what we were talking about earlier, that classrooms are complex and messy. When we were doing classroom design experiments they were complex and messy, so what should we really be attending to, be focusing on? It is a way of looking on what is happening in the classroom and what the kids are up to and what the teachers are up to. A way of looking that could inform the revision and improvement of your design. So it is an attempt to develop that, and make the classroom appear less messy.

# Notes
1 http://peabody.vanderbilt.edu/departments/tl/teaching_and_learning_research/mist/index.php

# An interview with Christopher Winch

*Interviewed by Merete Wiberg, Nina B. Dohn, Oliver Kauffmann, Ane Qvortrup and Peder Holm-Pedersen*

Christopher Winch (1949) is professor of educational philosophy and policy at Kings College in London.

He is the author of several articles and books, including his pioneering study of human learning *The Philosophy of Human Learning* from 1998. Winch is convinced that a philosophical treatment of learning is necessary 'because of the distorted way in which learning has been treated by many psychologists and those educationists who have been influenced by them". (Winch 1998 p.1). The book not only gives a comprehensive philosophical analysis of the phenomenon and concept of learning, it also presents Winch's own views on learning, with decided inspiration from Wittgenstein.

Winch is an active participant in contemporary discussions on learning. He questions some of the prevalent trends in education, and is critical of concepts such as 'learning how to learn' and 'learning styles'.

As an aspect of his interest in the philosophy of learning, Christopher Winch also has done considerable research and writing in the area of vocational and professional education. In the book *Dimensions of Expertise* (2010) Winch explores the concept of expertise. His analysis, though, also offers interesting and valuable perspectives on the concept of learning. The book contains analyses of Wittgenstein's notion of rule-following, tacit knowing (Polanyi), knowing that and how (Ryle), as well as a discussion of the theory of expertise expounded by Dreyfus&Dreyfus.

The interview took place at Kings College, London on January 23, 2015, during the course of a visit to Christopher Winch and his colleagues. The interview was conducted by Merete Wiberg (int 1), Nina B. Dohn (int. 2), Oliver Kauffmann (Int. 3), Ane Qvortrup (int.4) and Peder Holm-Pedersen (Int.5).

In the course of the interview, we asked Christopher Winch to discuss how theories of learning can help us to understand the phenomenon of learning. In addition, we were interested in hearing how a change of focus from the concept of learning to the concept of expertise has helped him to understand the phenomenon of learning.

## Interview: Christopher Winch, 23 January 2015

### 1. Your shift of focus from learning to expertise.

INT1: *How do you see the relationship between learning and expertise and why did you shift your focus from learning to expertise? And how does the concept of expertise help us to understand the concept of learning?*

CW: Well, it was really because of my interest in vocational and professional education. I have done a lot of work in that area, and I have had a particular interest in the debates in epistemology about how we "know that" (Ryle). I thought these debates had a significant bearing on questions of expertise. So this is what partially explains my change of focus. You also asked how, and whether, the concept of expertise helps us to understand the concept of learning. I would put things the other way around: as we gain more clarity around our conceptions of learning, we are perhaps better able to understand expertise and "know-how". A central preoccupation of my book *Dimensions of Expertise* is how one can make sense of the relationship between having command over a body of systematic knowledge, and having the ability to make decisions in a professional context.

INT1: *Could you elaborate on your views about how the concept of learning helps us to understand expertise?*

CW: I think it is particularly issues around 'learning-how' which raises interesting questions in this regard. This was not so clear to me at the time when I wrote *The Philosophy of Human Learning*. Ryle draws attention to these issues when he talks about intelligence epithets, and how we evaluate actions and judgements. This is really important for an understanding of expertise. I tend to regard expertise as a sort of family resemblance concept. I have never attempted to produce a definition of expertise, and I am very sceptical as to whether it's possible. But on the other hand, it does seem to be possible to identify some key features of expertise: in the first place, that expertise is subject to normative evaluation; and secondly, that there is a continuum from being a novice to becoming an expert. Both these features have to be accounted for. The concept and phenomenon of learning is really important for understanding the transition from the novitiate to expertise. We also have to make sense of the ability to apply these intelligence epithets to performances. We not only learn to become better at doing things; we also learn how to apply evaluative vocabulary to our own actions, and the actions of others.

INT1: *Would you say that the concept of expertise helps us to better understand this normative dimension, a sense which perhaps is lacking in the concept of learning?*

CW: I think it is another aspect of the normative. The prevailing emphasis has been on constitutive judgement: *what* makes this something, rather than something else. Whereas it seems clear that normative evaluation is a constitutive element of talk about know-how. It is this element which allows us to distinguish know-how from mere physical ability, for example. But there is also a normative framework involved in evaluation, when we determine what counts as a good, or an expert, or an excellent performance, as opposed to an ordinary one, or the performance of a novice. Normative criteria are different than those employed in constitutive judgement. Something can be constitutively x without necessarily being evaluated as excellent.

## 2. Theories of learning

INT1: *Do you have a favourite theory of learning and, if so, which one and why? You state in Philosophy of Human Learning that grand theories of learning are useless. Do you still think that this is the case?*

CW: Well, I would rather say, that all of them that have been produced so far are of very limited value; that is a more polite way of putting it. I thought the discussion yesterday was helpful in clarifying the distinction between producing a categorical framework for understanding, which is important, though a notion not free from difficulties, and the idea that one can arrive at a universal explanatory account of learning. I maintained in *Philosophy of Human Learning* that the latter has not been done, despite various claims to the contrary. I think it is pretty unlikely that it ever could be done. This is not to say that we cannot construct explanatory frameworks about learning, but I think you have to start in a much less ambitious way, from the outset. For example, I think we know a lot more about how children learn to read than we did say sixty years ago, and that is one example of real progress.

INT2: *In your book on expertise, you seem to argue that differences among domains of knowledge and know-how makes grand theories of learning impossible. Is that a correct understanding of your position? In other words, that being an expert in one domain is quite different than being an expert in another domain?*

CW: It is partly the reason, I think. My argument suggests that even if you could construct a very general theory of learning, it would be of limited applicability, given the diversity of domains, and the wide variety of contexts in which learning takes place. But I think my main critique in *Philosophy of Learning* was this: that those theories that we do have, which make very grand claims, do so on a very, very limited empirical base, and very often, the conceptual foundations of the theories have not been clearly thought through.

INT2: *Right. I agree that there is something flawed in those theories, but you seem to have a more principled scepticism towards grand theories of learning, such that even if one had an extensive empirical basis and a sound conceptual foundation, a grand theory of learning would be difficult, if not impossible to establish. So I suspect your scepticism must have something to do with differences in subject domains. Or perhaps it has to do with something else altogether?*

CW: I think it has mostly to do with the point Eraut raised about the significance of differences in domain. Moreover, if you go back to Ryle's discussion of intelligence epithets, he is pretty clear that you only really learn to apply them when you are thoroughly immersed in concrete contexts. Conceptual shifts happen all the time when you move from one domain to the other. If you think, for example, of the creative writer, that would be a term of approbation... creative accounting is probably not. So the issue of domains is really important. I'm not saying that it is impossible for someone to arrive at a general theory of learning, but my assumption would be, that it would be at such a level of generality as to be of little practical use.

INT2: *That seems to imply that the first principle of a general theory of learning would be an insistence on the importance of immersion. Immersion of the subject within a domain is a necessary condition for learning. Is that right?*

CW: Yes. And the other point I think is the one about context ... learning is context dependent.

INT2: *You see those as two different points, immersion and context?*

CW: Yes I do really. To take an example like reading, I think there are all kinds of factors that can affect a child's ability to and willingness to read. And they are very often dependent on specific features of the environment.

INT2: *Right. So on the one hand, we have immersion in a domain, and on the other, immersion in a context. But these two spheres will interact, will they not? E.g., isn't the way you immerse yourself in a domain dependent on the way you immerse yourself in a context?*

CW: I guess so, yes.

INT3: *You are obviously right in pointing out the problems involved in building grand theories of learning in relation to differences of context. But if we approach learning from the point of view of Ryle's account of "knowing-how", can one not say that he is silent about the body's role, about what really, in an ontological sense, grounds our dispositions to know and to learn. What is the connection, for example, between 'knowing-how', and our abilities? The latter are still bodily abilities. Aren't we leaving something out of the picture here?*

CW: We are physically embodied agents, and to that extent, the body has to be taken into account. I think where I part company with Ryle is that he appears to think that any admission that there might exist a sphere of inner activity which affects action leads right into Cartesianism. He is extremely reluctant to do justice to that phenomenon. And that is the problem with the Rylean account. I don't have any problems with the idea of embodied agency. But if you're trying to dismiss the inward aspects of human cognition, then I think you are missing something very important. And I think that omission has quite a considerable bearing on the notion of expertise. You probably are acquainted with the so- called fluency theories of expertise by Dreyfus and others. In their account of expert performance, they neglect cognitive activity and judgement. I think that is a serious mistake.

## 3. Learning, training and instruction

INT1: *In The Philosophy of Human Learning, you criticize Rousseau for his dismissal of the importance of training and instruction (p.39). How do you- in the light of some of the considerations you raised in Dimensions of Expertise - look at the relationship between learning, instruction and training?*

CW: I don't believe my views on that issue have changed significantly in the period you mention. I think there are some aspects of training which depend on instruction. I didn't really bring that out in *The Philosophy of Human Learning*. But if you think of vocational education or professional education, you will see that it contains both bodies of knowledge, which mandate certain courses of action, as well as ways and means of justifying those courses of action. It seems clear that in any programme, let's say, for example, a programme of vocational education, there are elements both of instruction *and* training, as well as various ways of combining them. So we would expect to see instruction and training, as well as a variety of other kinds of pedagogical activities, within a broader umbrella which I call vocational education. That dimension of learning and education didn't receive much attention in *The Philosophy of Human Learning* because it wasn't my main focus of interest in the book. I don't think my views on that subject have changed that much over time, but I think they need to be adapted to take account of practical learning and expertise.

INT1: *So it's not sufficient just to be in the context to learn, one also has to receive instruction?*

CW: Again, you don't want to generalize too much. But if you think of the logic of modern occupations, that of the " German Berufe", for example, they are really built up around that idea. That's their philosophical basis.

INT4: *Could you elaborate more on the conception of instruction? What is instruction, and more precisely, what constitutes good instruction?*

CW: Well, let's take the example of teacher education. It is probably also the case in Denmark, that people complain that educational theory does not have much relevance for practice. It is clearly a challenge for those involved in curriculum design to bring theory into an intimate relation with practice. Instruction in educational theory is necessary, but it must be such so as to help illuminate what teachers are actually doing in the classroom. It should give prospective teachers a means for both raising questions about the validity of the theories, as well as for raising questions about instructional practice. In my view, there has to be an intimate relationship between these two elements in vocational programs. I am aware that attention is being given to this issue by the Swiss, for example. I believe that in the German Cantons, where the dual system has been the norm, one is now moving towards a situation where the first year of the program is spent entirely in the classroom. Why? Because recent and rapid changes in working conditions makes it more difficult for people to just insert themselves into the workplace.

INT1: *Lave and Wenger have spoken a great deal about 'learning when you participate'. Does this notion of learning involve and include instruction, or is there something lacking in this theory of situational learning?*

CW: I think there is. What it reminds me most of is Oakeshott's account of learning how to be a politician in national politics. First you are a part of the community; it's there you pick up the normative structures, and the relevant moves and attitudes you will need later as a politician. You learn by gradually inserting yourself into the local context of the community. And that seems to be the kind of model that Lave and Wenger also work with in their example of the tailor. But as a working model, it doesn't fit at all well with other forms of education. I think it is a bit of a romanticized and selective description of reality.

INT2: *I don't think Lave and Wenger would necessarily abandon the idea of instruction. They would simply insist that the instructor should be in the work-place all the time, so that you would have peer- to -peer instruction. This in turn would eliminate the need for classroom instruction, with the result that you wouldn't have the dual system you mentioned above. But you would still have situational instruction.*

CW: I think in that respect their views resemble Ryle's somewhat. They don't want to deny the place of instruction, but it never actually plays any part in their own descriptions of learning.

INT2: *Indeed, it only plays a role in the context of participation itself. Of course, we say things while we participate, but the language of instruction in this case is not decontextualized. If we put it elsewhere then we are doing something essentially different. We are learning new school practices instead of vocational practices.*

CW: Yes. The emphasis for them is on participation, rather than instruction. Although I think they leave theoretical space for workplace-based instruction in their model, they don't seem too anxious to explore the implications of it ...

## 4. Current discussions of learning in society

INT1: *I know you have examined the concepts of "learning to learn" and "learning styles". Which of the current discussions or conceptions of* learning do you consider important – in the UK, Europe and in other places? And which conceptions do you consider problematic?

CW: Well, I think you have already mentioned some of them.

INT1: *Why do you think they are problematic?*

CW: For example, I think there is very little empirical evidence to support the notion of learning styles. I think that point is quite well established now. In the case of learning to learn, as I hope I have shown in one of my articles, the claims are confused. We don't actually know what concretely is implied and claimed by the concept; it seems to me to be something fairly trite on closer inspection... normally the examples given come from the province of literacy and numeracy, or from moral education and the development of certain character attributes. The concept of learning to learn isn't some kind of a magic bullet. Finally, one might consider theories of brain-based learning. Again you have to look very carefully at what is being claimed by the theory. I would argue that to the extent that the theory employs a representational account of how the brain works, there is conceptual confusion. I think these are the three most dominant theories or paradigms that are currently in circulation in the educational system in this country, and there are powerful and influential figures pushing them. Though I don't know that much about it, the latest theory on the educational scene is the idea that you can develop memory very powerfully. I haven't looked much at the literature, but on the face of it, there doesn't seem to be much conceptual confusion, unless one bases one's approach to learning on some kind of storehouse conception of memory.

INT1: *So it seems that it is not researchers who are discussing these things or proposing these concepts. Or is it?*

CW: Well, actually, I think it is. You may know more about it than I do.

INT3: *I would like to ask a follow-up question on the topic of brain-based learning. I am curious about the comment you made regarding representationalism- specifically, that it involved a form of conceptual confusion. Could you elaborate on that?*

CW: I think representationalism involves making the claim that one can describe the workings of the brain in representational terms. The brain represents itself to itself and so on. This logic implies in turn that the brain uses a representational framework of propositions. I try to argue in *The Philosophy of Human Learning*, on the basis of Wittgenstein's private language argument, that that doesn't really make a great deal of sense. Of course, I am not sure how much Hacker would agree with that conclusion. I believe his focus is on the mereological fallacy, as you know. He has been under some attack for that. It's worth noting that he has been called a "Linguistic Policeman". In addition, there is a rather more sophisticated objection from Rom Harré. I think there are potential problems with dismissing representationalism solely on the grounds of the mereological fallacy.

INT3: *Doesn't this impasse result in a potential danger? Namely, that in one corner, we have people working with the paradigm of brain-based learning running the show... And here we are, sitting in the other corner, talking about conceptual confusion. Even if we might be right about that as philosophers, it's the others who run the show. Can you say a bit more about that?*

CW: It is a bit of a political problem. I think philosophers, as you know, are very often regarded with suspicion, sometimes with good reason. I think in the case of the philosophy of education there has been an unfortunate tendency to be generally dismissive of empirical work, and even to suggest that none of it is of any use. And that's led to alienation between psychologists and sociologists and philosophers. So I certainly don't think we should let philosophers get away scot free in this situation. But from what I can see of the attempt to engage in discussion with the neuroscientific community, the blame isn't solely on the philosophers' side. Hacker made a serious effort to work with an established neuroscientist to set out some of the problems. I know from talking to people in the neuroscientific community that there are dissident voices. But, as in all areas where there is a dominant paradigm, your career can suffer if you kick against it too much, it is difficult to argue for something contrary to the conventional wisdom. I think the challenge posed by Bennett and Hacker to the dominant paradigm (Bennett & Hacker, 2003), eds.]

was simply dismissed with too little care, for they were right to pose it.

## 5. The role of expertise in the welfare state

INT5: *I was wondering if you could say something about the current role of expertise in society today. In particular, I would like to hear your comments about the way welfare professions and semi professions, like nursing, teaching and so on, are being managed. For instance, what dimensions of expertise does new public management favor? Do modern welfare states provide good conditions for developing the kind of expertise you write about?*

CW: I think conditions are difficult under new public management, where one of the premises appears to be, that there aren't very high levels of trust between managers and workers. If you take the kind of approach adopted in the dual system, the worker is expected to be both autonomous, and to be able to work in teams with other people. As you probably know, the Germans emphasize the skill element of Fertigkeiten and what they call Fähigkeiten [Winch, 2010, p. 73]. Are those distinctions present in Danish as well? In this approach, planning, evaluating, coordinating, communicating are all extremely important elements of one's professional competence. They can't just be reduced to skills. There is another piece of Ryle's work which is much less well known, called *On Thinking*, which calls attention to this. I have learned a lot from it. Ryle put his finger on something which is often overlooked in English philosophical discourse. It is very much here in the German one. So to answer your question: to have independent workers who can coordinate and cooperate horizontally rather than vertically, we don't need large layers of management. One can be trusted to get on with the job, not to act in a self interested way, to be a good professional. That kind of trust doesn't seem to be much encouraged under new public management.

INT5: *So these dimensions of expertise are under pressure in the current way of managing the welfare state as you see it?*

CW: Yes. I mean, in this country, it has always been less emphasized.

INT5: *Does that mean that we are seeing another kind of expertise developing within welfare professions? To be an expert under the prevailing conditions might be something quite different than the kind of expertise you have been talking about.*

CW: I think there are different sorts of things going on. For example, in occupations like nursing, you will see much more emphasis on the regulation of higher education, where nurses are actually required to undergo higher education. But paradoxically, in countries like Britain, it doesn't lead to their being excluded from very strict performance management systems. So although in theory, higher education should enable personnel to enjoy higher levels of autonomy, in practice autonomy is not so well regarded, because it conflicts with the regime of performance management. It is a serious issue. Take teaching, for example. When teachers are held accountable, they may lose their jobs if they don't produce results. This ensures that they are going to be focused almost entirely on satisfying the demands of management. As a consequence, they may not attend to other things they believe, and have been taught to believe, are important to fulfilling their professional responsibilities. I don't think anyone has a good answer to that dilemma. I was watching a House of Commons Select Committee on education where this problem was pointed out to our Secretary of State by the Chair of the committee. No answer came, because there isn't one under the current system. As long as we work within the logic of a performance regime, we take account of its demands. Under that kind of regime, one always tries to gain advantages and avoid negative consequences. So it becomes a game of cat and mouse.

INT2: *Isn't your distinction between being an expert and excellence of action of relevance here? You seem to argue that it is quite possible to be an expert in performance management, without being an actual expert in a profession. In that case, you wouldn't necessarily be performing excellent actions, because you would be performing actions that normatively weren't the ones that you should be performing, as a nurse for example.*

CW: Yes. A thing that has happened in the educational system in Britain is perhaps of relevance here. We have seen a performance regime in school for years. If you look over the history of it, you see at first the establishment of a set of performance criteria. Pretty soon afterwards, schools learn how to take advantage of them. They produce the intended outcomes. In the next round, the criteria are further refined, and then the same thing happens all over again. The latest re-iteration of criteria has been done very thoroughly. What we have now is a very elaborate system of performance criteria for secondary schools which is intended to eliminate the possibility of gaming all together. One can conclude that whoever devised that system is an expert in performance management.

INT2: *This state of affairs cannot be considered to be something positive, because it doesn't lead to excellent actions.*

CW: The whole framework of assumptions around which the system is based has got problems.

INT2: *Exactly.*

CW: One can still be a kind of expert, but at the price of actually discounting the expertise of the people whose performances one is going to manage. That's where the problem lies.

INT5: *It is pretty much the same in Denmark, I guess. We see a new kind of expert there, one you might call "the evidence expert" or "the expert who knows best practice". This would be a professional who is able to base his practice on evidence, or, at the very least, one whose practice is informed by some knowledge of best practice. Do you see that kind of figure here in England as well? How does the figure of "the evidence expert" fit into your treatment of the different dimensions of expertise?*

CW: I think evidence-based and evidence-informed are different. There is a joke about precisely this distinction. We have all heard about something called evidence-based policymaking. Someone has remarked that it usually in reality is more like policy-based evidence making. There is a lot of truth in that comment. Once again, teaching is quite interesting as an example, because the dominant conception is that teaching is a craft, and you learn it "Lave and Wenger style". But at the same time, we hear the rhetoric about evidence-based practice. If we know what works – that's the other phrase - then we can tell teachers what to do. One simply devises a set of protocols, which are mandated by the evidence, give the teachers the protocols, and say, do this! For example, we claim to know that synthetic phonics works as a method for teaching reading. Therefore, on that basis we can devise teacher- proof programs and put them into effect. You see many examples of that kind of logic. But under it, the ability of the teacher to make judgments about what they are doing, or should be doing, is very restricted, and mostly limited to minor matters, such as the timing and sequencing of activities, rather than on making judgments about the needs of individual children. It seems that evidence-based teaching has found its own niche. On the other hand, evidence- informed teaching, where you use the evidence as an ingredient in your own making of judgments, is much less recognized. It's one of the jobs of a university to say that we need to recognize the value of that, and to argue that universities are an indispensable means for developing this capacity.

INT5: *What kind of skills would a teacher need to learn to make the transition from being simply an evidence-based teacher, to one who knows and is able to use the relevant research in his teaching practice, as one ingredient among others? What kind of knowledge or skills would an expert teacher need to be able to do that?*

CW: Your question leads back to that point that was made earlier about expertise. First of all, teachers need to be able to understand the research. I don't think teacher education, as it is done in Britain at the moment, gives them the ability to do that. Secondly, teachers need to be able to make judgments as to what bearing that research has on what they're doing. So for example, if they only read meta- studies of education, like John Hattie's, that is not really going to help them deal with problems in a classroom. In other words, they need to understand the implications- if any -of the research for what they are doing, and to formulate their own course of action on the basis of that understanding. That is where the link between theory and practice is important. It enables you to make judgments on the basis of what you've read and understood.

INT4: *Could one perhaps describe the difference between these two kinds of teachers' use of the evidence as the difference between responsibility and accountability?*

CW: Yes... I think teachers who tackle their work informed by evidence are still accountable for what they do, but in a different way. One might be asked: "Why did you make this or that judgment"? The answer will probably be something like this: "that in terms of the alternatives available to me, and the constraints present etc. it seemed to me at the time to be the best course of action to take". One relies on one's professional judgment, rather than on some protocol dictated by a performance regime.

INT2: *That teacher would likely have some explaining to do higher up in the system, because he or she would have to argue why it wasn't enough to just tick off the boxes. It's easier to be accountable upwards in the system when you just follow the protocol. So the distinction you made previously makes sense.*

CW: Well, let's take an example: Teachers are accountable under a performance regime for producing good exam results; they are not accountable for giving good advice about possible careers to children. You might say, professionally, they ought to be, because they adhere to a professional ethic that says one ought to attend to the needs of the children. But in terms of the accountability regime, they are not held accountable, just as they are not held responsible either.

## 6. The concept of learning

INT1: *Let's return to the concept of learning. Do you think knowledge of theories of learning actually helps teachers? As you know, theories of learning are not often evidence-informed.*

CW: I think they have to. I argue in my forthcoming book, that whatever happens, teachers always act on the basis of theories. As Keynes once said...business men...you think they're talking common sense, but they are actually working on the basis of some outmoded economic theory. Teachers who seem to be making very pragmatic judgments are all the time making assumptions, more or less. They justify their own justifications, on the basis of theoretical assumptions they are not fully aware of. That is a dangerous situation. It is one of the problems with the craft notion of teaching. Gramsci said that common sense is sedimented ideology and theory. If teachers only relied on common sense, that would be a really bad situation. Therefore, teachers do need to know theories. They also need to know the theories' strengths and weaknesses, and whether they are conceptually coherent.

INT5: *Could you give a more specific example of the relation between the knowledge of learning theories and the practice of teachers? Why is that relation so important?*

CW: Let me give you an example from my own teaching career . When I started teaching, the theories of Basil Bernstein on verbal deficit and working class educational achievement were very influential. I remember looking at some notes the Head of the school made at the first school I taught in. The note said that children start school without any language at all, which is obviously nonsense. That is a good example of the influence of a theory on school practice. It can really affect your perception of reality, in this case, in quite a negative way.

## 7. Rule-following in relation to learning and expertise

INT1: *I think rule-following is an important concept in your first book, The Philosophy of Human Learning. How does Wittgenstein's concept of rule-following help us to understand learning? Or does it help us?*

CW: Yes, I think it does, though I think you need to extend his account. I think that Wittgenstein was probably more concerned with how one participates in a practice and what constitutes a practice, than he was concerned with issues that have to do with how one improves within a practice. It's clear that more work needs to be done in this area. Of course, Ryle began to look into some of these issues, but he only touched upon the developmental dimensions of learning within a practice. I would say that there are norms governing the transition from novicehood to expertise. But it is probably unlikely that they can be adequately captured in a set of discursive norms. Looking at things more broadly, I would endorse the Baker and Hacker account of rule-governed activity in "Language, Sense and Nonsense" in one of their Wittgenstein commentaries, where they describe the various kinds of normative practices which jointly constitute the normative framework in which people operate, as a form of rule-governed activity. I think their thinking also takes account of the kind of objections made by people like MacIntyre against Peter Winch, for example. Smoking or sitting down or walking are not obviously rule-governed activities, in the conventional sense of the term. But they are certainly also activities subject to normative constraints at the very least, and probably normative prescriptions as well to a certain extent.

INT2: *But sometimes we might have norms and rules that we are only more or less aware of. And we might get into situations where we feel somehow that we should not merely follow our conventional norms, that the situation we're in demands something else. So my question is: what governs our judgment in those kinds of situations? In other words, how do we normatively judge our own norms?*

CW: Well, do you know the novel by Tom Wolfe called "Bonfire of the Vanities"? There is a lot in it about people who fall foul of the law, people down and out, people from black communities and so on. One of the things Wolfe does is to describe people's behavior in court. When someone is a defendant, you would normally expect their demeanor to be anxious and respectful and so on. At one point, he describes this young man coming in to the courtroom with a sort of swagger, where you go walking on the balls of your feet. He calls it a 'pimp roll'. So this guy comes into the courtroom, doing the pimp roll. In effect, he is consciously deviating from the kind of normative expectations we have of people in that situation, because he wants to make a point. He is more interested in what his peers think about him then he is about what the judge thinks. So I think that would be an example of the kind of situation you described before.

INT2: *But then he is still doing it because of norms of his peers, rather than the norms of the courtroom?*

CW: Yes, he has decided that he is going to do it that way, rather than the other way. He has got his own reasons for doing what he does.

## 8. Training and conditioning

INT3: *You distinguish between training and conditioning in your book* The Philosophy of Human Learning. *From your perspective, training involves rules and, therefore, norms. This seems to suggest there is a difference between 'mere conditioning' and training. Obviously, conditioning exists. It has a function, right? But isn't there a gap between conditioning and training, building your argument, as you do, upon Wittgenstein? And doesn't conditioning in one way or another play a role in learning?*

CW: Conditioning is a term that applies both to animals and humans I think. It is probably easiest to see the gap between conditioning and training with humans. With regards to your question, are you trying to imply that there is some kind of continuity between conditioning, training and activities. I think there probably is. I think there are cases where you move from being conditioned to do certain things to being able to be trained to do certain things. Again, perhaps one example might be Strawson's account of how children learn to react to resentment in the early stages of their moral formation. First, we have reactive behaviour on the part of adults. This in turn leads to reactive behaviour on the part of children. These patterns of reaction again become the foundation, if you like, for the ability to be trained in certain activities. So, I wouldn't argue that there was an absolutely impermeable distinction between the two.

INT3: *My question might be related to something we talked about earlier, when we discussed Ryle and his silence regarding the role of the body in cognition, when I used the term "the ground for dispositions". If we adopt the Wittgensteinian perspective, we will ask questions like" how does the infant get in to this more or less closed circle of rule-following, or" how does he gain entry into concrete life-forms" et cetera. These kinds of questions point at conditions of early human life... where we might get some help from biology and psychology. But*

*Ryle and Wittgenstein are notoriously afraid of dealing with empirical science.*

CW: The growth of the ability to speak and to understand is extremely important here. Ryle does actually draw a distinction between drilling and training, which is pretty much the same as the distinction that I've been trying to draw. And as far as I recall, Ryle argues the two are different, but he does not argue that there is no possible transition between the two. But, as you suggest, he does not actually give us an account of how you get from the state where someone is capable of being conditioned, to one where the person is capable of being trained. And certainly one of the capacities which make the transition possible will be the ability to understand- to understand what was being conditioned, and how that can be trained into something which is more than mere conditioning. I think an account of this transition has to involve an account of the child's growing mastery of language in various contexts.

## 9. Training, action and reflection

INT3: *We also have a couple of questions on the role of awareness, or consciousness. You consider the kind of learning associated with training as more closely linked with action than with reflection and knowledge (The Philosophy of Human Learning, p.56). This seems to give the impression that training doesn't involve conscious awareness. There are plenty of examples of inculcating a type of expertise through action without conscious awareness. So what is the relation between conscious awareness and training?*

CW: Any account of professional judgment, I think, has got to give due place to the phenomenon of people arriving at a decision consciously in some kind of ratiocinating process. I think if you can't do that, then there is something seriously missing in your account of it. Some writers on expertise, I think Ryle actually, and Dreyfus too, try and avoid this issue. I don't think it can be avoided. And I don't think it needs be avoided either, because I don't think admitting the reality of rational processes necessarily entails that you are a Cartesian, as Ryle appears to think. My own preferred way of approaching this issue would be to take the kind of view that Peter Geach took in "Mental Acts", although I would also include other elements from a Wittgensteinian perspective. My position also has very strong affinities with Vygotsky's view of the transition from outer to inner speech; that is, that we first learn to assert discursively in outer speech, and then afterwards, as a secondary ability, we learn to do it inwardly. I suggest one should conceive of judgment as something analogous to assertion, with the difference that the former primarily refers to inward activity (if one can use that term without too much confusion).

INT3: *You seem, then, to be turning the normal path of intuition around. Isn't this in line with Wilfrid Sellars and his considerations about Ryle and 'the Rylean ancestors': First, we are immersed in society and then we learn and make tools. Finally, we can use those tools to understand the process and explain ourselves as beings having minds.*

CW: Yes, and lastly be able to do that as a purely internal act. I think that is the way forward. I think these considerations are important for expertise, because you need to be able to account for the occasions where someone is confronted with a complex, unusual situation that they haven't come across before, and where they have to formulate a course of action. Perhaps it doesn't matter so much how they might subsequently explain their actions, if they are asked to justify what they did. What will come to expression in that case is the quality of the justification afterwards, not what actual mental processes they went through prior to acting. It does seem important that we allow for the possibility that people do think things through in this way, and that very often it constitutes an important condition of professional judgment. I don't think it is same thing as reflecting while acting. The idea that you can do this sort of thing in the middle of carrying out an action seems unrealistic; it is more likely these kinds of episodes usually take place at some level of detachment from the actual activity.

INT1: *So you better like the often-used concept: reflection on action?*

CW: Yes, that's right. Or also: reflection before action.

INT2: *But sometimes while acting you have to act more intuitively, in the heat of the moment, so to speak. Afterwards, you will likely be able to rationalize what you did, but the fact is, you did act, and probably with good reason. What would you call the form of judgment made in that kind of situation? If it is not reflection in action, then what is it? It is one thing to supply the arguments beforehand; quite another to come with them afterwards. But given that one did act, and that one acted accountably and responsibly and well in the situation, what is one doing if the judgment actually is only articulated afterwards?*

CW: I think there is clearly a distinction between thoughtful and non-thoughtful action, and I'd be happy to use that distinction when dealing with the sorts of cases you describe. But again, as Wittgenstein said, 'Thinking is a widely ramified concept'. It doesn't entail that one has to go through some sort of conscious representational action in order to act thoughtfully, or to think while acting.

INT3: *How would you avoid the fallacies of representationalism, that is, of having to judge and represent your own mental states? I think you obviously want to avoid the pitfalls of representationalism as a first-level description of mental states – of mentality as such – but when you are reflecting on your own cognition, don't you need a means of representing your own mental states?*

CW: I don't have a problem with that. My problem lies with describing the brain as a user of representations.

INT1: *Where would you locate the process of representation? If it is not there in the brain, where else could it be?*

CW: We do have representational abilities, and these are the prerequisites of representation, which is an important point.

INT5: *Could you elaborate on something you were discussing previously with Interviewer 2, where professionals act in the heat of the moment. In some way, one can say there is knowledge in play. There is some process of performing and knowing occurring in the action. How do you conceptualize that situation? There is both action and knowledge, but there doesn't seem to be much reflection involved in the process. You just do something because you have to do something. Somehow it seems to be a good idea. How would you view or describe that situation?*

CW: Quite a lot of our abilities can be described discursively but they are not completely described discursively. I think that includes both capacities connected with acquaintance or perception and also capacities associated with knowing how to do things. So we have capacities which we are not fully aware of, always. They are not present to our conscious minds. And for which our explanatory abilities are just incomplete or inadequate to fully describe them. That is the harmless version, if you like, of what are termed the tacit elements of knowledge. The capacities we have outrun our ability to describe how we use them. When someone is asked why they did such and such in the heat of the moment, some sort of explanation and justification is called for. Depending on the context, it might be an inquiry, if something has gone badly wrong. The focus will then be on the quality of the explanation, rather than on trying to establish exactly what was going on in the person's mind at the time. To what extent one accepts the justification and explanation offered, I guess, depends on the circumstance.

INT1: *Maybe this point has some connection with Vygotsky's view of developing tools when we are trying to explain something, and how this process can help us to develop our ways of thinking.*

CW: Yes, you are right. I think it does, because it involves a kind of reflection on action as well. One asks oneself: Why did I do that? That can lead to greater self knowledge.

INT2: *If you had to point at one learning theorist, would Vygotsky be your favourite?*

CW: I have never been very happy with the actual accounts given of scaffolding, for example. As a conceptual framework, though, I think it is more promising than some of the other existing frameworks. I have never seen a Vygotskian approach really used as well as it might have been. For some reason, it has always seemed disappointing to me. I don't quite know why that is.

INT1: *I think there has been a lot of focus on scaffolding. People tend to forget all the other things Vygotsky said.*

INT3: *Can I go back to the question of consciousness? Do you have any independent ideas on the notion of consciousness? Obviously, there is a difference between tacit and non tacit knowledge, just as there is a difference between conscious and non-conscious behaviour, or between conditioning and training These differences exist. But what about consciousness as such, and its possible role in mental causation? I am curious to hear your comments about that.*

CW: I think it is implicit in what I have said. There are clear cases of what you might want to call mental causation. Cases where somebody considers alternative courses of action, argues merits and demerits, maybe to themselves, maybe to someone else ... and on that basis, acts. I don't see anything particular problematic about that.

INT 3: *I am thinking of the standard ontological issues.*

CW: Perhaps you mean some of the ones Ryle raises. There is the regress argument, for example: if you avow something, then you must know how to avow, which assumes that you know that such and such is a way to avow, and so on.

INT 3: *I am referring both to the ontological problem of the explanatory gap, and the ontological question about what consciousness is as such. Maybe you wouldn't put it like that; maybe you don't agree with this way of posing the question about the nature of consciousness. Previously, it seemed that you were saying that Ryle had got it wrong, because he opted for the dichotomy of dualism and non-dualism, excluding the possibility that there might be something in between. So that is what I am thinking of- the standard ontological question.*

CW: I suppose my view would be similar to that of Strawson, that a human being is a primitive category to which p-predicates apply. I would be happy with that. You keep on asking for an explanation, how one might explain our capacity for judgment. I have explained why I think Ryle's account is unsatisfactory. What more do you want? Of course, that is not going to satisfy a lot of philosophers or psychologists.

INT1: *When you talk about judgments, are you referring to a certain theory? What kind of theoretical explanation would you give of judgment?*

CW: I think the best explanation I've seen is Peter Geach's. I think it needs elaboration because he only deals with the case of assertion; he doesn't, for example, extend his account to supposition, or to the processes of reasoning that lead to conclusions. But I don't think it would be philosophically problematic to extend his account.

INT 1: *Many refer to Aristotle's concept of phronesis, or something like it. Does that make sense to you?*

CW: Yes, as long as judgment takes account of the concrete situation people are in. I think phronesis also covers the phenomenon of the *way* in which people do things, not necessarily when they are ratiocinating or contemplating their actions, but when they are acting thoughtfully. I think phronesis, generally speaking, has to do with the way in which something is done. It is not an added extra, as Ryle would say, or a parallel activity that goes on alongside action.

INT3: *How one views it might also depend on one's (philosophical) training, you might say.*

CW: I do think phronesis is something more than prudence. Some people describe it as prudence. There seems to me to be a distinction between regarding the virtue in itself, and then considering how it is actually exercised.

INT1: *In Denmark we talk often about forms of knowledge. You seem to use the concept in another way. In your book, it seems more to signify subjects or disciplines ...*

INT2: *... Like the German "Fach" or "Fach Gebiet". Is that correct?*

CW: Yes, that is right. I have been very influenced by Hirst's theory of the forms of knowledge. I just think that it tries to do things at too high a level of generality. That's one problem. The other problem is that it doesn't take sufficient account of the more practically oriented subjects, for example, the ability to speak a foreign language. Unfortunately, when Hirst revised his position, he went completely off in the other direction, and argued that what really matters are practices, without offering any account at all about how knowledge might inform practices. So, in a sense, he is a bit like Ryle there. I think it was a mistake for Hirst to abandon the idea of forms of knowledge. I think, as I mentioned, there was a problem with generality. There was also the problem of not taking sufficient account of practical subjects. He probably also needed to look more into the question of how knowledge of a "Fach" might affect action. In my view, those things could have been done.

INT 2: *Danish is very similar to German and we often struggle with translating the term "faglighed", which is "Fachlichkeit". I think that what you are actually trying to get at with the term 'forms of knowledge' is what we mean by "faglighed". Does that make sense?*

CW: Yes I think so.

INT 2: *It is a field of knowledge for a subject, which includes systematic knowledge, as well as the ways of applying systematic knowledge in different situations and from different perspectives - a Weltanschauung, a way the subject views the world. Does that make sense?*

CW: It does. But there is something else which Hirst does not bring out as much as he could, which is the fact that subject expertise does involve a lot of know-how. It involves the ability to find your way around the subject, to grasp the connection between concepts, make material inferences and so on. It is unfortunate that he didn't develop that side of it, because then he would have seen more clearly that subject expertise has a lot in common with know-how. I think people who talk about learning outcomes forget that as well. They think that knowledge can be adequately described in terms of someone's ability to state propositions and understand their relationships.

## References

Bennett, M., & Hacker, P. M. S. (2003). *Philosophical Foundations of Neuroscience.* Oxford: Blackwell.

Winch, Christopher (1998). *The Philosophy of Human Learning.* London and New York: Routledge.

Winch, Christopher (2010). *Dimensions of Expertise.* London: Continuum.

# An interview with Knud Illeris

*Interviewed by Mikala Hansbøl and Gerd Christensen*

## About Knud Illeris
Knud Illeris (1939-) is Professor Emeritus of Lifelong learning at the Danish School of Education, Honourable adjunct professor at Teachers College, Columbia University, and an inducted member of the International Adult Education Hall of Fame.

He is the author of numerous articles and books and, since the late 1960's, he has worked on questions like "How does human learning function?" and "What happens when intended learning fails or becomes distorted?" (Illeris, 2015). In 2007, (2006 in Denmark) Illeris published the book "How We Learn: learning and non-learning in school and beyond" in which he presented an updated version of what he calls a comprehensive and coherent learning theory – a new edition is expected to be published in September 2016. One of the central elements of his theory, and perhaps one of the best-known of his ideas, is his conception of the learning triangle, in which learning is represented as the intersection of content, incentives and interaction in a concrete context. Illeris' work is remarkable for the way it strives to understand learning empirically as progression and regression, with continual movements back and forth between the two poles in an increasingly fluid world. Illeris adopts an eclectic approach to learning, and his inspiration stems from a variety of sources. He developed his own position by compiling and developing a wide variety of theories, such as: perspectives interested in student-centred education (e.g., Jean Piaget, Thomas Nissen and Carl Rogers); the Frankfurter School, combining Marx-inspired understandings of society and Freudian understandings of the individual (e.g., Oskar Negt, Thomas Leithäuser, and Thomas Ziehe). Donald Schön's work on the reflexive practitioner and David Kolb's theory of experiential learning have also had a significant influence on Illeris' thinking. In his later work, Illeris has been inspired by the notion of transformative learning, as can be found, for example, in the work of Jack Mezirow, and by Peter Jarvis's approach to learning.

Illeris is, and has been for many years, highly influential in the field of education, both in Denmark and internationally, where his empirical research, as well as theoretical work, have influenced educational policies, and inspired numerous educational programs. Illeris's groundbreaking work on problem-oriented learning and participatory direction was one of the major sources of inspiration for the development of the then (1972) new University Centre of Roskilde. The latter emphasizes the importance of the students' self-directed, problem-solving activity in learning, and it sees project-oriented group-work as the central study activity of the university. Illeris has also been an influential figure in relation to vocational education, where he has developed empirically-inspired theories of vocational training, which aimed simultaneously at the development of 'general' qualifications and personal development.

With his book "Learning in the Competition State" (Illeris, 2014, in Danish), Illeris continues to contribute to our understanding of how important the discussion of the concept of learning is to the field of education and educational research. As he himself states:

> "... genuine learning theory is about how learning takes place and functions in various situations and conditions, and not about how it can be streamlined as an industrial production process – simply because learning is an entirely human, and in no way industrial, matter" (2015).

The following interview was conducted as a historical-biographical interview, and it took the form of a conversation with Illeris, where our primary interest lay in the task of understanding the 'engine room' underlying the wide variety of his work and ideas on education. We wanted to obtain deep insight into Illeris' thinking on learning, the development of competence, education and practice. And we were interested in exploring the course of his theoretical development, tracing developments in his learning theory and understanding of learning, as it finds expression in his work, from its beginning up until today.

The interview was conducted at Roskilde University on March 2nd, 2015.

# Interview with Knud Illeris

I: *When we consider your work as a whole, it has an incredibly broad scope. When looking at your work throughout your life it gives us an idea of the range of the concepts and ideas you have developed. The interesting thing is that in the process, we get pieces of the puzzle, which help us to understand what your engagement with the problem of learning has been all about.*

K: I have noticed that something has begun to happen to our conceptions of learning since around the turn of this century (even though my latest book on learning first came out in 2006). Even then, the whole idea of learning was beginning to lose ground to the concept of education. It seems clear to me that what has happened is that when education is discussed, those who aren't in the teaching profession believe that learning and education are identical. Most people seem to believe that if one is educated as something or other, then one has learned everything that stands in the course descriptions and teaching objectives. Whether one has learned the subject matter well, or badly, or not at all, nobody seems to know; what good and poor learning is, again, nobody seems to know; and what is necessary for learning to be useful and used in practice, no one seems to care too much about either. What authorities are really interested in is, how many students complete their courses and graduate, and perhaps, what kind of marks and test results they have achieved, for they believe that gives a concrete indication of what they can do. In my opinion, this supposition has no basis in reality.

I: *You say that the concept of learning has largely been replaced by "the concept of education". How does the idea of competence fare in that connection?*

K: It has suffered the same fate. If one reads all the OECD literature on the subject, the discussion actually ends on a note of agreement. The Ministry of Education has made what is called the Danish set of quality standards. As far as I can tell, there is about 10,000 different kinds of competence named in the standards, but these find no real equivalents in what the current system of education actually qualifies one to do. That one becomes qualified in relation to certain competencies means little more than that the curriculum attached to a particular course of study is supposed to provide people with these abilities. The whole thing is quite technocratic... Of course, students have passed some tests, and one can not deny the fact that they may have acquired certain competencies. But, firstly, that is no guarantee that they in fact possess them, and secondly, the question can be asked, on what level they have them. Originally, when the notion of competence first made its appearance, it meant what one was actually capable of in praxis. But when one lines up 10,000 competencies neatly in a row, what is going on is little more than a form of self-deception, where one comes to believe that one is capable of almost anything.

I: *Yes, and in some sense the notion seems to be taken out of context. As I understand the term competence, context is an important part of it.*

K: That's certain. Whether something is learned well or not is not unimportant... Bertel Haarder (a former Danish Minister of Education) often used the criteria of whether learning was better or worse. He actually used the term "learning" sometimes. But he unequivocally identified the quality of learning with test results, for example, with PISA results.

I: *How could we approach and understand learning. Is it a process whereby we are "informed", or is it a process where the learner is active? Could you comment on that? These conceptual differences and developments are in themselves quite interesting.*

K: I am currently doing some historical work, and I see that one actually began to use the former term in the first half of the 1990's; the concept was sort of just thrown into the ring at the time. Learning conceived as the process of receiving knowledge implies the notion that something is inserted or put into us; linguistically, it puts the learner in the position of receiver. I argue strongly for the term learning, understood as an active process. There is nothing or no one that can teach anything into me, not even the best teacher in the world. I am the one who learns, who takes it in.

I: *Back in the 70's, in your books on project work, you seemed to employ the term learning more in the sense of "being informed". But you probably meant learning in the sense in which you employ the term today?*

K: Yes, that is right. But the word "learning" did not exist in the Danish academic literature at the time. One can say that it is an anglification, that is, a term taken from English. I do not know how it happened, but I do know, that when I read the word learning a dozen times or so, I thought it actually works better.

I: *It is also more precise in relation to the point you make in your books, that is, that students need to be active in some way if they are to learn anything, and make it their own, isn't that right?*

K: You are absolutely right with regards to the notion that one should be active; the idea began to make its appearance already in the 1950's, but only first really came to stay in the '70's. The shift towards using the concept of competence happened somewhat later, even though its original meaning is entirely in keeping with the above mentioned conception of learning.

I: *Yes, instead of the concept of qualification one adopted...*

K: The concept of qualification is kind of a middle thing which existed in a phase of transition, and I was very fascinated with the term at the time. But when competence appeared as an idea, I was not hard to convince, though many of my good colleagues still kept their distance from it, similarly with regards to it's supposed place of origin. One thought at the time that the idea had something to do with OECD, and that got people on their toes. But that the notion originated there does not necessarily mean the idea is bureaucratic. In the meantime, that point of the term has been lost.

I: *You point out something in your books... I'm thinking about the three parameters or axis you see in relation to the concept of learning. Learning seems always to have a societal dimension, something that is bound up with concrete contexts, isn't that right? I see the same feature present in the notion of competence. Is it also present in the more passive sense of learning as "receiving information"?*

K: I do not know. I will say there were people who were proponents of the term "indlæring"... (i.e. "learning in"). I think I have to say in any case no. The term "indlæring"[1] in Denmark in the 1970's was used precisely in the same way that one uses the term learning today. I do not know how exactly one came to insert the prefix "ind" in the word. I think maybe it derives from German, but the difference between 'lehren' and 'lernen' has also been the subject of unending debate. And of course, there is also the difference between teaching and learning, but here we don't have to worry about any 'ind' in these terms...

I: *I find that quite interesting, that there was really no difference between how one used the term "indlæring", and the way one uses the term learning today. Can you elaborate upon that in relation to educational policy, for instance?*

K: When I say that it was used in that sense, I simply mean it is the word that was used. The discussion about whether learning should be understood primarily as something receptive, or as something active, is much older. It can certainly be traced back to Dewey, and also to Piaget. I do not know what the equivalent term is in French, but the French concept of learning was normally translated as 'indlæring' in Danish. The Danish educational researcher Thomas Nissen wrote a little book called 'Indlæring og Pædagogik'. It's by far the best book written in Danish on the subject. In it, he just uses the term 'indlæring'- and that's that! So, in my opinion, the linguistic change refers to a change in understanding. That change in understanding was there at the time, and one can still say today that the situation is somewhat fluid. That is to say, learning around the middle of the past century was understood as something one received, which is also often the case today. One could say that there is more debate around the issue today, but it is the bureaucracy that decides these things.

I: *I have also noticed an increasing use of the term in the last two and a half years and it is still thought-provoking that one seems to meet the term 'indlæring' more and more often.*

K: I had the same thought myself recently, a week or so ago, when I fell over the same term again.

I: *That is interesting, maybe because it indicates there is not the same level of reflective awareness around the terms one employs, and what kind of historical undertones they bring with them.*

K: Yes, either that, or the fact that one wanted to make a clear distinction between learning and 'indlæring'.

I: *If it is done consciously, it does not make it any less interesting.*

K: I really doubt that that's the case. It is more an atmosphere, something that is in the air. And it is really something that hangs in the air today. Whoever you talk to now, whether it be parents, or teachers of whatever kind, seems to have this belief that it is the teachers who teach the students something. And the corollary is, that students are simply receptors.

I: *Hasn't one always seen things that way? Maybe in educational settings one has had the idea that students are responsible for their own learning, and need to be active etc. etc. But in one way or another, parents have surely always thought, that if their child can not do what he is supposed to do, it is the teacher's fault.*

K: I am sure you are right, generally speaking. But in educational circles, where people take a more than everyday interest in pedagogy, for a period of around 30 years, the dominant paradigm had been one which understood learning as the student's active appropriation of the subject matter. I believe that one can still find proponents for this view. It is one of the theories I hold on to hopefully, and which I still hope is so much a part of our blood here in Denmark, that if one went into a Danish classroom, you would see teacher behaviour that was in conformity with this conception of learning. I am especially thinking about the public schools. But I have also recently done some work with high school teachers, and even though they as a group have never been particularly passionate about pedagogy, they also understand what I am talking about here. There is still a contradiction between what is discussed 'higher up' in the system, especially at the political-administrative level, and what is actually going on in schools. But I doubt whether the newly-educated teachers which are entering the field will see things this way.

I: *You referred before to technocracy in connection with the notion of competence, and I started thinking about how, in relation to the influence of context and culture upon learning processes, these shape our concepts in different ways at different times, and how technology, and the material resources that follow in its wake, have significance for how we move in and out of this domain. It is an area I am particularly interested in. When you use the term technocratic, I can not help thinking that some of these matters maybe also have something to do with certain developments that have taken place since the turn of the century. I am thinking of the increased focus on new technology, especially digital technology. Could you say something about this area, as it is not something you have written a great deal about in your work to date.*

K: I feel somewhat on shaky ground here, as I have not had the chance to do work in that area for many years. I have previously worked with the Danish researcher Lone Dirckinck-Holmfeldt, and it is her I would point to as a possible reference. Where I encounter technology is in a high school context, where students have all kinds of small gadgets, which often are a source of irritation. Of course, one can learn through the use of computers, but even then, it is still the individual person who learns; the computer screen is simply the medium which presents the material to be learned.

I: *So it is just an instrument like so many other things?*

K: Fundamentally, as I understand things, it is only the mode which mediates the flow and form of input that has changed. At the same time, I would be the first to insist that the context in which learning occurs is also a part of the learning process. And if the context is shaped by the texts or the pictures one is supposed to learn something from, as a kind of substitute for a teacher, or by the social media such as Facebook, or by similar media which permit a kind of communicative exchange, I do not really have anything specific to say about how these factors might eventually influence learning. I have not worked with these things in practice. The whole of the development of my theory of learning has taken place in conjunction with practical experience. And this experience has largely been derived from my work with vocational courses of study, partly first from Vocational Education[2] (EFG), later from the 10 years I was at Adult Vocational Training Centres.[3] There, one had the opportunity to experience first-hand some of the things most theoreticians do not have much knowledge about. And this has contributed to an understanding of learning that has many facets to it.

I: *Yes, you also speak about the affective dimension of learning, for instance, the significance of the emotional aspect in education. It allows us to speak about what can be called resistance-to-learning.*

K: I refer both to motivation in the positive sense, as engagement, but also to resistance and defence. Not the least my experience in the area of vocational education has taught me its' significance.

K: The fact that the content, the context, the situation, and the emotions connected with them are part of an integrated whole, and that this finds expression in learning outcomes, is, in my opinion, the most ground-breaking insight found in my understanding of learning. It is not just that motivation is seen as the catalyst of learning, motivation is part and parcel of the *way* an individual learns; hence, it also becomes a part of the results of learning. I remember the time when this first hit me; there was a fellow called Furth, who had plucked 3 of Piaget's formulations taken from different places in his work, and he set them up, one after the other. It was plain to see that they represented 3 slightly different understandings. Piaget's understanding of the significance of the emotions had changed over time, without he, or anybody else, noticing it. So, one could ask the question: what is the correct understanding in this instance? The correct interpretation is that the emotional or motivational dimension always is an integral part of the result(s) of learning. Piaget has the example of two boys, who both learn that two and two makes four, just simple mathematics really. Both will be able to use what they've learned in a similar way, both would get the same results in a PISA test, but for one of the boys, mathematics is simply essential to his understanding of the world, while for the other, it is just a pile of crap that he's been forced to learn. And it is true enough what Piaget writes, that two and two still are four for both of them, but the contexts in which they can use that knowledge, and what they can use it for, differs greatly.

I: *Yes, and likewise in regards to their future development (or lack thereof) as mathematicians... Another thing I'd like to ask about concerns the concept of activity. When you say that students must be active in order to learn, it has often hit me that there are many different concepts of activity that come into play. There is the concept of activity that Piaget works with, which involves cognitive activity, and, of course, also activity in relation to primarily a material environment. Then, there is the concept of activity you use in connection with the pedagogy of the project-form, which in addition implies that one addresses a societal problem of some kind, at the same time that one does something in practice. Could you say something about these different notions of activity?*

K: I am willing to acknowledge that pure cognition does not appear to me to be what the term implies. The classic example is the person who is trying to solve some kind of a mathematical problem. You can call it, if you wish, a purely cognitive activity, as the person is actively trying to solve the problem. It is still an activity, but of course, not of the same kind as a practical activity. But there is an affective dimension present in both cases. The boy is enthusiastic about solving math problems, just as another could get just as excited doing crossword puzzles. The other possible association could be likened to a kind of slavish experience. I sit down and work on this problem because I have to; it does not really interest me in the least. I will try and get the right answer, because of the consequences of a wrong one, but what the actual result is, I could not care less. These kinds of examples represent extremes, but what I really would like to use them for is to say, that the active aspect of learning is always present. So the tendency to distinguish between the active and the passive can quickly become linguistic hair-splitting. Activity is always present. One can learn something even if one is not at all interested in the subject matter, but in that case, it is only superficial learning that is going on, and what is learned is much more likely to be forgotten. An important criterion for measuring the quality of learning is when, or in what situations, one thinks about it, which is something different than what PISA measures. It is the transferability problematic that comes into play here. I would like to use the example of reading the newspaper. For up to half the articles, a chemist might get associations that would remind him of various kinds of pollution; for very many of our daily activities, a chemist would be able to use his knowledge of chemistry, where 99% of the ordinary readers would be unable to do so. This implies, that if one has appropriated and learned chemistry in this way, it has become part of one's identity, and so much so, that one can think of the chemical consequences, or implications, of observed relations in a wide variety of situations, where we others can it. I think we all have learned some rudimental chemistry, but how many of us think of chemistry when we are standing at home cleaning the kitchen table? Some of us may think of hygiene, but that is not the same thing. We may know more or less about hygiene, but a chemist thinks of hygiene in terms of formulas. So the quality of learning, its true aim, is expressed in when, and how often, one thinks about it, when and in which situations one makes connections to what one has learned.

I: *Yes, and is that what is implied in the notion of learning by experience, at least partially?*

K: Learning by doing is based on the same thought, just said 'in other words'.

I: *When one discusses different forms of teaching, one can also mention the situation where students simply sit down and listen to the teacher, where they are not really active. It seems it is necessary for them to do something if learning is to be optimal.*

K: Students who sit in the class and listen dutifully to their teacher probably learn to some degree what is being taught. But depending upon their level of engagement and their intellectual prerequisites, what is learned can vary considerably. Let us say, there are 30 students sitting in the class, and the teacher talks for half an hour, and this results in 30 different outputs, 30 different learning outcomes. The contents of what is learned in each case also differs, which can also be reflected in differing test results, which in turn may also contain other qualitative differences that a test can't bring to light.

I: *In your latest article, you mention that your work has been met with both discussion and criticism. That is of course unavoidable in a long career. Were you able to use the critique constructively?*

K: I have received very little criticism with regards to my conception of learning. I have never met anyone, and by that I mean anyone, that has come up and said to me that my model of learning is mistaken. But I have been met with some critique of the contextual relations I set the model into. The criticism is based in one way or another upon the understanding that sees learning as essentially the learning of a curriculum.

I: *More precisely, you mean that...?*

K: ...that the consequence of curriculum-based teaching is not a particularly intelligent way of encouraging learning. I argue that point more or less directly, and indirectly, and there are, of course, some to whom that assertion does not sit well with. Some think that 'of course, that is the way it is', while there are others who, deep inside, have a sense that 'that is not the way things are'. But the pedagogical critique I have received has aligned itself with a traditional understanding of learning. And, of course, political interests also come into play. I employ my conception of learning in a variety of contexts, some of which have political over-and-undertones. There are, of course, others who desire something else again, and who think that people should learn something other than what I think they should learn. This tendency has grown very strong over the last few years. The competition-state's conception of learning centres, in the final analysis, on the production of competencies that can be used to bolster our competitive position internationally. First, I simply disagree with the premise, that that is what we should be striving for. Secondly, that approach to education is certainly not one which looks at things from a human point of view. That deficiency in itself may have negative effect on our ability to compete. A much more creative school, a much more active school. A school much less concerned with evaluation and grading and compiling statistics would be steps in the right direction; if one loosened the reins, and returned to things as they were 20 or 30 years ago, one would get a far greater return on one's investment in upgrading the qualifications of the working force. In addition, it would have the consequence that there would be more individuals who could use their creativity in the workplace.

Something I have often noticed, and commented upon, is that the people who do not like my conception of learning are either those who take a very academic approach to the subject, or they are technocrats. Businessmen, on the other hand, especially those from the productive sectors, look at it with much interest. I worked for 10 years in the organization 'Project Plan', where we focused upon the learning environment at the workplace, and our approach was very much in line with the thinking of progressive business professionals. What I really want to say, is that all of those people who believe in measuring everything according to whether it contributes to our ability to compete internationally, never actually get around to creating a school and a system of education which will live up to that standard, because they believe, for example, in the power of incitements. I think the enormous significance marks have received at the high school level results in poorer learning; what one learns is how to get good marks. If what you want is for people afterwards to work creatively with more advanced courses of study, then high school has to do things differently. The funny thing is that it actually has begun to develop in that direction.

The high school is not so much concerned with rote and repetition as it once was, but we are seeing some signs of change now where marks again are placed in the foreground, a step in the wrong direction in my view.

I: *You said something about learning becoming impoverished before, as well as something about good and bad learning, and about defence mechanisms and resistance. Can you elaborate on what you mean by good and bad learning, and why, for example, it is so important to focus upon the phenomena of learning resistance?*

K: I think you have found a citation that deals precisely with motivation, haven't you? It is there where I point out the connection between education and learning: "The most important question a teacher or a counsellor can ask himself is "what significance does this subject matter have for people's lives and situations?" (Interview with Illeris on transformative learning (2013), 2015: http://runningwithnolegs.com/knud-illeris/)

Your insight and intuition have enabled you to find the citation which expresses exactly what I want to say. In relation to teaching, it is probably the most important thing of all. Furthermore, it is something I have experimented a great deal with, together with teachers, always with other teachers. I know a moving story about 3 high school teachers who teach the most hated subject of all at the secondary level - the study of ancient societies, a compulsory subject. Three young men from the provincial periphery of Denmark got together and tried to discuss how to do something about it; after all, it was not very pleasant for them to have to teach the subject, and it was quite likely that, in the not-too-distant future, the course would either be discontinued, or it would cease to be compulsory. It happened that they agreed to look more closely at the curriculum, and what professionals in the area had to say; then, they divided the material in three and went home, and tried to identify the places where the study of ancient societies might have something to say to the life-situations and problems of their students. The first big surprise was that all three came back with a long list of suggestions! There were a lot of possibilities. The second was that when they put it into practice, despite of course varying results, generally speaking the activity level in the classroom rose dramatically. And the third, not unsurprising, consequence was that the students spent more energy on preparation, with the result that they got higher marks in the end. I would say this is a pretty strange and ironic example, because in my opinion, I think we could quite easily live without ancient studies.

This just told me that in almost every context you can think of, there exists the possibility of relating the subject matter to the group of people who have to learn it, thereby creating the conditions for a living engagement with it.

I: *Yes, and for relevance - a sense of relevance.*

K: That idea points to the level of didactics. But in any case it creates the engagement necessary to create qualitatively better learning.

I: *It is also a question about formation, and the relationship between education and learning.*

K: The concept of education is simply capable of multiple interpretations. It both covers something I am crazy about, and something that I can not swallow. I am not an opponent of what one can refer to as the formative[4] processes in education, because often, when one uses the term formation, one means the same thing as I do when I use the term competencies. And I mean *real* competencies. Where the substance of what is learned is integrated with a sense of personal relevance and engagement. If that is what is meant by education and formation, then I am all for it. But I do not use the word myself, because it seems to suggest 'high culture' for some, but not for others. Some people use the term to imply that education has to involve the whole person, and if that is the case, it is fine by me; others use it as an expression of quality defined by one's social class, as a way of indicating cultural power.

I: *Education is a concept that has become increasing significant, because one of the things that characterizes some of the ongoing discussions at primary school, is the tendency to employ the concept of learning without explaining more closely what is meant by the term. Moreover, we do not take the time to discuss the reason(s) for our schools' existence. What kind of human beings and what kind of society do we want? I consider these questions to be central to the whole discussion on learning, and the answers depend on what underlying concepts of knowledge you are operating with. In the didactically very technical, result-oriented system we have, it becomes important to take up precisely these issues. Not from the perspective of high culture, but precisely to arrive at more fundamental discussions of education, and our school's 'raison d'etre'.*

K: If you use the term education in that sense, you are likely to understand learning in a contrary sense. Learning is what can be put to good use on a PISA test, whereas education refers to qualitative formation, to the cultivation of personal qualities, etc. etc. But if learning is defined as mere training and repetition, not only does it reduce learning to 'indlæring', it becomes merely technical - rote learning, or something similar.

I: *I also take the term up because I want to look at what it includes. One sense of learning refers to internal processes going on in the human subject. I consider these in reality to be psychological, and they refer to a relationship between the individual and the world. But, moreover, also the discussion of the determination of learning's contents seems important: that is, what the relations are between the fact of appropriation, the content of what we appropriate, and the qualities of that content seen in relationship to the kind of society we want to create. As you say, there is an appeal to an ideal in relation to the contents of what is to be learned, as well as to the choice of the content itself. Can you say something about the relation between learning and content, and about the relationship of the latter to what we want to accomplish.*

K: In the first place, all learning has a content. You can not speak about learning without it being learning something. All content, in turn, bears some relation to the learner, and that relationship is very important for engagement, and thus the quality of learning. Society has an interest that it's members all acquire a certain common corpus of knowledge, as well as that its' professionals and technicians, whatever their kind, appropriate a more concretely defined set of concepts and skills. There can not really be any doubt about that. It's not always the case that this 'content' is in accord with what the learners are actually engaged in learning. But then one can say, that one of the problems is, that the contents found in curriculum outlines are chosen partly out of a qualitative evaluation of what is useful in different contexts, and partly with an eye to traditional and customary parameters which may no longer be valid in reality. I have myself participated in committees whose purpose was to discuss the contents of the curriculum with professionals in their respective subjects. These experts could not do it properly. They had difficulty distinguishing between the parts of their subject which were fair to pour into the heads of their students, from those parts which were not. That is one problem. At the other end of the spectrum, there is the problem which occurs in daily life in the classroom, where teachers have the reasonable desire that the students should learn something that they may not think is worth learning.

This is unavoidable, and the little quote mentioned before, which asks us to find the place where the engagement of the students lie, is the answer to that problem. So, the answer is really two-sided. There has to be some kind of content, but a good part of the content in the majority of courses of study is chosen badly, in my opinion. On the other hand, it is the teacher's task to ensure a correspondence between the contents of the curriculum, and the capacities and capabilities of the students. This task would be easier if there was not so much unnecessary information that professionals have entangled themselves with. I have a short story to tell in this connection. Many years ago, when I was taught mathematics at high school level, I got into a discussion with a progressive high school principal. We both were members of a committee that was supposed to redefine the curriculum for mathematics at the gymnasium, and there was a subject domain that was called 'imaginary numbers'. Imaginary numbers are what the name suggests, imaginary, numbers that do not exist in the real world. I myself knew, as did my colleagues, that everyone was afraid of getting a question on this subject at exam time; furthermore, we knew that almost anyone who did was sure to break his or her neck on it, because the subject is so abstract that you have to be a real mathematician to find it interesting and comprehensible. I argued against retaining this particular aspect of mathematics, and for the idea that it was necessary to cut down the curriculum. At the end, the principal, who had in any case the power to decide what was included, and what was not, decided "it should remain, because it's such a beautiful piece of mathematics". So, it stayed. And every year, you can be sure there will be students who get low marks when that area comes out as their exam question.

That example expresses unequivocally the circumstance that experts in a particular subject often have difficulty in understanding, that some of the things they believe to be integral and important to their subject, are not for that reason necessarily so.

I: *Can't something be important, simply because they consider it important?*

K: That view causes a lot of problems. But in all humility, I believe I learned from my experiences at the time, when we also had other subjects to consider, and where I, for instance, sat in on discussions about geography. I felt there was a real dialogue, where we discussed things, each from his own point of view, where we tried to decide what was worth keeping, and what could better be let go. A real dialogue, particularly compared with my previous example, with the postulate that "I'm right because I am a mathematician".

I: *Could we talk more about the question of what is good and bad learning, and the theme of the competition-state. This also fits in well with what we have said earlier about the normative dimension - about whether it's a necessary part of all learning. Everything you had a hand in starting with regards to problem-based learning processes also pointed to the desirability of having critical capabilities, as well as having something one could refer to as 'democratic formation'. I think there are additional dimensions to subject content that go beyond mere intellectual knowledge, which have more to do with being a citizen in our society. And this has relevance in relation to the variety of the good, and not so good, possibilities for learning that exist, yes...?*

K: In the final analysis, you ca not speak about good or bad learning independently of the context, but the discussions always ends up revolving around the relation between content and the kind of appropriation that takes place. When all is said and done, good learning expresses itself in the circumstance that one comes to think about what one has learned in situations where it actually can be put to good use. If one has learned something that has relevance only in contexts one never will meet, it is possibly good learning, but in the end quite superficial.

I: *I am led to think about something here that is extremely interesting. If good learning is only a question of being able to recall some definite content, it is pretty close to being a form of manipulation or indoctrination. Doesn't good learning also have to do with preparing and helping those in question to take a critical stance towards learning, and towards the desirability of opposition? To create a person who can both choose for or against things. The crux of the issue, is whether we take pains to ensure that our young people are able to reflect upon the choices presented to them. That seems to be the essence of the logic of competitive thinking, that we all have to run in the same direction in order to reach comparable standpoints, and this seems to have something to do with what you are referring to when you speak of good and bad learning.*

K: I am a little in doubt as to which level I should address. There can be disjunctions and discord at many levels. But I mean a standard for determining good learning has to do with when and how often one thinks about what one has learned, for I think this gives us, if you wish, an exact criterion we can use, as opposed to the one offered by tests. It is not a test, it is reality that decides what is good and what is bad learning. Good learning is characterized by the quality that it is integrated with some kind of engagement, with a positive attitude towards what has been learned. This engagement, or positive attitude, can be acquired by reading in a book. But in the first place, personal engagement would not happen nearly as often when reading a book, as it would if one is placed in a context which encourages one to be active in relation to learning. And even though the material to be learned comes from the outside, it can be presented in a way that is measured and inspiring, so that the material is communicated in a broad variety of ways.

I wish to return to a point I have often made, that people in the world of business, who really are immersed in contexts where the ability to compete means something, are the strongest advocates for the necessity of having employees that can think independently, who are critical, engaged, and all the other positive terms one can come up with. It's not there that the one finds opposition. If we really want to strive for the goal of increasing our ability to compete, then we are going about it in the wrong way. We are simply making a mistake. There is much more to gain in a system that builds on project-work and problem-solving and similar processes; one can, of course, also make demands on this kind of system. For example, that it should deal with matters one finds relevant. This criterion is sometimes not met in practice, where one can see really good projects being done that do not have relevance anywhere, or for anything.

So, one can say, that through these processes one can develop 'generally' one's critical sense, or something like that. I am not so sure about that. The critical sense that develops and grows in relation to something concrete has more to offer in the long run, I think. It is certainly not the case that what is desired is something one-dimensional. If you have to produce thumb tacks, maybe it is possible to find one way that is the best. But that is not the way it is with human understanding and qualities, which involve reciprocity and interaction. Partly because of humanistic reasons, and partly because of political reasons, we need our courses of study to encourage more personal development, or more autonomy, or whatever you want to call it. And we need these things both in the sphere of human culture, and in the competitive arena. The contradiction lies in another place. It is between those who think only in terms of productivity and making better and bigger sausage factories, and those who really understand what it is all about.

Something that always happens to someone like me, when I insist that learning should contribute to personal development, is that people believe I am excluding the possibility of it having a real content. That is just nonsense! There is no contradiction between the two, they go hand in hand.

A new edition of my book on learning is going to be released in the spring 2016. I have in the course of recent years written a series of books on the subject of learning, and I have now tried to distil the essence of what I have written, and put that in the new edition. There are already some things I think I should have done a little differently, but that is always the way it is.

I: *Is there something we have not talked about yet that you want to mention now?*

K: There is something about competence, something about transformative learning, and something about the competition-state. These are the things I have most recently been engaged with. We have not talked yet about transformative learning.

I: *One thing that hit me when I tried to look over your activities over time had to do with the perspectives of people with limited education, a group sometimes referred to as "low-skilled". It seems like this group somehow interests you; more recently, you have looked closely at vocational education, and have focused upon barriers to learning, and upon different conceptions of it. It's not these things which occupy a central position in modern learning theory or didactics. I think it could be interesting to hear you speak more about some of these things.*

K: I am happy to hear that. For actually the question of barriers to learning, or "non-learning" as Jarvis calls it, is at least as important and worthy of attention as learning is, and maybe even more so. Maybe teachers need to know more about why there are always some who do not learn what they should, and that can always be unfolded in more detail. I think it is important to distinguish between three kinds of barriers to learning. There is incorrect learning, which springs from misunderstanding, and there is that which comes from inadequate attention - the latter can be remedied if the need arises. I still makes reference to a very old investigation that showed that all people carry around the results of faulty learning, which is no serious misfortune; if one happens to need some of it, and it is flawed, one can always make the necessary corrections. But I include that type here, because if you listen to the conversation of teachers in their staff rooms, it is almost always faulty learning they are referring to, or 'mislearning' as I term it in my writings. But this is not very problematic, because such learning can rather easily be corrected if it should be necessary. The important kinds of learning barriers are 'learning defence', which is extremely widespread today and has to be so because we are overloaded with so much information that we cannot possibly take all of it in, and 'learning resistance', which we practice when we are confronted with something which is personally unacceptable. It was actually fairly late in the game when I first began to distinguish clearly between these three maintypes of non-learning or faulty learning. It was actually in connection with my first book on learning, which came out in 1999.

Erecting defences against learning is absolutely necessary for us. So much information is thrown at us; just go home and listen to the news tonight, and your head will be filled with all kinds of information about so many things, stuff which, by and large, is pretty insignificant if you look at the bigger picture. On top of that, we are ceaselessly bombarded with things we could learn, but do not; and those who are unable to mobilize their defences end up in a psychiatric ward really quickly. They are vulnerable, and they are unable to distinguish between what is useful and what is not. That is a threatening situation. If you go back to the roots of it, this problem was discovered partly by a French philosopher by the name of Lefevre, and later on in the 1950's developed further by German Thomas Leithhauser. My thesis is that it was first during that period that the ordinary working man, farmer, or housewife began to be so bombarded with all sorts of information that they no longer were able to deal with it all. These two researchers called this phenomenon 'everyday consciousness'. This state of affairs has developed to such an extent that we all need to have a form of well structured defence that clears the field, so to speak.

There are some things that are captured by one's defences that could well have been put to good use. One must accept that, because it is necessary to have the capacity for defence, and it has to work, more or less automatically, most of the time. Also for the reason that we do not have the capability of deciding, for example, as we are watching the news, "Is this something I can put to good use?" The stream of input/information just keeps on coming, and one's automatic defence mechanisms keep much of it at a distance, but once in a while one comes to say "hey! there was something that interested me". To the extent that things work more or less that way, it becomes enormously important that we have the capacity to defend ourselves. Of course, there is the case of teachers of certain subjects, who are of the opinion that too many students have an overly-active set of defences with regards to their own subjects, geography for example, probably for the reason that a good many students find the subject not especially interesting. As long as they know that New York is located in America, they know enough to get by.

That is probably OK. But the geography teacher does not agree, because he or she feels their job implies something else. I consider this form of defence against learning not only as something necessary, but also as something good for both teachers and students, something they need to get a handle on. And we do that by discussing the more significant types of educational decisions, so that we clear the field, and get a grip on the things that really matter. Of course, there will always be some individuals who are better at managing their defences than others, and how exactly one can improve in that regard is a good question...I think the first precondition is becoming aware of the problem.

I: *And to acknowledge that there is one?*

K: Yes, that is exactly what I mean. Get a grip on it, admit that it is there. I have pointed out in other places that most people, those with limited education included, are for the most part open to reasonable arguments. They are actually in most instances interested in discussing what they themselves find worth learning. They would like for their parents to say to them, that there are things worth making an extra effort to learn. Especially if the parents are sometimes able to say that, "that stuff there, you don't need to worry too much about".

I: *Then you have resistance to learning.*

K: Resistance, well, that is something else again. The capacity for defence is simply there, and a lot goes on, and some things get simply caught in the process. Resistance is something that springs up when you get in a situation you feel called to resist, and which you cannot accept...where you encounter something you believe is not good for yourself. There are, of course, individual differences. Some have low thresholds, others have high thresholds etc. etc. Both in everyday life, and in the school system, we can say it is important, that one both has and uses the power of resistance, and that we are aware of this to such a degree that we do not uncritically accept whatever comes along. It is naturally uncomfortable for the teacher when he or she meets real resistance. In that case, it is important to be able to distinguish between the kind of resistance for which there are good reasons, and the kind of resistance for which there are not.

I have an example that I often resort to, it has to do with a high school student who I once interviewed. She said about one of her teachers that "I can not learn anything from that man". Why is that?", I asked. She replied, "He reminds me a lot of my older brother". A totally personal reason. And though I could see that that explanation didn't help her in any way, she really was caught in a hard position. She had a know-it-all for a brother. But in other cases, resistance can be in its place; and then the teacher can learn from the fact that there is resistance against one thing or the other, something which is real, and fantastically characteristic of the learning process as a whole. There are teachers who can handle that, whom I know, and it is they who are capable of understanding that resistance bears engagement within itself, and that that kind of engagement often provokes and encourages significant learning - maybe another kind of learning than what was originally intended. I have met teachers who, the first time around, when they met resistance at first rejected it, but who then afterwards approached the student in question and initiated a dialogue about it. And I have an example of an adult vocational training teacher who had the ability to deal with opposition, and the persons who effectively resisted, in such a way that it was integrated, which led to the result that both they, and the others in the class, got a lot more out of it, because the resistance in some way was accepted and worked through. That is probably one of the most demanding of the challenges one can meet as a teacher... I do not believe there is an awful lot of teachers who master it.

I: *But it does happen?*

K: Yes, it does, and it is a wonderful thing to experience, how it is possible to tackle resistance so well. And by tackling a situation of resistance, I do not only mean that one makes things work despite opposition, but that one turns it around, so that it proves to be useful to the learners.

## Notes

1. The Danish term is 'indlæring' (in-learning/learning in) which if taken literally refers to learning as something which comes into the student. Until the 90's there wasn't a Danish equivalent to 'Learning'. In the 90's the Danish word 'læring' appeared and to some extent replaced the concept of 'indlæring'. [eds.]
2. In Danish Erhvervsfaglig Grunduddannelse (EFG)
3. In Danish Arbejdsmarkedsuddannelser (AMU)
4. Formative processes/formation refer to the Danish concept 'dannelse' which is the same as the German concept Bildung[eds]

## References

Illeris, K. (2003). *Three Dimensions of Learning: Contemporary learning theory in the tension field between the cognitive, the emotional and the social.* Frederiksberg: Roskilde University Press.

Illeris, K. (2007 [2006]): *How We Learn: learning and non-learning in school and beyond.* London: Routledge.

Illeris, K. (ed.) (2014): *Læring i konkurrencestaten – kapløb eller bæredygtighed.* Frederiksberg: Samfundslitteratur.

Illeris, K. (2015): The Development of a Comprehensive and Coherent Theory of Learning. European Journal of Education, Vol. 50, No. 1, p. 29-40. Available at: http://onlinelibrary.wiley.com/doi/10.1111/ejed.12103/epdf

*Translation from Danish by Glenn Doucette*

# An interview with Anna Sfard

*Interviewed by Ane Qvortrup and Merete Wiberg*

## About Anna Sfard

Anna Sfard is Professor and Head of Department of Mathematics Education at the Faculty of Education, The University of Haifa. Sfard's area of research is in the domain of the learning sciences, with particular focus on the relation between thinking, communication and learning.

She is the author of several books and articles, including the article "On Two Metaphors for Learning and the Dangers of Choosing Just One" (Sfard 1998). This article is generally acknowledged to be an important and influential contribution in the field of learning theory. Sfard draws on metaphor theory as a source of inspiration, and she uses the metaphor as a conceptual tool to classify the foundational principles at work in theories of learning. She argues that theories of learning can be classified predominantly as either acquisition-oriented or participation-oriented, though she acknowledges that most theories of learning use elements of both metaphors. She argues in the paper that both metaphors are useful in understanding the phenomenon of learning.

Currently, Sfard has come to advocate a decidedly more participationist vision of learning. Her studies of mathematical thinking and education are clearly inspired by sociocultural theories of learning. Her recent work focusses on culture, communication and discourse, and on how we actually communicate about learning. According to Sfard, the understanding and learning of mathematics arises from discursive practices. The discussion of the problem of how one defines learning is important in the research of Anna Sfard because it contributes in her view to a better understanding of the relationship between theoretical categories of learning and the actual practice of teaching.

The following interview was conducted as an email interview between Anna Sfard and Ane Qvortrup and Merete Wiberg in the period from February to April 2015.

## Interview with Anna Sfard

## Metaphors in educational research

**Ane & Merete:** *In your paper* On Two Metaphors for Learning and the Dangers of Choosing Just one *(Sfard 1998), you use metaphors as a methodological tool for understanding our thinking on learning. Where did that idea come from?*

**Anna:** I guess my interest in metaphors comes from two places. The first source is my childhood home, my family and, more generally, the *milieu* in which I grew up. I was born into discourses saturated with metaphors. In my native environment, one wouldn't simply say she was "in a hurry" – the person would claim that, as far as she could tell, "her things" were "burning"; and the straightforward "I'd run away" would be replaced with "I'd run to the place where the pepper grows" or even "I'd go to the place where crayfish spend their winters". Yes, for whatever you could think about, one had a whole assortment of metaphors. This omnipresence of figurative expressions created a fertile soil for an interest in language and its special devices. But it was not until I was already a researcher in mathematics education that what had been ready-at-hand turned into an object of explicit reflection.

The catalyst of this change came in the form of two formative events. First, I read Michael Reddy's seminal paper *Conduit Metaphor* (Reddy, 1979). Then, at a conference,[1] I heard about two, at that time relatively recent books with the intriguing titles, *Women, fire and dangerous things* (Lakoff, 1987) and *The body in the mind* (Johnson, 1987). I got enchanted with the ideas reportedly presented in these volumes, and this led to the study of all the publications by George Lakoff and Mark Johnson I could get my hands on. In particular, I was fascinated by their jointly written slim volume with the telling title *The metaphors we live by* (Lakoff & Johnson, 1980). I devoured all these goodies one by one. At some point, the critical mass of bigger and smaller insights accumulated and I had this 'aha' effect, a kind of sudden illumination: I saw that, metaphors were the generators of our mathematical thinking, perhaps of *all* our thinking! It was through metaphorical projection that mathematical concepts, especially those that refer to the so called "mathematical objects" – numbers, sets, functions and so on – came into being. Why hadn't I seen this earlier? After this epiphany, I was like a new mother who sees babies everywhere. I started noticing metaphors in literally every utterance I heard. Even words as elementary as *before* and *after*, when used in the context of time rather than space, appeared to me metaphorical.

Ane & Merete: *Could you elaborate on that? What did you gain from seeing most of our concepts, mathematical or otherwise, as metaphorical? What did you know now that you did not know before?*

Anna: Above all, I now could say more, much more, about the phenomenon called *reification*, which I noticed already in the 1980's while doing my PhD research and have been studying ever since. It now became clear to me that the activity of turning a process into objects, which is extremely frequent in mathematics, was simply a special case of metaphorical projection. When we replace our talk on mathematical operations with one on abstract entities, we get a better sense of the intangible world of mathematics. Indeed, by populating the mathematical universe with objects, we make it in the image of the much more familiar physical reality, where processes are usually performed on objects and produce objects. Ample evidence in support of this insight came shortly afterwards, when I interviewed mathematicians and asked them the "simple" question: "What kind of experience makes you say that you managed to understand a piece of mathematics?" The interviewees' responses were replete with direct and indirect references to metaphor, which they presented mostly as a device that "makes things fall into place", turns complex mathematical ideas into "visible at a glance", and even endows abstract "things" with "human physiognomies". In the light of all this, it was only natural to speak about "reification as the birth of a metaphor", which I actually did while summarizing the results of these interviews (Sfard, 1994).[2]

Ever since these conversations with mathematicians, metaphors have been present in my mind either explicitly or in a kind of subconscious stand-by, always ready to jump into full view at short notice. Over the years, they have served me generously in my research on mathematical learning. Through theoretical reflection and empirical research, I have become more and more cognizant of how metaphors shape our mathematical ideas, and of how these figurative projections mold our decisions and actions.

This awareness went hand in hand with the decision to think about learning mathematics as changing a discourse. Within this framework, thinking was conceived as a multimodal discursive activity: the activity of communicating with oneself. This "discursive" approach to cognition entailed a particular understanding of what metaphor and reification are all about and why they are closely related. Metaphor, which was first defined by Aristotle as calling something by a name that belongs to something else, was now seen as occurring whenever parts of a familiar discourse were used in conjunction with another, seemingly unrelated form of talk. This rendering made it clear that metaphors are a tool for *creating* new discourses rather than just for embellishing existing ones. Reification became one of such metaphorical generative acts. It was the discursive device for turning expressions about *acting* into much more concise expressions about *things*. Whereas the utterances of the former type were saturated with verbs, utterances of the latter type were composed mainly of *nouns*. Reification was usually accompanied by yet another discursive move, called *alienation*: the procedure of eliminating the human actor by using reifying nouns in the place of the grammatical subject. Thus, instead of saying "I add 2 and 3 and get 5" one could now say impersonally "2 plus 3 equals 5". When combined, reification and alienation generated "objectified" talk, one that presented mathematical objects, the products of our own discursive constructions, as if they were a part of the non-human world, not much different, in this respect, from stars, trees and rivers. So this is, more or less, how I came to understand that metaphors, through reification and alienation, play a central role in mathematical thinking and its development, both historically and ontogenetically.

Ane & Merete: *In your 1998 paper you analyzed the role of metaphors, not in mathematics or physics, but in the discourse on learning. How did it happen that you also began to speak about metaphors and their role in research on learning?*

Anna: I just realized that there was no reason to think that all the phenomena I gleaned from my studies on mathematical thinking were restricted to that particular discourse. At closer inspection, reification and alienation turned out to be frequent occurrences in almost any type of talk I could think of, and in particular, in the one I was immersed in on an everyday basis: the discourse of research on learning, whether mathematical or any other. Take such common learning-related expressions as "acquiring knowledge" or "constructing concepts". The verbs *acquire* or *construct* signify, first and foremost, physical activities, and this implies that while using the nouns *knowledge* and *concept*, we draw on the discourse about the world of tangible things. I could see that far from being a strictly mathematical procedure, metaphor of object allows us to tell stories about the world around us, thus helping us to make sense of what we see. Moreover, rather than just serving as a tool for narrating reality, it creates this reality in the first place.

Once I became alert to the metaphorical nature of our most common expressions about learning, I also realized that as "natural" as this "acquisitionist" talk appeared to be, there were alternatives. For one thing, we could return to speaking in verbs rather than build our sentences around nouns. Thus, we could say "This kid *has always dealt successfully* with tasks involving functions" instead of saying "He has *acquired* the *concept* of function"; or we could claim that "She can *tell* a lot about historical events" rather than just saying "She *has* historical *knowledge*". And then, as I started looking around, it turned out that this alternative was not purely theoretical. During the time I was wondering about the phenomena of reification and alienation in discourses about people and their actions, the relatively disobjectified discourse on learning was already well underway. This was due mainly to the work of Vygotsky and his followers, and to their particular answer to the question of "What is it that changes when a person learns?" While acquisitionists would answer that question by pointing at changes in *knowledge, concepts* and *mental schemes*, Vygotskians identified *participation in historically established human activities* as the main object of learning-induced change. No wonder that the "participationist" approach, grounded in a metaphor for learning so different from the one that underlay the acquisitionist discourse, was producing a totally new discourse on all those phenomena that we consider unique to humans.

Ane & Merete: *In that paper, after you describe the strengths and weaknesses of the acquisition and participation metaphors respectively, you end up suggesting that both metaphors are useful for understanding learning. Do you still think that both metaphors are useful for understanding learning – and if so/if not so – why?*

Anna: I feel that there were many misunderstandings about the call for peace and reconciliation issued in that paper. I must have not been clear enough. So, before I disclose my preferences, let me explain what I was trying to say.

That article was my contribution to the debate about "paradigm wars", which was taking place on the pages of *Educational Researcher* at that time. Participants in that heated conversation were arguing for either a cognitivist or a situative vision of learning. My aim was, above all, to pour some water on the fire by questioning some of the unspoken epistemological assumptions this debate seemed to be grounded upon. Basically, I had the feeling that the participants, mostly unconsciously, were drawing on the *monological* vision of research, the one that, according to Bakhtin, features the researcher as "ventriloquist" of the world. Indeed, most of the discussants were talking as if their professional narratives about reality were dictated by this reality itself. I wanted to make them aware of their own assumptions, while also arguing for the alternative stance, the one that some writers, under Bakhtin's influence, describe as *dialogic* or *multivocal*. You can also call this approach *postmodern*, if you wish.

To describe the dialogic project, as I see it, it will be helpful to use a metaphor (this should hardly surprise you, I guess?). Consider this: If you agree that the researcher's job is to forge stories that help us go about our daily affairs, you may also agree that, in many respects, these stories are to the world what clothes are to our bodies. For one thing, they are human-made rather than being a part of the world itself. They are also supposed to "fit" what they are meant to "cover". Although there is no "perfect fit" – no ultimate story about the world – it is also not true that any story goes.[3] Some narratives may be entirely inappropriate, just like a dress that is three sizes too small. For other stories, the "coverage" may seem so accurate that we start mistaking the "clothes" for the world's own skin. And there is another important parallel: our choice of stories is no less a matter of fashion (and, in the background, of our desired identities) than is our selection of garments. In a nutshell, I was trying to say that the "paradigms", or discourses, in which we engage while doing research on learning are neither perfect for all purposes, nor even equally good for most of them, and this means that we can never be fully satisfied with a single framework. In that paper, exposing metaphors underlying the existing research on learning helped me to sharpen this message. Indeed, I was able to show that one of the identified metaphors had disadvantages of which the other was free, but it also had advantages that were lacking in the other. What can constitute a more convincing argument for having many dresses than showing that no single dress can be good for *every* occasion?

I still believe in what I said in that paper and I do not think I am contradicting myself when I say that right now, the participation metaphor is my favorite one (I qualified this declaration with "right now", because true to my 1998 self, I am always aware that this may change). As I said, the call for the coexistence of multiple discourses does not imply that all frameworks are made equal or that they are equally appropriate for all contexts. At the present moment I do believe that participationism is more beneficial – or perhaps less harmful – for my purposes than acquisitionism. Let me explain why.

When you follow acquisitionists and speak about phenomena in terms of objects rather than processes, you imply that whatever you are studying has at least some of the characteristics that we usually associate with objects. As a result, your thinking about learning becomes shaped by what you are able to say about objects, and especially about those with which you are most familiar: the objects that you came to know through bodily, physical experience. This kind of projection may be of little consequence in mathematics or physics, but if we talk about people, it is probably less benign. Indeed, it can have considerable ramifications for people's lives. The problem is that when objectifying human phenomena, we never pause to ask ourselves which properties of concrete entities may be preserved and which should be given up. While it is true that some of the uncontrolled entailments of the objectifying metaphor are harmless, or may even bring useful insights, others can be dangerous.

The talk about *discalculia* or, more generally, on *learning disability*, which is very popular these days, is a good example of this latter possibility. We are tempted to use these words whenever we face a child who has a long history of poor scholarly performance. Succumbing to the urge for objectification, we begin speaking in nouns and adjectives that indicate a property of the learner (*learning disability*), as opposed to using verbs and adverbs that make us concentrate on properties of the learners' actions (e.g., she *performs poorly*). Without realizing it, we begin to be guided by the implicit message of the objectified discourse: properties of a person, unlike those of her actions, are more likely to be given by nature than shaped by people, to be general rather than context-dependent (after all, one remains the same person wherever she goes), and to be permanent rather than transient. This view of the student's difficulty may to lead to consequential decisions: we are likely to direct those with a "learning disability" towards a segregated life trajectory, where they will have little chance to further their mathematical education in a substantial manner. In this way, our talk about learning disability becomes a self-fulfilling prophecy: we create the undesirable reality, rather than just reacting to it.

To sum up, I feel that in the discourse of research on learning, unlike that of mathematics, the negative consequences of objectification probably outweigh the gains. Indeed, translating the properties of human action into properties of the actor often leads to decisions that may have a negative impact on the learners' lives. In my view, these possible negative consequences overshadow all the "good" things that come with objectification.

Ane & Merete: *Let us try to rephrase/interpret what you have written until now. In the beginning phase of your research, you perceived reification as a metaphor which was very suitable for understanding mathematics education. A problem with this way of understanding human processes such as learning (as opposed to those one meets in mathematics) is that the researcher's discourse becomes noun-oriented. In consequence, we are stuck with metaphors that may lead to an understanding of human learning as passive and static. Also, you say: 'The problem is that when objectifying human phenomena, we never pause to ask ourselves which properties of concrete entities may be preserved and which should be given up'. Speaking about learning in verbs instead of nouns may not only help us to understand learning in another way, it also helps us to understand students/learners differently. Does this summary reflect your thinking?*

Anna: Yes, you have said what I wanted to say, and you said it better than I did.

Ane & Merete: *OK, so now our question is this: How does thinking about learning in verbs, that is, in terms of actions, help us to understand human beings differently? Is it because this way of understanding human learning helps us to see students (with or without disabilities) in a more dynamic way? Is it possible that the conceptualization of learning as a change in the way we do things may change our view of human beings?*

Anna: Yes to all you said. If we speak about learners in terms of what they are *doing* rather than what they *are* or *have*, not only do we protect ourselves from straying into places we don't want to visit, but we also inevitably change our answer to the question of what it means to be human. It may take more than a few words to make this point so please be patient with me while I try to do so.

I want to begin with a somewhat unusual definition of humanity. But before I spell it out, I want you to think about your own answer to the old question of what is this one thing that makes us humans stand out so clearly within the animal kingdom. By "one thing" I mean the uniquely human property that allows us to make a distinction between ourselves and other species in an unequivocal way. You may be surprised to find out that this seemingly obvious question has no obvious answer. And the fact is that it puzzled and challenged generations of thinkers. Whatever special human feature was identified over the course of time, it always turned out that there was some animal species in which this property appeared in a nascent form, to say the least. This, it seems to me, is bound to happen as long as one is trying to make the distinction by comparing the individual human being to representatives of other types of animals. The definition I now wish to offer circumvents this difficulty by changing the scale: instead of focusing on a single human individual, I propose to take a "long-distance", telescopic look at humanity as a whole. When you alter your perspective in this way, you immediately realize that we are the only animal species that changes its ways of doing things from one generation to the next. Once articulated, this fact may appear trivial, but nonetheless, it has never been considered as the feature that *defines* humanness. Now, think about it: historical transformations can be seen in almost everything we do, be it our activity of feeding ourselves, organizing our habitats, moving from one distant place to another, communicating with other members of our own species – the list is practically inexhaustible. Another important thing to note is that historical changes in our forms of life entail constant increase in the complexity of our activities. While saying this, I do not mean that our ways of doing things become more laborious, time consuming or difficult. Sometimes, the opposite is the case. Here, the noun *complexity* refers to the amount of developments that must have occurred before an activity could be performed. Most of these prior advances are due to people whom the present performer never met. Note also that since each of the prerequisite contributions may have prerequisites of its own, the growth of complexity becomes a non-linear, quickly accelerating phenomenon.

Let me say it again: Our seemingly unlimited capacity for building on what has been done before is where we differ most strongly from all the other creatures in the animal kingdom. This vision of the gist of humanness may resolve an old dilemma, but it also leads to new questions: What is this special something that we have and other animals don't? What is this uniquely human property that allows our innovations to live longer than the innovators themselves, and that turn every innovation into a basis for a new one, to be introduced by the next generation of innovators?

This last query is exactly the point where the participationist vision of learning proves more powerful than the acquisitionist. This claim may raise some brows, if only because it is far from obvious what learning, the activity carried out by and among individuals and consisting in reproducing old ways of knowing rather than creating new ones, has to do with innovating and with the *historical* aggregation of complexity. True, the growth of complexity is a phenomenon that can be observed in the process of *individual* learning. As stated time and again by all thinkers who have tried to fathom the mechanisms of human development, new knowing emerges from what has been known before. It is also quite clear that individuals have the means to preserve their own former achievements and to build on them whenever the need arises. And yet, as long as one thinks about learning as an acquisition – as a change in the contents of an individual mind that originate in the outside world and are then accumulated inside one's skull – the products of continuous change are, of necessity, only as durable as the individual's life. Moreover, as long as learning is seen as occurring in the "conversation" between the individual and the world, there is no reason to expect far reaching differences in the amount of complexity various individuals manage to accumulate. All this indicates that acquisitionism has no way of dealing with the question of what makes it possible for an individual achievement to transcend the boundaries of the achiever's physical existence. This approach has no explanation for the fact that the endpoint of one's learning becomes the learner's successors' starting point.

This is exactly where participationism, with its vision of learning as the process of changing ways of acting in the world, comes in handy. Before I present my argument, let me note some relevant implications of this definition. First, the most basic form of learning, the one that constitutes the primary goal of schooling, can be described as the process by which one turns into one's own some of the patterns of acting that already exist in society. In this process, the learner may become able to perform competently, and on her own accord, such historically shaped activities as preparing food, dressing, communicating with others, solving mathematical problems or doing biological research.[4] If we think about learning in this way, *interactions with other people come to the fore as the primary source of learning*. Indeed, these historically shaped ways of acting cannot be found in any other place. Of course, also non-human reality plays a role in the process of learning. After all, only those forms of acting survive which have proved helpful in dealing with whatever was going on around us. Still, participationism reverses the roles of the two types of interaction: whereas acquisitionism views individual, spontaneous interaction with the world as the primary source of learning and hence the interaction with other humans as just secondary, participationism implies the opposite: what people around us say and do comes first and the world serves mainly as but a touchstone by which the viability of learning can be tested and regulated. The second implication is that *historical change can now count as a special case of learning*. This claim is an immediate consequence of the definition that equates learning with a durable change in patterns of acting, and of the fact that patterns of acting can appear at any level: at the level of an individual actor, of a small group, of a community or of society as a whole. When it comes to transformations in such patterns, one can thus speak about individual-ontogenetic change or about societal-historical transformation. The first type of change is tantamount to *individual learning*, whereas the latter one may be referred to as *societal learning*.[5] If that is so, we can now say that it is the *propensity for societal learning* that constitutes the defining feature of humanness.

I'm now ready to return to the question *What is it that makes humanity conducive to historical change?* This query can now be rephrased as *What makes humans capable of societal learning?* At closer inspection, the participationist rendering of the concept of learning, as discussed above, simply dissolves this puzzle. The inherently collective nature of learning and our resulting propensity for passing on innovation from one generation to the next, is now the *defining feature* of human learning. To put it in a somewhat different way, since people learn first and foremost from other people, it is only natural that whatever helpful form of acting is developed by an individual or a team, is immediately taken up by others. One can also say, somewhat metaphorically, that what appears as two kinds of change – individual learning and societal learning – is, in fact, a pair of differing images of a single phenomenon, obtained by zooming in on the phenomenon and then zooming out again. Thus, the answer to our question is now simple: It is our untameable propensity for learning from one another that makes us capable of societal learning and, in the final analysis, becomes the source of all things human.

You may be wondering why I needed this longish story to arrive at what may seem to be a rather obvious conclusion. You may also be surprised that this is the narrative I chose to try and answer your question of how participationism changes our vision of what it means to be human. To this, let me say that I needed this story to explain what I meant when I said that participationism, as opposed to acquisitionism, pictures learning as an *inherently social activity* and portrays human beings as *inherently social creatures*. You may still object that all this sounds trivial. Nowadays, you can find declarations about "inherently social" nature of learning in almost any educational publication. And yet, according to my reading – and I have developed a great sensitivity to unspoken assumption underlying these kind of statements – not every author who says things like these believes the story about humans that I just told. Indeed, in many cases, claims about the "inherently social character" of anything related to human beings proves, on closer reading, to be little more than an add-on to the good old acquisitionist discourse.[6] The discourse I am trying to promote is *incommensurable* with acquisitionism. In this discourse, the statement "learning is inherently social" stops being a cliché and regains its deep and proper meaning intended by participationists: not only is the "object of learning" situated "on the social plane", as famously stated by Vygotsky, but also the learning subject can no longer be viewed as a lone individual. Individual learning, even if it takes place in the learner's home and away from other people, is, necessarily, an interpersonal affair. Humanity emerges from this rendering as a complex system of individual agents. None of our moves can be properly understood unless we keep in mind that, throughout our lives, we negotiate the perennial tension between our individuality and the fact of our being a part of a bigger whole.

## Notes

1. This happened at the 1991 annual meeting of The International Group for the Psychology of Mathematics Education, PME, that took place in Assisi, Italy. Lakoff and Johnson's book were mentioned by Willi Dörfler (1991) in his plenary address.
2. A similar conviction was expressed some time later by Lakoff and Núñez in their well-known volume *Where mathematics comes from*. And yet, as I soon will make clear, the epistemological and ontological assumptions of these authors differ considerably from the foundational principles of my own approach..
3. "Anything goes" is the slogan which, in the eyes of the objectors, encapsulates the postmodernist stance. The critics see this postulation as deriving from the postmodernist rejection of the idea of "absolute truth". But "anything goes" does not follow from "no story is true in an absolute manner", just as the claim that every dress is equally good for me does not follow from the fact that no dress fits me in an "absolute" fashion (see also Sfard 2012).
4. Vygotsky referred to this conversion of the activity of others into one's own as *internalization* and his followers often use the term *appropriation to refer to this process*. Because of the objectifying undertones of both these terms, I prefer the word *individualization*.
5. Note that the acquisitionist definition does not allow for such an extension of the notion of learning. According to the acquisitionist definition, the change that happens when a person learns occurs in her mental schema, and mental schemas, unlike ways of acting, are not anything that can be observed at both the individual and the collective level.
6. Jean Lave uses the term *Cognition Plus View (CPV)* while speaking about this kind of acquisitionist discourse with slight participationist touches.

## References

Dörfler, W. (1991). Meaning: Image schemata and protocols. In F. Furinghetti (Ed.), *Proceedings of the 15th PME International Conference, 1*, p. 17-32.

Johnson, M. (1987). *The body in the mind: The bodily basis of meaning, imagination, and reason.* Chicago: University of Chicago Press.

Lakoff, G., & Johnson, M. (1980). *The metaphors we live by.* Chicago: University of Chicago Press.

Lakoff, G. (1987). *Women, fire and dangerous things: What categories reveal about the mind.* Chicago: University of Chicago Press.

Reddy, M. J. (1979). The conduit metaphor: A case of frame conflict in our language about language. In: A. Ortony (Ed.), *Metaphor and thought.* New York: Cambridge University Press.

Sfard, A. (1994). Reification as a birth of a metaphor. *for the learning of mathematics, 14*(1), p. 44-55.

Sfard, A. (1998). Two metaphors for learning and the dangers of choosing just one. *Educational Researcher, 27*(2), p. 4-13.

Sfard, A. (2012). Research problems in mathematics education revisited: New clothes – and no emperor. *for the learning of mathematics, 32* (2), p. 3-5.

Sfard, A. (to appear). Learning, commognition and mathematics. In: D. Scott & E. Hargreaves (Eds.), *The Sage Handbook of Learning.* London: Sage.

# Contributors

**Ane Qvortrup** is associate professor at Department for the Study of Culture, University of Southern Denmark. Her research areas are teaching and general didactics, curriculum and curriculum theory and learning. Her research is informed by the complex-sensitive approach offered by second-order systems theory.

**Merete Wiberg** is associate professor at Danish School of Education, Aarhus University, Denmark. Her research area is philosophy of education, theory of learning, moral learning and ethical formation.

**Gerd Christensen** is associate professor at Department of Media, Cognition and Communciation, Copenhagen University. Main research interests are group psychology, group work, problem-based project studies at universities, and the philosophy of science and the methodologies of the humanities and the social sciences.

**Mikala Hansbøl** is docent at the research group Digital Learning Resources at Department of Education, Metropolitan University College, Copenhagen, Denmark. Her research is informed by empirical philosophy and philosophy of technology, and primary research area is shifting movements and relationships between digitalization and society, teaching and learning.

**Esben Nedenskov Petersen** is associate professor of philosophy at Department for the Study of Culture, University of Southern Denmark. His main research interests are epistemology, philosophy of language, philosophy of science, and the philosophy of the humanities and social sciences.

**Caroline Schaffalitzky de Muckadell** is associate professor of philosophy at Department for the Study of Culture, University of Southern Denmark. Her research areas include philosophy of religion and theories of concepts and definitions.

**Rolf Hvidtfeldt** is a PhD-student in philosophy at Department for the Study of Culture, University of Southern Denmark. His main interests include (the philosophy of) science, psychiatry, psychology, concepts, language, and interdisciplinarity.

**Nina Bonderup Dohn** is associate professor at Department of Design and Communication, University of Southern Denmark. Her research bridges epistemology and learning theory, both theoretically and pragmatically, with a special focus on the use of ICT for learning.

**Oliver Kauffmann** is associate professor at Danish School of Education, Aarhus University, Denmark. His research areas are philosophy of mind and theories of learning. He has a particular interest in developing a scientifically informed realist approach to the learning capacities of the mind.

**Steen Beck** is associate professor at Department for the Study of Culture, University of Southern Denmark. His research areas are theories of learning, general didactics and student culture.

**Klaus Nielsen** is professor at Department of Psychology, Aarhus University, Denmark. His research areas are learning theory, situated learning and apprenticeship.

**Tina Bering Keiding** is associate professor at Centre for Teaching Development and Digital Media, Aarhus University, Denmark. Her research area is higher education with special focus on curriculum and didactics.

**Torben Spanget Christensen** is associate professor at Department for the Study of Culture, University of Southern Denmark. His research areas are didactics in social science subjects, assessment and ethnographic research in writing in the school subjects.

**Rie Troelsen** is associate professor at the Centre for Teaching and Learning at University of Southern Denmark. Her research interests are higher education teaching and learning in general and learning spaces in particular.

**Maj Sofie Rasmussen** is a PhD student at the Danish School of Education, Aarhus University, Denmark and VIA University College, Aarhus. Her research area is (dis)engagement, passion and marginalizing processes in lower secondary school.

**Peder Holm-Pedersen** is a PhD student at Department for the Study of Culture, University of Southern Denmark. His research areas are teacher education and professional development.